American 24-Karat Gold

24 Classic American Short Stories

Third Edition

Yvonne Collioud Sisko

Middlesex County College

Illustrations by
John Seymour and Ted Sisko

PEARSON
Longman

New York   San Francisco   Boston
London   Toronto   Sydney   Tokyo   Singapore   Madrid
Mexico City   Munich   Paris   Cape Town   Hong Kong   Montreal

Vice President and Editor in Chief: Joe Terry
Acquisitions Editor: Kate Edwards
Editorial Assistant: Lindsey Allen
Marketing Manager: Thomas DeMarco
Senior Supplements Editor: Donna Campion
Production Manager: Savoula Amanatidis
Project Coordination, Text Design, and Electronic
     Page Makeup: Electronic Publishing Services Inc., NYC
Cover Design Manager: John Callahan
Cover Designer: Maria Ilardi
Cover Image: Cover image courtesy of Getty Images, Inc.
Senior Manufacturing Buyer: Dennis J. Para
Printer and Binder: Courier–Stoughton
Cover Printer: Courier–Stoughton

For permission to use copyrighted material, grateful acknowledgment is made
to the copyright holders on pp. 431–432, which are hereby made part of this
copyright page.

Library of Congress Cataloging-in-Publication Data
Sisko, Yvonne Collioud.
  American 24-karat gold : 24 classic American short stories / Yvonne Collioud
Sisko; illustrations by John Seymour and Ted Sisko.—3rd ed.
    p. cm.
  Includes bibliographical references and index.
  ISBN-13: 978-0-205-61765-4
  ISBN-10: 0-321-36523-2
1. College readers. 2. English language—United States—Rhetoric—Problems,
exercises, etc. 3. Report writing—Problems, exercises, etc. 4. Short stories,
American. I. Title: American twenty four-karat gold. II. Title.
  PE1417.S454 2009
  808'. 0427—dc22

                                                                    2007052430

Please visit us at www.ablongman.com

ISBN-13: 978-0-205-61765-4
ISBN-10: 0-205-61765-4

1 2 3 4 5 6 7 8 9 10—CS—11 10 09 08

Why Do You Need this New Edition?

If you're wondering why you should buy this new edition of *American 24-Karat Gold* here are 7 good reasons!

1. Contains **5 new stories** from Amy Tan, Alice Walker, O. Henry, Max Brand, and Kate Chopin that are interesting and engaging.

2. An alternate organization that includes a **new "Relationships" thematic category** provides for more challenging study.

3. **Stories have been re-arranged** to progress more accurately in terms of difficulty to assist you in your reading comprehension.

4. New *Setting* Assignment focuses on props in the story to increase awareness of this literary element.

5. New assignment for *Literary Elements* asks you to apply the elements to your understanding of the story.

6. New *Foreshadowing, Irony and/or Symbolism* Assignment asks you to reach even deeper in reconstructing each story.

7. New additions to the **definitions in the glossary** assist your word attack skills.

To Teddy and Laura and Alex and George,
who give me joy every day of my life.

Contents

Old Phoenix overcomes challenge after challenge as she takes the reader on her journey to town.

In this lively story, Migene Gonzalez-Wippler portrays a childhood experience with a religious system that combines Christian and African beliefs.

❦ Joseph Bruchac   "Bone Girl"   122

Old traditions lead to new changes in this spirited tale.

❦ Mark Twain   "Strong Temptations—Strategic Movements— The Innocents Beguiled"   137

Told with humor and irony, this is the classic tale of Tom Sawyer painting the fence.

❦ Edgar Allan Poe   "The Cask of Amontillado"   151

Edgar Allan Poe walks the reader through the homicidal mind in this classic story of revenge wherein darkness increases with the subterranean descent.

O. Henry   "The Last Leaf"   228

We share friendship and devotion in this stirringly poignant tale.

Frank Stockton   "The Lady or the Tiger?"   242

The reader expects resolution, but Frank Stockton leaves the reader holding her or his breath.

Chapter 4   Irony   257

Kate Chopin   "The Story of an Hour"   258

Kate Chopin turns marital assumptions upside down with her ironic twist.

Chapter 5   Extended Short Story Study   339

🍃 William Faulkner   "A Rose for Emily"   340

The reader experiences the very wretchedness of William Faulkner's decaying South through Emily and her relationships.

🍃 Nathaniel Hawthorne   "Dr. Heidegger's Experiment"   358

In this tale set amid dark and ominous surroundings, Nathaniel Hawthorne questions change with light humor, irony, and even a touch of magic.

🍃 Edgar Allan Poe   "The Masque of the Red Death"   377

Writing over a hundred year ago, Edgar Allan Poe uses the supernatural with a vengeance that forebodes today's plight with AIDS.

Intent and/or Tone
Contents

Here is a general listing of stories by theme, although most of these stories do not easily fit into one category or another. For example, Twain's story of Tom Sawyer painting the fence can as easily be placed in *Triumph of the Spirit, Irony, Social Commentary*, or *Humor*.

TRIUMPH OF THE SPIRIT

These stories inspire and offer insight into the human condition:

HUMOR

Told with a light touch and humor, these stories tickle the reader's funny bone:

IRONY

These stories come with unexpected twists:

SOCIAL COMMENTARY

These stories examine societal and/or cultural issues:

RELATIONSHIPS

These stories explore interpersonal relations:

EERIE

These stories visit the worlds of the macabre or the supernatural:

Chronological
Contents

Foreword

*A*merican 24-Karat Gold originally grew out of necessity and, today, has become a teaching tool used around the world to teach students how to read, write, and think about literature—and here, specifically, the rich experience of American literature. Years ago while simultaneously teaching courses on world literature, composition, and developmental studies, I searched far and wide for a concise and affordable collection of American short stories that would be a logical culmination in New World study for world literature, provide rich prompts for composition, and supply a literary answer to the question, "But what do they *read*?" for developmental studies. I found none. Instead, I found comprehensive monographs (all O. Henry, and so forth), ponderous tomes for advanced short story courses, or weighty collections of esoteric writings by obscure writers. Nowhere was there a concise and diverse collection of America's best. And putting the collection together was not enough. In order to make this collection accessible for students, we added extensive and comprehensive support materials. Thus, *American 24-Karat Gold* originally evolved to meet these challenges and, as noted, is now successfully expanding the literary lexicons of students around the world. Further, through extensive field-testing, we have found that student success rates in both reading and writing have dramatically improved by using the many teaching and learning options that *American 24-Karat Gold* provides.

Now this third edition maintains the consistently effective and efficient pedagogical apparatus formats found in prior editions. Based on lengthy observations and the aforementioned extensive field-testing, every exercise, every assignment, and every comprehension structure has been most carefully designed to maximize learning for the student and efficiency for the teacher. For this new edition, several new stories appear which have demonstrated great student success. For the contents, *Intent and/or Tone Contents* has the new *Relationships* category. Further, the stories have been rearranged in the *Intent and/or Tone Contents* and within each chapter *per se*, so that the stories more accurately progress from more accessible to more difficult. And for the Journal, several new assignments appear that expand student focuses and increase student thinking. I hope you and your students enjoy the changes.

Thankfully, I have had much support in creating this and all my books. First, I deeply thank Lucille Alfieri, Betty Altruda, Jim Bernarducci, Debbie Brady, Santi Buscemi, Wilson Class, Gert Coleman, Jamie Daley, Sallie DelVecchio, Leah Ghiradella, Evelyn and Kristin Honey, Vernie Jarocki, Jim Keller, Angelo Lugo, Ben Marshall, JoAnne McWilliams, Albert Nicolai,

Renee Price, Ellen Shur, Helena Swanicke, Shirley Wachtel, Nancy Zavoluk, and Dan Zimmerman—all dear friends and colleagues—for their ever ready interest and guidance. Next, I deeply thank Andre Gittens, Liz Oliu, and Esther Young, librarians at Middlesex who always find the impossible for me. I deeply thank Bernie Weinstein, Dan O'Day, Eileen Kennedy, Bill Evans, Howard Didsbury, Carol Kouros-Shaffer, and Carla Lord—my mentors who continually inspire me to push further and further. I thank the reviewers of the text: Marsha Nourse, Dean College; Marge Morian, Boyle-Dean College; Charlene Aldrich, Trident Technical College; Evelyn Koperwas, Broward Community College; Karla Nast, Cy-Fair College; Patty Valenziano, Prairie State College; Anna Apple, Cy-Fair College; and JoAnn Foriest, Prairie State College.

Of course, special thanks go to my mom Margaret and to my sisters Michelle, Dodee, and Alice, who always adjust to my I've-got-to-get-this-done days. Really special thanks go to my brother-in-law John, whose illustrations light my books. Super thanks go to my husband George, who now asks where—and not when—dinner is. And super, super thanks go to my beautiful children. Thank you, son-in-law Dave—well, we all thank you and Teddy for the many technical tantrums you have solved. Thank you, Teddy, for your illustrations, your patient wisdom, and—most of all—your infectious laugh. Thank you, Laura, for your radiant and boundless enthusiasm that ever lights my life. And thank you little grandson Alex—you are utter and sheer joy.

And very, very special thanks go to Joe Terry, Kate Edwards, and Lindsey Allen—my wonderful editors and staff at Pearson Longman. As *American 24-Karat Gold* has evolved, so also have other books applying the same extensive pedagogical formats and offering you even more options. *A World of Short Stories* offers short stories from around the world. *Looking at Literature* offers short stories, a play, and a novel. *Sterling Stories* offers highly accessible and very short stories. Longman's new *Annotated Editions*, for which I serve as Series Editor, offer classic novels with chapters surrounded by all the pedagogical support materials surrounding the short stories. And the forthcoming *Mastering Literature* will offer a comprehensive literature anthology with—of course—all the pedagogical support materials that our students need.

And most of all, thank *you* for choosing this book—I truly, truly hope you enjoy using this book as much as I have enjoyed developing it.

YVONNE COLLIOUD SISKO

Preface

To the Student

It seems that human beings have always loved a good story. In fact, anthropologists tell us that story telling has been used to teach rules and inspire ideas for millennia.

This book is filled with good stories, or narratives or narrations, from some of post-Columbian America's greatest storytellers. Read these stories to gain knowledge about past and present American attitudes. Read them to gain knowledge about yourself, for good stories also offer us information about ourselves. But most of all, read these stories to enjoy them. Stories have a way of taking us into new worlds and offering universals, the feelings we all can understand.

However, the stories in this book are designed to do more than just expose you to each story itself. Each story in *American 24-Karat Gold* is surrounded with exercises that will help you better understand each story. Each story includes:

- **Vocabulary Exercises**—Vocabulary exercises help you define the words you need to know for the story, before you even read it.
- **Questions**—Questions help guide you through the story.
- **Biography**—A biography of the story's author provides you information about the author's life, style, and other works.
- **Journal**—After reading, you can record and organize your thoughts about the story in a journal.
- **Follow-up Questions**—You can demonstrate what you've learned about the story in follow-up questions.
- **Discussion Questions**—These questions ask you to reach deeper and to react to the story.
- **Writing Ideas**—Writing ideas help guide your own writing.

To understand better how this book works, turn to the Sample Lesson on page 1 and work your way through it. You'll find that you will be actively participating in this book, which will make understanding and appreciating the stories easier and more rewarding for you.

Welcome to *American 24-Karat Gold*! Read this book, study it, and—most of all—enjoy it.

To the Teacher

For the third edition, several great new stories have been added that have proven to be very successful with the over two thousand students who have field-tested them, these students representing one of the most culturally diverse counties in the nation. For the contents, the new *Relationships* category has been added to the *Intent and/or Tone Contents* table. Further, the stories, both in the *Intent and/or Tone Contents* table and within the chapters themselves, have been rearranged so that the stories more accurately progress from more accessible to more difficult. For the Journal, new assignments have been added to expand student focuses and extend student thinking.

The greatest assets of *American 24-Karat Gold* are its participatory lessons and the many options these lessons offer you. Certainly, the literature is the core of this book, but the pedagogical materials that surround each story require students to participate actively in every story. Simultaneously, these materials offer you a choice of multiple, administratively efficient diagnostic and assessment tools. Each entry is a self-contained lesson, and all the stories are consistently formatted, thereby offering students clear expectations and offering you multiple options.

Sample Lesson

American 24-Karat Gold starts out with an applied **Sample Lesson**. The Sample Lesson can be used in class, *or* it can be assigned as homework. Written in simple and accessible language, this introductory lesson walks students through the basic story format, using Kate Chopin's "Ripe Figs." This lesson, as all lessons, opens with Pre-Reading Vocabulary—Context and Pre-Reading Vocabulary—Structural Attack to help students define important words used in the story. Pre-Reading Questions set purpose, and an author biography supplies relevant background information.

After reading "Ripe Figs," students learn notation strategies that they can then apply to the subsequent readings. With the story completed, students move on to the Journal exercises, which are comprehensive and participatory studies of the story. The Sample Lesson explains the tasks in each Journal section, offers sample answers to get students started, and introduces relevant literary terminology.

With the Journal completed, students now have an active, working understanding of "Ripe Figs." They can then move on to three sets of Follow-up Questions. These questions consistently use multiple assessment formats: (1) ten multiple-choice questions objectively assessing comprehension, (2) five significant quotations subjectively assessing comprehension, and (3) two essay questions subjectively assessing comprehension. Discussion Questions encourage debate and can be discussed in class or written. Each story ends with Writing suggestions. In the Sample Lesson, students are introduced to pre-writing and outlining strategies. In subsequent stories, students will find multiple writing prompts.

I suggest that you work through the Sample Lesson in class, for it is here that you will find the dynamics and possibilities of this book encapsulated.

Chapter Structure

The stories in *American 24-Karat Gold* are arranged into five topical chapters, based on and reinforcing the literary terminology the student has already encountered in the Sample Lesson. While all stories contain combinations of these terms and/or elements, each of the chapters focuses on one or more specific terms and/or elements by beginning with a restatement of the term(s) and then by presenting the stories that have been specifically chosen to demonstrate the term(s) and/or element(s). Chapter 1 focuses on characters and conflicts, Chapter 2 focuses on setting and props, Chapter 3 focuses on plot and foreshadowing, and Chapter 4 focuses on irony. Chapter 5 focuses on symbolism, but it is different from the other chapters. The more complex stories in Chapter 5 bring together all that students have learned in earlier chapters and are intended to challenge advanced students.

Within each chapter, you have many options:

1. You can assign these chapters in any order.
2. You can also assign the stories within each chapter in any order. Generally, the stories within each chapter progress from more accessible to more difficult, but the strengths of each class vary, and what may seem more accessible to one group may be more difficult for another.
3. You can assign all the stories in a chapter or any number you prefer.
4. You can ignore all of these suggestions and assign any story at your discretion.
5. You can use one of the alternative tables of contents. Selecting from the *Intent and/or Tone Contents* can make for interesting study. The *Chronological Contents* offers an historical perspective for more thematic or sophisticated study, wherein the stories move, generally, from Puritan moral and supernatural concerns to laic human affairs and, with Gonzalez-Wippler, Bruchac, and Hughes, back to spiritual concerns. In this context, students visit the Mississippi with Twain, the disillusionment after World War I with the modernists, and cultural concerns with contemporary writers.
6. How *I* Use This Book, located in Appendix B, is intended to offer you some teaching options.

Story Structure

Each entry in *American 24-Karat Gold* is set amid carefully designed teaching materials, and because the format is consistent, you will be able to find the material easily. These materials were discussed generally in the overview of the Sample Lesson above, but here we look at them more closely.

Pre-Reading Materials

Each story selection begins with pre-reading materials. The pre-reading materials prepare students for reading stories while offering you insights into their vocabulary mastery and study habits.

Pre-Reading Vocabulary—Context presents words that are crucial to understanding the story. These words have been chosen to make the story accessible to students and may or may not be the most sophisticated words in the story. For more sophisticated study, all potentially troublesome words in any given story are presented in the Instructor's Manual, where you will find words listed in the order in which they appear in the story so that you can easily locate them and identify them for students in the story's text.

Pre-Reading Vocabulary—Structural Attack offers structural analysis exercises. These words were chosen not for their sophistication, but because they help students apply structural analysis skills. Thus, before students start the story, they have defined at least 20 words in context and 10 to 30 words by structural analysis. The need for distracting glossed words and marginal definitions is thereby eliminated, because students are well prepared by the pre-reading vocabulary to attack the story.

Third, **Pre-Reading Questions** offer food for thought as students enter the story. The author's **Biography** provides not only biographical background, but also additional information about the author's other works.

Journal

After students have read and annotated the story, the **Journal** then draws them into active reflection and participation.

- **MLA Works Cited**—Students record the reading in MLA Works Cited entry format, using the generic model provided.
- **Main Characters(s)**—Students separate, describe, and defend the character(s) they have selected as main character(s) (applying and reinforcing the separation of main ideas from supporting details).
- **Supporting Characters**—Students separate, describe, and defend the characters they have selected as supporting characters (applying and reinforcing the separation of main ideas from supporting details).
- **Setting**—Students describe the story's setting(s) and prop(s) (applying and reinforcing inference skills).
- **Sequence**—Students outline the story's events in order (applying and reinforcing sequencing and outlining skills).
- **Plot**—Students summarize the story's events in no more than three sentences (applying and reinforcing the separation of main ideas from supporting details, as well as summary skills).
- **Conflicts**—Students identify and explain the relevant conflicts (applying and reinforcing inference and judgment skills).
- **Significant Quotations**—Students explain the importance of five quotations that are central to the story (applying and reinforcing inference skills) and learn MLA parenthetical citation format.
- **Literary Elements**—Students reflect upon and explain the literary elements of each chapter as they are relevant to each story (applying and reinforcing judgment and synthesizing skills).
- **Foreshadowing, Irony, and/or Symbolism**—Students identity and explain these literary devices as each may apply to each story (applying and reinforcing sequencing, inference, and/or judgment skills).

The Journal is a comprehensive cognitive workout for students. In the Journal, students reflect on the story, sort out the details, and organize the story's components while applying and reinforcing the comprehension skills noted above. You can collect any part or all of the Journal to check on student progress. The wealth of diagnostic information in the Journal will enable you to spot misunderstandings, illogical thinking, and so forth, that may compromise comprehension. Requiring a completed Journal for classroom participation also assures you of students prepared to discuss the story.

Follow-up Questions

The Journal is followed by three follow-up question formats. The Follow-up Questions are designed for assessment, but they can also be used for small-group or class discussion. All of these questions are intended to measure comprehension; they purposely avoid literary controversy.

- **10 Short Questions** offer ten multiple-choice questions.
- **5 Significant Quotations** ask students to explain the importance of five quotations that are central to the story and usually different from the five quotations in the Journal.
- **2 Comprehensive Essay Questions** provide two essay prompts.

The Follow-up Questions offer you multiple, efficient assessment options. You may decide to use some questions for discussion or some for testing. If you are trying to establish standardization, the section of 10 Short Questions is applicable for standardization, measuring comprehension efficiently by psychometrically employing ten questions with three choices each.

Discussion Questions

Each story provides two thought-provoking questions. Unlike the Follow-up Questions, **Discussion Questions** encourage reflection, personal opinion, and/or literary debate. Again, you may choose to have students discuss these in class or write the answers.

Writing Prompts

Each work concludes with options for **Writing**. Here, two prompts for personal writing are included. Then, under **Further Writing**, you will find prompts for more advanced, research-oriented writing. These prompts may be literary (compare and contrast this story with another in this book, with another by this author, with one by another author, and so forth) or topical research suggestions.

Instructor's Manual

The **Instructor's Manual (IM)** offers valuable resources for teachers. In addition to an overview of the book's pedagogy, the IM offers additional information on each story.

1. The entry for each story starts with a brief overview and suggestions for appropriate readers.

2. Next, each entry offers an extensive list of all potentially troublesome words in the story, assembled with both the native speaker and the ESL student in mind. Words are listed in the order they appear in the story for easy location.
3. Under plot, each story is condensed to one sentence; you may find these summaries useful in selecting stories for assignment.
4. Suggested answers to the Journal and Follow-up Questions are provided. The suggested answers—suggested because these are, after all, literary pursuits and students' answers will vary—set parameters for correctness. The only areas that have clearly right or wrong answers are the MLA Works Cited entry and 10 Short Questions.

To order a copy of the Instructor's Manual, contact your Longman sales representative and request ISBN: 0-205-61769-7.

Some Final Notes

The materials in *American 24-Karat Gold*—the context and structural vocabulary exercises, the journal format, the three assessment options, the discussion questions, as well as many of the writing prompts—have been extensively field-tested by several thousand students. These field tests have taken place in one of the most culturally diverse counties in the nation—Middlesex County, New Jersey. Two results have occurred. First, the story lessons have not only increased all students' competencies but have also come to serve as a basis for acculturation discussions with ESL and international students. Second, the pedagogical materials have been streamlined to maximize learning efficacy and to minimize administrative inefficiency.

It should also be noted that, although copyright restrictions apply, we have elided offensive words wherever feasible.

Last, but certainly not least, we must address the stories themselves. The richness of the literature speaks for itself, and the stories have been carefully chosen to present the best of American short stories by some of America's foremost writers. Increasingly, we are seeing students who have never heard of O. Henry or Mark Twain, let alone Faulkner, Hurston, or Hughes. This collection sets out to expand the basic literary lexicon of today's entering college student.

Two criteria were used to select the stories in this anthology: first, that the author is a recognized American writer and, second, that the story is important, accessible, or interesting. Tom Sawyer painting the fence? It's in here. The irony of O. Henry and the macabre aura of Poe? They're in here. This is America and America's best.

I sincerely hope you and your students enjoy reading these stories as much as I have enjoyed discovering them, rediscovering them, and working with them.

YVONNE COLLIOUD SISKO

A SAMPLE LESSON

Ripe Figs

by

Kate Chopin

The best way to learn how to use something is to do just that—to use it. This sample lesson presents a very short work, "Ripe Figs" by Kate Chopin, to demonstrate how this book works. This sample lesson presents all the materials that surround each story. Generally, each reading starts with pre-reading activities that are designed to make your reading easier, and ends with a journal, follow-up questions, discussion questions, and writing assignments that are designed to improve your understanding. This sample lesson also introduces the elements of a narrative—elements that you will be using throughout this book.

Let's begin.

Ripe Figs
KATE CHOPIN

PRE-READING VOCABULARY
CONTEXT

Use context clues to define these words before reading. Use a dictionary as needed.

The words that are critical for your understanding of the reading are presented at the beginning of each reading. These are not necessarily the most difficult words. Rather, they are words that you will need to know to understand the reading more easily.

The **Pre-reading Vocabulary—Context** exercises present words in sentences. You should try to define each word by using the **context clues** in the sentence. Note that the first eight words have been defined as examples for you. Look at sentence 1. The word here is "fig," and the clues let you know that this is something "small" and "purple" that grows "on a tree" and is "delicious." Since "delicious" implies it is something to eat and since fruit grows on a tree, we can define a "fig" as "a small, purple fruit that grows on a tree." Using this same strategy, check the meanings of the next seven words. Then use the clues and define the remaining words.

1. The small, purple *figs* grow on a tree and are delicious. *Fig* means
   a small, purple fruit that grows on a tree
   .

2. Some may say "mom" or "mama" for "mother," while the French
   may say *"mère"* or *"maman."* *Mère* or *maman* means
   a name for "mother"
   .

3. The campers rowed their boat slowly through the reeds along the side
   of the *bayou. Bayou* means   a slow-moving body of water
   .

4. The children licked the long *sugar cane* they found in the field. *Sugar
   cane* means   a stick-like food
   .

5. The elderly person's fingers seemed to cross each other in *gnarled*
   knots from old age and arthritis. *Gnarled* means
   knotted and crisscrossed
   .

6. Ted is so *patient*; he doesn't mind if Laura takes two hours to do her hair. *Patient* means willing to wait   .

7. There is a stone *statue* of a little boy in the middle of the garden. *Statue* means a carved or sculpted figure   .

8. The tiny *humming-bird's* wings moved so quickly that you could not see them. *Humming-bird* means a small bird with rapidly moving wings   .

9. Dave was *disconsolate* after he lost the championship game. *Disconsolate* means   .

10. Kings and queens usually walk in a very dignified and *stately* manner. *Stately* means   .

11. Furniture is often first covered in a simple *muslin* under the fine fabric to protect the fabric. *Muslin* means   .

12. The haze of color often drawn around a saint's head is called a halo or *aureole*. *Aureole* means   .

13. In spite of all the upset and confusion, Alex stayed cool and *placid*. *Placid* means   .

14. The bride's dishes are fine *porcelain* decorated with tiny flowers and trimmed in gold. *Porcelain* means   .

15. I will go to see my aunt, *Tante* Lena, to celebrate her birthday. *Tante* means   .

16. I love the large yellow *chrysanthemums* that bloom in a fall garden. *Chrysanthemum* means   .

PRE-READING VOCABULARY
STRUCTURAL ATTACK

Define these words by solving the parts. Use the Glossary or a dictionary as needed.

The **Pre-reading Vocabulary—Structural Attack** exercises present words that you know but that may look strange or have altered meanings because of added parts. Here you will want to look for and define the **root**, or core, word. Then look for and define the **prefix**, or part added to the front of the word. Finally, look for and define the **suffix**, or part added to the end of the word.

Prefixes (added to the front) and suffixes (added to the end) are called **affixes**. By defining the root and the affixes, you should be able to define each of these words with little trouble. For instance, look at the first vocabulary word. The very simple word "ripe" has two suffixes (–en, –ing) that can be added to it, which change the word's meaning from "ready" or "mature" to "getting ready" or "maturing." Or words may combine to become a **compound word**. Look at the fourth word. "Summer" and "time" combine to mean "warm time of the year."

Using these same strategies, take each word apart, and define it by using the roots and affixes. The next two words are defined for you also. Try the last three on your own. See the Glossary (page 425) for affix definitions.

1. ripening   *becoming ripe or mature*
2. la Madone   *mother or Holy Mother*
3. restless   *active; cannot rest*
4. summertime
5. godmother
6. plumpest

PRE-READING QUESTIONS

Try answering these questions as you read.

Before reading, it is always helpful to start with a purpose. Use the reading's title and any other relevant information to set up questions to answer while you are reading. Answering these questions will make your reading easier and more efficient, so that you do not have to reread and reread to understand the narrative.

Each reading starts with **Pre-reading Questions** to set your purpose. Keep these questions in mind as you read.

Who are the main characters? Supporting characters?

What does Babette want?

What does Maman want?

What does the title mean?

Ripe Figs

KATE CHOPIN

Before each narrative, a brief **biography** provides some information about the author. In addition to learning about the author's life, you may also pick up information that will help you in reading the narrative. The biography may also list other works by the author, in case you would like to read more by that author.

Read Kate Chopin's biography. It tells you, among other things, that she writes about the people she met in Louisiana and that she likes to use "symbols and images from nature." Both of these pieces of information will come in handy as you read "Ripe Figs."

Kate O'Flaherty Chopin was born in St. Louis in 1851 to an affluent family. Although her father died when she was young, her widowed mother gave young Kate a taste of independence. In 1870 Kate married Oscar Chopin and moved to New Orleans and then Natchitoches Parish. Here she met the Creoles, Acadians, and African Americans she would later write about. Oscar died in 1882, and by 1884 she sold the plantation, gathered her five children, and returned home to St. Louis, where she began to write for popular women's magazines. Influenced noticeably by Guy de Maupassant's sense of irony and Henrik Ibsen's social comment, Chopin wrote stories, often touched with rich symbols and images from nature, that question societal assumptions and dictates. The Awakening remains her master work, although short stories such as "Desiree's Baby" and "The Kiss" offer Chopin at her most terse. Chopin died in 1904.

Now it is time to turn to the reading. As you read, keep the following suggestions in mind. Don't just let your eyes go over words. Instead, *get involved—get out a pen or pencil and highlighters, and use them!*

1. First, *circle the name of each character*, or highlight each in a different color. The first step in understanding a narrative is knowing *whom* it is about.
2. Second, underline or highlight in yet another color all the hints that let you know *where and when* the narrative takes place. The second step in understanding a narrative is knowing *where and when* it takes place.
3. Third, *number each event* in the narrative as it occurs. Number these events in the margin or right in the text. The third step in understanding a narrative is knowing *what* is happening.
4. Fourth, *make notes*—ideas, questions to be answered later, and so on—in the margin. These are ideas you can return to later, and they may help you understand the *how* and/or *why* of the narrative.
5. Fifth, but certainly not least, always *reread the title*. The title often gives you information that is helpful in understanding the narrative.

Maman-Nainaine said that when the figs were ripe Babette might go to visit her cousins down on the Bayou-Lafourche where the sugar cane grows. Not that the ripening of figs had the least thing to do with it, but that is the way Maman-Nainaine was.

2   It seemed to Babette a very long time to wait; for the leaves upon the trees were tender yet, and the figs were like little hard, green marbles.

3   But warm rains came along and plenty of strong sunshine, and though Maman-Nainaine was as patient as the statue of la Madone, and Babette as restless as a humming-bird, the first thing they both knew it was hot summertime. Every day Babette danced out to where the fig-trees were in a long line against the fence. She walked slowly beneath them, carefully peering between the gnarled, spreading branches. But each time she came away disconsolate again. What she saw there finally was something that made her sing and dance the whole day long.

4   When Maman-Nainaine sat down in her stately way to breakfast, the following morning, her muslin cap standing like an aureole around her white, placid face, Babette approached. She bore a dainty porcelain platter, which she set down before her godmother. It contained a dozen purple figs, fringed around with their rich, green leaves.

5   "Ah," said Maman-Nainaine arching her eyebrows, "how early the figs have ripened this year!"

6   "Oh," said Babette. "I think they have ripened very late."

7   "Babette," continued Maman-Nainaine, as she peeled the very plumpest figs with her pointed silver fruit-knife, "you will carry my love to them all down on Bayou-Lafourche. And tell your Tante Frosine I shall look for her at Toussaint—when the chrysanthemums are in bloom."

Now turn to the marked copy of "Ripe Figs" in Figure 1. The first half has already been noted for you. Take out your pen, pencil, and/or highlighters, and using the strategies listed above, complete the notes on "Ripe Figs." Note how effective the notations in Figure 1 are. It's important to know that Chopin uses nature to reflect life, so this is underlined in the biography. The title is "Ripe Figs," so figs (which are a delicate fruit) must somehow relate to the story. Babette and Maman-Nainaine are in the center of the story, and the cousins and Tante Frosine are also involved. Hints like "figs" and "Bayou," as well as information in the biography, all indicate that this story is probably taking place in the South, in Louisiana. The events are numbered in sequence: (1) Babette wants to go visiting, but Maman says not yet; (2) Babette must wait for the figs to ripen; (3) the figs ripen, and Babette now can go; and (4) Maman will go in the fall. Now it is easier to see that two things are ripening or maturing here: Babette and the figs. Thus, the ripening figs reflect Babette's maturing. When the figs are ripe, she is also ripe–or mature enough—to go visiting. By using the information from the biography and title and combining this information with the story's characters, setting, and events, you can see that as the figs ripen, Babette grows older and becomes ready to travel. Add your own notes in paragraphs 4 through 7.

FIGURE 1
Marked Copy of "Ripe Figs"

Ripe Figs

KATE CHOPIN

Kate O'Flaherty Chopin was born in St. Louis in 1851 to an affluent family. Although her father died when she was young, her widowed mother gave young Kate a taste of independence. In 1870 Kate married Oscar Chopin and moved to New Orleans and then Natchitoches Parish. Here she met the Creoles, Acadians, and African Americans she would later write about. However, Oscar died in 1882, and by 1884 she sold the plantation, gathered her five children, and returned home to St. Louis, where she began to write for popular women's magazines. Influenced noticeably by Guy de Maupassant's sense of irony and Henrik Ibsen's social comment, Chopin wrote stories, often touched with rich symbols and <u>images from nature,</u> that question societal assumptions and dictates. Her brief novel <u>The Awakening</u> remains her master work, although stories such as "Desiree's Baby" and "The Kiss" offer Chopin at her most terse. Chopin died in 1904.

Maman-Nainaine said that when the figs were ripe Babette might go to visit her cousins down on the <u>Bayou-Lafourche</u> where the <u>sugar cane grows.</u> Not that the ripening of figs had the least thing to do with it, but that is the way Maman-Nainaine was.

    1. CAN VISIT WHEN FIGS RIPEN

2   It seemed to Babette a very long time to wait; for the leaves upon the trees were tender yet, and the figs were like little hard, green marbles.

3   But <u>warm rains</u> came along and plenty of <u>strong sunshine</u>, and though Maman-Nainaine was as patient as the statue of la Madone, and Babette as restless as a humming-bird, the first thing they both knew it was <u>hot summertime</u>. Every day Babette danced out to where the fig-trees were in a long line against the fence. She walked slowly beneath them, carefully peering between the gnarled, spreading branches. But each time she came away disconsolate again. What she saw there finally was something that made her sing and dance the whole long day.

    2. WAIT FOR FIGS TO GROW

4   When Maman-Nainaine sat down in her stately way to breakfast, the following morning, her muslin cap standing like an aureole around her white, placid face, Babette approached. She bore a dainty porcelain platter, which she set down before her godmother. It contained a dozen purple figs, fringed around with their rich, green leaves.

5   "Ah," said Maman-Nainaine arching her eyebrows, "how early the figs have ripened this year!"

6   "Oh," said Babette. "I think they have ripened very late."

7   "Babette," continued Maman-Nainaine, as she peeled the very plumpest figs with her pointed silver fruit-knife, "you will carry my love to them all down on Bayou-Lafourche. And tell your Tante Frosine I shall look for her at Toussaint—when the chrysanthemums are in bloom."

Ripe Figs
JOURNAL

Once you have finished reading and making your notes on the reading, the **Journal** allows you to record and organize all the relevant information. Here you will be able to record, to organize, to reflect upon, and to make sense out of all the details that can make a reading challenging.

1. MLA Works Cited

Using this model, record your reading here.

Author's Last Name, First Name. "Title of the Story." <u>Title of the Book</u>. *3rd ed. Ed. First Name Last Name. City: Publisher, year. Pages of the story.*

Whenever you refer to or use anyone else's words or ideas, you must give that person credit. Failing to give credit is called **plagiarism**. Plagiarism can result in failing an assignment, failing a course, and even being removed from school.

To give credit appropriately, it is helpful to learn the format used to credit works of literature and, in this sample, short stories are literature. This format has been created by the MLA, which is short for Modern Language Association. The **MLA Works Cited entry** you use here is the same form you will be using in your other English classes.

The MLA entry is really a very simple form. All you have to do is follow the model given. Note that, unlike paragraphs, the first line starts at the left margin and each line *after* that is indented. Also note that, generally, titles of major works and/or collections are underlined, while titles of shorter works and/or entries within a collection are put in quotation marks. Try doing this on your own. When you finish, your MLA Works Cited entry should look like the following:

Chopin, Kate. "Ripe Figs." <u>American 24-Karat Gold</u>. 3rd ed. Ed. Yvonne C. Sisko. New York: Pearson Longman, 2009. 7.

2. Main Character(s)

Characters are the creatures that create, move, or experience the actions of a narrative. We normally think of characters as alive, animated beings, such as humans or animals, who can participate in the action, although some characters will surprise you. A character may also be called an **actor, player, person, personage,** or **persona**.

Characters fall into two categories: main characters and supporting characters. Generally, a **main character** is central to the action. A **supporting character** may encourage the action and is usually not present as much, or as central to the action, as the main character. Sometimes it is difficult to decide if a character is main or supporting. For instance, in a murder mystery, the victim may appear at the beginning or not at all, but the entire narrative is about solving her or his murder. Is the victim a main character because the entire narrative is all about her or him, or is s/he a supporting character because s/he is simply not around much? Both answers may be correct. In literature there are not always so much right or wrong answers as there are explanations, analyses, and debates. The correctness of your answers may depend on how well you explain your choices.

Characters may also be considered protagonists or antagonists. "Pro" means "for," and the **protagonist** is the hero or heroine, the character we **empathize** with or share feelings with, the character we root for. "Anti" means "against," and the **antagonist** is the villain, the enemy of the protagonist, the character we do not like, the character we root against. In "Ripe Figs," our sympathies are with Babette and her longing for adventure; she is the protagonist. Maman, who sets limits on Babette, is the antagonist. Here, these two characters are members of a seemingly close family and love each other, but in other narratives the protagonist and antagonist may not be such close relatives and/or friends.

The author speaks to us through her or his characters. When an author writes using "I" or "we," this is called a **first-person narrative**. The first person makes a story very immediate. The character who tells the story is called the **narrator**. If the author addresses the reader directly using "you," this narrative technique is called a **second-person narrative**. Second person is not used often today. Finally, if the author uses "he," "she," "it," or "they" to tell the narrative, this narrative technique is called a **third-person narrative**. This is the most common narrative form, with the author seeming to be more of an observer and less of a participant in the story. In "Ripe Figs," both Babette and Maman are observed as "she." The story is thus told in the third person; the author is the narrator who observes but does not enter the narrative.

With these understandings, turn to the **Main Character(s)** and **Supporting Characters** entries in the Journal. Note that we have already filled in Babette, briefly describing her and noting her important place in the story. Who else should be here? Add an entry in which you describe and defend Maman as a main character.

Note: When discussing literature, always use the **present tense**. Although a narrative may have been written a thousand years ago, each time a narrative is read the characters and actions come to life and are alive right now, so keep your discussions of the characters and events in the present tense.

Describe each main character, and explain why you think each is a main character.

Babette is a young girl who lives with her godmother and wants to go visit her cousins. She is a main character because the story is about her wants and her godmother's rules.

3. Supporting Characters

Now fill in the **Supporting Characters** entry. This has been started for you. Certainly, the cousins support the action because they are the reason Babette wants to travel. Who else should be here? Add an entry in which you describe and defend Tante Frosine as a supporting character. Remember from your context studies that "tante" means "aunt," so Tante Frosine is probably the cousins' mother.

Describe each supporting character, and explain why you think each is a supporting character.

Babette's cousins are supporting characters. Although we never see them, they are the reason for the story's conflict.

4. Setting

Setting is a catch-all term that describes the **time, place**, and surroundings of a narrative. In a short story, the setting is usually, although not always, limited. The story usually takes place in a shorter amount of time than in a longer work, and fewer places are involved. In a novel, there may be more time and more places.

Props go along with the setting. Props (short for "properties") are the inanimate objects in a narrative. Props sometimes take on the qualities of characters.

Now turn to the **Setting** entry. You already have a head start because the place, Louisiana, is described. But you still have several things to do. First, you need to add when the story takes place. Check the biography for when Chopin lived, and remember that traveling seems to be a very big accomplishment in this story, unlike it is in today's world of easy car transportation. Second, think about props and mention the figs, which are certainly part of this story. Here, the place has been done for you. Now, add your descriptions of the time and any relevant props.

Describe the setting(s) and any relevant prop(s).

This must be set in the South because figs are a delicate fruit, because the French words sound like words spoken in Louisiana, and because the biography says that Chopin wrote about the South.

5. Sequence

A narrative is based around a simple skeleton of events called a **plot**. Around this basic plot, a logical order of events or **sequence** occurs that builds tension or, in mysteries, suspense. In narratives we call all the events in the sequence a **story line**. The plot is the bare framework, while the sequence supplies the details that make each narrative unique.

Have you ever gone to the movies and watched the end credits roll while you were still waiting for the movie to get going? You looked at the person sitting next to you, felt cheated, and asked, "What happened?" What happened is that, somewhere along the line, the storyteller failed.

In a well-written narrative, one event logically leads to another, and then to another, and so on, so that each word and action counts and builds tension that carries your interest. The tension peaks at the **climax** and then resolves in the **dénouement**. When any of these pieces are missing, poorly developed, or unbelievable, we are disappointed. (Movie sequels, in fact, purposely stop at the climax and before the dénouement so that we will return for the next episode.) A very simple story line appears in Figure 2.

FIGURE 2
Simple Story Line

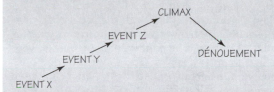

Record information about sequence and plot in the Journal. In the **Sequence** entry, you are asked to outline all the events in order. The outline is started for you, with Babette's desire to go visiting and Maman's restriction. Now look at your numbered notes on the story, and complete the outline. Add as many events as you feel are necessary.

Outline the events of the story in order.

I. Babette wants to go visiting, but Maman-Nainaine says she must wait for the figs to ripen.

II.

III.

IV.

6. Plot

Next, in the **Plot** entry, summarize all these events into one sentence. Summarizing makes you look back over the reading and reflect on what you have read. Remember, this is the bare framework of the narrative, so keep it short.

Tell the story in no more than one sentence.

7. Conflicts

Conflicts are the disagreements between the characters. Conflicts build the tension in a narrative. Many types of conflicts are possible. The conflict may be **human versus human**, as when a character(s) is pitted against another character(s). The conflict may be **human versus society**, as when a character(s) struggles against a group, community, or social structure. The conflict may be **human versus technology**, as when a character(s) vies with the tools of science or machines of society. The conflict may be **human versus nature**, as when a character(s) battles with the forces of nature. The conflict may be **human versus the supernatural**, as when a character(s) vies with God or gods or demons. Finally, the conflict may be **human versus herself/himself**, as when a character wrestles with her or his own internal and self-defeating **flaw**. More often than not, a story will contain a combination of these conflicts.

Let's now turn to the **Conflicts** entry. Human versus human, in Babette's struggle with Maman's restriction, is already noted. What other types of conflicts are present in the story? How about human versus nature in Babette's wanting the figs to mature rapidly, and human versus herself in Babette's impatience? Add these and explain them in your Journal entry.

Identify and explain all the conflicts involved here.

Human versus human applies to Babette wanting to go and Maman-Nainaine stopping her.

8. Significant Quotations

By now, you already understand the narrative well. You have identified the pieces and pulled them together. Now you need to reflect on the narrative. In this section, you will find quotations from key parts of the narrative. By explaining why each quotation is important to the reading, you can deepen your understanding.

First, look up the quotation in the reading text. Underline it and note what is important about this moment in the reading. Then, record the importance of this moment. Tell who is speaking and why this quotation is important to the action in the reading. The first one has been done for you. Now, complete the rest. Record the page number for practice with **MLA parenthetical citation**.

Explain the importance of each of these quotations. Record the page number in the parentheses.

a. "Maman-Nainaine said that when the figs were ripe Babette might go to visit her cousins down on the Bayou-Lafourche where the sugar cane grows" (7).

This quotation sets the tension in the story between Babette and Maman-Nainaine and between Babette and nature. Babette wants to visit her cousins, but she must wait until the figs—and she—are ripe or mature enough to go.

b. "Every day Babette danced out to where the fig-trees were in a long line against the fence" (   ).

c. "What she saw there finally was something that made her sing and dance the whole day long" (   ).

    d. "'Ah,' said Maman-Nainaine arching her eyebrows, 'how early the figs have ripened this year!'" ( ).

    e. "'And tell your Tante Frosine I shall look for her at Toussaint—when the chrysanthemums are in bloom'" ( ).

9. Literary Elements

By now, you have become familiar with identifying characters, conflicts, settings, props, sequences, plots, and so forth. These terms or ideas, along with others you will meet, are called **literary elements**. You will see that the chapters in this book stress specific elements. Here you are asked to decide why each story is placed in the chapter in which it appears.

    For instance, let's say that "Ripe Figs" had been placed in the *Characters and Conflicts* chapter. "Ripe Figs" not only has characters and conflicts, but it certainly also has a setting and important props, and it certainly has events leading up to a climax. Yet in looking over the whole story, we can see that this story is largely a character study focused on impatient Babette and the conflicts her impatience entails. Thus, here you will want to focus on why characters and conflicts are so important in this story. Likewise, for every other story, you will focus on the chapter's literary element(s) and explain why the element(s) is (are) important to the story. Sometimes you may even disagree with the placement and, if you disagree, explain why you disagree and where else you would place the story. The important thing is that you explain the story in terms of the given element(s). Now, explain why characters and conflicts are so important in "Ripe Figs." Then explain any other chapter(s) in which you feel "Ripe Figs" might also fit.

Look at this chapter's title [here, we are using Characters and Conflicts] and explain why you think this story is placed in this chapter. Explain in which other chapter(s) you might place this story, as relevant to the literary element(s) of that chapter.

10. Foreshadowing, Irony, and/or Symbolism

Other elements that may enhance a narrative are foreshadowing, irony, and/or symbolism.

Foreshadowing is a technique some authors use to help explain or predict events to come. The author may sprinkle information or hints throughout the narrative to help predict actions that are yet to happen.

Irony is found in the difference between what *is* and what *should be*. Irony may be bitter—you work and work and work, and someone new, who has done nothing, arrives at your job and gets the promotion you deserve. Irony may be humorous—you wake up late and race around knowing you will be late for class, only to get to school and find out that your class has been canceled. Irony may even be providential—you sleep in and miss your bus only to find out that the bus has been in an accident and you are still safe at home. Think of ironies as unexpected twists in time, places, or events.

Symbols are objects or characters that represent something beyond their face value. For instance, an American flag is really nothing more than pieces of cloth sewn together, but the American flag represents the pride and glory and industry of America. By looking beyond the surface, you will find many examples of symbolism in literature.

In **Foreshadowing, Irony, and/or Symbolism**, you will want to discuss one of these elements. Here, let's focus on the symbols in this story, and there are several. First and foremost, the figs represent maturity and reflect Babette's growth. Second, the **seasons** are relevant here. Summer is youthful Babette's time, while fall is the older Maman's and Tante Frosine's time. In literature, spring may represent birth or rebirth or youth; summer may represent youth or the full blossom of life; fall may represent middle age; and winter may represent the later years. Here Chopin gives us clues to the characters' ages by using the seasons. The chrysanthemums (flowers that bloom in the fall) represent the time for Babette's elders.

Although foreshadowing and irony are not particularly relevant to this story, be aware that Kate Chopin is known for her ironic twists. "The Kiss" and "The Story of an Hour" (pages 193 and 261) take wonderfully unexpected turns. And, of course, here the ripening figs foreshadow Babette's growth.

Explain examples of foreshadowing, irony, and/or symbolism in this story.

FOLLOW-UP QUESTIONS

10 SHORT QUESTIONS

Follow-up questions are designed to measure your comprehension of each reading. In the first set of questions, **10 Short Questions**, you will see ten multiple-choice entries aimed at measuring your comprehension.

Notice that you are instructed to "select the <u>best</u> answer." In some readings, more than one answer will be correct; it is your job to choose the <u>best</u> answer. The first five have been done for you here.

The answer to question 1 is "a" because Babette is the younger of the two. We know this because Babette's actions and the information from the story—Maman means "mother" and Maman is Babette's godmother—imply that Babette is younger and Maman is older. The answer to question 2 is "b" for the same reasons listed in the answer to question 1. The answer to question 3 is "c" because we are clearly told that Maman is the godmother. The cousins are in Babette's age group and are whom she wants to visit; there is no mention of a sister in the story. The answer to question 4 is "a" because, as the story implies, figs need a warm summer and rain to grow; neither "cold" nor "desert" fit the story's setting. The answer to question 5 is "c," because we are clearly told about Babette's "restlessness" as opposed to Maman's "patience."

Now complete questions 6 through 10 on your own. The correct answers appear on page 21.

Select the <u>best</u> answer for each.

_a_ 1. Babette is
    a. younger than Maman.
    b. older than Maman.
    c. the same age as Maman.

_b_ 2. Maman-Nainaine is
    a. younger than Babette.
    b. older than Babette.
    c. the same age as Babette.

_c_ 3. Maman-Nainaine is Babette's
    a. sister.
    b. cousin.
    c. godmother.

_a_ 4. "Ripe Figs" is probably set in
    a. a warm climate.
    b. a cold climate.
    c. a desert climate.

_c_ 5. Babette
    a. does not wait for the figs.
    b. waits calmly for the figs.
    c. waits impatiently for the figs.

____ 6. Maman
    a. does not wait for the figs.
    b. waits calmly for the figs.
    c. waits impatiently for the figs.

____ 7. The figs symbolize
    a. Maman's maturing.
    b. Babette's maturing.
    c. Babette's cousins' maturing.

____ 8. We can infer that Maman is relatively
   a. poor.
   b. middle class.
   c. well off.

____ 9. We can infer that the cousins live
   a. nearby.
   b. a distance away.
   c. very, very far away.

____ 10. The chrysanthemums tell us that Maman is
   a. very young.
   b. very old.
   c. in her middle years.

5 SIGNIFICANT QUOTATIONS

Approach these **5 Significant Quotations** by reflecting on the reading. The quotations are important and central to the reading. Remember you are demonstrating how well you have understood the reading, so explain why each quotation is important as completely as you can.

The first quotation here has already been done for you. Now, explain the significance of the remaining four. (The answers are on page 21.)

Explain the importance of each of these quotations.

1. "Maman-Nainaine said that when the figs were ripe Babette might go to visit her cousins down on the Bayou-Lafourche where the sugar cane grows."

    This sentence sets the tension in the story between Babette and Maman-Nainaine and between Babette and nature. Babette wants to visit her cousins, but she must wait until the figs—and she—are ripe or mature enough.

2. "It seemed to Babette a very long time to wait; [. . .]."

3. "But warm rains came along and plenty of strong sunshine, and though Maman-Nainaine was as patient as the statue of la Madone, and Babette as restless as a humming-bird, the first thing they both knew it was hot summertime."

4. "It [the platter] contained a dozen purple figs, fringed around with their rich, green leaves."

5. "'Babette,' continued Maman-Nainaine, as she peeled the very plumpest figs with her pointed silver fruit-knife, 'you will carry my love to them all down on Bayou-LaFourche.'"

2 COMPREHENSION ESSAY QUESTIONS

The **2 Comprehension Essay Questions** offer opportunities for extended essays. Your teacher may assign one or both for individual assignment or for group discussion. Gather your thoughts and respond, demonstrating what you have learned from the reading. Note that none of these questions asks how well you liked the reading or even if you liked it at all. The intention here is very simply to find out what you have understood in the reading.

Note that the directions ask you to "use specific details and information from the story." This does not mean that you have to memorize the reading, but it does mean that you should know the characters and events in the reading. Look at question 1. It asks you to explain the title, so for this essay question, you will want to review the story's events and the relevance of the figs. Now look at question 2. It asks you to focus on the ages involved in the story, and for this you will want to discuss the ages of Babette and her cousins as opposed to those of Maman and Tante Frosine, remembering the references to summer and fall in the story.

Use specific details and information from the story to answer these questions as completely as possible.

1. How does the title relate to the story? Explain the significance of the title using specific details and information from the story.

2. What is the relevance of age in this story? Use specific details and information from the story to support your explanation.

DISCUSSION QUESTIONS

Now that you have read and studied the narrative, **Discussion Questions** are two questions that are always focused on the narrative and that are designed to help you think about the narrative. Here, you may be asked to share your opinions or reactions to elements in the narrative. Notice that you are instructed to "be prepared to discuss these questions in class." Although your teacher may ask you to discuss these questions as a class or to write the answers independently, your thoughtful answers should reflect what you have learned about the reading. The first one has been started for you.

Here, you need to reflect on the story and on your own youth. You need to identify and explain what characteristics you think Babette possesses that are youthful. Of course, when one thinks of youth, one thinks of energy, and you might want to discuss Babette's activities that require lots of energy, such as being physically busy and active, surrounding oneself with busy friends, and so forth. Related to energy, one thinks of impatience when one thinks of youth, and you may want to discuss Babette's impatience with the figs and Maman and travelling. Finally, the curiosity to explore or, in this case, to travel may also be a sign of youth, and you may want to discuss Babette's desire to travel. Think if there is anything else you might want to add to question 1.

Then, reflect on the story and on your own observations of mature people. Complete question 2 on your own.

Be prepared to discuss these questions in class.

1. What characteristics mark Babette's youth?

> One characteristic of youth is having lots of energy. Babette is continually in motion, expending a great deal of physical energy. She is also looking forward to visiting with her cousins, and visiting also requires a great deal of energy. With all this energy, another characteristic of youth is impatience. Babette is impatient with Maman, wanting to speed the ripening of the figs to suit Maman's rules. Babette is also impatient with the figs themselves, as she spends much time and energy checking and wishing them into ripening. And Babette is impatient to travel. Curiosity and inquisitiveness are often associated with the young, and Babette has both the energy and the curiosity to look forward to this trip.

2. What characteristics mark Maman's maturity?

WRITING

Each narrative ends with a final section of **Writing** prompts. The first two prompts offer suggestions for personal writing. The prompts under **Further Writing** are designed with research in mind. These may suggest comparing and contrasting the reading with other readings in this book or with other narratives the author or another author has written, or they may suggest other research topics. Your teacher will guide you through the writing process.

At this point, a few words about the writing process are in order. Writing does not start with a pen or pencil; it starts with ideas. Before you start writing, jot down ideas, and then organize them. Here are two **pre-writing strategies** to get the ideas flowing:

1. On a clean sheet of paper, write one key word based on the topic you plan to write about. Now look at the key word, and start listing every word that this key word brings to mind. Avoid sentences or even phrases, as they take longer to write and can break your train of thought. Just write words—lots of words, the more the merrier. When you run out of words, look back at the key word, and write more words. When you finish, you will have a whole list of ideas to start thinking about for your essay. This process is called **free associating** or **brainstorming.**

2. On a clean sheet of paper, draw a circle. Inside that circle, write one key word about the topic on which you plan to write. Now look at the key word, and start tagging other, related words onto the circle. Then tag words onto the tag words, and so on. When you get stuck, look back at the key word, and add more words. When you finish, you will have groups of words—ideas—to start thinking about for your essay. This process is called **grouping, networking**, or **clustering.**

Once you have the ideas—and you should have plenty from either of these pre-writing strategies—the next step is to organize them into an **outline**. Do not worry about Roman numerals at this stage. Rather, develop logical groupings of these ideas into a working outline. You may find that there are words/ideas in your pre-write that you do not want to use. Cross these out. You may also find ideas in your outline that are out of place. Number and renumber the groups to make them work for you. (Your instructor may want you to formalize your outline later, but at this point the important thing is to find an organization that works for you.)

Look at the first writing prompt below. It asks you, first, to discuss one specific maturing process you have experienced and, second, to relate this process to a reflective image, much like the figs in our story. In Figure 3 both a cluster and an outline on the topic, "Getting a License," are demonstrated, but you may want to try "Learning to Ride a Bike" or "Graduating from High School" or any other maturing process you prefer.

FIGURE 3
Sample Cluster and Outline

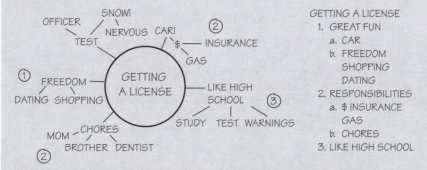

To prepare the pre-writing cluster and outline shown in Figure 3, we first tagged ideas onto "License" and then tagged ideas onto ideas. Second, we looked for a logical order and numbered and renumbered the cluster. Third, we transferred these numbers into the informal, working outline. Finally, we looked back over what we had and decided that getting a license was like attending high school, because of all the preparation and responsibility involved in getting a license. With these ideas initiated and organized, we are now ready to write an intelligent and orderly essay.

Now try your hand at the other writing prompts.

Use each of these ideas for writing an essay.

1. We all go through maturing processes. Think of a specific process you have experienced. Then think of something that reflects your process, much like the figs reflect Babette's growth. Write an essay on your own growing up process, relating it to a continuing symbol.

2. Age has an effect on all of us. Write about a specific incident when age affected you or someone you know.

Further Writing

1. Read Kate Chopin's "The Storm" (available in a library), and compare and contrast the images of nature in "The Storm" with those in "Ripe Figs."

2. Read Kate Chopin's "The Kiss" (page 193), and compare Nathalie in "The Kiss" with Calixta in "The Storm."

Answers to
10 Short Questions

6. b. We are clearly told Maman is "patient" and not "impatient."
7. b. We know Babette is the one growing and "maturing."
8. c. Their genteel life, her leisurely breakfast, and the "silver fruit-knife" all imply wealth.
9. b. Bayou-Lafourche, in Louisiana, and Maman's reluctance to let Babette go at all both imply that this is, on the one hand, not "near by" and, on the other hand, not "very, very far away." The middle choice is the best choice here.
10. c. Again, we have discussed literary seasons and the middle choice is the best choice here. Spring or summer would refer to youth, and winter would refer to old age. Chrysanthemums bloom in the fall, and fall represents middle age.

Answers to
5 Significant Quotations

2. You should note that this sets up the central tension of Babette having to wait for the figs to ripen so that she can go visiting.
3. You should comment on Babette's "restlessness" and Maman's patience. This is not an easy wait for Babette.
4. You should explain that this is the moment of climax. The figs are ripe. You should explain that the ripe figs represent Babette's maturing and she now is old enough/mature enough/ripe enough to travel to see her cousins.
5. You should note that this is the story's resolution, the dénouement. Babette may now travel.

Notes

CHAPTER 1

Characters and Conflicts

Characters are the creatures that create, move, or experience the actions of a story. We normally think of characters as alive, animated beings, such as humans or animals, who can participate in the action. A character may also be called an **actor**, **player**, **person**, **persona**, or **personage**.

Characters fall into two categories: main characters and supporting characters. Generally, a **main character** is central to the action. A **supporting character** may encourage the action and is usually not present as much, or as central to the action, as the main character. Sometimes, it is difficult to decide if a character is main or supporting. For instance, in a murder mystery the victim may only appear at the beginning of the story or not at all, but the entire story is about solving her or his murder. Is the victim a main character because the entire story is about her or him, or is s/he a supporting character because s/he simply is not present? Both answers may be correct. In literature there are not always so much right or wrong answers as there are explanations, analyses, and debates. The correctness of your answers may depend on how well you explain your choices.

The author speaks to us through her or his characters. When an author writes using "I" or "we," this is called a **first-person narration**. The first-person makes a story very immediate. The character who tells the story is called the **narrator**. If the author addresses the reader directly using "you," this narrative technique is called a **second-person narration**. The second-person is not used often in American literature. Finally, if the author uses "he," "she," "it," or "they" to tell the story, this narrative technique is called a **third-person narration**. This is the most common narrative form, with the author seeming to be more of an observer and less of a participant in the story. The stories in this chapter are told in the third person, except Migene Gonzalez-Wippler's "Yoruba," Amy Tan's "Two Kinds," and Edgar Allan Poe's "The Tell-Tale Heart." Notice how immediate and how different Gonzalez-Wippler's, Tan's, and Poe's stories are.

Characters may also be considered protagonists or antagonists. "Pro" means "for," and the **protagonist** is the hero or heroine, the character we

empathize with, or share feelings with, the character we root for. "Anti" means "against," and the **antagonist** is the villain, the enemy of the protagonist, the character we do not like, the character we root against. Be aware that authors like to play with these roles. You may be sympathetic to one character and then find that the author turns things upside down and you no longer like the character.

When we talk about protagonists and antagonists, we need to talk about conflicts. **Conflicts** are the disagreements between characters. Conflicts build the tension in a story. Many types of conflicts are possible. The conflict may be **human versus human**, as when a character(s) is pitted against another character(s). Notice the conflict between the old man and the narrator in "The Tell-Tale Heart." The conflict may be **human versus society**, as when a character(s) struggles against a group, community, or social structure. Notice how the narrator struggles with the expectations of her community in "Two Kinds." The conflict may be **human versus herself/himself**, as when a character wrestles with her or his own internal and self-defeating **flaw**. Notice the flaw in the narrator of "The Tell-Tale Heart." The conflict may be **human versus technology**, as when a character(s) vies with the tools of science or machines of society. This conflict is at the very core of "There Will Come Soft Rains." The conflict may be **human versus nature**, as when a character(s) battles with the forces of nature. Notice Old Phoenix's struggle in "A Worn Path." Finally, the conflict may be **human versus the supernatural**, as when a character(s) vies with God or gods or demons. Notice the narrator's struggle in "Yoruba." You will discover this conflict again when you read later stories. More often than not, a story will contain a combination of these conflicts.

Stories in this chapter focus on characters and are called **character studies**. In a character study, the emphasis is on getting to know each character, and the action of the story is used to help you understand each character better. Eudora Welty takes you through Old Phoenix's persistence, Migene Gonzalez-Wippler takes you through the narrator's concerns, and Amy Tan takes you through the narrator's struggles. Then Edgar Allan Poe, whose stories are invariably character studies, works his sinister magic as he walks you through insanity. In reading Poe, keep asking yourself which character is the protagonist and which is the antagonist. And finally, Ray Bradbury turns all our assumptions about characters upside down as inanimate objects and machines take on the qualities of characters. The living, breathing family and even the dog become merely supporting characters or properties in this story centered on technology.

Now it is time to turn to the stories. Enjoy the characters you meet.

A Worn Path

Eudora Welty

Pre-reading Vocabulary
Context

Use context clues to define these words before reading. Use a dictionary as needed.

1. The cook wore a full *apron* to cover his clothes. *Apron* means

   _____.

2. The *thicket* of bushes was so dense that only the little rabbits could live under it. *Thicket* means _____.

3. When he walked, the elderly man used a slender *cane* made of oak to steady himself. *Cane* means _____.

4. The land was quite even until it dipped into a *hollow* near the stream. *Hollow* means _____.

5. The *thorn* on the rose stem stuck Gert in the finger. *Thorn* means

   _____.

6. When Leisha performed in front of hundreds of people, she was so nervous that her hands were *trembling*. *Trembling* means

   _____.

7. Whether Teddy could pass chemistry or not became a personal *trial* for him. *Trial* means _____.

8. As the lions finished their meal, the *buzzards* flew overhead and then waited to finish what was left. *Buzzard* means _____.

9. A figure made of straw stuffed into clothes so it looks like a person and scares birds out of a field is called a *scarecrow*. *Scarecrow* means

   _____.

10. The cool water of the *spring* bubbled up from an underground source. *Spring* means _____.

11. Laura was lost in thought as she *meditated* on her new job. *Meditate* means _____.

12. Workers worked for three years to build the tall *tower* with the clock at the top. *Tower* means_____.

13. The tall building looked like a tower as it stood so straight and *erect*. *Erect* means _____.

14. George knew he was close to home when he saw the tall, cone-shaped *steeple* on top of the church. *Steeple* means _____.

15. Whenever she can, Sallie donates to *charity*, with her time and money, in order to help the poor. *Charity* means_____.

16. When Lucille felt ill, she went to the drugstore and bought *medicine* which she could take to feel better. *Medicine* means

    _____.

17. Graduation ceremonies, with their formal speeches and many well-dressed people, are very *dignified* events. *Dignified* means

    _____.

18. The *lye* Tim was mixing to make soap got on his skin and burned it. *Lye* means _____.

19. He is so *obstinate* and never listens to anyone else's ideas or suggestions. *Obstinate* means _____.

20. Jamie decided to buy Megan a *windmill*, a hand-held toy with paddles that turn in the wind. *Windmill* means _____.

PRE-READING VOCABULARY
STRUCTURAL ATTACK

Define these words by solving the parts. Use the Glossary or a dictionary as needed.

1. pinewoods
2. shoe-laces
3. numberless
4. pearly
5. acceptable
6. barbed-wire
7. overhead
8. gunshot
9. crisscrossed
10. clockwork
11. forgiveness

PRE-READING QUESTIONS

Try answering these questions as you read.

Who is Old Phoenix?

What does she do?

What do her actions tell you about her?

A Worn Path

EUDORA WELTY

Eudora Welty was born in Jackson, Mississippi in 1909. After studying at Mississippi State College for Women, the University of Wisconsin, and the Columbia University Graduate School of Business, she returned to the South and eventually turned to writing. Her stories present a much more pleasant view of the South than William Faulkner's, and the triumphs of her always-interesting characters inspire us all. Her other works include <u>The Collected Stories of Eudora Welty</u> and <u>The Optimist's Daughter</u>, which won the Pulitzer Prize in 1972.

It was December—a bright frozen day in the early morning. Far out in the country there was an old Negro woman with her head tied in a red rag, coming along a path through the pinewoods. Her name was Phoenix Jackson. She was very old and small and she walked slowly in the dark pine shadows, moving a little from side to side in her steps, with the balanced heaviness and lightness of a pendulum in a grandfather clock. She carried a thin, small cane made from an umbrella, and with this she kept tapping the frozen earth in front of her. This made a grave and persistent noise in the still air, that seemed meditative like the chirping of a solitary little bird.

2   She wore a dark striped dress reaching down to her shoe tops, and an equally long apron of bleached sugar sacks, with a full pocket: all neat and tidy, but every time she took a step she might have fallen over her shoe-laces, which dragged from her unlaced shoes. She looked straight ahead. Her eyes were blue with age. Her skin had a pattern all its own of numberless branching wrinkles and as though a whole little tree stood in the middle of her forehead, but a golden color ran underneath, and the two knobs of her cheeks were illuminated by a yellow burning under the dark. Under the red rag her hair came down on her neck in the frailest of ringlets, still black, and with an odor like copper.

3   Now and then there was a quivering in the thicket. Old Phoenix said, "Out of my way, all you foxes, owls, beetles, jack rabbits, coons, and wild animals! . . . Keep out from under these feet, little bobwhites. . . . Keep the big wild hogs out of my path. Don't let none of those come running my direction. I got a long way." Under her small black-freckled hand her cane, limber as a buggy whip, would switch at the brush as if to rouse up any hiding things.

4   On she went. The woods were deep and stiff. The sun made the pine needles almost too bright to look at, up where the wind rocked. The cones dropped as light as feathers. Down in the hollow was the mourning dove—it was not too late for him.

5   The path ran up a hill. "Seem like there is chains about my feet, time I get this far," she said, in the voice of argument old people keep to use with themselves. "Something always take a hold of me on this hill—pleads I should stay."

6   After she got to the top she turned and gave a full, severe look behind her where she had come. "Up through pines," she said at length. "Now down through oaks."

7   Her eyes opened their widest, and she started down gently. But before she got to the bottom of the hill a bush caught her dress.

8   Her fingers were busy and intent, but her skirts were full and long, so that before she could pull them free in one place they were caught in another. It was not possible to allow the dress to tear. "I in the thorny bush," she said. "Thorns, you doing your appointed work. Never want to let folks pass—no sir. Old eyes thought you was a pretty little *green* bush."

9   Finally, trembling all over, she stood free, and after a moment dared to stoop for her cane.

10   "Sun so high!" she cried, leaning back and looking, while the thick tears went over her eyes. "The time getting all gone here."

11   At the foot of this hill was a place where a log was laid across the creek.

12   "Now comes the trial," said Phoenix.

13   Putting her right foot out, she mounted the log and shut her eyes. Lifting her skirt, levelling her cane fiercely before her, like a festival figure in some parade, she began to march across. Then she opened her eyes and she was safe on the other side.

14   "I wasn't as old as I thought," she said.

15   But she sat down to rest. She spread her skirts on the bank around her and folded her hands over her knees. Up above her was a tree in a pearly cloud of mistletoe. She did not dare to close her eyes, and when a little boy brought her a little plate with a slice of marble-cake on it she spoke to him. "That would be acceptable," she said. But when she went to take it there was just her own hand in the air.

16   So she left that tree, and had to go through a barbed-wire fence. There she had to creep and crawl, spreading her knees and stretching her fingers like a baby trying to climb the steps. But she talked loudly to herself: she could not let her dress be torn now, so late in the day, and she could not pay for having her arm or leg sawed off if she got caught fast where she was.

17   At last she was safe through the fence and risen up out in the clearing. Big dead trees, like black men with one arm, were standing in the purple stalks of the withered cotton field. There sat a buzzard.

18   "Who you watching?"

19   In the furrow she made her way along.

20   "Glad this not the season for bulls," she said, looking side-ways, "and the good Lord made his snakes to curl up and sleep in the winter. A pleasure I don't see no two-headed snake coming around that tree, where it come once. It took a while to get by him, back in the summer."

21   She passed through the old cotton and went into a field of dead corn. It whispered and shook and was taller than her head. "Through the maze now," she said, for there was no path.

22   Then there was something tall, black, and skinny there, moving before her.

23   At first she took it for a man. It could have been a man dancing in the field. But she stood still and listened, and it did not make a sound. It was as silent as a ghost.

24   "Ghost," she said sharply, "who be you the ghost of? For I have heard of nary death close by."

25   But there was no answer—only the ragged dancing in the wind.

26   She shut her eyes, reached out her hand, and touched a sleeve. She found a coat and inside that an emptiness, cold as ice.

27   "You scarecrow," she said. Her face lighted. "I ought to be shut up for good," she said with laughter. "My senses is gone, I too old. I the oldest people I ever know. Dance, old scarecrow," she said, "while I dancing with you."

28   She kicked her foot over the furrow, and with mouth drawn down, shook her head once or twice in a little strutting way. Some husks blew down and whirled in streamers about her skirts.

29   Then she went on, parting her way from side to side with the cane, through the whispering field. At last she came to the end, to a wagon track where the silver grass blew between the red ruts. The quail were walking around like pullets, seeming all dainty and unseen.

30   "Walk pretty," she said. "This the easy place. This the easy going."

31   She followed the track, swaying through the quiet bare fields, through the little strings of trees silver in their dead leaves, past cabins silver from weather, with the doors and windows boarded shut, all like old women under a spell sitting there. "I walking in their sleep," she said, nodding her head vigorously.

32   In a ravine she went where a spring was silently flowing through a hollow log. Old Phoenix bent and drank. "Sweet-gum makes the water sweet," she said, and drank more. "Nobody know who made this well, for it was here when I was born."

33   The track crossed a swampy part where the moss hung as white as lace from every limb. "Sleep on, alligators, and blow your bubbles." Then the track went into the road.

34   Deep, deep the road went down between the high green-colored banks. Overhead the live oaks met, and it was as dark as a cave.

35   A black dog with a lolling tongue came up out of the weeds by the ditch. She was meditating, and not ready, and when he came at her she only hit him a little with her cane. Over she went in the ditch, like a little puff of milk-weed.

36   Down there, her senses drifted away. A dream visited her, and she reached her hand up, but nothing reached down and gave her a pull. So she lay there and presently went to talking. "Old woman," she said to herself, "that black dog come up out of the weeds to stall you off, and now there he sitting on his fine tail, smiling at you."

37   A white man finally came along and found her—a hunter, a young man, with his dog on a chain.

38   "Well, Granny!" he laughed. "What are you doing there?"

39   "Lying on my back like a June-bug waiting to be turned over, mister," she said, reaching up her hand.

40   He lifted her up, gave her a swing in the air, and set her down. "Anything broken, Granny?"

41   "No sir, them old dead weeds is springy enough," said Phoenix, when she had got her breath. "I thank you for your trouble."

42   "Where do you live, Granny?" he asked, while the two dogs were growling at each other.

43   "Away back yonder, sir, behind the ridge. You can't even see it from here."

44   "On your way home?"

45   "No, sir, I going to town."

46   "Why, that's too far! That's as far as I walk when I come out myself, and I get something for my trouble." He patted the stuffed bag he carried, and there hung down a little closed claw. It was one of the bob-whites, with its beak hooked bitterly to show it was dead. "Now you go on home, Granny!"

47   "I bound to go to town, mister," said Phoenix. "The time come around."

48   He gave another laugh, filling the whole landscape. "I know you old colored people! Wouldn't miss going to town to see Santa Claus!"

49   But something held Old Phoenix very still. The deep lines in her face went into a fierce and different radiation. Without warning, she had seen with her own eyes a flashing nickel fall out of the man's pocket onto the ground.

50   "How old are you, Granny?" he was saying.

51   "There is no telling, mister," she said, "no telling."

52   Then she gave a little cry and clapped her hands and said, "Git on away from here, dog! Look! Look at that dog!" She laughed as if in

admiration. "He ain't scared of nobody. He a big black dog." She whispered, "Sic him!"

53   "Watch me get rid of that cur," said the man. "Sic him, Pete! Sic him!"

54   Phoenix heard the dogs fighting, and heard the man running and throwing sticks. She even heard a gunshot. But she was slowly bending forward by that time, further and further forward, the lids stretched down over her eyes, as if she were doing this in her sleep. Her chin was lowered almost to her knees. The yellow palm of her hand came out from the fold of her apron. Her fingers slid down and along the ground under the piece of money with the grace and care they would have in lifting an egg from under a sitting hen. Then she slowly straightened up, she stood erect, and the nickel was in her apron pocket. A bird flew by. Her lips moved. "God watching me the whole time. I come to stealing."

55   The man came back, and his own dog panted about them. "Well, I scared him off that time," he said, and then he laughed and lifted his gun and pointed it at Phoenix.

56   She stood straight and faced him.

57   "Doesn't the gun scare you?" he said, still pointing it.

58   "No, sir, I seen plenty go off closer by, in my day, and for less than what I done," she said, holding utterly still.

59   He smiled, and shouldered the gun. "Well, Granny," he said, "You must be a hundred years old, and scared of nothing. I'd give you a dime if I had any money with me. But you take my advice and stay home, and nothing will happen to you."

60   "I bound to go on my way, mister," said Phoenix. She inclined her head in the red rag. Then they went in different directions, but she could hear the gun shooting again and again over the hill.

61   She walked on. The shadows hung from the oak trees to the road like curtains. Then she smelled wood-smoke, and smelled the river, and she saw a steeple and the cabins on their steep steps. Dozens of little black children whirled around her. There ahead was Natchez shining. Bells were ringing. She walked on.

62   In the paved city it was Christmas time. There were red and green electric lights strung and crisscrossed everywhere, and all turned on in the daytime. Old Phoenix would have been lost if she had not distrusted her eyesight and depended on her feet to know where to take her.

63   She paused quietly on the sidewalk where people were passing by. A lady came along in the crowd, carrying an armful of red-, green-, and silver-wrapped presents; she gave off perfume like the red roses in hot summer, and Phoenix stopped her.

64   "Please, missy, will you lace up my shoe?" She held up her foot.

65   "What do you want, Grandma?"

66   "See my shoe," said Phoenix. "Do all right for out in the country, but wouldn't look right to go in a big building."

67   "Stand still then, Grandma," said the lady. She put her packages down on the sidewalk beside her and laced and tied both shoes tightly.

68   "Can't lace 'em with a cane," said Phoenix. "Thank you, missy. I doesn't mind asking a nice lady to tie up my shoe, when I gets out on the street."

69   Moving slowly and from side to side, she went into the big building and into a tower of steps, where she walked up and around and around until her feet knew to stop.

70   She entered a door, and there she saw nailed up on the wall the document that had been stamped with the gold seal and framed in the gold frame, which matched the dream that was hung up in her head.

71   "Here I be," she said. There was a fixed and ceremonial stiffness over her body.

72   "A charity case, I suppose," said an attendant who sat at the desk before her.

73   But Phoenix only looked above her head. There was sweat on her face, the wrinkles in her skin shone like a bright net.

74   "Speak up, Grandma," the woman said. "What's your name? We must have your history, you know. Have you been here before? What seems to be the trouble with you?"

75   Old Phoenix only gave a twitch to her face as if a fly were bothering her.

76   "Are you deaf?" cried the attendant.

77   But then the nurse came in.

78   "Oh, that's just old Aunt Phoenix," she said. "She doesn't come for herself—she has a little grandson. She makes these trips just as regular as clockwork. She lives away back off the old Natchez Trace." She bent down. "Well, Aunt Phoenix, why don't you just take a seat? We won't keep you standing after your long trip." She pointed.

79   The old woman sat down, bolt upright in the chair.

80   "Now, how is the boy?" asked the nurse.

81   Old Phoenix did not speak.

82   "I said, how is the boy?"

83   But Phoenix only waited and stared straight ahead, her face very solemn and withdrawn into rigidity.

84   "Is his throat any better?" asked the nurse. "Aunt Phoenix, don't you hear me? Is your grandson's throat any better since the last time you came for the medicine?"

85   With her hands on her knees, the old woman waited, silent, erect and motionless, just as if she were in armor.

86   "You mustn't take up our time this way, Aunt Phoenix," the nurse said. "Tell us quickly about your grandson, and get it over. He isn't dead, is he?"

87   At last there came a flicker and then a flame of comprehension across her face, and she spoke.

88   "My grandson. It was my memory had left me. There I sat and forgot why I made my long trip."

89   "Forgot?" The nurse frowned. "After you came so far?"

90   Then Phoenix was like an old woman begging a dignified forgiveness for waking up frightened in the night. "I never did go to school, I was too old at the Surrender," she said in a soft voice. "I'm an old woman without an education. It was my memory fail me. My little grandson, he is just the same, and I forgot it in the coming."

91   "Throat never heals, does it?" said the nurse, speaking in a loud, sure voice to Old Phoenix. By now she had a card with something written on it, a little list. "Yes. Swallowed lye. When was it—January— two-three years ago—"

92   Phoenix spoke unasked now. "No, missy, he not dead, he just the same. Every little while his throat begin to close up again, and he not able to swallow. He not get his breath. He not able to help himself. So the time come around, and I go on another trip for the soothing medicine."

93   "All right. The doctor said as long as you came to get it, you could have it," said the nurse. "But it's an obstinate case."

94   "My little grandson, he sit up there in the house all wrapped up, waiting by himself," Phoenix went on. "We is the only two left in the world. He suffer and it don't seem to put him back at all. He got a sweet look. He going to last. He wear a little patch quilt and peep out holding his mouth open like a little bird. I remembers so plain now. I not going to forget him again, no, the whole enduring time. I could tell him from all the others in creation."

95   "All right." The nurse was trying to hush her now. She brought her a bottle of medicine. "Charity," she said, making a check mark in a book.

96   Old Phoenix held the bottle close to her eyes and then carefully put it into her pocket.

97   "I thank you," she said.

98   "It's Christmas time, Grandma," said the attendant. "Could I give you a few pennies out of my purse?"

99   "Five pennies is a nickel," said Phoenix stiffly.

100   "Here's a nickel," said the attendant.

101   Phoenix rose carefully and held out her hand. She received the nickel and then fished the other nickel out of her pocket and laid it

beside the new one. She stared at her palm closely, with her head on one side.

102   Then she gave a tap with her cane on the floor.

103   "This is what come to me to do," she said. "I going to the store and buy my child a little windmill they sells, made out of paper. He going to find it hard to believe there such a thing in the world. I'll march myself back where he waiting, holding it straight up in his hand."

104   She lifted her free hand, gave a little nod, turned round, and walked out of the doctor's office. Then her slow step began on the stairs, going down.

A Worn Path

JOURNAL

1. **MLA Works Cited**   *Using this model, record this story here.*

   *Author's Last Name, First Name. "Title of the Story." <u>Title of the Book</u>.
   3rd ed. Ed. First Name Last Name. City: Publisher, year. Pages of
   the story.*

2. **Main Character(s)**   *Describe each main character, and explain why you
   think each is a main character.*

3. **Supporting Characters**   *Describe each supporting character, and explain why
   you think each is a supporting character.*

4. **Setting**   *Describe the setting(s) and any relevant prop(s).*

5. Sequence   *Outline the events of the story in order.*

6. Plot   *Tell the story in no more than two sentences.*

7. Conflicts   *Identify and explain all the conflicts involved here.*

8. Significant Quotations   *Explain the importance of each of these quotations. Record the page number in the parentheses.*

   a. "She wore a dark striped dress reaching down to her shoe tops, and an equally long apron of bleached sugar sacks [. . .]" (   ).

   b. "Without warning, she had seen with her own eyes a flashing nickel fall out of the man's pocket onto the ground" (   ).

    c. "Old Phoenix would have been lost if she had not distrusted her eyesight and depended on her feet to know where to take her" (   ).

    d. "'Oh, that's just old Aunt Phoenix,' she said. [. . .]. 'She makes these trips just as regular as clockwork'" (   ).

    e. "'I going to the store and buy my child a little windmill they sells, made out of paper'" (   ).

9. **Literary Elements** *Look at this chapter's title and explain why you think this story is placed in this chapter. Explain in which other chapter(s) you might place this story, as relevant to the literary element(s) of that chapter.*

10. **Foreshadowing, Irony, and/or Symbolism** *Explain examples of foreshadowing, irony, and/or symbolism in this story.*

FOLLOW-UP QUESTIONS

10 SHORT QUESTIONS

Select the best answer for each.

____ 1. Old Phoenix probably is
wearing
   a. fine clothing.
   b. old clothing.
   c. formal clothing.

____ 2. Old Phoenix probably
   a. does not care about her
   clothing.
   b. wants to buy new clothing.
   c. is concerned about her
   clothing.

____ 3. The hunter
   a. hands a nickel to Old
   Phoenix.
   b. drops the nickel on
   purpose.
   c. does not hand the coin to
   Old Phoenix.

____ 4. When Old Phoenix sees the
coin, she
   a. quietly takes the coin.
   b. does not see the coin.
   c. returns the coin to the
   hunter.

____ 5. Old Phoenix's journey to
town is
   a. a difficult trip for her.
   b. an easy trip for her.
   c. an uneventful trip for her.

____ 6. Old Phoenix's trip to town is
   a. a short trip.
   b. a long trip.
   c. a weekly trip.

____ 7. Old Phoenix
   a. has been to the doctor's
   office before.
   b. has never been to the
   doctor's office before.
   c. does not get into the
   doctor's office.

____ 8. Old Phoenix
   a. offers the nickel for the
   medicine.
   b. does not get the medicine.
   c. gets the medicine for free.

____ 9. Old Phoenix
   a. is willing to accept charity.
   b. insists on paying for all she
   receives.
   c. accepts only what she
   finds.

____ 10. Old Phoenix is probably
   a. rich.
   b. poor.
   c. middle class.

5 SIGNIFICANT QUOTATIONS

Explain the importance of each of these quotations.

1. "Old Phoenix said, 'Out of my way, all you foxes, owls, beetles, jack rabbits, coons, and wild animals! [. . .]. I got a long way.'"

2. "A white man finally came along and found her—a hunter, a young man, with his dog on a chain."

3. "Then she smelled wood-smoke, and smelled the river, and she saw a steeple and the cabins on their steep steps."

4. "She entered a door, and there she saw nailed up on the wall the document that had been stamped with the gold seal and framed in the gold frame [. . .]."

5. "'I going to the store and buy my child a little windmill they sells, made out of paper.'"

2 COMPREHENSION ESSAY QUESTIONS

Use specific details and information from the story to answer these questions as completely as possible.

1. The Phoenix is a mythical bird that could not die. After it flew into fire, it would rise from the ashes and come alive again. Why has Welty named her character "Old Phoenix"? Use specific details and information from the story.

2. How does the title relate to the story? Explain the significance of the title using specific details and information from the story.

DISCUSSION QUESTIONS

Be prepared to discuss these questions in class.

1. From what you have read, exactly how old do you think Old Phoenix is? Use specific information from the story to make your assessment.

2. Why do you think the hunter is in the story? The lady on the street? The nurse?

WRITING

Use each of these ideas for writing an essay.

1. Often students want to describe a person by looks, but here we learn about Old Phoenix through her actions. Write an essay describing someone you know, using mainly conversation with or the words of that person.

2. No matter what, Old Phoenix persists. Write an essay describing a time when you or someone you know persisted in achieving something.

Further Writing

1. Compare and contrast this story with William Faulkner's "A Rose for Emily" (page 344).

2. Compare and contrast Old Phoenix with Tom Sawyer in the story by Mark Twain (page 140).

Yoruba

MIGENE GONZALEZ-WIPPLER

PRE-READING VOCABULARY CONTEXT

Use context clues to define these words before reading. Use a dictionary as needed.

1. When Ben's mother went to work, his *nanny* saw to it that he was dressed and fed and ready for school each day. *Nanny* means

   _____.

2. The rainstorm was *mammoth*, covering over half the country with clouds and rain. *Mammoth* means _____.

3. Services, or *masses*, are usually celebrated daily at the Catholic church in town. *Mass* means _____.

4. Maureen put all her clothes in her closet, picked up all her belongings, and generally kept her room *immaculate. Immaculate* means

   _____.

5. To keep from getting a sunburn, Jennifer walked through town with a large pink *parasol* that looked like an umbrella. *Parasol* means

   _____.

6. Since it was the weekend, Lisa broke from her usual weekday *routine* and went to the mall instead of going to work. *Routine* means

   _____.

7. Margaret loved the beautiful beads on the *rosary* chain she used to count her prayers as she said them. *Rosary* means

   _____.

8. Since they had never met before, Allison *introduced* her brother Jacob to her friend Zachary. *Introduce* means _____.

9. Plowing the field and then later harvesting the crops was hard work for the poor *peasant*. *Peasant* means _____.

10. Ashley and Caitlin love going to the *beach* where they make sandcastles and swim in the ocean. *Beach* means

_____.

11. Hatem planned to take Rte. 1, but Rte. 1 was blocked and the *detour* took him way out of his way. *Detour* means_____.

12. Reid decided to *initiate* his own baseball team and started it by sending out flyers to his friends to encourage them to join. *Initiate* means _____.

13. The priest *anointed* the baby's head with holy water when he blessed the baby. *Anointed* means_____.

14. To keep her gown from getting wet in the rain, Missy put on a large *mantle* that flowed from her shoulders over her gown. *Mantle* means _____.

15. My *mammy* gave birth to me and has taken care of me ever since I was born. *Mammy* means _____.

16. The pastor of our church offered a *blessing* to all the new babies by saying a prayer for them. *Blessing* means _____.

17. A human baby grows for nine months within her or his mother's *womb*. *Womb* means _____.

18. With more rain than usual and mild weather, the farm produced a huge *bounty* of more food than ever. *Bounty* means

_____.

19. Karen *exchanged* the red shoes for the white ones when she knew she would not wear the red. *Exchanged* means _____.

20. Mary Beth *adores* the beautiful new dollhouse Donald built especially for her. *Adore* means_____.

Pre-reading Vocabulary
Structural Attack

Define these words by solving the parts. Use the Glossary or a dictionary as needed.

1. marketplace
2. shantytown
3. sundress
4. sunbonnet
5. majestically
6. fiery
7. unusually
8. compilation
9. obediently
10. throaty
11. luxurious
12. voluminous
13. undercurrent
14. fruitless
15. impassioned
16. encrusted

Pre-reading Questions

Try answering these questions as you read.

Who is María?

Who is Yemayá?

What is Yoruba?

Yoruba

MIGENE GONZALEZ-WIPPLER

> **Migene Gonzalez-Wippler** is a resident of Puerto Rico. She is a recognized authority on the Santeria religion. This story is taken from her book, <u>The Santeria Experience</u>. More of her writing can be found in <u>Santeria: African Magic in Latin America</u>.

A recibo, tucked in a fold of Puerto Rico's northeastern coast, is one of the oldest towns in the western hemisphere. Originally an Indian village ruled by a Taíno chieftain called Aracibo, it was founded by the Conquistadores in 1616.

2   In the late nineteen forties, when I was three years old, my mother hired María, a black woman of mammoth proportions, to be my nanny. María's skin was like shiny mahogany with almost iridescent tones, and her smile was radiant, I never saw María angry or sad, and if she was ever prey to these dismal human moods, she was quite adept at hiding them from me. I thought her very beautiful, and soon I would take my meals only if María ate with me and would not fall asleep unless María sat by my side.

3   María took me everywhere she went. To the marketplace where she did our daily shopping and to the shantytown where her numerous family lived. To daily mass, for she was a devout Catholic, and to the neighborhood store where she placed her occasional bets with the numbers. My mother took a dim view of these escapades, but I was so healthy and so happy in María's care that my mother eventually relented and let her take full charge of me.

4   Each morning María would put me in a frothy sundress with a matching sunbonnet, white sandals, and socks which she bleached daily to ensure their whiteness. Underneath the bonnet, my long black

hair would be meticulously braided and tied with silk ribbons matching the color of my dress. María was partial to the scent of Parma violets, and all my clothes exuded a faint violet fragrance.

5   Once my morning toilet was finished, María would march me proudly into our dining room, where my parents and grandparents would make proper sounds of praise and admiration at my dazzling pulchritude. Then, under María's watchful eyes, I would sit to breakfast without wrinkling my skirts or soiling my ruffles. After a substantial breakfast, María sailed majestically out of the house with me in tow, her long, immaculate skirts crackling with starch. On her shoulder was a huge parasol to protect us from the fiery Caribbean sun, while from her wrist dangled a fan to bring us relief from the stifling heat. Since air conditioning had barely made its appearance on the island, the fan was more than an ornament. But female vanity had long turned a necessary instrument into a thing of beauty, and fans had become the objects of both pride and delight, some of them made of fine sandalwood and hand-painted with exquisite landscapes by renowned artists. Others were of peacock or ostrich feathers, or of Chantilly lace embroidered with seed pearls. María had purchased her fan from a merchant marine sailor who had brought if from Spain. Its unusually wide span was of ebony, carved with intricate flowery designs and highlighted with delicate touches of color that made the flower patterns dance with light.

6   It was María who first taught me that with a flick of the wrist and the opening and closing of a fan, a woman can tell an admirer that she is angry or jealous, that she welcomes his advances or finds him a crashing bore. María taught me all this and more during the twelve years I remained in her care.

7   I was thrilled at the idea of going to school, which opened the day after I turned five, and talked about it incessantly with María. My mother had promised me an especially nice party to celebrate my birthday, and my grandfather had a famous designer in San Juan make a special dress of pink organdy, hand-embroidered with tiny flowers and musical notes. The shoes and socks were also pink, as were the silk ribbons for my hair. But early in the morning, María dressed me in an old white dress and took me to mass. She did not take me in to my family and have breakfast with them. I kept questioning the departure from our daily routine, but María said to be silent and do as I was told.

8   After mass was over, María brought me to an altar over which stood a statue of the Virgin Mary. While I knelt down before the image, María pulled from her capacious handbag a large wooden rosary, and proceeded to pass the beads. She stood behind me, praying in muted tones, with her hand on my shoulder as if she were introducing me to the Virgin.

9   Even if you don't pray the litanies, a compilation of fifty-three Hail
Mary and seven Pater-nosters is a lengthy business if you are a child of
five. My stomach was empty. My knees ached and throbbed and threatened to buckle, and I had to keep balancing my weight first on the one
knee, then on the other. I must have presented a most unhappy picture
to Our Blessed Lady. But not once did I think to complain to María.
One did not question her orders; one simply did what one was told.

10   It was already midmorning when we left the church. My knees
were functioning again after María rubbed them briskly with her handkerchief, but my stomach was grumbling louder than ever.

11   "María, are we going to the market place or back home?"

12   "I know you're tired and hungry," she said evasively, opening her
parasol and pulling me under it. "But you must never let your body tell
you what to do. It must obey you, not the other way around."

13   I trotted obediently by her side. "But how does my body tell me
what to do?"

14   "By making you feel things," she answered. "It makes you feel
hungry, so you eat. Tired, so you sit down. Sleepy, so you go to bed.
Sometimes it makes you feel angry, so you scream and yell and stomp
your feet."

15   My face colored, remembering my occasional temper tantrums.

16   "But, María, then my body isn't good."

17   "Oh yes it is, *florecita* [little flower]. Because of your body, you can
see the sky and the sun and the sea. You can smell the perfume of the
flowers and sing and play, and love your mother and father."

18   "And you," I added, drawing closer to her.

19   "And me," she laughed her great throaty laugh. "But you see, *florecita*, your body is like a little child. It must be taught good habits and
to obey. It must learn we can't always eat when we're hungry or sit
down when we're tired or sleep when we're sleepy. And the best way to
teach your body these things is by sometimes not doing the things it
wants you to do. Not always," she emphasized. "Only sometimes."

20   "Like now?" I asked.

21   "Like now."

22   We reached the bus stop. With delight, I thought we were going
home, where I could eat some breakfast and play before my party in the
afternoon.

23   "But I will only eat a little," I promised myself, remembering
María's words, "and I will play with only one doll."

24   But I was not to eat a little breakfast or play with any dolls that
morning.

25   The bus chugged along the country road to our home. Palm trees
and banana plants heavy with fruit grew profusely on both sides of the

road, as did the brilliant blossoms of the hibiscus, the poinciana, and the bougainvillea. To our left, gently sloping hills alternated with narrow valleys carpeted in a dazzling variety of greens. To our right, the Atlantic melted with the sky in a majestic display of aquamarine and gold. A few peasant huts, known as *bohíos*, were scattered on the hillside, while on the ocean side rose elegant, luxurious *quintas* of white stucco ornamented with costly mosaics and Spanish ironwork.

26   We were still about ten minutes from home when María pulled the cord to get off. Before I knew what was happening I found myself standing by the road, watching the bus disappear in the distance. María opened her parasol and gathered her parcels together.

27   Directly in front of us was a rough path, largely overgrown with vegetation. María and I trudged along this path until we emerged directly onto a part of the beach hidden from the main road by a series of large boulders imbedded in the sand. Among the dunes grew a profusion of tropical sea grapes, their hard, bitter fruit shining like amethysts among their harsh round leaves. Some palm trees bent their trunks so close to the sand one could easily grab the clusters of coconut growing among the fan-shaped leaves.

28   We stopped under the shadow of a palm while María removed my shoes and socks, her own heavy brogans, and the thick cotton stockings she always wore. Thus barefoot we trampled through the warm sand.

29   I did not bother to ask María the reason for our detour, used as I was to being taken along on all her outings. I had the vague feeling this surprise visit to the beach I had always admired from a distance, but never had walked on before, was María's birthday present to me. Intoxicated by the sharp, tangy smell of the sea, I wanted to stay on the shore for the rest of my life.

30   When we finally arrived at the water's edge, María set her parcels down, closed her parasol, and then calmly proceeded to tear the clothes from my body.

31   I felt no shame. María washed and dressed me every day and put me to sleep every night. I had stood naked in front of her many times before. I had not yet learned to be ashamed of my own body. But her action had a certain ominous authority that made me feel destitute and vulnerable beyond description. Deprived of more than my own clothes, I felt stripped of identity, of a sense of being. It was as if I had died somehow, standing there on the golden sand, with the sun like a halo around me and the taste of salt water on my lips. I stood there in shock and utter humiliation, tears rolling steadily down my cheeks. I did not understand María's actions, but I knew there was always a reason for everything she did. (Many years later I would find an echo of María's teachings, in the philosophies of some of the world's greatest religions,

especially Zen Buddhism. When María tore my clothes and left me naked facing the sea, without any sense of ego or identity, she was echoing Zen's concept of the perfect Initiate, who must be "devoid of selfhood, devoid of personality, devoid of identity, and devoid of separate identity.")

32   Out of her handbag's unfathomable depths, María extracted a bottle of sugarcane syrup and the red handkerchief, tied in a knot, where she kept all her loose change. Only then did she turn to look at me, all at once the picture of consternation.

33   "Ah, my little flower, don't cry. You afraid of María? You think María can hurt you?" She rocked me gently against her bosom as she spoke her soothing words. "Why, my *florecita*, María would cut out her heart for you. María could never hurt you."

34   Slowly my tears stopped flowing. I lifted my wet face from her shoulder. I felt I could question her now.

35   "Why, María?" I asked, with still trembling lips. "Why did you do that?"

36   "Because I want you to be protected from all harm. Now that you're going to school, you'll be alone, *florecita*, without María to watch over you. You need protection, and only God and the Blessed Lady can give it to you and give you her blessings. And now I bring you to the Lady and her true power, the sea."

37   As she spoke, María opened the bottle of sugarcane syrup. Tasting it with her forefinger, she anointed my temples, lips, wrists, and ankles with the thick liquid. I automatically licked the heavy, cloying syrup on my lips.

38   "It's too sweet," I grimaced. "I don't like it."

39   "It has to be sweet for the Lady, as sweet as possible. Nothing can be too sweet for her."

40   María undid the knot of her red handkerchief. Counting seven pennies, she pressed them in my hand.

41   "Here, *florecita*," she said, closing my fingers around the coins. "This is the payment, *el derecho*, of the Lady. I give you seven pennies because seven is her number. You remember that. Seven is the number of the Lady, of Yemayá."

42   "Of who?" I asked, staring at the pennies. "What Lady are you talking about, María? The Blessed Lady is in the church and in heaven."

43   "Yes, *florecita*, but her true power is in the sea and the seawater. She stands in heaven, but where the bottom of her mantle touches the earth, it turns into the ocean. The waves and the sea foam are her ruffles and her lace. And here, in the sea, her name is Yemayá."

44   She enunciated the strange name carefully so that I could grasp its melodious rhythm, "Say it, *florecita*. Ye-ma-yá."

45   I repeated it after her. "It is the prettiest name I ever heard, María!"

46   "The prettiest name in the whole world," María laughed delight-edly. "It is the name of the Lady in African, in Yoruba. My mammy taught it to me. And now, my little flower, your black mammy teaches it to you." She took my hand gently and guided me to the water. "Come, let me show you how to salute Yemayá."

47   Lifting her voluminous skirts so that the waves would not wet them, she turned her body to the left and forced me to do the same. We both stood ankle-deep in the water, our bodies at right angles to the sea.

48   "See, *florecita*, you never enter into the ocean facing front. To do so is a challenge to Yemayá, it's like saying, 'I'm here, come get me.' So then maybe she does. Always, always enter on your side, better the right side. Then you say, '*Hekua, Yemayá, hekua.*' Say it, little flower."

49   I looked dubiously at the water, then at María. Like most Puerto Rican children I had been raised as a very strict Catholic, and I had the vague feeling that our parish priest would not approve of what María was saying. But my trust in her had been firmly reestablished and I did not want to offend her. "*Hekua, Yemayá, hekua,*" I repeated.

50   As soon as I repeated these words, I felt relieved and relaxed, as if an unseen link had been established between the sea and myself. My soul was overwhelmed by a great love for the sea, that has never stopped growing within me. I have never bathed in the sea again with-out remembering that incredible feeling of love illuminating my entire being.

51   "See, *florecita*," María said joyously. "Yemayá blesses you, she accepts you. She will always protect you now."

52   I looked up at her with wondering eyes. "Is that what *hekua* means?"

53   "Yes, *hekua* means blessings. And see how Yemayá blesses you?"

54   María pointed to the water frothing softly around my feet. Small whirlpools of foam enveloped my ankles, then my knees. Then sud-denly an unexpectedly huge wave rose from the sea like a great green arm. As the wall of water collapsed over my head, I heard María cry out, "The coins! The coins! . . . Let go the coins!"

55   I felt myself being drawn out to sea inside a glimmering cocoon, with the rushing sound of a thousand crystal bells. I opened my arms to embrace the sea, and the seven pennies fell from my fingers. Almost immediately, the water receded and the waves resumed their usual gentle motion. I stood as before, ankle-deep in foamy water, blinking at the morning sunshine.

56   I recall little of what happened inside the water. The lingering memory is one of silky green depths, of sun rays shining through the water; of softness, warmth and safety. It was almost as if I had returned

to the womb of the world, and felt reluctant to be born anew. This episode at the beach was my first initiation in the Yoruba religion known as Santería.

57   María used to tell me that the presence of Yemayá is always much stronger in very deep waters. Off the north coast of Puerto Rico, in an area known as Bronson's Deep, the ocean floor plunges down to 27,000 feet. Measured from this depth, the mountains of Puerto Rico would be among the highest in the world, with an approximate height of 31,500 feet. Anything that falls within these waters is lost forever—says the legend—unless Yemayá is offered a prize in exchange for her bounty. Truly, her demands are modest. Seven shiny copper pennies, a bit of sugarcane syrup, and sometimes a few candles are enough to please her. Perhaps it is not the value of the gift that Yemayá really wants, but the faith with which it is given.

58   In these same waters, on August 16, 1977, off the coast of San Juan, an incident took place which was fully reported in the San Juan *Star*. For several weeks I had been in one of the hotels lining El Condado Avenue, working against a deadline on one of my books. One afternoon, a friend went snorkeling in the deep waters off the San Juan coast. When he returned several hours later, he had a tragic story to tell.

59   A family from nearby Santo Domingo had come to visit Puerto Rico for the first time. Their thirteen-year-old son disregarded the warnings of the dangerous undercurrents surrounding the coast of San Juan, and the great depths of the waters, and he swam out far from shore. Probably too weak to fight against the currents, the boy suddenly sank under the water and did not surface again. Local lifeguards and members of the Police Rescue Squad tried to locate his body, but all their efforts proved fruitless.

60   The story spread throughout El Condado, and all the hotels sent out search parties to find the body. The boy's mother was determined not to leave her son's body in the sea, as she wanted to bring it back to Santo Domingo for proper burial. But late in the afternoon of the following day, the authorities called off the search. All the desperate entreaties of the boy's mother fell on deaf ears. The police were sure the powerful undercurrents in these waters had driven the body toward the ocean floor or wedged it in one of the reef's many underwater crevices. But the mother asked to go along with a search party—the very last one, she pleaded. If the body was not found during this last search, she would not insist any further.

61   After some consideration, the authorities agreed. As the story unfolded in the San Juan *Star*, she brought along with her four white candles. When the boat had gone sufficiently out to sea, she asked the

officers to stop the engines. Here, she felt, they would find her son's body. More to humor her than for any other reason, the Rescue Squad officers stopped the boat's engines.

62   The mother then approached the boat's gunwale and began an impassioned plea to the sea. Kneeling on deck, her hands linked together in prayer, tears streaming down her face, she called out to the sea to return her son's body to her. Reminding the sea that the boy was dead, she proposed that it exchange his body for the candles she had brought along. Since four candles are burned around a coffin, these also represented her dead son.

63   As she spoke, she pulled the candles from her handbag and threw them overboard. A few minutes later, the Rescue Squad officers aboard the boat watched, aghast, as the boy's body surfaced on the same spot where the candles had sunk into the water.

64   Had María been aboard that boat, she would not have been at all surprised. Without any doubts she would have stated that Yemayá, the Great Supernal Mother, had taken pity on another mother and had accepted the exchange willingly, and with her blessings. As to the apparent cruelty of the sea in taking the boy's life, María would have probably answered that the sea had been kind, saving him from a life of suffering and giving him eternal life instead.

65   María held the view that life was an illusion. So, for that matter, was death.

66   "It's just another way of life, *florecita*," she would say. "A far better way of life."

67   I would wrinkle my forehead. "But María, then why do we live this life? Wouldn't it be better to die and live in a better life in the other world instead?"

68   "No, *florecita*, we're here for a reason. We're here to learn to become better so that we can enjoy that other, better life. If we're bad here, we don't go to the better life after this one. Instead, we have to come back, again and again, until we learn to be good."

69   This simple explanation is exactly the same as the theory of reincarnation expressed by Buddha to his disciple Subhuti in the Diamond Sutra:

70   "Furthermore, Subhuti, if it be that good men and good women . . . are downtrodden, their evil destiny is the inevitable retributive result of sins committed in their mortal lives. By virtue of their present misfortunes, the reacting effects of their past will be thereby worked out, and they will be in a position to attain the Consummation of Incomparable Enlightenment."

71   The Consummation of Incomparable Enlightenment was the same concept expressed by María as a "better life in the other world."

72   After she took me out of the water, María dried me, braided my hair and tied it with pink silk ribbons, and then dressed me, with the pink organdy dress my grandfather had given me for my birthday. She seemed in very high spirits and hummed a popular tune. When I told her I was happy to have come to the sea and hoped that she would bring me back again, she laughed and hugged me.

73   "We'll see, *florecita*, we'll see," she said, putting the finishing touches on a satin bow. "But I'm happy that Yemayá has accepted you. Now you can go to school without María and no harm can come to you."

74   To my lips came a question that was burning in my mind. "María, why did you tear my clothes?"

75   She looked at me briefly. Her smiled widened, and she returned her attention to my hair.

76   "Why? Because you had to be presented to Yemayá without clothes, like a newborn baby. I tore the clothes to tell Yemayá you gave up your old life and wanted to start living again with her as your mother."

77   "And now my mother is not my mother anymore?" I asked in alarm, my eyes filling with tears.

78   María hugged me again, brushing away my tears with expert fingers.

79   "Of course she is, *florecita*. But she's your mother on earth, while Yemayá is your mother in heaven and in the sea."

80   "But who is Yemayá, the sea?" I asked, still confused.

81   "Yemayá is the Yoruba name of the Virgin Mary, *florecita*," explained María patiently. "She's the mother of all, of whites and blacks, of yellows and greens; of everybody. But in Africa she's always black because the people there are black, and she wants them to know she's black too."

82   "But María, the Virgin is not black, she's white. I've seen her in the church."

83   "No, *florecita*, the Virgin is like your ribbons. She has many colors. Sometimes she's white, sometimes yellow, sometimes she's red, sometimes black. It depends on the color of the people who adore her. She does this to tell the world she loves everybody the same, no matter what their color is. To the Yorubas she's always black because they're black."

84   "Who are the Yorubas, María?"

85   María paused in the middle of a braid, her eyes lost in reverie.

86   "The Yorubas were a great black people." She continued her braiding. "My mammy was Yoruba," she said, with evident pride. "She come to Puerto Rico 1872, year before abolition."

87   When she spoke of her mother, which was often, María reverted to broken Spanish, with African words interspersed. "She comes with two hundred fifty Yorubas from Ife, that's the name of Yoruba land in black country," she added. "Come from Africa, they did, in them slave boats.

In chains they brought them, the mean slave merchants—*los negreros*. Many of the black people die on boat, of hunger and sickness, but mostly of broken heart. Yorubas is proud people. Don't like white man."

88   "I'm white, María," I reminded her sadly.

89   "No you aren't, *florecita*," María cried, holding me tight against her. "You aren't white, and you aren't black. You're like the sun and the stars—all light, no color."

90   She finished tying the last ribbon and stood up with great efforts from her stooped position. Her usually immaculate clothes were drenched with seawater and covered with sand, but she paid no attention to them.

91   "Old María is not as strong as she used to be," she grunted, flexing her back. "Not like my mammy. My mammy real strong," she said with relish. "She only ten when she come to island. But white man leave my mammy alone. She knew how to talk to the *orishas*."

92   "What is *orisha*, María?" I asked.

93   "*Orisha?*" she mused. "Yemayá is *orisha*. Elegguá is *orisha*. Changó is *orisha*. *Orisha* is a saint, a force of the good God. But come," she added, taking me by the hand. "It's no good to ask too many questions all at once. Later, I'll tell you more."

94   "But María," I insisted, "Are there many . . . *orishas?*"

95   "As many as the grains of sand on the beach. But I only know a dozen or two. There are too many. Someday you'll know them too. But now is time to get back home, *florecita*, or your mammy will be really worried. And then your cake will be eaten, your presents gone, and the ice cream melted."

96   The thought of the promised birthday party came rushing back to my five-year-old mind, erasing all thoughts about the shadowy *orishas*, the Yorubas, and even the black Virgin known as Yemayá.

97   The pink shoes and socks remained in María's handbag until we emerged from the sand into the path that led back to the road. Free from their confinement, I ran ahead of María toward the bus stop, oblivious of my fine embroidered dress, pigtails dancing in the sun, my small feet encrusted with wet sand. She followed behind me slowly, dragging her heavy brogans, her parcels, and her parasol, tired but always smiling.

Yoruba

Journal

1. **MLA Works Cited**   *Using this model, record this story here.*

   Author's Last Name, First Name. "Title of the Story." <u>Title of the Book</u>. 3rd ed. Ed. First Name Last Name. City: Publisher, year. Pages of the story.

2. **Main Character(s)**   *Describe each main character, and explain why you think each is a main character.*

3. **Supporting Characters**   *Describe each supporting character, and explain why you think each is a supporting character.*

4. **Setting**   *Describe the setting(s) and any relevant prop(s).*

5. Sequence *Outline the events of the story in order.*

6. Plot *Tell the story in no more than two sentences.*

7. Conflicts *Identify and explain all the conflicts involved here.*

8. Significant Quotations *Explain the importance of each of these quotations. Record the page number in the parentheses.*

a. "In the late nineteen forties when I was three years old, my mother hired María [. . .]" ( ).

b. "I was thrilled at the idea of going to school [. . .]" ( ).

c. "We both stood ankle-deep in the water, our bodies at right angles to the sea" (   ).

d. "The mother then approached the boat's gunwale and began an impassioned plea to the sea" (   ).

e. "'But she's your mother on earth, while Yemayá is your mother in heaven and in the sea'" (   ).

9. **Literary Elements** *Look at this chapter's title and explain why you think this story is placed in this chapter. Explain in which other chapter(s) you might place this story, as relevant to the literary element(s) of that chapter.*

10. **Foreshadowing, Irony, and/or Symbolism** *Explain examples of foreshadowing, irony, and/or symbolism in this story.*

FOLLOW-UP QUESTIONS
10 SHORT QUESTIONS

Select the <u>best</u> answer for each.

_____ 1. María is the narrator's
  a. mother.
  b. grandmother.
  c. nanny.

_____ 2. The narrator's family
  probably
  a. is poor.
  b. is well-off.
  c. lives on a farm.

_____ 3. María is probably
  a. a lively and colorful
     person.
  b. a quiet person.
  c. considered usual by the
     narrator's family.

_____ 4. María is
  a. a large woman.
  b. a small woman.
  c. of unknown size.

_____ 5. María practices and is
  described as a "devout"
  a. Buddhist.
  b. Protestant.
  c. Catholic.

_____ 6. For the ritual by the water,
  the narrator
  a. is stripped of her old
     clothes.
  b. enters the water front first.
  c. wears her new clothes.

_____ 7. The narrator is anointed in
  sugarcane syrup
  a. because it is good for her.
  b. because she likes it.
  c. because it is sweetness to
     offer Yemayá.

_____ 8. María takes the narrator to
  the beach
  a. to harm her.
  b. to protect her.
  c. to drown her.

_____ 9. According to the story, the
  boy's body
  a. is lost forever.
  b. is returned in exchange for
     seven pennies.
  c. is returned in exchange for
     four candles.

_____ 10. The ritual at the beach
  a. is an act of revenge.
  b. is an act of love.
  c. is an act of hatred.

5 SIGNIFICANT QUOTATIONS

Explain the importance of each of these quotations.

1. "My mother took a dim view of these escapades, but I was so healthy
   and so happy in María's care that my mother eventually relented and
   let her take full charge of me."

2. "I was thrilled at the idea of going to school, which opened the day
   after I turned five, and talked about it incessantly with María."

3. "As the wall of water collapsed over my head, I heard María cry out, 'The coins! The coins! . . . Let go the coins.'"

4. "A few minutes later, the Rescue Squad officers aboard the boat watched, aghast, as the boy's body surfaced on the same spot where the candles had sunk into the water."

5. "'But I'm happy that Yemayá has accepted you.'"

2 COMPREHENSION ESSAY QUESTIONS

Use specific details and information from the story to answer these questions as completely as possible.

1. What is the ritual at the beach from María's standpoint? Use specific details and information from the story to support your description.

2. What is the ritual at the beach from the narrator's standpoint? Use specific details and information from the story to support your description.

DISCUSSION QUESTIONS

Be prepared to discuss these questions in class.

1. How is the religion in this story like and unlike Christianity? How does it compare to your own religion?

2. Why is this story named "Yoruba"?

WRITING

Use each of these ideas for writing an essay.

1. Many of us have superstitions. Describe a superstition you or someone that you know has, and tell the effects this superstition has had on you or on the person you know.

2. Religion and/or spirituality may also have many effects on us. Tell about a specific time that religion or spirituality affected you or someone you know.

Further Writing

1. This story offers one form of adapted Christianity. Research other forms of adapted Christianity found in The Caribbean.

2. Compare the rituals in this story with the ritual found in Canto XXXI of Purgatoria by Dante Alighieri (available in a library).

Two Kinds

Amy Tan

Pre-reading Vocabulary Context

Use context clues to define these words before reading. Use a dictionary as needed.

1. When Jay learned to play the piano by the time he was two years old, his teacher called Jay his "little *prodigy*." *Prodigy* means _____.

2. *Shirley Temple*, with her bouncing curls and endearing smile, arguably became the model for child movie stars. *Shirley Temple* means

   _____.

3. Alex's parents had great *expectations* for him and were sure he would pass all his courses and become a doctor. *Expectation* means

   _____.

4. Ellen looked at her *reflection* in the mirror and decided she needed more lipstick after eating. *Reflection* means_____.

5. Josh had absolutely no interest in the show on television, so he became *bored* with it and fell asleep. *Bored* means_____.

6. Years ago, Ed Sullivan hosted a television show with many different acts, including Elvis and the Beatles and the Beach Boys, on the *Ed Sullivan Show*. *Ed Sullivan Show* means_____.

7. After her beautiful dance, the ballerina placed one foot in back of the other and slowly bowed in a graceful *curtsy*. *Curtsy* means _____.

8. With its long keyboard and deep, wooden shell for vibrating strings, the *piano* is considered by many to be the perfect musical instrument. *Piano* means _____.

9. When one cannot hear, the loss of one's hearing may be referred to as *deafness*. *Deaf* means_____.

10. No matter how hard she tried, Jodi made too many *mistakes* on her test and these errors caused her to fail the test. *Mistake* means

    _____.

11. Ted is a strong swimmer and, after winning so many first-place medals, he is now considered the *champion* of his league. *Champion* means_____.

12. Rachel has many *talents*, as she can sing and dance and play the piano in addition to getting all A's in school. *Talent* means _____.

13. In order to get their act together, the band members met every night to play and *practice* each and every song they would perform. *Practice* means_____.

14. Lauren finally bought her little boy a toy to stop her *pleading* child from begging and crying. *Pleading* means _____.

15. Lin Su became very nervous when she got up on the stage and looked out to see all the people in the *audience*. *Audience* means

    _____.

16. Laura has the voice of an angel and, since she never hits a *wrong note*, she has been hired to sing in the movies. *Wrong note* means _____.

17. Ming Nu plays the violin beautifully and is very happy to get up in front of an audience at a violin *recital* and perform. *Recital* means

    _____.

18. Sarah expects her dog to follow her every command and demands complete *obedience* from her dog. *Obedience* means _____.

19. After Andy's baseball team won the league championship, he brought home a tall, bronze *trophy* to set on his desk. *Trophy* means _____.

20. Barbara has completed everything she wanted to do in her life and is now *contented* to relax, kick back, and enjoy life. *Contented* means

    _____.

PRE-READING VOCABULARY
STRUCTURAL ATTACK

Define these words by solving the parts. Use the Glossary or a dictionary as needed.

1. instantly
2. immediately
3. pursing
4. uneven
5. tiptoes
6. imaginings
7. remarkable
8. Chinatown
9. disappointed
10. willful
11. listlessly
12. foghorn
13. embraceless
14. mesmerizing
15. lilting
16. sauciness
17. housekeeping
18. ungrateful
19. invisible
20. unreachable
21. nonsense
22. obediently
23. pianist
24. discordant
25. bragging
26. closeness
27. foolishly
28. secondhand
29. showpiece
30. memorize
31. daydreamed
32. unison
33. enthusiastically
34. nervousness
35. envisioned
36. bewitched
37. stricken
38. anchored
39. unicycle
40. unlocked
41. nonchalantly
42. frighteningly
43. lifeless
44. inevitable
45. forgiveness
46. disproved
47. tuner
48. reconditioned

PRE-READING QUESTIONS

Try answering these questions as you read.

What does the mother want?

What does the narrator want?

What happens?

Two Kinds

AMY TAN

Born in 1952 in Oakland, California to parents who had recently immigrated to the United States from China, Amy Tan would go on to pursue her interests in language. Although her mother wanted Tan to become a physician, Tan ultimately graduated from California State University at San Jose with a bachelor's degree in English and then a master's degree in linguistics. Turning her interests to writing, she joined the Squaw Valley Community of Writers and later produced her masterwork, The Joy Luck Club. Tan's writing often explores the conflicts surrounding both cultural and intergenerational issues. Her writings can be found in many collections, including the interrelated stories in The Joy Luck Club, which includes "Two Kinds."

M y mother believed you could be anything you wanted to be in America. You could open a restaurant. You could work for the government and get good retirement. You could buy a house with almost no money down. You could become rich. You could become instantly famous.

2   "Of course, you can be prodigy, too," my mother told me when I was nine. "You can be best anything. What does Auntie Lindo know? Her daughter, she is only best tricky."

3   America was where all my mother's hopes lay. She had come to San Francisco in 1949 after losing everything in China: her mother and father, her family home, her first husband, and two daughters, twin baby girls. But she never looked back with regret. Things could get better in so many ways.

4   We didn't immediately pick the right kind of prodigy. At first my mother thought I could be a Chinese Shirley Temple. We'd watch Shirley's old movies on TV as though they were training films. My mother would poke my arm and say, "*Ni kan*. You watch." And I would see Shirley tapping her feet, or singing a sailor song, or pursing her lips into a very round O while saying "Oh, my goodness."

5   "*Ni kan*," my mother said, as Shirley's eyes flooded with tears. "You already know how. Don't need talent for crying!"

6   Soon after my mother got this idea about Shirley Temple, she took me to the beauty training school in the Mission District and put me in the hands of a student who could barely hold the scissors without shaking. Instead of getting big fat curls, I emerged with an uneven mass of crinkly black fuzz. My mother dragged me off to the bathroom and tried to wet down my hair.

7   "You look like Negro Chinese," she lamented, as if I had done this on purpose.

8   The instructor of the beauty training school had to lop off these soggy clumps to make my hair even again. "Peter Pan is very popular these days," the instructor assured my mother. I now had hair the length of a boy's, with curly bangs that hung at a slant two inches above my eyebrows. I liked the haircut, and it made me actually look forward to my future fame.

9   In fact, in the beginning I was just as excited as my mother, maybe even more so. I pictured this prodigy part of me as many different images, and I tried each one on for size. I was a dainty ballerina girl standing by the curtain, waiting to hear the music that would send me floating on my tiptoes. I was like the Christ child lifted out of the straw manger, crying with holy indignity. I was Cinderella stepping from her pumpkin carriage with sparkly cartoon music filling the air.

10   In all of my imaginings I was filled with a sense that I would soon become perfect. My mother and father would adore me. I would be beyond reproach. I would never feel the need to sulk, or to clamor for anything.

11   But sometimes the prodigy in me became impatient. "If you don't hurry up and get me out of here, I'm disappearing for good," it warned. "And then you'll always be nothing."

12   Every night after dinner my mother and I would sit at the Formica-topped kitchen table. She would present new tests, taking her examples from stories of amazing children that she read in *Ripley's Believe It or Not* or *Good Housekeeping, Reader's Digest*, or any of a dozen other magazines she kept in a pile in our bathroom. My mother got these magazines from people whose houses she cleaned. And since she cleaned many houses each week, we had a great assortment. She would look through them all, searching for stories about remarkable children.

13   The first night she brought out a story about a three-year-old boy who knew the capitals of all the states and even of most of the European countries. A teacher was quoted as saying that the little boy could also pronounce the names of the foreign cities correctly. "What's the capital of Finland?" my mother asked me, looking at the story.

14   All I knew was the capital of California, because Sacramento was the name of the street we lived on in Chinatown. "Nairobi!" I guessed, saying the most foreign word I could think of. She checked to see if that might be one way to pronounce *Helsinki* before showing me the answer.

15   The tests got harder—multiplying numbers in my head, finding the queen of hearts in a deck of cards, trying to stand on my head without using my hands, predicting the daily temperatures in Los Angeles, New York, and London. One night I had to look at a page from the Bible for three minutes and then report everything I could remember. "Now Jehoshaphat had riches and honor in abundance and . . . that's all I remember, Ma," I said.

16   And after seeing, once again, my mother's disappointed face, something inside me began to die. I hated the tests, the raised hopes and failed expectations. Before going to bed that night I looked in the mirror above the bathroom sink, and when I saw only my face staring back—and understood that it would always be this ordinary face—I began to cry. Such a sad, ugly girl! I made high-pitched noises like a crazed animal, trying to scratch out the face in the mirror.

17   And then I saw what seemed to be the prodigy side of me—a face I had never seen before. I looked at my reflection, blinking so that I could see more clearly. The girl staring back at me was angry, powerful. She and I were the same. I had new thoughts, willful thoughts—or, rather, thoughts filled with lots of won'ts. I won't let her change me, I promised myself. I won't be what I'm not.

18   So now when my mother presented her tests, I performed listlessly, my head propped on one arm. I pretended to be bored. And I was. I got so bored that I started counting the bellows of the foghorns out on the bay while my mother drilled me in other areas. The sound was comforting and reminded me of the cow jumping over the moon. And the next day I played a game with myself, seeing if my mother would give up on me before eight bellows. After a while I usually counted only one bellow, maybe two at most. At last she was beginning to give up hope.

19   Two or three months went by without any mention of my being a prodigy. And then one day my mother was watching the *Ed Sullivan Show* on TV. The TV was old and the sound kept shorting out. Every time my mother got half-way up from the sofa to adjust the set, the sound would come back on and Sullivan would be talking. As soon as she sat

down, Sullivan would go silent again. She got up—the TV broke into loud piano music. She sat down—silence. Up and down, back and forth, quiet and loud. It was like a stiff, embraceless dance between her and the TV set. Finally, she stood by the set with her hand on the sound dial.

20   She seemed entranced by the music, a frenzied little piano piece with a mesmerizing quality, which alternated between quick, playful passages and teasing, lilting ones.

21   "*Ni kan*," my mother said, calling me over with hurried hand gestures. "Look here."

22   I could see why my mother was fascinated by the music. It was being pounded out by a little Chinese girl, about nine years old, with a Peter Pan haircut. The girl had the sauciness of a Shirley Temple. She was proudly modest, like a proper Chinese child. And she also did a fancy sweep of a curtsy, so that the fluffy skirt of her white dress cascaded to the floor like the petals of a large carnation.

23   In spite of these warning signs, I wasn't worried. Our family had no piano and we couldn't afford to buy one, let alone reams of sheet music and piano lessons. So I could be generous in my comments when my mother badmouthed the little girl on TV.

24   "Play note right, but doesn't sound good!" my mother complained. "No singing sound."

25   "What are you picking on her for?" I said carelessly. "She's pretty good. Maybe she's not the best, but she's trying hard." I knew almost immediately that I would be sorry I had said that.

26   "Just like you," she said. "Not the best. Because you not trying." She gave a little huff as she let go of the sound dial and sat down on the sofa.

27   The little Chinese girl sat down also, to play an encore of "Anitra's Tanz," by Grieg. I remember the song, because later on I had to learn how to play it.

28   Three days after watching the *Ed Sullivan Show* my mother told me what my schedule would be for piano lessons and piano practice. She had talked to Mr. Chong, who lived on the first floor of our apartment building. Mr. Chong was a retired piano teacher, and my mother had traded housecleaning services for weekly lessons and a piano for me to practice on every day, two hours a day, from four until six.

29   When my mother told me this, I felt as though I had been sent to hell. I whined, and then kicked my foot a little when I couldn't stand it anymore.

30   "Why don't you like me the way I am?" I cried. "I'm *not* a genius! I can't play the piano. And even if I could, I wouldn't go on TV if you paid me a million dollars!"

31   My mother slapped me. "Who ask you to be genius?" she shouted. "Only ask you be your best. For you sake. You think I want you to be genius? Hnnh! What for! Who ask you!"

32   "So ungrateful," I heard her mutter in Chinese. "If she had as much talent as she has temper, she'd be famous now."

33   Mr. Chong, whom I secretly nicknamed Old Chong, was very strange, always tapping his fingers to the silent music of an invisible orchestra. He looked ancient in my eyes. He had lost most of the hair on the top of his head, and he wore thick glasses and had eyes that always looked tired. But he must have been younger than I thought, since he lived with his mother and was not yet married.

34   I met Old Lady Chong once, and that was enough. She had a peculiar smell, like a baby that had done something in its pants, and her fingers felt like a dead person's, like an old peach I once found in the back of the refrigerator; its skin just slid off the flesh when I picked it up.

35   I soon found out why Old Chong had retired from teaching piano. He was deaf. "Like Beethoven!" he shouted to me. "We're both listening only in our head!" And he would start to conduct his frantic silent sonatas.

36   Our lessons went like this. He would open the book and point to different things, explaining their purpose: "Key! Treble! Bass! No sharps or flats! So this is C major! Listen now and play after me!"

37   And then he would play the C scale a few times, a simple chord, and then, as if inspired by an old unreachable itch, he would gradually add more notes and running trills and a pounding bass until the music was really something quite grand.

38   I would play after him, the simple scale, the simple chord, and then just play some nonsense that sounded like a cat running up and down on top of garbage cans. Old Chong would smile and applaud and say, "Very good! But now you must learn to keep time!"

39   So that's how I discovered that Old Chong's eyes were too slow to keep up with the wrong notes I was playing. He went through the motions in half time. To help me keep rhythm, he stood behind me and pushed down on my right shoulder for every beat. He balanced pennies on top of my wrists so that I would keep them still as I slowly played scales and arpeggios. He had me curve my hand around an apple and keep that shape when playing chords. He marched stiffly to show me how to make each finger dance up and down, staccato, like an obedient little soldier.

40   He taught me all these things, and that was how I also learned I could be lazy and get away with mistakes, lots of mistakes. If I hit the wrong notes because I hadn't practiced enough, I never corrected myself. I just kept playing in rhythm. And Old Chong kept conducting his own private reverie.

41   So maybe I never really gave myself a fair chance. I did pick up the basics pretty quickly, and I might have become a good pianist at that young age. But I was so determined not to try, not to be anybody different, and I learned to play only the most ear-splitting preludes, the most discordant hymns.

42   Over the next year I practiced like this, dutifully in my own way. And then one day I heard my mother and her friend Lindo Jong both talking in a loud, bragging tone of voice so that others could hear. It was after church, and I was leaning against a brick wall, wearing a dress with stiff white petticoats. Auntie Lindo's daughter, Waverly, who was my age, was standing farther down the wall, about five feet away. We had grown up together and shared all the closeness of two sisters, squabbling over crayons and dolls. In other words, for the most part, we hated each other. I thought she was snotty. Waverly Jong had gained a certain amount of fame as "Chinatown's Littlest Chinese Chess Champion."

43   "She bring home too many trophy," Auntie Lindo lamented that Sunday. "All day she play chess. All day I have no time do nothing but dust off her winnings." She threw a scolding look at Waverly, who pretended not to see her.

44   "You lucky you don't have this problem," Auntie Lindo said with a sigh to my mother.

45   And my mother squared her shoulders and bragged: "Our problem worser than yours. If we ask Jing-mei wash dish, she hear nothing but music. It's like you can't stop this natural talent."

46   And right then I was determined to put a stop to her foolish pride.

47   A few weeks later Old Chong and my mother conspired to have me play in a talent show that was to be held in the church hall. But then my parents had saved up enough to buy me a secondhand piano, a black Wurlitzer spinet with a scarred bench. It was the showpiece of our living room.

48   For the talent show I was to play a piece called "Pleading Child," from Schumann's *Scenes From Childhood*. It was a simple, moody piece that sounded more difficult than it was. I was supposed to memorize the whole thing. But I dawdled over it, playing a few bars and then cheating, looking up to see what notes followed. I never really listened to what I was playing. I daydreamed about being somewhere else, about being someone else.

49   The part I liked to practice best was the fancy curtsy: right foot out, touch the rose on the carpet with a pointed foot, sweep to the side, bend left leg, look up, and smile.

50   My parents invited all the couples from their social club to witness my debut. Auntie Lindo and Uncle Tin were there. Waverly and her

two older brothers had also come. The first two rows were filled with children either younger or older than I was. The littlest ones got to go first. They recited simple nursery rhymes, squawked out tunes on miniature violins, and twirled hula hoops in pink ballet tutus, and when they bowed or curtsied, the audience would sigh in unison, "*Awww*," and then clap enthusiastically.

51   When my turn came, I was very confident. I remember my childish excitement. It was as if I knew, without a doubt, that the prodigy side of me really did exist. I had no fear whatsoever, no nervousness. I remember thinking, This is it! This is it! I looked out over the audience, at my mother's blank face, my father's yawn, Auntie Lindo's stiff-lipped smile, Waverly's sulky expression. I had on a white dress, layered with sheets of lace, and a pink bow in my Peter Pan haircut. As I sat down, I envisioned people jumping to their feet and Ed Sullivan rushing up to introduce me to everyone on TV.

52   And I started to play. Everything was so beautiful. I was so caught up in how lovely I looked that I wasn't worried about how I would sound. So I was surprised when I hit the first wrong note. And then I hit another, and another. A chill started at the top of my head and began to trickle down. Yet I couldn't stop playing, as though my hands were bewitched. I kept thinking my fingers would adjust themselves back, like a train switching to the right track. I played this strange jumble through to the end, the sour notes staying with me all the way.

53   When I stood up, I discovered my legs were shaking. Maybe I had just been nervous, and the audience, like Old Chong, had seen me go through the right motions and had not heard anything wrong at all. I swept my right foot out, went down on my knee, looked up, and smiled. The room was quiet, except for Old Chong, who was beaming and shouting, "Bravo! Bravo! Well done!" But then I saw my mother's face, her stricken face. The audience clapped weakly, and as I walked back to my chair, with my whole face quivering as I tried not to cry, I heard a little boy whisper loudly to his mother, "That was awful," and the mother whispered, "Well, she certainly tried."

54   And now I realized how many people were in the audience—the whole world, it seemed. I was aware of eyes burning into my back. I felt the shame of my mother and father as they sat stiffly through the rest of the show.

55   We could have escaped during intermission. Pride and some strange sense of honor must have anchored my parents to their chairs. And so we watched it all: The eighteen-year-old boy with a fake moustache who did a magic show and juggled flaming hoops while riding a unicycle. The breasted girl with white makeup who sang an aria from *Madame Butterfly* and got an honorable mention. And the eleven-year-old boy

who won first prize playing a tricky violin song that sounded like a busy bee.

56   After the show the Hsus, the Jongs, and the St. Clairs, from the Joy Luck Club, came up to my mother and father.

57   "Lots of talented kids," Auntie Lindo said vaguely, smiling broadly.

58   "That was somethin' else," my father said, and I wondered if he was referring to me in a humorous way, or whether he even remembered what I had done.

59   Waverly looked at me and shrugged her shoulders. "You aren't a genius like me," she said matter-of-factly. And if I hadn't felt so bad, I would have pulled her braids and punched her stomach.

60   But my mother's expression was what devastated me: a quiet, blank look that said she had lost everything. I felt the same way, and everybody seemed now to be coming up, like gawkers at the scene of an accident, to see what parts were actually missing.

61   When we got on the bus to go home, my father was humming the busy-bee tune and my mother was silent. I kept thinking she wanted to wait until we got home before shouting at me. But when my father unlocked the door to our apartment, my mother walked in and went straight to the back, into the bedroom. No accusations. No blame. And in a way, I felt disappointed. I had been waiting for her to start shouting, so that I could shout back and cry and blame her for all my misery.

62   I had assumed that my talent-show fiasco meant that I would never have to play the piano again. But two days later, after school, my mother came out of the kitchen and saw me watching TV.

63   "Four clock," she reminded me, as if it were any other day. I was stunned, as though she were asking me to go through the talent-show torture again. I planted myself more squarely in front of the TV.

64   "Turn off TV," she called from the kitchen five minutes later.

65   I didn't budge. And then I decided. I didn't have to do what my mother said anymore. I wasn't her slave. This wasn't China. I had listened to her before, and look what happened. She was the stupid one.

66   She came out of the kitchen and stood in the arched entryway of the living room. "Four clock," she said once again, louder.

67   "I'm not going to play anymore," I said nonchalantly. "Why should I? I'm not a genius."

68   She stood in front of the TV. I saw that her chest was heaving up and down in an angry way.

69   "No!" I said, and I now felt stronger, as if my true self had finally emerged. So this was what had been inside me all along.

70   "No! I won't!" I screamed.

71   She snapped off the TV, yanked me by the arm and pulled me off the floor. She was frighteningly strong, half pulling, half carrying me

toward the piano as I kicked the throw rugs under my feet. She lifted me up and onto the hard bench. I was sobbing by now, looking at her bitterly. Her chest was heaving even more and her mouth was open, smiling crazily as if she were pleased that I was crying.

72   "You want me to be someone that I'm not!" I sobbed. "I'll never be the kind of daughter you want me to be!"

73   "Only two kinds of daughters," she shouted in Chinese. "Those who are obedient and those who follow their own mind! Only one kind of daughter can live in this house. Obedient daughter!"

74   "Then I wish I weren't your daughter. I wish you weren't my mother," I shouted. As I said these things I got scared. It felt like worms and toads and slimy things crawling out of my chest, but it also felt good, that this awful side of me had surfaced, at last.

75   "Too late change this," my mother said shrilly.

76   And I could sense her anger rising to its breaking point. I wanted to see it spill over. And that's when I remembered the babies she had lost in China, the ones we never talked about. "Then I wish I'd never been born!" I shouted. "I wish I were dead! Like them."

77   It was as if I had said magic words. Alakazam!—her face went blank, her mouth closed, her arms went slack, and she backed out of the room, stunned, as if she were blowing away like a small brown leaf, thin, brittle, lifeless.

78   It was not the only disappointment my mother felt in me. In the years that followed, I failed her many times, each time asserting my will, my right to fall short of expectations. I didn't get straight As. I didn't become class president. I didn't get into Stanford. I dropped out of college.

79   Unlike my mother, I did not believe I could be anything I wanted to be. I could only be me.

80   And for all those years we never talked about the disaster at the recital or my terrible declarations afterward at the piano bench. Neither of us talked about it again, as if it were a betrayal that was now unspeakable. So I never found a way to ask her why she had hoped for something so large that failure was inevitable.

81   And even worse, I never asked her about what frightened me the most: Why had she given up hope? For after our struggle at the piano, she never mentioned my playing again. The lessons stopped. The lid to the piano was closed, shutting out the dust, my misery, and her dreams.

82   So she surprised me. A few years ago she offered to give me the piano, for my thirtieth birthday. I had not played in all those years. I saw the offer as a sign of forgiveness, a tremendous burden removed.

83   "Are you sure?" I asked shyly. "I mean, won't you and Dad miss it?"

84   "No, this your piano," she said firmly. "Always your piano. You only one can play."

85   "Well, I probably can't play anymore," I said. "It's been years."

86   "You pick up fast," my mother said, as if she knew this was certain. "You have natural talent. You could be genius if you want to."

87   "No, I couldn't."

88   "You just not trying," my mother said. And she was neither angry nor sad. She said it as if announcing a fact that could never be disproved. "Take it," she said.

89   But I didn't at first. It was enough that she had offered it to me. And after that, every time I saw it in my parents' living room, standing in front of the bay window, it made me feel proud, as if it were a shiny trophy that I had won back.

90   Last week I sent a tuner over to my parents' apartment and had the piano reconditioned, for purely sentimental reasons. My mother had died a few months before, and I had been getting things in order for my father, a little bit at a time. I put the jewelry in special silk pouches. The sweaters she had knitted in yellow, pink, bright orange—all the colors I hated—I put in mothproof boxes. I found some old Chinese silk dresses, the kind with little slits up the sides. I rubbed the old silk against my skin, and then wrapped them in tissue and decided to take them home with me.

91   After I had the piano tuned, I opened the lid and touched the keys. It sounded even richer than I remembered. Really, it was a very good piano. Inside the bench were the same exercise notes with handwritten scales, the same secondhand music books with their covers held together with yellow tape.

92   I opened up the Schumann book to the dark little piece I had played at the recital. It was on the left-hand page, "Pleading Child." It looked more difficult than I remembered. I played a few bars, surprised at how easily the notes came back to me.

93   And for the first time, or so it seemed, I noticed the piece on the right-hand side. It was called "Perfectly Contented." I tried to play this one as well. It had a lighter melody but with the same flowing rhythm and turned out to be quite easy. "Pleading Child" was shorter but slower; "Perfectly Contented" was longer but faster. And after I had played them both a few times, I realized they were two halves of the same song.

Two Kinds

JOURNAL

1. **MLA Works Cited**   *Using this model, record this story here.*

   Author's Last Name, First Name. "Title of the Story." <u>Title of the Book</u>. 3rd ed. Ed. First Name Last Name. City: Publisher, year. Pages of the story.

2. **Main Character(s)**   *Describe each main character, and explain why you think each is a main character.*

3. **Supporting Characters**   *Describe each supporting character, and explain why you think each is a supporting character.*

4. **Setting**   *Describe the setting(s) and any relevant prop(s).*

5. **Sequence**   *Outline the events of the story in order.*

6. **Plot**   *Tell the story in no more than two sentences.*

7. **Conflicts**   *Identify and explain all the conflicts involved here.*

8. **Significant Quotations**   *Explain the importance of each of these quotations. Record the page number in the parentheses.*
   a. "America was where my mother's hopes lay" (   ).

   b. "Three days after watching the *Ed Sullivan Show* my mother told me what my schedule would be for piano lessons and piano practice" (   ).

   c. "If I hit the wrong notes because I hadn't practiced enough, I never corrected myself" (   ).

d. "My parents invited all the couples from their social club to witness my debut" (   ).

e. "And for the first time, or so it seemed, I noticed the piece on the right-hand side" (   ).

9. **Literary Elements**   *Look at this chapter's title and explain why you think this story is placed in this chapter. Explain in which other chapter(s) you might place this story, as relevant to the literary element(s) of that chapter.*

10. **Foreshadowing, Irony, and/or Symbolism**   *Explain examples of foreshadowing, irony, and/or symbolism in this story.*

FOLLOW-UP QUESTIONS

10 SHORT QUESTIONS

Select the <u>best</u> answer for each.

____ 1. The mother is
    a. native to America.
    b. an immigrant to America.
    c. not in America.

____ 2. The mother has had
    a. an easy life.
    b. a hard life.
    c. an unknown life.

____ 3. The mother wants her daughter
    a. to be successful.
    b. to be happy.
    c. to live in China.

____ 4. The mother first sees the piano as a route
    a. in the movies.
    b. at the talent show.
    c. on television.

____ 5. The narrator must learn
    a. to dance like Shirley Temple.
    b. to sing like Shirley Temple.
    c. to play the piano.

____ 6. The narrator practices
    a. very hard.
    b. very poorly.
    c. not at all.

____ 7. At the talent show, the mother
    a. plays the piano.
    b. has invited all her friends.
    c. is delighted in the end.

____ 8. At the talent show, the narrator
    a. thinks she can do well.
    b. thinks she will fail.
    c. knows she will fail.

____ 9. The mother wants her daughter to be
    a. pleasant.
    b. happy.
    c. obedient.

____ 10. In the end, the piano seems to become a sign of
    a. forgiveness.
    b. furniture.
    c. firewood.

5 SIGNIFICANT QUOTATIONS

Explain the importance of each of these quotations.

1. " 'Of course, you can be prodigy, too,' my mother told me when I was nine."

2. "She had talked to Mr. Chong, who lived on the first floor of our apartment building."

3. "But I was so determined not to try, not to be anybody different, and I learned to play only the most ear-splitting preludes, the most discordant hymns."

4. "I was so caught up in how lovely I looked that I wasn't worried about how I would sound. So I was surprised when I hit the first wrong note."

5. " 'Only two kinds of daughters,' she shouted in Chinese. 'Those who are obedient and those who follow their own mind!' "

2 COMPREHENSION ESSAY QUESTIONS

Use specific details and information from the story to answer these questions as completely as possible.

1. How are the narrator and the mother different? Use specific details and information from the story to support your ideas.

2. Although seemingly defiant, how does the narrator show respect for her mother? Use specific details and information from the story to support your answer.

DISCUSSION QUESTIONS

Be prepared to discuss these questions in class.

1. What are the "two kinds"? People? Ambitions? Daughters? Something else?

2. Do you agree or disagree with the mother's goals? Why?

WRITING

Use each of these ideas for writing an essay.

1. We have all wanted to be good at something. Select one goal you have had and tell how well you have—or have not—accomplished this and what impact this has had on you.

2. We have all experienced generation gaps. Using specific examples and illustrations, describe an instance when your age impacted you or those around you.

Further Writing

1. Research your own family's immigration patterns. Record where your family members first immigrated to and, then later, where they relocated in America. Record the occupations the members took up in these areas. Explain the location and occupational patterns or—equally significant—the lack of patterns in your family.

2. Related to the idea above, research the general patterns of immigration and occupations as they apply to your specific ancestral heritage (e.g., Irish patterns, Chinese patterns, Cherokee patterns, and so forth). Now compare your family's specific immigration and occupational patterns with those of your heritage group(s).

The Tell-Tale Heart

EDGAR ALLAN POE

PRE-READING VOCABULARY
CONTEXT

Use context clues to define these words before reading. Use a dictionary as needed.

1. The movie was so terrible that it was *dreadful*. *Dreadful* means

   _____.

2. The smell of dinner may *sharpen* one's appetite. *Sharpen* means

   _____.

3. After too much use, the knife became *dull*. *Dull* means

   _____.

4. A *vulture* circled overhead, waiting to eat the dead animal. *Vulture*

   means _____.

5. Not being able to separate reality from fantasy is just plain *mad*. *Mad*

   means _____.

6. To see down the dark hallway, Betty used a *lantern*. *Lantern* means

   _____.

7. The cat *cunningly* hid in the closet so that she could jump out and

   scare us. *Cunningly* means _____.

8. The sudden, loud noise *startled* Juan. *Startle* means

   _____.

9. Albert bought new wooden *shutters* to filter the light in each window.

   Shutters means _____.

10. Renée was in *awe* when she actually met the rock superstar. *Awe* means _____.

11. Shirley was *furious* when her dog tore up her favorite, brand new shoes. *Furious* means _____.

12. The smog *enveloped* the city, making it very hard to see. *Envelop* means _____.

13. As he got tired of waiting, Jim's tapping fingers beat a continual *tattoo* on the countertop. *Tattoo* means _____.

14. When Kathy saw the mouse run across her foot, she let out a loud *shriek*. *Shriek* means _____.

15. John *muffled* the loud noise with earplugs. *Muffle* means

    _____.

16. After the funeral, the *corpse* was buried in the old cemetery. *Corpse* means _____.

17. After running the mile, Aimée could feel her heart beat and sensed its every *pulsation*. *Pulsation* means _____.

18. The mechanic had to *dismember* the car to get to the fan belt. *Dismember* means _____.

19. After money suddenly was found to be continuously missing, we developed a *suspicion* that the new employee was stealing. *Suspicion* means _____.

20. Although Bruce was very upset after his accident, he *dissembled* well and had us all believing that he was not upset at all. *Dissemble* means _____.

PRE-READING VOCABULARY
STRUCTURAL ATTACK

Define these words by solving the parts. Use the Glossary or a dictionary as needed.

1. causeless
2. unperceived
3. stealthily
4. distinctness
5. motionless
6. uncontrollable
7. precaution
8. concealment
9. hastily

PRE-READING QUESTIONS

Try answering these questions as you read.

Who are the characters in the story?

How does the narrator want you to feel about him?

Sanity is defined as being able to recognize reality, while insanity is defined as not being able to recognize reality. What does this tell you about the narrator?

What hints does Poe give you for the startling ending?

The Tell-Tale Heart

EDGAR ALLAN POE

Edgar Allan Poe was born in 1809 and orphaned at a young age. He was adopted by John Allan, a rather militaristic businessman from Richmond, Virginia. Adoption by a person of means was not uncommon and would have been fortunate for the young Poe, except that his free spirit and his father's precision clashed. John Allan provided Poe with study at the University of Virginia—but Poe withdrew, due to drinking problems—and then at West Point—but Poe was dismissed, due to a disciplinary problem. Poe later married his very young cousin, Virginia Clemm, but the probable nonconsummation of this marriage and the early death of young Virginia contributed to Poe's idealization of both real and imagined women. His life, in fact, was one of continual disappointments. After Virginia's death, Poe sank into intermittent depressions, suffered bouts of insanity, and experienced hallucinations. Writing for many others, he wanted to publish his own magazine, but this dissolved in financial failure. He eventually died in Baltimore in 1849.

However, it is from these very problems that Poe's genius soars. He envelops the reader with his perceived worlds of the sane and insane, the rational and macabre, with equal ease. Credited with developing the modern mystery form, Poe's every word and every action draw the reader in, mixing reality with irreality, sane with insane. His other works include "The Pit and the Pendulum" and "The Fall of the House of Usher."

True! nervous—very, very dreadfully nervous I had been and am; but why *will* you say that I am mad? The disease had sharpened my senses—not destroyed—not dulled them. Above all was the sense of hearing acute. I heard all things in the heaven and in the earth. I heard many things in hell. How, then, am I mad? Hearken! and observe how healthily—how calmly I can tell you the whole story.

2   It is impossible to say how first the idea entered my brain; but once conceived, it haunted me day and night. Object there was none. Passion there was none. I loved the old man. He had never wronged me. He had never given me insult. For his gold I had no desire. I think it was his eye! yes, it was this! He had the eye of a vulture—a pale blue eye, with a film over it. Whenever it fell upon me, my blood ran cold; and so by degrees—very gradually—I made up my mind to take the life of the old man, and thus rid myself of the eye forever.

3   Now this is the point. You fancy me mad. Madmen know nothing. But you should have seen *me*. You should have seen how wisely I proceeded—with what caution—with what foresight—with what dissimulation I went to work! I was never kinder to the old man than during the whole week before I killed him. And every night, about midnight, I turned the latch of his door and opened it—ah, so gently! And then, when I had made an opening sufficient for my head, I put in a dark lantern, all closed, closed, so that no light shone out, and then I thrust in my head. Oh, you would have laughed to see how cunningly I thrust it in! I moved it slowly—very, very slowly, so that I might not disturb the old man's sleep. It took me an hour to place my whole head within the opening so far that I could see him as he lay upon his bed. Ha!— would a madman have been so wise as this? And then, when my head was well in the room, I undid the lantern cautiously—oh, so cautiously—cautiously (for the hinges creaked)—I undid it just so much that a single thin ray fell upon the vulture eye. And this I did for seven long nights—every night just at midnight—but I found the eye always closed; and so it was impossible to do the work; for it was not the old man who vexed me, but his Evil Eye. And every morning, when the day broke, I went boldly into the chamber, and spoke courageously to him, calling him by name in a hearty tone, and inquiring how he had passed the night. So you see he would have been a very profound old man, indeed, to suspect that every night, just at twelve, I looked in upon him while he slept.

4   Upon the eighth night I was more than usually cautious in opening the door. A watch's minute hand moves more quickly than did mine. Never, before that night, had I *felt* the extent of my own powers—of my sagacity. I could scarcely contain my feelings of triumph. To think that there I was, opening the door, little by little, and he not even to

dream of my secret deeds or thoughts. I fairly chuckled at the idea; and perhaps he heard me; for he moved on the bed suddenly, as if startled. Now you may think that I drew back—but no. His room was as black as pitch with the thick darkness (for the shutters were close fastened, through fear of robbers), and so I knew that he could not see the opening of the door, and I kept pushing it on steadily, steadily.

5   I had my head in, and was about to open the lantern, when my thumb slipped upon the tin fastening, and the old man sprang up in bed, crying out, "Who's there?" I kept quite still and said nothing. For a whole hour I did not move a muscle, and in the meantime I did not hear him lie down. He was still sitting up in the bed listening—just as I have done, night after night, hearkening to the death watches in the wall.

6   Presently I heard a slight groan, and I knew it was the groan of mortal terror. It was not a groan of pain or of grief—oh, no!—it was the low stifled sound that rises from the bottom of the soul when overcharged with awe. I knew the sound well. Many a night, just at midnight, when all the world slept, it has welled up from my own bosom, deepening, with its dreadful echo, the terrors that distracted me. I say I knew it well. I knew what the old man felt, and pitied him, although I chuckled at heart. I knew that he had been lying awake ever since the first slight noise, when he had turned in his bed. His fears had been ever since growing upon him. He had been trying to fancy them causeless, but could not. He had been saying to himself—"It is nothing but the wind in the chimney—it is only a mouse crossing the floor," or "It is merely a cricket which has made a single chirp." Yes, he had been trying to comfort himself with these suppositions: but he had found all in vain. *All in vain*; because Death, in approaching him, had stalked with his black shadow before him, and enveloped the victim. And it was the mournful influence of the unperceived shadow that caused him to feel—although he neither saw nor heard—to *feel* the presence of my head within the room.

7   When I had waited a long time, very patiently, without hearing him lie down, I resolved to open a little—a very, very little crevice in the lantern. So I opened it—you cannot imagine how stealthily, stealthily—until at length a single dim ray, like the thread of the spider, shot from out the crevice and fell upon the vulture eye.

8   It was open—wide, wide open—and I grew furious as I gazed upon it. I saw it with perfect distinctiveness—all a dull blue, with a hideous veil over it that chilled the very marrow in my bones; but I could see nothing else of the old man's face or person; for I had directed the ray as if by instinct, precisely upon the damned spot.

9   And have I not told you that what you mistake for madness is but overacuteness of the senses?—Now, I say, there came to my ears a low,

dull, quick sound, such as a watch makes when enveloped in cotton. I knew *that* sound well, too. It was the beating of the old man's heart. It increased my fury, as the beating of a drum stimulates the soldier into courage.

10   But even yet I refrained and kept still. I scarcely breathed. I held the lantern motionless. I tried how steadily I could maintain the ray upon the eye. Meantime the hellish tattoo of the heart increased. It grew quicker and quicker, and louder and louder every instant. The old man's terror *must* have been extreme! It grew louder, I say louder every moment!—do you mark me well? I have told you that I am nervous: so I am. And now at the dead hour of the night, amid the dreadful silence of that old house, so strange a noise as this excited me to uncontrollable terror. Yet, for some minutes longer I refrained and stood still. But the beating grew louder, louder. I thought the heart must burst. And now a new anxiety seized me—the sound would be heard by a neighbor! The old man's hour had come! With, a loud yell, I threw open the lantern and leaped into the room. He shrieked once—once only. In an instant I dragged him to the floor, and pulled the heavy bed over him. I then smiled gaily, to find the deed so far done. But, for many minutes, the heart beat on with a muffled sound. This, however, did not vex me; it would not be heard through the wall. At length it ceased. The old man was dead. I removed the bed and examined the corpse. Yes, he was stone, stone dead. I placed my hand upon the heart and held it there many minutes. There was no pulsation. He was stone dead. His eye would trouble me no more.

11   If still you think me mad, you will think so no longer when I describe the wise precautions I took for the concealment of the body. The night waned, and I worked hastily, but in silence. First of all I dismembered the corpse. I cut off the head and the arms and the legs.

12   I then took up three planks from the flooring of the chamber, and deposited all between the scantlings. I then replaced the boards so cleverly, so cunningly, that no human eye—not even his—could have detected anything wrong. There was nothing to wash out—no stain of any kind—no blood spot whatever. I had been too wary for that. A tub had caught all—ha! ha!

13   When I had made an end of these labors, it was four o'clock—still dark as midnight. As the bell sounded the hour, there came a knocking at the street door. I went down to open it with a light heart—for what had I *now* to fear? There entered three men, who introduced themselves, with perfect suavity, as officers of the police. A shriek had been heard by a neighbor during the night; suspicion of foul play had been aroused; information had been lodged at the police office, and they (the officers) had been deputed to search the premises.

14   I smiled—for *what* had I to fear? I bade the gentlemen welcome. The shriek, I said, was my own in a dream. The old man, I mentioned, was absent in the country. I took my visitors all over the house. I bade them search—search *well*. I led them, at length, to *his* chamber. I showed them his treasures, secure, undisturbed. In the enthusiasm of my confidence, I brought chairs into the room, and desired them *here* to rest from their fatigues, while I myself, in the wild audacity of my perfect triumph, placed my own seat upon the very spot beneath which reposed the corpse of the victim.

15   The officers were satisfied. My *manner* had convinced them. I was singularly at ease. They sat, and while I answered cheerily, they chatted of familiar things. But, erelong, I felt myself getting pale and wished them gone. My head ached, and I fancied a ringing in my ears: but still they sat and still chatted. The ringing became more distinct— it continued and became more distinct; I talked more freely to get rid of the feeling; but it continued and gained definiteness—until, at length, I found that the noise was *not* within my ears.

16   No doubt I now grew *very* pale—but I talked more fluently, and with a heightened voice. Yet the sound increased—and what could I do? It was *a low, dull, quick sound—much such a sound as a watch makes when enveloped in cotton.* I gasped for breath—and yet the officers heard it not. I talked more quickly—more vehemently; but the noise steadily increased. I arose and argued about rifles, in a high key and with violent gesticulations; but the noise steadily increased. Why *would* they not be gone? I paced the floor to and fro with heavy strides, as if excited to fury by the observations of the men—but the noise steadily increased. Oh, God! what *could* I do? I foamed—I raved—I swore! I swung the chair upon which I had been sitting, and grated it upon the boards, but the noise arose over all and continually increased. It grew louder—louder—*louder!* And still the men chatted pleasantly, and smiled. Was it possible they heard not? Almighty God!—no, no! They heard!—they suspected!—they *knew!*—they were making a mockery of my horror!—this I thought, and this I think. But anything was better than this agony! Anything was more tolerable than derision! I could bear those hypocritical smiles no longer! I felt that I must scream or die! and now—again!—hark! louder! louder! louder! *louder!*

17   "Villains!" I shrieked, "dissemble no more! I admit the deed!—tear up the planks! here, here!—it is the beating of his hideous heart!"

The Tell-Tale Heart

JOURNAL

1. **MLA Works Cited**   *Using this model, record this story here.*

   Author's Last Name, First Name. "Title of the Story." <u>Title of the Book</u>. 3rd ed. Ed. First Name Last Name. City: Publisher, year. Pages of the story.

2. **Main Character(s)**   *Describe each main character, and explain why you think each is a main character.*

3. **Supporting Characters**   *Describe each supporting character, and explain why you think each is a supporting character.*

4. **Setting**   *Describe the setting(s) and any relevant prop(s).*

5. Sequence   *Outline the events of the story in order.*

6. Plot   *Tell the story in no more than two sentences.*

7. Conflicts   *Identify and explain all the conflicts involved here.*

8. Significant Quotations   *Explain the importance of each of these quotations. Record the page number in the parentheses.*

    a. "The disease had sharpened my senses—not destroyed—not dulled them" (   ).

    b. "He had the eye of a vulture—a pale blue eye, with a film over it" (   ).

c. "Upon the eighth night I was more than usually cautious in opening the door" (   ).

d. "And have I not told you that what you mistake for madness is but over-acuteness of the senses?—Now, I say, there came to my ears a low, dull, quick sound, such as a watch makes when enveloped in cotton" (   ).

e. "I gasped for breath—and yet the officers heard it not" (   ).

9. **Literary Elements**   *Look at this chapter's title and explain why you think this story is placed in this chapter. Explain in which other chapter(s) you might place this story, as relevant to the literary element(s) of that chapter.*

10. **Foreshadowing, Irony, and/or Symbolism**   *Explain examples of foreshadowing, irony, and/or symbolism in this story.*

FOLLOW-UP QUESTIONS

10 SHORT QUESTIONS

*Select the **best** answer for each.*

_____ 1. The narrator thinks
   a. he is sane.
   b. he is insane.
   c. he is normal.

_____ 2. The narrator wants you to think
   a. he is sane.
   b. he is insane.
   c. he is sane and more clever than most.

_____ 3. At first, the narrator is
   a. kind to the old man.
   b. unkind to the old man.
   c. unfeeling toward the old man.

_____ 4. The old man is
   a. unkind to the narrator.
   b. like a father figure to the narrator.
   c. the narrator's brother.

_____ 5. The narrator probably shares
   a. no relationship with the old man.
   b. a formal working relationship with the old man.
   c. a family-like relationship with the old man.

_____ 6. The narrator
   a. hates the old man.
   b. loves the old man.
   c. does not care about the old man.

_____ 7. The narrator
   a. hates the old man's eye.
   b. loves the old man's eye.
   c. does not care about the old man's eye.

_____ 8. The narrator
   a. has planned well.
   b. has not planned well.
   c. does not tell the reader about his plans.

_____ 9. The only person(s) who can hear the heartbeat is (are)
   a. the police.
   b. the old man.
   c. the narrator.

_____ 10. At first, the police
   a. do not suspect the narrator.
   b. do suspect the narrator.
   c. know the old man is dead.

5 SIGNIFICANT QUOTATIONS

Explain the importance of each of these quotations.

1. "True! nervous—very, very dreadfully nervous I had been and am; but why *will* you say that I am mad?"

2. "I think it was his eye! yes, it was this!"

3. "You fancy me mad. Madmen know nothing. But you should have seen *me*."

4. "And this I did for seven long nights—every night just at midnight—but I found the eye always closed; and so it was impossible to do the work; [. . .]."

5. " 'Villains!' I shrieked, 'dissemble no more! I admit the deed!—tear up the planks! here, here!—it is the beating of his hideous heart!'"

2 COMPREHENSION ESSAY QUESTIONS

Use specific details and information from the story to answer these questions as completely as possible.

1. How does the title relate to the story? Explain the significance of the title using specific details and information from the story.

2. What are all the events that happen during the narrator's confession? Use specific details and information from the story for your explanation.

DISCUSSION QUESTIONS

Be prepared to discuss these questions in class.

1. What characteristics of the homicidal mind do you think this story presents?

2. How does Poe's biography relate to the story? Use specific details from the biographical blurb and the story to support your ideas.

WRITING

Use each of these ideas for writing an essay.

1. At one time or another, we have all been so scared that we could hear our own heartbeat. Tell the story of a time when you were so scared that you could hear your heartbeat.

2. The narrator is very sure that what he is doing is very clever. Describe a time when you or someone you know was sure of being right when, in fact, what you or she or he was doing was wrong.

Further Writing

1. Compare and contrast the narrator in this story with Montresor in Edgar Allan Poe's "The Cask of Amontillado" (page 154).

2. Research today's use of the insanity plea in criminal actions. Poe's story offers an insightful anecdote for this study.

There Will Come Soft Rains

RAY BRADBURY

PRE-READING VOCABULARY
CONTEXT

Use context clues to define these words before reading. Use a dictionary as needed.

1. The principal *ejected* the student from school who was always in trouble. *Eject* means _____.

2. The *relay* runners passed the torch from one runner to the next. *Relay* means _____.

3. When rabbits live underground, they live in what is called a *warren*. *Warren* means _____.

4. The scientist created a *robot* with arms like a man so it could put the dishes in the dishwasher. *Robot* means _____.

5. The atomic bomb gave off deadly *radioactive* particles. *Radioactive* means _____.

6. The chef baked the rolls too long and *charred* their bottoms. *Char* means _____.

7. A *silhouette* is usually a picture of a black profile set on a white background. *Silhouette* means _____.

8. The extremely large wave was of *titanic* size. *Titanic* means

   _____.

9. When Ted studied *mechanical* engineering, he learned how machines work and how to invent new ones. *Mechanical* means

   _____.

10. Reading books and saying prayers before bedtime are our children's *rituals*. *Ritual* means _____.

11. The air flowed through the open *vent*. *Vent* means

    _____.

12. To get rid of excess trash, the township burned it in an *incinerator*. *Incinerator* means _____.

13. Jess sunbathed on the lovely concrete *patio* in back of her house. *Patio* means _____.

14. Cinderella's busy mice rapidly *scurried* past the sleeping cat. *Scurry* means _____.

15. When it broke, the glass shattered into a million dangerous and flying pieces, like *shrapnel*. *Shrapnel* means _____.

16. The hot water *scalded* the young plants. *Scald* means

    _____.

17. When Kristin called for silence, all the talking *ceased*. *Cease* means

    _____.

18. Hundreds of rocks fell down the mountainside in a roaring *avalanche*. *Avalanche* means _____.

19. The *frantic* mother searched everywhere for her lost child until she found him. *Frantic* means _____.

20. After the building burned to the ground, the workers returned to search through the *rubble* for valuables. *Rubble* means

    _____.

PRE-READING VOCABULARY
STRUCTURAL ATTACK

Define these words by solving the parts. Use the Glossary or a dictionary as needed.

1. emptiness
2. payable
3. acrawl
4. windowpane
5. self-protection

6. senselessly
7. uselessly
8. summer-starched
9. trapdoor
10. remote-control

PRE-READING QUESTIONS

Try answering these questions as you read.

Who or what are the characters in the story?

What has happened?

What is happening now?

What is the scene Bradbury is painting?

There Will Come Soft Rains

Ray Bradbury

Ray Bradbury was born in 1920 in Waukegan, Illinois, but was raised in Los Angeles. Already writing science fiction in high school, he published his first story in 1941. With a continuing dialectic dynamic, his writings discuss the relationship between humans and the machines and/or destruction we create. Taken from <u>The Martian Chronicles</u>, this story remains one of his more noted short stories.

The house was a good house and had been planned and built by the people who were to live in it, in the year 1980. The house was like many another house in that year; it fed and slept and entertained its habitants, and made a good life for them. The man and wife and their two children lived at ease there, and lived happily, even while the world trembled. All of the fine things of living, the warm things, music and poetry, books that talked, beds that warmed and made themselves, fires that built themselves in the fireplaces of evenings, were in this house, and living there was a contentment.

2   And then one day the world shook and there was an explosion followed by ten thousand explosions and red fire in the sky and a rain of ashes and radioactivity, and the happy time was over.

3   In the living room the voice clock sang, *tick-tock, seven A.M. o'clock, time to get up!* as if it were afraid nobody would. The house lay empty. The clock talked on into the empty morning.

4   The kitchen stove sighed and ejected from its warm interior eight eggs, sunny side up, twelve bacon slices, two coffees, and two cups of hot cocoa. *Seven nine, breakfast time, seven nine.*

5   "Today is April 28th, 1985," said a phonograph voice in the kitchen ceiling. "Today, remember, is Mr. Featherstone's birthday. Insurance, gas, light, and water bills are due."

6   Somewhere in the walls, relays clicked, memory tapes glided under electric eyes. Recorded voices moved beneath steel needles:

7   *Eight one, run, run, off to school, off to work, run, run, tick-tock, eight one o'clock!*

8   But no doors slammed, no carpets took the quick tread of rubber heels. Outside, it was raining. The voice of the weather box on the front door sang quietly: *Rain, rain, go away, rubbers, raincoats for today.* And the rain tapped on the roof.

9   At eight thirty the eggs were shriveled. An aluminum wedge scraped them into the sink, where hot water whirled them down a metal throat which digested and flushed them away to the distant sea.

10   *Nine fifteen*, sang the clock, *time to clean.*

11   Out of warrens in the wall, tiny mechanical mice darted. The rooms were acrawl with the small cleaning animals, all rubber and metal. They sucked up the hidden dust, and popped back in their burrows.

12   *Ten o'clock.* The sun came out from behind the rain. The house stood alone on a street where all the other houses were rubble and ashes. At night, the ruined town gave off a radioactive glow which could be seen for miles.

13   *Ten fifteen.* The garden sprinkler filled the soft morning air with golden fountains. The water tinkled over the charred west side of the house where it had been scorched evenly free of its white paint. The entire face of the house was black, save for five places. Here, the silhouette, in paint, of a man mowing a lawn. Here, a woman bent to pick flowers. Still farther over, their images burned on wood in one titanic instant, a small boy, hands flung in the air—higher up, the image of a thrown ball—and opposite him a girl, her hands raised to catch a ball which never came down.

14   The five spots of paint—the man, the woman, the boy, the girl, the ball—remained. The rest was a layer of charcoal.

15   The gentle rain of the sprinkler filled the garden with falling light.

16   Until this day, how well the house had kept its peace. How carefully it had asked, "Who goes there?" and getting no reply from rains and lonely foxes and whining cats, it had shut up its windows and drawn the shades. If a sparrow brushed a window, the shade snapped up. The bird, startled, flew off! No, not even an evil bird must touch the house.

17   And inside, the house was like an altar with nine thousand robot attendants, big and small, servicing, attending, singing in choirs, even though the gods had gone away and the ritual was meaningless.

18   A dog whined, shivering, on the front porch.

19   The front door recognized the dog's voice and opened. The dog padded in wearily, thinned to the bone, covered with sores. It tracked mud on the carpet. Behind it whirred the angry robot mice, angry at having to pick up mud and maple leaves, which, carried to the burrows, were dropped down cellar tubes into an incinerator which sat like an evil Baal in a dark corner.

20   The dog ran upstairs, hysterically yelping at each door. It pawed the kitchen door wildly.

21   Behind the door, the stove was making pancakes which filled the whole house with their odor.

22   The dog frothed, ran insanely, spun in a circle, biting its tail, and died.

23   It lay in the living room for an hour.

24   *One o' clock.*

25   Delicately sensing decay, the regiments of mice hummed out of the walls, soft as blown leaves, their electric eyes glowing.

26   *One fifteen.*

27   The dog was gone.

28   The cellar incinerator glowed suddenly and a whirl of sparks leaped up the flue.

29   *Two thirty-five.*

30   Bridge tables sprouted from the patio walls. Playing cards fluttered onto pads in a shower of pips. Martinis appeared on an oaken bench.

31   But the tables were silent, the cards untouched.

32   At four thirty the tables folded back into the walls.

33   *Five o'clock.* The bathtubs filled with clear hot water. A safety razor dropped into a wall mold, ready.

34   *Six, seven, eight, nine o'clock.*

35   Dinner made, ignored, and flushed away; dishes washed; and in the study, the tobacco stand produced a cigar, half an inch of gray ash on it, smoking, waiting. The hearth fire bloomed up all by itself, out of nothing.

36   *Nine o'clock.* The beds began to warm their hidden circuits, for the night was cool.

37   A gentle click in the study wall. A voice spoke from above the crackling fireplace:

38   "Mrs. McClellan, what poem would you like to hear this evening?"

39   The house was silent.

40   The voice said, "Since you express no preference, I'll pick a poem at random." Quiet music rose behind the voice. "Sara Teasdale. A favorite of yours, as I recall."

41   *There will come soft rains and the smell of*
42   *   the ground,*
43   *And swallows circling with their shimmering*
44   *   sound;*

45   *And frogs in the pools singing at night,*
46   *And wild plum-trees in tremulous white.*

47   *Robins will wear their feathery fire*
48   *Whistling their whims on a low fence-wire;*

49   *And not one will know of the war, not one*
50   *Will care at last when it is done.*

51   *Not one would mind, neither bird nor tree,*
52   *If mankind perished utterly.*

53   *And Spring herself, when she woke at dawn,*
54   *Would scarcely know that we were gone.*

55   The voice finished the poem. The empty chairs faced each other between the silent walls, and the music played.
56   At ten o'clock, the house began to die.
57   The wind blew. The bough of a falling tree smashed the kitchen window. Cleaning solvent, bottled, crashed on the stove.
58   "Fire!" screamed voices. "Fire!" Water pumps shot down water from the ceilings. But the solvent spread under the doors, making fire as it went, while other voices took up the alarm in chorus.
59   The windows broke with heat and the wind blew in to help the fire. Scurrying water rats, their copper wheels spinning, squeaked from the walls, squirted their water, ran for more.
60   Too late! Somewhere, a pump stopped. The ceiling sprays stopped raining. The reserve water supply, which had filled baths and washed dishes for many silent days, was gone.
61   The fire crackled upstairs, ate paintings, lay hungrily in the beds! It devoured every room.
62   The house was shuddering, oak bone on bone, the bared skeleton cringing from the heat, all the wires revealed as if a surgeon had torn the skin off to let the red veins quiver in scalded air. Voices screamed, *"Help, help, fire, run!"* Windows snapped open and shut, like mouths, undecided. Fire, run! the voices wailed a tragic nursery rhyme, and the silly Greek chorus faded as the sound-wires popped their sheathings. Ten dozen high, shrieking voices died, as emergency batteries melted.

63   In the other parts of the house, in the last instant under the fire avalanche, other choruses could be heard announcing the time, the weather, appointments, diets, playing music, reading poetry in the fiery study, while doors opened and slammed and umbrellas appeared at the doors and put themselves away—a thousand things happening like the interior of a clockshop at midnight, all clocks striking, a merry-go-round of squeaking, whispering, rushing, until all the film spools were burned and fell, and all the wires withered and the circuits cracked.
64   In the kitchen, an instant before the final collapse, the stove, hysterically hissing, could be seen making breakfasts at a psychopathic rate, ten dozen pancakes, six dozen loaves of toast.

65   The crash! The attic smashing kitchen down into cellar and sub-
cellar. Deep freeze, armchairs, film tapes, beds, were thrown in a cluttered mound deep under.

66   Smoke and silence.

67   Dawn shone faintly in the east. In the ruins, one wall stood alone.
Within the wall, a voice said, over and over again and again, even as the
sun rose to shine upon the heaped rubble and steam:

68   "Today is April 29th, 1985. Today is April 29th, 1985. Today is . . ."

There Will Come Soft Rains

Journal

1. **MLA Works Cited**   *Using this model, record this story here.*

   Author's Last Name, First Name. "Title of the Story." <u>Title of the Book</u>. 3rd ed. Ed. First Name Last Name. City: Publisher, year. Pages of the story.

2. **Main Character(s)**   *Describe each main character, and explain why you think each is a main character.*

3. **Supporting Characters**   *Describe each supporting character, and explain why you think each is a supporting character.*

4. **Setting**   *Describe the setting(s) and any relevant prop(s).*

5. Sequence   *Outline the events of the story in order.*

6. Plot   *Tell the story in no more than three sentences.*

7. Conflicts   *Identify and explain all the conflicts involved here.*

8. Significant Quotations   *Explain the importance of each of these quotations. Record the page number in the parentheses.*

  a. "The house stood alone on a street where all the other houses were rubble and ashes" (   ).

  b. "Here the silhouette, in paint, of a man mowing a lawn. Here, a woman bent to pick flowers" (   ).

c. "Delicately sensing decay, the regiments of mice hummed out of the walls, soft as blown leaves, their electric eyes glowing" (   ).

d. *"There will come soft rains and the smell of*
        the ground, [. . .].
    And Spring herself, when she woke at dawn,
    Would scarcely know that we were gone'" (   ).

e. "Somewhere, a pump stopped" (   ).

9. **Literary Elements**   *Look at this chapter's title and explain why you think this story is placed in this chapter. Explain in which other chapter(s) you might place this story, as relevant to the literary element(s) of that chapter.*

10. **Foreshadowing, Irony, and or Symbolism**   *Explain examples of foreshadowing, irony, and/or symbolism in this story.*

FOLLOW-UP QUESTIONS

10 SHORT QUESTIONS

Select the <u>best</u> answer for each.

____ 1. The mice are
   a. animals.
   b. robots.
   c. rodents.

____ 2. The house works
   a. by human command.
   b. by human touch.
   c. automatically.

____ 3. Breakfast is made by
   a. humans.
   b. machines.
   c. animals.

____ 4. The house is cleaned by
   a. humans.
   b. machines.
   c. animals.

____ 5. The family is
   a. dying.
   b. alive.
   c. vaporized.

____ 6. The massive destruction is caused by
   a. a fire.
   b. a thunderstorm.
   c. a nuclear explosion.

____ 7. The dog is
   a. ill and dies.
   b. healthy and lives.
   c. unaffected.

____ 8. The dog is
   a. incinerated.
   b. buried.
   c. fed.

____ 9. The house
   a. continues to stand.
   b. burns to the ground.
   c. explodes.

____ 10. The poem predicts that
   a. nature will go on.
   b. the world is destroyed.
   c. the house will be rebuilt.

5 SIGNIFICANT QUOTATIONS

Explain the importance of each of these quotations.

1. "And then one day the world shook and there was [. . .] a rain of ashes and radioactivity, and the happy time was over."

2. "Out of warrens in the wall, tiny mechanical mice darted."

3. "The entire face of the house was black, save for five places."

4. "*'There will come soft rains and the smell of the ground, [. . .].*
   And Spring herself, when she woke at dawn,
   Would scarcely know that we were gone.'"

5. "The bough of a falling tree smashed the kitchen window. Cleaning solvent, bottled, crashed on the stove."

2 COMPREHENSION ESSAY QUESTIONS

Use specific details and information from the story to answer these questions as completely as possible.

1. One of Bradbury's themes is the destruction of war. How does he demonstrate this here? Use specific details and information from the story.

2. Another of Bradbury's themes is that the machines we create will destroy us. How does he demonstrate this here? Use specific details and information from the story.

DISCUSSION QUESTIONS

Be prepared to discuss these questions in class.

1. What is Bradbury's central thesis? Use specific details from the story to support your ideas.

2. In a Hegelian dialectic, a given (the thesis) produces that which will destroy it (the antithesis) and this results in whole new construct (the synthesis). How does this story demonstrate this dialectic form?

WRITING

Use each of these ideas for writing an essay.

1. Select one or two machines you depend on and tell how they help you. Explain your dependence on these machines.

2. Select one or two machines you depend on and tell how they hinder you. Explain your dependence on these machines.

Further Writing

1. This story portrays the effects of war. Compare and contrast this story with Ambrose Bierce's "An Occurrence at Owl Creek Bridge" (available in a library).

2. Bradbury's calamity is not the only threat to our world. Research ozone depletion, the greenhouse effect, or an endangered animal species, all of which are man-made problems.

CHAPTER 2

Setting and Props

Setting is the catch-all term that describes the time, place, and surroundings of a story. The surroundings include the mood or the tone of the story and even the inanimate objects that support the action of the story. In a short story, the setting is usually, although not always, limited. The story usually takes place in a shorter amount of time than in a longer work, and fewer places are involved.

The **time** during which a story takes place may be a historical period, such as the ancient, medieval, or modern period, or it may be an era, such as the Roaring Twenties, the Depression, the Civil War, or a world war. The time period may be a season—spring, summer, winter, or fall—or it may be a rainy, sunny, planting, or harvesting period or part of a day, such as daytime or nighttime. "To Build a Fire," for instance, will make more sense to you if you know that it is set during an extremely cold winter.

Place is the location where a story is set. That "Everyday Use" is set in the country, that "Bone Girl" is set near a reservation, that "Strong Temptations—Strategic Movements—The Innocents Beguiled" is set on a fenced property in the South, that "The Cask of Amontillado" is set in a large home in Italy, and that "To Build a Fire" is set to the far north are important to the events of each story.

Mood or **tone** sets the general feeling of the story. A bright setting that is filled with sunlight and light breezes sets a much different mood or tone than a decaying, haunted house. Think of setting <u>Pet Sematary</u> on a bright, sun-filled beach; it would not work. Notice that the rural atmosphere is central in "Everyday Use." Notice that the steadfast location is crucial in "Bone Girl." In "Strong Temptations—Strategic Movements—The Innocents Beguiled," the outdoor setting is bright and airy and sets a light-hearted feeling. Edgar Allan Poe, a master of overwhelming atmospheres, draws the reader deeper and deeper into dampness and gloom. And in "To Build a Fire," the pristine beauty of the outdoors creates the very threat of the story.

Props (short for "properties") are the inanimate objects in a story. Props sometimes take on the qualities of characters. In a story of renown by the French master, Guy de Maupassant, a woman loses a diamond necklace and then devotes ten years of her life to paying for the replacement necklace, only to find that the original necklace was a fake and she has wasted ten years of her life for nothing. The prop, the necklace, is the very core of the story. In the stories in this chapter, the quilt is central in "Everyday Use," the flowing locks are necessary in "Bone Girl," the fence is crucial in "Strong Temptations—Strategic Movements—The Innocents Beguiled," the wine is essential to "The Cask of Amontillado," and the energy of fire is central in "To Build a Fire."

Enjoy the times and places to which these stories take you.

Everyday Use

ALICE WALKER

PRE-READING VOCABULARY
CONTEXT

Use context clues to define these words before reading. Use a dictionary as needed.

1. The boy's leg became *lame* after he smashed his kneecap. *Lame* means _____.

2. Heather is a beautiful young woman, and no one would ever call her *homely*. *Homely* means _____.

3. Brian and Andy stood in *awe* of the beautiful woman and were so overcome that they did not say a word. *Awe* means _____.

4. Not to know is to be *ignorant*. *Ignorant* means _____.

5. The fire *blazed* white hot as they watched. *Blaze* means

   _____.

6. The characters in *Dumb and Dumber* act like *dimwits*. *Dimwit* means _____.

7. The cows lazily wandered the grassy *pasture*. *Pasture* means

   _____.

8. The hot water was *scalding* to the touch. *Scalding* means

   _____.

9. The *lye* Ben was boiling to make soap ate through the counter. *Lye* means _____.

10. The reds and oranges in her dress were so *loud* that they hurt my eyes. *Loud* means _____.

11. When the wind blew, the little leaves *trembled*. *Tremble* means _____.

12. The scared puppy was *cowering* in the corner. *Cower* means

    _____.

13. When Anna cooked the pasta too long, the pasta became sticky and *limp*. *Limp* means _____.

14. The dictator forced his *oppressed* nation to follow his every rule. *Oppress* means _____.

15. After Karen put milk in the *butter churn*, the milk sat in the wooden pot waiting to be stirred into butter. *Butter churn* means

    _____.

16. Dave used a sharp knife to *whittle* the little boat out of an old piece of wood. *Whittle* means _____.

17. Katherine went *rifling* through her dresser drawers looking for the ring she had lost. *Rifling* means _____.

18. A *quilt* is a large bed covering often made out of little pieces of material sewn together. *Quilt* means _____.

19. After Pia spilled the boiling water on her hand, she had bubbly *scars* all over her hand. *Scar* means _____.

20. The historical memory of a group or family is called its *heritage*. *Heritage* means _____.

PRE-READING VOCABULARY
STRUCTURAL ATTACK

Define these words by solving the parts. Use the Glossary or a dictionary as needed.

1. everyday
2. wavy
3. irregular
4. hopelessly
5. soft-seated
6. sporty
7. man-working
8. mercilessly
9. nightfall
10. uncooked
11. farthest
12. papery
13. make-believe
14. good-naturedly
15. rawhide
16. washday
17. faultfinding
18. salt-lick
19. artistic
20. priceless

PRE-READING QUESTIONS

Try answering these questions as you read.

What does the title mean?

Who are the main characters in the story? Supporting characters?

How are the characters different?

Why are the quilts so important?

Everyday Use

Alice Walker

Alice Walker was born in rural Eatonton, Georgia in 1944. She suffered an eye injury at the age of eight that was not surgically repaired until she was fourteen. Avoiding others because of her injury, Walker turned to writing poetry and to observing relationships among others. She later attended Spelman College in Atlanta and Sarah Lawrence College in New York. She returned south to Mississippi as a teacher and became active in civil rights. Here she met Melvyn Leventhal, whom she married in 1967. Her writings present the often heroic struggles of African American women, and her novel <u>The Color Purple</u> received the Pulitzer Prize for fiction and the American Book Award. Her writings are available in many collections.

2   *For your grandma*

F I will wait for her in the yard that Maggie and I made so clean and wavy yesterday afternoon. A yard like this is more comfortable than most people know. It is not just a yard. It is like an extended living room. When the hard clay is swept clean as a floor and the fine sand around the edges lined with tiny, irregular grooves, anyone can come and sit and look up into the elm tree and wait for the breezes that never come inside the house.

3   Maggie will be nervous until after her sister goes: she will stand hopelessly in corners homely and ashamed of the burn scars down her arms and legs, eyeing her sister with a mixture of envy and awe. She thinks her sister had held life always in the palm of one hand, that "no" is a word the world never learned to say to her.

4   You've no doubt seen those TV shows where the child who has "made it" is confronted, as a surprise, by her own mother and father, tottering in weakly from backstage. (A pleasant surprise, of course: What would they do if parent and child came on the show only to curse out and insult each other?) On TV mother and child embrace and smile into each other's faces. Sometimes the mother and father weep, the child wraps them in her arms and leans across the table to tell how she would not have made it without their help. I have seen these programs.

5   Sometimes I dream a dream in which Dee and I are suddenly brought together on a TV program of this sort. Out of a dark and soft-seated limousine I am ushered into a bright room filled with many people. There I meet a smiling, gray, sporty man like Johnny Carson who shakes my hand and tells me what a fine girl I have. Then we are on the stage and Dee is embracing me with tears in her eyes. She pins on my dress a large orchid, even though she has told me once that she thinks orchids are tacky flowers.

6   In real life I am a large, big-boned woman with rough, man-working hands. In the winter I wear flannel nightgowns to bed and overalls during the day. I can kill and clean a hog as mercilessly as a man. My fat keeps me hot in zero weather. I can work outside all day, breaking ice to get water for washing. I can eat pork liver cooked over the open fire minutes after it comes steaming from the hog. One winter I knocked a bull calf straight in the brain between the eyes with a sledge hammer and had the meat hung up to chill before nightfall. But of course all this does not show on television. I am the way my daughter would want me to be: a hundred pounds lighter, my skin like an uncooked barley pancake. My hair glistens in the hot bright lights.

Johnny Carson has much to do to keep up with my quick and witty tongue.

7   But that is a mistake. I know even before I wake up. Who ever knew a Johnson with a quick tongue? Who can even imagine me looking a strange white man in the eye? It seems to me I have talked to them always with one foot raised in flight, with my head turned in whichever way is farthest from them. Dee, though. She would always look anyone in the eye. Hesitation was no part of her nature.

8   "How do I look, Mama?" Maggie says, showing just enough of her thin body enveloped in pink skirt and red blouse for me to know she's there, almost hidden by the door.

9   "Come out into the yard," I say.

10   Have you ever seen a lame animal, perhaps a dog run over by some careless person rich enough to own a car, sidle up to someone who is ignorant enough to be kind to him? That is the way my Maggie walks. She has been like this, chin on chest, eyes on ground, feet in shuffle, ever since the fire that burned the other house to the ground.

11   Dee is lighter than Maggie, with nicer hair and a fuller figure. She's a woman now, though sometimes I forget. How long ago was it that the other house burned? Ten, twelve years? Sometimes I can still hear the flames and feel Maggie's arms sticking to me, her hair smoking and her dress falling off her in little black papery flakes. Her eyes seemed stretched open, blazed open by the flames reflected in them. And Dee. I see her standing off under the sweet gum tree she used to dig gum out of; a look of concentration on her face as she watched the last dingy gray board of the house fall in toward the red-hot brick chimney. Why don't you do a dance around the ashes? I'd wanted to ask her. She had hated the house that much.

12   I used to think she hated Maggie, too. But that was before we raised the money, the church and me, to send her to Augusta to school. She used to read to us without pity; forcing words, lies, other folks' habits, whole lives upon us two, sitting trapped and ignorant underneath her voice. She washed us in a river of make-believe, burned us with a lot of knowledge we didn't necessarily need to know. Pressed us to her with the serious way she read, to shove us away at just the moment, like dimwits, we seemed about to understand.

13   Dee wanted nice things. A yellow organdy dress to wear to her graduation from high school; black pumps to match a green suit she'd made from an old suit somebody gave me. She was determined to stare down any disaster in her efforts. Her eyelids would not flicker for

minutes at a time. Often I fought off the temptation to shake her. At sixteen she had a style of her own: and knew what style was.

14   I never had an education myself. After second grade the school was closed down. Don't ask me why: in 1927 colored asked fewer questions than they do now. Sometimes Maggie reads to me. She stumbles along good-naturedly but can't see well. She knows she is not bright. Like good looks and money, quickness passed her by. She will marry John Thomas (who has mossy teeth in an earnest face) and then I'll be free to sit here and I guess just sing church songs to myself. Although I never was a good singer. Never could carry a tune. I was always better at a man's job. I used to love to milk till I was hoofed in the side in '49. Cows are soothing and slow and don't bother you, unless you try to milk them the wrong way.

15   I have deliberately turned my back on the house. It is three rooms, just like the one that burned, except the roof is tin; they don't make shingle roofs any more. There are no real windows, just some holes cut in the sides, like the portholes in a ship, but not round and not square, with rawhide holding the shutters up on the outside. This house is in a pasture, too, like the other one. No doubt when Dee sees it she will want to tear it down. She wrote me once that no matter where we "choose" to live, she will manage to come see us. But she will never bring her friends. Maggie and I thought about this and Maggie asked me, "Mama, when did Dee ever *have* any friends?"

16   She had a few. Furtive boys in pink shirts hanging about on wash-day after school. Nervous girls who never laughed. Impressed with her they worshiped the well-turned phrase, the cute shape, the scalding humor that erupted like bubbles in lye. She read to them.

17   When she was courting Jimmy T she didn't have much time to pay to us, but turned all her faultfinding power on him. He *flew* to marry a cheap gal from a family of ignorant flashy people. She hardly had time to recompose herself.

18   When she comes I will meet—but there they are!

19   Maggie attempts to make a dash for the house, in her shuffling way; but I stay her with my hand. "Come back here," I say. And she stops and tries to dig a well in the sand with her toe.

20   It is hard to see them clearly through the strong sun. But even the first glimpse of leg out of the car tells me it is Dee. Her feet were always neat-looking, as if God himself had shaped them with a certain style. From the other side of the car comes a short, stocky man. Hair is all over his head a foot long and hanging from his chin like a kinky

mule tail. I hear Maggie suck in her breath. "Uhnnnh," is what it sounds like. Like when you see the wriggling end of a snake just in front of your foot on the road. "Uhnnnh."

21   Dee next. A dress down to the ground, in this hot weather. A dress so loud it hurts my eyes. There are yellows and oranges enough to throw back the light of the sun. I feel my whole face warming from the heat waves it throws out. Earrings, too, gold and hanging down to her shoulders. Bracelets dangling and making noises when she moves her arm up to shake the folds of the dress out of her armpits. The dress is loose and flows, and as she walks closer, I like it. I hear Maggie go "Uhnnnh" again. It is her sister's hair. It stands straight up like the wool on a sheep. It is black as night and around the edges are two long pigtails that rope about like small lizards disappearing behind her ears.

22   "Wa-su-zo-Tean-o!" she says, coming on in that gliding way the dress makes her move. The short stocky fellow with the hair to his navel is all grinning and he follows up with "Asalamalakim, my mother and sister!" He moves to hug Maggie but she falls back, right up against the back of my chair. I feel her trembling there and when I look up I see the perspiration falling off her chin.

23   "Don't get up," says Dee. Since I am stout it takes something of a push. You can see me trying to move a second or two before I make it. She turns, showing white heels through her sandals, and goes back to the car. Out she peeks next with a Polaroid. She stoops down quickly and lines up picture after picture of me sitting there in front of the house with Maggie cowering behind me. She never takes a shot without making sure the house is included. When a cow comes nibbling around the edge of the yard she snaps it and me and Maggie *and* the house. Then she puts the Polaroid in the back seat of the car, and comes up and kisses me on the forehead.

24   Meanwhile Asalamalakim is going through the motions with Maggie's hand. Maggie's hand is as limp as a fish, and probably as cold, despite the sweat, and she keeps trying to pull it back. It looks like Asalamalakim wants to shake hands but wants to do it fancy. Or maybe he don't know how people shake hands. Anyhow, he soon gives up on Maggie.

25   "Well," I say. "Dee."

26   "No, Mama," she says. "Not 'Dee,' Wangero Leewanika Kemanjo!"

27   "What happened to 'Dee'?" I wanted to know.

28   "She's dead," Wangero said. "I couldn't bear it any longer being named after the people who oppress me."

29   "You know as well as me you was named after your aunt Dicie," I said. Dicie is my sister. She named Dee. We called her "Big Dee" after Dee was born.

30   "But who was *she* named after?" asked Wangero.

31   "I guess after Grandma Dee," I said.

32   "And who was she named after?" asked Wangero.

33   "Her mother," I said, and saw Wangero was getting tired. "That's about as far back as I can trace it," I said. Though, in fact, I probably could have carried it back beyond the Civil War through the branches.

34   "Well," said Asalamalakim, "there you are."

35   "Uhnnnh," I heard Maggie say.

36   "There I was not," I said, "before 'Dicie' cropped up in our family, so why should I try to trace it that far back?"

37   He just stood there grinning, looking down on me like somebody inspecting a Model A car. Every once in a while he and Wangero sent eye signals over my head.

38   "How do you pronounce this name?" I asked.

39   "You don't have to call me by it if you don't want to," said Wangero.

40   "Why shouldn't I?" I asked. "If that's what you want us to call you, we'll call you."

41   "I know it might sound awkward at first," said Wangero.

42   "I'll get used to it," I said. "Ream it out again."

43   Well, soon we got the name out of the way. Asalamalakim had a name twice as long and three times as hard. After I tripped over it two or three times he told me to just call him Hakim-a-barber. I wanted to ask him was he a barber, but I didn't really think he was, so I didn't ask.

44   "You must belong to those beef-cattle peoples down the road," I said. They said "Asalamalakim" when they met you, too, but didn't shake hands. Always too busy: feeding the cattle, fixing the fences, putting up salt-lick shelters, throwing down hay. When the white folks poisoned some of the herd the men stayed up all night with rifles in their hands. I walked a mile and a half just to see the sight.

45   Hakim-a-barber said, "I accept some of their doctrines, but farming and raising cattle is not my style." (They didn't tell me, and I didn't ask, whether Wangero [Dee] had really gone and married him.)

46   We sat down to eat and right away he said he didn't eat collards and pork was unclean. Wangero, though, went on through the chitlins and corn bread, the greens and everything else. She talked a blue streak over the sweet potatoes. Everything delighted her. Even the fact that we still used the benches her daddy made for the table when we couldn't afford to buy chairs.

47   "Oh, Mama!" she cried. Then turned to Hakim-a-barber. "I never knew how lovely these benches are. You can feel the rump prints," she said, running her hands underneath her and along the bench. Then she gave a sigh and her hand closed over Grandma Dee's butter dish. "That's it!" she said. "I knew there was something I wanted to ask you if I could have." She jumped up from the table and went over in the corner where the churn stood, the milk in it clabber by now. She looked at the churn and looked at it.

48   "This churn top is what I need," she said. "Didn't Uncle Buddy whittle it out of a tree you all used to have?

49   "Yes," I said.

50   "Uh huh," she said happily. "And I want the dasher, too."

51   "Uncle Buddy whittle that, too?" asked the barber.

52   Dee (Wangero) looked up at me.

53   "Aunt Dee's first husband whittled the dash," said Maggie so low you almost couldn't hear her. "His name was Henry, but they called him Stash."

54   "Maggie's brain is like an elephant's," Wangero said, laughing. "I can use the churn top as a centerpiece for the alcove table," she said, sliding a plate over the churn, "and I'll think of something artistic to do with the dasher."

55   When she finished wrapping the dasher the handle stuck out. I took it for a moment in my hands. You didn't even have to look close to see where hands pushing the dasher up and down to make butter had left a kind of sink in the wood. In fact, there were a lot of small sinks; you could see where thumbs and fingers had sunk into the wood. It was beautiful light yellow wood, from a tree that grew in the yard where Big Dee and Stash had lived.

56   After dinner Dee (Wangero) went to the trunk at the foot of my bed and started rifling through it. Maggie hung back in the kitchen over the dishpan. Out came Wangero with two quilts. They had been pieced by Grandma Dee and then Big Dee and me had hung them on the quilt frames on the front porch and quilted them. One was in the Lone Star pattern. The other was Walk Around the Mountain. In both of them were scraps of dresses Grandma Dee had worn fifty and more years ago. Bits and pieces of Grandpa Jarrell's paisley shirts. And one teeny faded blue piece, about the piece of a penny matchbox, that was from Great Grandpa Ezra's uniform that he wore in the Civil War.

57   "Mama," Wangero said sweet as a bird. "Can I have these old quilts?"

58   I heard something fall in the kitchen, and a minute later the kitchen door slammed.

59   "Why don't you take one or two of the others?" I asked. "These old things was just done by me and Big Dee from some tops your grandma pieced before she died."

60   "No," said Wangero. "I don't want those. They are stitched around the borders by machine."

61   "That's make them last better," I said.

62   "That's not the point," said Wangero. "These are all pieces of dresses Grandma used to wear. She did all this stitching by hand. Imagine!" She held the quilts securely in her arms, stroking them.

63   "Some of the pieces, like those lavender ones, come from old clothes her mother handed down to her," I said, moving up to touch the quilts. Dee (Wangero) moved back just enough so that I couldn't reach the quilts. They already belonged to her.

64   "Imagine!" she breathed again, clutching them closely to her bosom.

65   "The truth is," I said, "I promised to give them quilts to Maggie, for when she marries John Thomas."

66   She gasped like a bee had stung her.

67   "Maggie can't appreciate these quilts!" she said. "She'd probably be backward enough to put them to everyday use."

68   "I reckon she would," I said. "God knows I been saving 'em for long enough with nobody using 'em. I hope she will!" I didn't want to bring up how I had offered Dee (Wangero) a quilt when she went away to college. Then she had told me they were old-fashioned, out of style.

69   "But they're *priceless!*" she was saying now, furiously; for she has a temper. "Maggie would put them on the bed and in five years they'd be in rags. Less than that!"

70   "She can always make some more," I said. "Maggie knows how to quilt."

71   Dee (Wangero) looked at me with hatred. "You just will not understand. The point is these quilts, *these* quilts!"

72   "Well," I said, stumped. "What would *you* do with them?"

73   "Hang them," she said. As if that was the only thing you *could* do with quilts.

74   Maggie by now was standing in the door. I could almost hear the sound her feet made as they scraped over each other.

75   "She can have them. Mama," she said, like somebody used to never winning anything, or having anything reserved for her. "I can 'member Grandma Dee without the quilts."

76   I looked at her hard. She had filled her bottom lip with checkerberry snuff and it gave her face a kind of dopey, hangdog look. It was

Grandma Dee and Big Dee who taught her how to quilt herself. She stood there with her scarred hands hidden in the folds of her skirt. She looked at her sister with something like fear but she wasn't mad at her. This was Maggie's portion. This was the way she knew God to work.

77   When I looked at her like that something hit me in the top of my head and ran down to the soles of my feet. Just like when I'm in church and the spirit of God touches me and I get happy and shout. I did something I never had done before: hugged Maggie to me, then dragged her on into the room, snatched the quilts out of Miss Wangero's hands and dumped them into Maggie's lap. Maggie just sat there on my bed with her mouth open.

78   "Take one or two of the others," I said to Dee.

79   But she turned without a word and went out to Hakim-a-barber.

80   "You just don't understand," she said, as Maggie and I came out to the car.

81   "What don't I understand?" I wanted to know.

82   "Your heritage," she said. And then she turned to Maggie, kissed her, and said, "You ought to try to make something of yourself, too, Maggie. It's really a new day for us. But from the way you and Mama still live you'd never know it."

83   She put on some sunglasses that hid everything above the tip of her nose and her chin.

84   Maggie smiled; maybe at the sunglasses. But a real smile, not scared. After we watched the car dust settle I asked Maggie to bring me a dip of snuff. And then the two of us sat there just enjoying, until it was time to go in the house and go to bed.

Everyday Use

JOURNAL

1. **MLA Works Cited**   *Using this model, record this story here.*

   *Author's Last Name, First Name. "Title of the Story." Title of the Book. 3rd ed.
   Ed. First Name Last Name. City: Publisher, year. Pages of the story.*

2. **Main Character(s)**   *Describe each main character, and explain why you
   think each is a main character.*

3. **Supporting Characters**   *Describe each supporting character, and explain why
   you think each is a supporting character.*

4. **Setting**   *Describe the setting(s) and any relevant prop(s).*

5. Sequence   *Outline the events of the story in order.*

6. Plot   *Tell the story in no more than two sentences.*

7. Conflicts   *Identify and explain all the conflicts involved here.*

8. Significant Quotations   *Explain the importance of each of these quotations. Record the page number in the parentheses.*

a. "Sometimes I can still hear the flames and feel Maggie's arms sticking to me, her hair smoking and her dress falling off her in little black papery flakes" (   ).

b. "At sixteen she had a style of her own: and knew what style was" (   ).

c. "Out she peeks next with a Polaroid. [. . .]. She never takes a shot without making sure the house is included" (   ).

d. " 'I can use the churn top as a centerpiece for the alcove table,' she said, sliding a plate over the churn, 'and I'll think of something artistic to do with the dasher' " (   ).

e. " 'Maggie can't appreciate these quilts!' she said. 'She'd probably be backward enough to put them to everyday use' " (   ).

9. **Literary Elements**   *Look at this chapter's title and explain why you think this story is placed in this chapter. Explain in which other chapter(s) you might place this story, as relevant to the literary element(s) of that chapter.*

10. **Foreshadowing, Irony, and/or Symbolism**   *Explain examples of foreshadowing, irony, and/or symbolism in this story.*

FOLLOW-UP QUESTIONS

10 SHORT QUESTIONS

Select the best answer for each.

_____ 1. Maggie is Dee's
   a. mother.
   b. cousin.
   c. sister.

_____ 2. The narrator is Dee's
   a. mother.
   b. cousin.
   c. sister.

_____ 3. The prettiest one is
   a. Maggie.
   b. Dee.
   c. the narrator.

_____ 4. Dee
   a. did not care about the house she grew up in.
   b. liked the house she grew up in.
   c. disliked the house she grew up in.

_____ 5. The one who has been scarred in the fire is
   a. Maggie.
   b. Dee.
   c. the narrator.

_____ 6. The one who is shy is
   a. Maggie.
   b. Dee.
   c. the narrator.

_____ 7. Dee wants the quilts because
   a. she wants to use them.
   b. she likes the colors in them.
   c. she wants to show them off.

_____ 8. Maggie wants the quilts because
   a. she wants to use them.
   b. she likes the colors.
   c. she wants to show them off.

_____ 9. Dee's changed attitude is
   a. a sincere interest in her background.
   b. a sincere interest in the quilts.
   c. for show.

_____ 10. The narrator is sympathetic to
   a. Dee.
   b. Maggie.
   c. the quilts.

5 SIGNIFICANT QUOTATIONS

Explain the importance of each of these quotations.

1. "Why don't you do a dance around the ashes? I'd wanted to ask her. She had hated the house that much."

2. "Impressed with her they worshipped the well-turned phrase, the cute shape, the scalding humor that erupted like bubbles in lye."

3. " 'No, Mama,' she said. 'Not "Dee," Wangero Leewanika Kemanjo!' "

4. " 'Mama,' Wangero said sweet as a bird. 'Can I have these old quilts?' "

5. "I did something I never had done before: hugged Maggie to me, then dragged her on into the room, snatched the quilts out of Miss Wangero's hands and dumped them into Maggie's lap."

2 Comprehension Essay Questions

Use specific details and information from the story to answer these as completely as possible.

1. How are the quilts central to the story? Explain the significance of the quilts using specific details and information from the story.

2. The mother and Maggie treat their heritage one way, while Dee treats it quite another. Using specific details and information from the story, how is each treatment different?

Discussion Questions

Be prepared to discuss these questions in class.

1. What are the humorous parts in this story? What makes them humorous?

2. Do you think there are any good reasons for Dee, in fact, to take the quilts? Why should she take them, or why not?

Writing

Use each of these ideas for writing an essay.

1. We all have special objects—a signed baseball, a good-luck charm, a prom memento. Write an essay that narrates the story of your favorite special object.

2. We all know insincere people like Dee who put on airs to impress others. Write a narrative essay contrasting your sincerity with the insincerity of another.

Further Writing

1. Compare and contrast the characters in "Everyday Use" with the characters in Dorothy Parker's "The Wonderful Old Gentleman" (page 285).

2. Dee in this story and Tom Sawyer in the selection from Mark Twain (page 140) both use ruses or pretenses to try to get what they want. Compare and contrast their manipulations and their goals.

Bone Girl

Joseph Bruchac

PRE-READING VOCABULARY
CONTEXT

Use context clues to define these words before reading. Use a dictionary as needed.

1. The miners dug a big ditch into the ground that became the *quarry* where they would mine for ore. *Quarry* means _____.

2. The government set aside specific land for the Native Americans to settle on and build their town in this *reservation* or, as they called it, "the *res*." *Reservation* or *res* means _____.

3. Little Mike is sometimes afraid of the ghosts or *spirits* and becomes scared on Halloween. *Spirit* means _____.

4. The murderer was *condemned* to spend the rest of his life in jail, alone, with no hope of freedom. *Condemned* means

   _____.

5. Native Americans are also referred to as *Indians*, a name that supposedly comes from Columbus's belief that he had found the water passage to India. *Indian* means _____.

6. When people die, they are normally taken to the *graveyard* or cemetery to be buried with others who have died. *Graveyard* means _____.

7. A particularly ugly or mean ghost may be referred to as a *ghoul*. *Ghoul* means _____.

8. Alice's *ancestors* came to America over two hundred years ago, and settled in New Jersey. *Ancestor* means _____.

9. Missy *dreaded* going to her boss's office because she was always afraid she would say the wrong thing. *Dread* means _____.

10. Michelle is very *familiar* with everyone in her family because she knows them all well and sees them often. *Familiar* means

_____.

11. Patrice is a real *neurotic* about her soap opera; she almost seems to think the characters are real. *Neurotic* means _____.

12. Allison has beautiful *blond* hair that is the color of pale yellow roses. *Blond* means _____.

13. In order to get across the river, John had to get in traffic and drive over the *bridge*. *Bridge* means _____.

14. Sarah was a very *shy* child who seemed afraid to speak to anyone, but now she talks to everyone. *Shy* means _____.

15. Tom thought he would create *romance* and invited his fiancée, Jacky, out for a candlelit dinner under the stars. *Romance* means

_____.

16. Jake is no *fool*; he studies carefully and is completely aware of all the people and events around him. *Fool* means _____.

17. Arjay loves *spooky* movies and enjoys reading ghost and horror stories. *Spooky* means _____.

18. A full *moon* lights the night sky with its reflection, even if it is hidden behind clouds. *Moon* means _____.

19. Laura has an exquisitely beautiful *face*; her eyes sparkle above her delicately shaped nose and bright smile. *Face* means

_____.

20. After the skin and muscles had rotted away, all that was left of the corpse's head was the *skull*. *Skull* means _____.

Pre-reading Vocabulary
Structural Attack

Define these words by solving the parts. Use the Glossary or a dictionary as needed.

1. outsiders
2. international
3. drainage
4. resurfaced
5. homeless
6. disconnected
7. development
8. flickering
9. goofing
10. staggering
11. old-fashioned
12. high-buttoned

Pre-reading Questions

Try answering these questions as you read.

Where does the narrator live?

How does the narrator feel about spirits?

What happens to the narrator?

Bone Girl

JOSEPH BRUCHAC

Joseph Bruchac is of Abenaki heritage. He shares his heritage in his many writings and in his role of the storyteller, a role and revered position that is absolutely essential to the transmission of culture within a tribe or community. He has told his stories around the world. Some of his other writings are <u>The Dawn Land</u> and <u>Turtle Meat</u>.

The Storyteller—Pueblo Statuette

There is this one old abandoned quarry on the reservation where she is often seen. Always late, late at night when there is a full moon. The kind of moon that is as white as bone.

2   Are ghosts outsiders? That is the way most white people seem to view them. Spirits who are condemned to wander for eternity. Ecto-plasmic remnants of people whose violent deaths left their spirits trapped between the worlds. You know what I mean. I'm sure. I bet we've seen the same movies and TV shows. Vengeful apparitions. Those are real popular. And then there is this one: scary noises in the background, the lights get dim, and a hushed voice saying "But what they didn't know was that the house had been built on an *Indian graveyard!*" And the soundtrack fills with muted tomtoms. Bum-bum-bum-bum, bum-bum-bum-bum.

3   Indian graveyards. White people seem to love to talk about them. They're this continent's equivalent of King Tut's tomb. On the one hand, I wish some white people in particular really were more afraid of them than they are—those people that some call "pot hunters," though I think the good old English word "ghoul" applies pretty well. There's a big international trade in Indian grave goods dug up and sold. And protecting them and getting back the bones of our ancestors who've been dug up and stolen and taken to museums, that is real important to us. I can tell you more about that, but that is another tale to tell another time. I'd better finish this story first.

4   Indian graveyards, you see, mean something different to me than places of dread. Maybe it's because I've spent a lot of time around real Indian graveyards, not the ones in the movies. Like the one the kids on our res walk by on their way to school—just like I used to. That cemetery is an old one, placed right in the middle of the town. It's a lot older than the oldest marker stones in it. In the old days, my people used to bury those who died right under the foundation of the lodge. No marker stones then. Just the house and your relatives continued to live there. That was record enough of the life you'd had. It was different from one part of the country to another, I know. Different Indian people have different ways of dealing with death. In a lot of places it still isn't regarded as the right thing to do to say the names of those who've died after their bodies have gone back into the earth. But, even with that, I don't think that Indian ghosts *are* outsiders. They're still with us and part of us. No farther away from us than the other side of a leaf that has fallen. I think Chief Cornplanter of the Seneca people said that. But he wasn't the only one to say it. Indian ghosts are, well, familiar. Family. And when you're family, you care for each other. In a lot of different ways.

5   Being in my sixties, now, it gives me the right to say a few things. I want to say them better, which is why I have taken this extension course in creative writing. Why I have read the books assigned for this class. But when I put my name on something I have written, when you see the name Russell Painter on it, I would like it to be something I am proud of. I worked building roads for a good many years and I was always proud that I could lay out a road just so. The crest was right and the shoulders were right and that road was even and the turns banked and the drainage good so that ice didn't build up. Roads eventually wear away and have to be resurfaced and all that, but if you make a road right then you can use it to get somewhere. So I would like to write in the same way. I would like any story I tell to get somewhere and not be a dead end or so poorly made that it is full of holes and maybe even throws someone off it into the ditch. This is called an extended metaphor.

6   You may note that I am not writing in the style which I have begun to call "cute Indian." There is this one Canadian who pretends to be an Indian when he writes and his Indians are very cute and he has a narrator telling his stories who is doing what I am doing, taking a creative writing course. My writing instructor is a good enough guy. My writing instructor would like me to get cuter. That is why he has had me read some books that can furnish me, as he put it, with some good "boilerplate models." But I think I have enough models just by looking at the people around me and trying to understand the lessons they've taught me. Like I said, as I said, being in my sixties and retired gives me the right to say some things. Not that I didn't have the right to say them before. Just that now I may actually be listened to when I start talking.

7   Like about Indian ghosts. Most of the real ghost stories I have heard from people in the towns around the res don't seem to have a point to them. It's always someone hearing a strange noise or seeing a light or the furniture moving or windows shutting or strange shapes walking down a hallway. Then they may find out later that someone died in that house a long time ago and that the spirit of that person is probably what has been making those weird things happen. Our ghost stories make sense. Or maybe it is more like our ghosts have a sense of purpose. I have a theory about this. I think it is because Indians stay put and white people keep moving around. White people bury their dead in a graveyard full of people they don't know and then they move away themselves. Get a better job in a city on the West Coast or maybe retire to Florida. And those ghosts—even if they've stayed in the family home—they're surrounded by strangers. I think maybe those ghosts get to be like the homeless people you see wandering around the streets in the big cities these days. Talking to themselves, ignored unless they really get into your face, disconnected and forgotten.

8   But Indian people stay put—unless they're forced to move. Like the Cherokees being forced out of the south or the way the Abenakis were driven out of western Maine or the Stockbridge people or, to be honest, just about every Indian nation you can name at one time or another. There's still a lot of forcing Indian people to move going on today. I could tell you some stories about our own res. Last year they were planning to put in a big housing development that would have taken a lot of land up on Turkey Hill. That little mountain isn't officially ours anymore, but we hope to get it back one day. And that development would have polluted our water, cut down a lot of trees we care about. Maybe someday I will write a story about how that housing develop-ment got stalled and then this "recession-depression" came along and knocked the bottom out of the housing market. So that development

went down the tubes. But some folks I know were involved in stopping that development, and they might get in trouble if I told you what they did. And I am digressing, my writing instructor is probably writing in the margin of this story right now. Except he doesn't understand that is how we tell stories. In circles. Circling back to the fact that Indian people like to stay put. And because we stay put, close to the land where we were born (and even though my one-story house may not look like much, I'm the fifth generation of Painters to live in it and it stands on the same earth where a log cabin housed four generations before that and a bark lodge was there when the Puritans were trying to find a stone to stand on), we also stay close to the land where we're buried. Close to our dead. Close to our ghosts—which, I assume, do not feel as abandoned as white ghosts and so tend to be a lot less neurotic. We know them, they know us, and they also know what they can do. Which often is, pardon my French, to scare the shit out of us when we're doing the wrong things!

9   I've got a nephew named Tommy. Typical junior high. He's been staying with my wife and me the last six months. Him and some of the other kids his age decided to have some fun and so they went one night and hid in the graveyard near the road, behind some of the bigger stones there. They had a piece of white cloth tied onto a stick and a lantern. They waited till they saw people walking home past the graveyard and as soon as they were close they made spooky noises and waved that white cloth and flashed the light. Just about everybody took off! I guess they'd never seen some of those older folks move that fast before! The only one they didn't scare was Grama Big Eel. She just paid no attention to it at all and just kept on walking. She didn't even turn her head.

10   Next night Tommy was walking home by himself, right past the same graveyard. As soon as he hit that spot a light started flickering in the graveyard and he could see something white.

11   "Okay, you guys!" he said. "I know you're there. You're not scaring me!" He kept right on going, trying not to speed up too much. He knew it was them, but he also wondered how come the light was a different color tonight and how they were able to make it move so fast through that graveyard.

12   As soon as he got home, the phone rang. It was one of his friends who'd been with him in the graveyard the night before, scaring people.

13   "Thought you scared me, didn't you?" Tommy said.

14   "Huh?" his friend answered. "I don't know what you mean. The guys are all here. They've been here the last two hours playing Nintendo. We were just wondering if you wanted to go back down to the graveyard again tonight and spook people."

15   After than, you can bet that Tommy stopped goofing around in the graveyard.

16   There's a lot more stories like that one. The best stories we can tell, though, are always the stories where the jokes are on ourselves. Which brings me to the story I wanted to tell when I started writing this piece.

17   When I came back home, retired here, I came back alone. My wife and I had some problems and we split up. There were some things I did here that weren't too bad, but I was drinking too much. And when they say there's no fool like an old fool, I guess I ought to know who they was talking about. I'd always liked the young girls too. Especially those ones with the blond hair. Right now if there's any Indian women reading this I bet they are about ready to give up in disgust. They know the type. That was me. Oh honey, sweetie, wait up for Grampa Russell. Lemme buy you another beer, lemme just give you a little hug, honey, sweetie. People were getting pretty disgusted with me. Nobody said anything. That would have been interfering. But when they saw me sleeping it off next to the road with a bottle in my hand, they must have been shaking their heads. I've always been real tough and even now I like to sleep outside, even when it gets cold. I have got me a bed in the field behind our house. But I wasn't sleeping in no bed in those days. I was sleeping in the ditches. Tommy wasn't living with me then or he would have been really ashamed of his Uncle Russell.

18   One Saturday night, I was coming home real, real late. There's a little bridge that is down about a mile from my house on one of the little

winding back roads that makes its way up to the big highway that cuts through the res. I had been at one of those bars they built just a hundred yards past the line. I'd stayed out even later than the younger guys who had the car and so I was walking home. Staggering, more like. The moonlight was good and bright, though, so it was easy to make my way and I was singing something in Indian as I went. That little bridge was ahead of me and I saw her there on the bridge. It was a young woman with long pale hair. Her face was turned away from me. She was wearing a long dress and it showed off her figure real good. She looked like she was maybe in her twenties from her figure and the way she moved. I couldn't see her face. I knew there was some girls visiting from the Cherokees and figured maybe she was one of them. Some of those southern Indian girls have got that long blond hair and you can't tell they're Indian till you see it in their face or the way they carry themselves. And from the way she moved she was sure Indian. And she was out looking for something to do late at night.

19   "Hey, honey!" I yelled. "Hey, sweetie, wait for me. Wait up."

20   She paused there on the bridge and let me catch up to her. I came up real close.

21   "Hi, sweetie," I said. "Is it okay if I walk with you some?"

22   She didn't say anything, just kept her head turned away from me. I like that. I've always liked the shy ones . . . or at least the ones who pretend to be shy to keep you interested. I put my arm around her shoulders and she didn't take it off; she just kept walking and I walked with her. I kept talking, saying the kind of no sense things that an old fool says when he's trying to romance a young girl. We kept on walking and next thing I knew we were at the old quarry. That was okay by me. There was a place near the road where there's a kind of natural seat in the stones and that's right where she led me and we sat down together.

23   Oh, was that moon bright! It glistened on her hair and I kept my left arm tight around her. She felt awfully cold and I figured she wouldn't mind my helping her get warm. I still had the bottle in my right hand and I figured that would get her to turn her head and look at me. I still hadn't seen her face under that long pale hair of hers.

24   "Come on, honey, you want a drink, huh?" But it didn't work. She kept her face turned away. So I decided that a drink wasn't what she wanted at all. "Sweetie," I said, "why don't you turn around and give old Grampa Russell a little kiss?"

25   And she turned her head.

26   They say the first time she was seen on the reservation was about two hundred years ago. She was dressed then the way she was that night. Her hair loose and long, wearing an old-fashioned long dress and wearing those tall high-button shoes. I should have recognized those

shoes. But no one ever does when they go to that quarry with her. They never recognize who she is until she turns her face to look at them. That skull face of hers that is all bone. Pale and white as the moon.

27   I dropped the bottle and let go of her. I ran without looking back and I'm pretty sure that she didn't follow me. I ran and I ran and even in my sleep I was still running when I woke up the next morning on the floor inside the house. That day I went and talked to some people and they told me what I had to do if I didn't want the Bone Girl to come and visit me.

28   That was two years ago and I haven't had a drink since then and with Mary and me having gotten back together and with Tommy living with us, I don't think I'll ever go back to those ways again.

29   So that is about all I have to say in this story, about ghosts and all. About Indian ghosts in particular and why it is that I say that Indian ghosts aren't outsiders. They're what you might call familiar spirits.

Bone Girl

JOURNAL

1. **MLA Works Cited**   *Using this model, record this story here.*

   Author's Last Name, First Name. "Title of the Story." <u>Title of the Book</u>. 3rd ed. Ed. First Name Last Name. City: Publisher, year. Pages of the story.

2. **Main Character(s)**   *Describe each main character, and explain why you think each is a main character.*

3. **Supporting Characters**   *Describe each supporting character, and explain why you think each is a supporting character.*

4. **Setting**   *Describe the setting(s) and any relevant prop(s).*

5. **Sequence**   *Outline the events of the story in order.*

6. **Plot**   *Tell the story in no more than two sentences.*

7. **Conflicts**   *Identify and explain all the conflicts involved here.*

8. **Significant Quotations**   *Explain the importance of each of these quotations. Record the page number in the parentheses.*

   a. "But, even with that, I don't think that Indian ghosts *are* outsiders" (   ).

   b. "I think it is because Indians stay put and white people keep moving around" (   ).

c. "'Huh?' his friend answered. 'I don't know what you mean. The guys are all here'" ( ).

d. "'Come on, honey, you want a drink, huh?'" ( ).

e. "I dropped the bottle and let go of her" ( ).

9. **Literary Elements**   *Look at this chapter's title and explain why you think this story is placed in this chapter. Explain in which other chapter(s) you might place this story, as relevant to the literary element(s) of that chapter.*

10. **Foreshadowing, Irony, and/or Symbolism**   *Explain examples of foreshadowing, irony, and/or symbolism in this story.*

FOLLOW-UP QUESTIONS

10 SHORT QUESTIONS

*Select the **best** answer for each.*

_____ 1. The narrator's heritage is
a. white.
b. Native American.
c. other.

_____ 2. The narrator is
a. married.
b. single.
c. divorced.

_____ 3. The narrator believes that Native spirits are
a. all warlike or hurtful.
b. scary.
c. an extension of life.

_____ 4. The narrator believes that Native spirits are
a. similar to Western spirits.
b. different from Western spirits.
c. irrelevant to the living.

_____ 5. The narrator's nephew
a. tries to scare people.
b. scares everyone.
c. does not believe in spirits.

_____ 6. The narrator's nephew seems to
a. become a ghost.
b. run into a ghost.
c. be scared by his friends.

_____ 7. The narrator is writing about this story
a. to clear his conscience.
b. to be a "cute Indian."
c. for a writing course.

_____ 8. The narrator has
a. always been happily married.
b. never been married.
c. some marital problems.

_____ 9. At first, the narrator does not think the Bone Girl is
a. an available young girl.
b. chilly from the weather.
c. a spirit.

_____ 10. After meeting with the Bone Girl, the narrator
a. mends his life.
b. continues his drinking and debauchery.
c. dies.

5 SIGNIFICANT QUOTATIONS

Explain the importance of each of these quotations.

1. "They're still with us and part of us. No farther away from us than the other side of a leaf that has fallen."

2. "I think it is because Indians stay put and white people keep moving around."

3. "He knew it was them, but he also wondered how come the light was a different color tonight and how they were able to make it move so fast through that graveyard."

4. "I still hadn't seen her face under that long pale hair of hers."

5. "That was two years ago [. . .]."

2 COMPREHENSION ESSAY QUESTIONS

Use specific details and information from the story to answer these questions as completely as possible.

1. How is the narrator's idea of staying "put" significant to this story? Use specific details and information from the story to support your answer.

2. How is the title relevant to the story? Use specific details and information from the story to support your answer.

DISCUSSION QUESTIONS

Be prepared to discuss these questions in class.

1. Would you describe the Bone Girl as helpful or frightful?

2. What do you believe about spirits, and how does your thinking compare with the narrator's thinking?

WRITING

Use each of these ideas for writing an essay.

1. The narrator tells us, "I have a theory about this. I think it is because Indians stay put and white people keep moving around" (page 127). Thinking of your own family or community, write an essay that refutes or substantiates the narrator's thinking.

2. The encounter with the Bone Girl helps the narrator to straighten out his life. Many of us have had, or know of someone who has had, the experience of a supernatural intervention. Write about a supernatural intervention you know about and explain the effects this has had on the person involved.

Further Writing

1. The narrator refers to his excessive drinking. Research the effects alcohol has had on Native American communities.

2. The Bone Girl seems to be a rather benevolent spirit. Compare and contrast her with the spirit in Edgar Allan Poe's "The Masque of the Red Death" (page 382).

Strong Temptations— Strategic Movements— The Innocents Beguiled

MARK TWAIN

PRE-READING VOCABULARY CONTEXT

Use context clues to define these words before reading. Use a dictionary as needed.

1. The children poured the water in a *bucket* in order to carry the water to the pool. *Bucket* means _____.

2. Ken painted the house using a solution of lime and water called *whitewash*. *Whitewash* means _____.

3. The *continents* of Asia, North America, and South America are all enormous land masses. *Continent* means _____.

4. Little Missy and Carrie had a wonderful time playing on the beach and just generally *skylarking* together. *Skylarking* means

_____.

5. Emanuel was not sure which suit to buy and *wavered* when he was at the counter, still unsure about which to purchase. *Waver* means

_____.

6. The sad woman looked so *melancholy* after she lost her dog. *Melancholy* means _____.

7. Robert went to *fetch* his mother at the train station. *Fetch* means

_____.

8. During the cruise, Jane got off the ship to take many exciting *expeditions* ashore. *Expedition* means _____.

9. In an even trade, the boys *exchanged* one baseball glove for another. *Exchange* means _____.

10. Chester improved his *straightened means* when he took a job and finally had money to spend. *Straightened means* means

_____.

11. The idea of painting the lawn's yellow spots green came as a great *inspiration* to Joe. *Inspiration* means _____.

12. During a lazy afternoon of floating around the pool, RoseAnn ran her fingers *tranquilly* and slowly through the water. *Tranquilly* means _____.

13. Helena is a good friend and never *ridicules* or makes fun of any of her friends. *Ridicule* means _____.

14. Pilar was so interested in the book that she became completely *absorbed* and did not notice anything around her. *Absorbed* means _____.

15. You could see the lazy boy's *reluctance* to help with all the work. *Reluctance* means _____.

16. Ali responded with *alacrity* to the wonderful invitation to see Springsteen for free. *Alacrity* means _____.

17. Little children, who are true *innocents*, are so pure and trusting that they believe everyone. *Innocent* means _____.

18. Don has always been able to earn a lot of money; he has never been *poverty-stricken*. *Poverty-stricken* means _____.

19. When Harold won all the money at the poker game, he *bankrupted* the other players. *Bankrupt* means _____.

20. After he took the job, Amar was *obliged* to show up on time. *Obliged* means _____.

PRE-READING VOCABULARY
STRUCTURAL ATTACK

Define these words by solving the parts. Use the Glossary or a dictionary as needed.

1. long-handled
2. topmost
3. steamboat
4. engine-bells
5. hurricane-deck
6. carelessly
7. poverty-stricken
8. passenger-coach

PRE-READING QUESTIONS

Try answering these questions as you read.

What are the "temptations"?

What are the "strategic movements"?

Who are "the innocents"?

What does Tom do?

What does Tom get everyone else to do?

Strong Temptations— Strategic Movements— The Innocents Beguiled

MARK TWAIN

Mark Twain was born Samuel Langhorne Clemens in 1835. Growing up in Hannibal, Missouri, he enjoyed a childhood filled with the glamour of riverboats and the mysteries of the Mississippi. His father died when he was twelve, and Clemens became a printer's apprentice. For ten years he set type for newspapers from Iowa to New York. In 1857 he returned to the Mississippi and became a riverboat pilot. With the coming of the Civil War and decreased river traffic, he headed west and became a journalist. While working for a Nevada newspaper, he adopted the name "Mark Twain," a term riverboat crews used in measuring water depth. In 1869 he journeyed to Europe. In 1890 he married Olivia Langdon and they moved to her hometown of Elmira, New York, where they built a sizable estate that, arguably, contributed to his later financial problems. During the 1890s he suffered the loss of his wife and a daughter as well as financial problems. He died in 1910.

Twain developed a uniquely American style, unstifled by European dictates and reflecting the frontier he explored. His happiest works are set in his fictional St. Petersburg, Missouri, and include <u>Tom Sawyer</u> and <u>The Adventures of Huckleberry Finn</u>. The death of his wife and daughter led to what is generally agreed as darker and more obscure writing, but this story from <u>Tom Sawyer</u> is a classic tale recognized as part of American lore, a story of inspired American ingenuity.

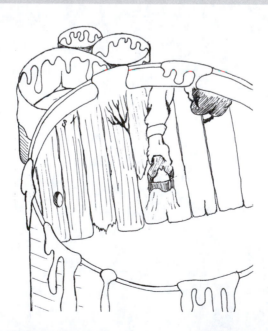

Saturday morning was come, and all the summer world was bright and fresh, and brimming with life. There was a song in every heart; and if the heart was young the music issued at the lips. There was cheer in every face and a spring in every step. The locust trees were in bloom and the fragrance of the blossoms filled the air. Cardiff Hill, beyond the village and above it, was green with vegetation, and it lay just far enough away to seem a Delectable Land, dreamy, reposeful, and inviting.

2   Tom appeared on the sidewalk with a bucket of whitewash and a long-handled brush. He surveyed the fence, and all gladness left him and a deep melancholy settled down upon his spirit. Thirty yards of board fence nine feet high. Life to him seemed hollow, and existence but a burden. Sighing he dipped his brush and passed it along the topmost plank; repeated the operation; did it again; compared the insignificant whitewashed streak with the far-reaching continent of unwhite washed fence, and sat down on a tree-box discouraged. Jim came skipping out at the gate with a tin pail, and singing "Buffalo Gals." Bringing water from the town pump had always been hateful work in Tom's eyes, before, but now it did not strike him so. He remembered that there was company at the pump. White, mulatto, and negro boys and girls were always there waiting their turns, resting, trading playthings, quarreling, fighting, skylarking. And he remembered that although the pump was only a hundred and fifty yards off, Jim never got back with a bucket of water under an hour—and even then somebody generally had to go after him. Tom said:

3   "Say, Jim, I'll fetch the water if you'll whitewash some."

4   Jim shook his head and said:

5   "Can't, Mars Tom. Ole missis, she tole me I got to go an' git dis water an' not stop foolin' roun' wid anybody. She say she spec' Mars Tom gwine to ax me to whitewash, an' so she tole me go 'long an' 'tend to my own business—she 'lowed *she'd* 'tend to de whitewashin'."

6   "Oh, never you mind what she said, Jim. That's the way she always talks. Gimme the bucket—I won't be gone only a minute. *She* won't ever know."

7   "Oh, I dasn't Mars Tom. Ole missis she'd take an' tar de head off'n me. 'Deed she would."

8   "*She!* She never licks anybody—whacks 'em over the head with her thimble—and who cares for that, I'd like to know. She talks awful, but talk don't hurt—anyways it don't if she don't cry. Jim, I'll give you a marvel. I'll give you a white alley!"

9   Jim began to waver.

10   "White alley, Jim! And it's a bully taw."

11   "My! Dat's a mighty gay marvel, *I* tell you! But Mars Tom I's powerful 'fraid ole missis—"

12   "And besides, if you will I'll show you my sore toe."

13   Jim was only human—this attraction was too much for him. He put down his pail, took the white alley, and bent over the toe with absorbing interest while the bandage was being unwound. In another moment he was flying down the street with his pail and a tingling rear, Tom was whitewashing with vigor, and Aunt Polly was retiring from the field with a slipper in her hand and triumph in her eye.

14   But Tom's energy did not last. He began to think of the fun he had planned for this day, and his sorrows multiplied. Soon the free boys would come tripping along on all sorts of delicious expeditions, and they would make a world of fun of him for having to work—the very thought of it burnt him like fire. He got out his worldly wealth and examined it—bits of toys, marbles, and trash; enough to buy an exchange of *work* maybe, but not half enough to buy so much as half an hour of pure freedom. So he returned his straightened means to his pocket, and gave up the idea of trying to buy the boys. At this dark and hopeless moment an inspiration burst upon him! Nothing less than a great, magnificent inspiration.

15   He took up his brush and went tranquilly to work. Ben Rogers hove in sight presently—the very boy, of all boys, whose ridicule he had been dreading. Ben's gait was the hop-skip-and-jump—proof enough that his heart was light and his anticipations high. He was eating an apple, and giving a long, melodious whoop, at intervals, followed by a deep-toned ding-dong-dong, ding-dong-dong, for he was personating a steamboat. As he drew near, he slackened speed, took the middle of the street, leaned far over to starboard and rounded to ponderously and with laborious pomp and circumstance—for he was personating the "Big Missouri," and considered himself to be drawing nine feet of water. He was boat, and captain, and engine-bells combined, so he had to imagine himself standing on his own hurricane-deck giving the orders and executing them:

16   "Stop her, sir! Ting-a-ling-ling!" The headway ran almost out and he drew up slowly toward the side-walk.

17   "Ship up to back! Ting-a-ling-ling!" His arms straightened and stiffened down his sides.

18   "Set her back on the stabboard! Ting-a-ling-ling! Chow! ch-chow-wow! Chow!" His right hand, meantime, describing stately circles—for it was representing a forty-foot wheel.

19   "Let her go back on the labboard! Ting-a-ling-ling! Chow-ch-chow-chow!" The left hand began to describe circles.

20   "Stop the stabboard! Ting-a-ling-ling! Stop the labboard! Come ahead on the stabboard! Stop her! Let your outside turn over slow! Ting-a-ling-ling! Chow-ow-ow! Get out that head-line! *Lively* now! Come—out with your spring-line—what're you about there! Take a turn round that stump with the bight of it! Stand by that stage, now—let her go!

Done with the engines, sir! Ting-a-ling-ling! *Sh't! sh't! sh't!*" (trying the gauge-cocks.)

21   Tom went on whitewashing—paid no attention to the steamboat. Ben stared a moment and then said:

22   "Hi-*yi! You're* up a stump, ain't you!

23   No answer. Tom surveyed his last touch with the eye of an artist; then he gave his brush another gentle sweep and surveyed the result, as before. Ben ranged up alongside of him. Tom's mouth watered for the apple, but he stuck to his work. Ben said:

24   "Hello, old chap, you got to work, hey?"

25   Tom wheeled suddenly and said:

26   "Why it's you Ben! I warn't noticing."

27   "Say—*I'm* going in a swimming, *I* am. Don't you wish you could? But of course you'd druther *work*—wouldn't you? Course you would!"

28   Tom contemplated the boy a bit, and said:

29   "What do you call work?"

30   "Why ain't *that* work?"

31   Tom resumed his whitewashing, and answered carelessly:

32   "Well, maybe it is, and maybe it ain't. All I know, is, it suits Tom Sawyer."

33   "Oh come, now, you don't mean to let on that you *like* it?"

34   The brush continued to move.

35   "Like it? Well I don't see why I oughtn't to like it. Does a boy get a chance to whitewash a fence every day?"

36   That put the thing in a new light. Ben stopped nibbling his apple. Tom swept his brush daintily back and forth—stepped back to note the effect—added a touch here and there—criticised the effect again—Ben watching every move and getting more and more interested, more and more absorbed. Presently he said:

37   "Say, Tom, let *me* whitewash a little."

38   Tom considered, was about to consent; but he altered his mind:

39   "No—no—I reckon it wouldn't hardly do, Ben. You see, Aunt Polly's awful particular about this fence—right here on the street, you know—but if it was the back fence I wouldn't mind and *she* wouldn't. Yes, she's awful particular about this fence; it's got to be done very careful; I reckon there ain't one boy in a thousand, maybe two thousand, that can do it the way it's got to be done."

40   "No—is that so? Oh come, now—lemme just try. Only just a little—I'd let *you*, if you was me, Tom."

41   "Ben, I'd like to, honest injun; but Aunt Polly—well Jim wanted to do it, but she wouldn't let him; Sid wanted to do it, and she wouldn't let Sid. Now don't you see how I'm fixed? If you was to tackle this fence and anything was to happen to it—"

42   "Oh, shucks, I'll be just as careful. Now lemme try. Say—I'll, give you the core of my apple."

43   "Well, here—. No Ben, now don't. I'm afeard—"

44   "I'll give you *all* of it!"

45   Tom gave up the brush with reluctance in his face but alacrity in his heart. And while the late steamer "Big Missouri" worked and sweated in the sun, the retired artist sat on a barrel in the shade close by, dangled his legs, munched his apple, and planned the slaughter of more innocents. There was no lack of material; boys happened along every little while; they came to jeer, but remained to whitewash. By the time Ben was fagged out, Tom had traded the next chance to Billy Fisher for a kite, in good repair; and when *he* played out, Johnny Miller bought in for a dead rat and a string to swing it with—and so on, and so on, hour after hour. And when the middle of the afternoon came, from being a poor poverty-stricken boy in the morning, Tom was literally rolling in wealth. He had beside the things before mentioned, twelve marbles, part of a Jew's-harp, a piece of blue bottle-glass to look through, a spool cannon, a key that wouldn't unlock anything, a fragment of chalk, a stopper of a decanter, a tin soldier, a couple of tadpoles, six firecrackers, a kitten with only one eye, a brass door-knob, a dogcollar—but no dog—the handle of a knife, four pieces of orange peel, and a dilapidated old window-sash.

46   He had had a nice, good, idle time all the while—plenty of company—and the fence had three coats of whitewash on it! If he hadn't run out of whitewash, he would have bankrupted every boy in the village.

47   Tom said to himself that it was not such a hollow world, after all. He had discovered a great law of human action, without knowing it—namely, that in order to make a man or a boy covet a thing, it is only necessary to make the thing difficult to attain. If he had been a great and wise philosopher, like the writer of this book, he would now have comprehended that Work consists of whatever a body is *obliged* to do, and that Play consists of whatever a body is not obliged to do. And this would help him to understand why constructing artificial flowers or performing on a treadmill is work, while rolling ten-pins or climbing Mont Blanc is only amusement. There are wealthy gentlemen in England who drive four-horse passenger-coaches twenty or thirty miles on a daily line, in the summer, because the privilege costs them considerable money; but if they were offered wages for the service, that would turn it into work and then they would resign.

48   The boy mused a while over the substantial change which had taken place in his worldly circumstances, and then wended toward headquarters to report.

Strong Temptations—
Strategic Movements—
The Innocents Beguiled

Journal

1. **MLA Works Cited**   *Using this model, record this story here.*

   Author's Last Name, First Name. "Title of the Story." <u>Title of the Book</u>.
   3rd ed. Ed. First Name Last Name. City: Publisher, year. Pages of
   the story.

2. **Main Character(s)**   *Describe each main character, and explain why you*
   think each is a main character.

3. **Supporting Characters**   *Describe each supporting character, and explain why*
   you think each is a supporting character.

4. **Setting**   *Describe the setting(s) and any relevant prop(s).*

5. Sequence   *Outline the events of the story in order.*

6. Plot   *Tell the story in no more than two sentences.*

7. Conflicts   *Identify and explain all the conflicts involved here.*

8. Significant Quotations   *Explain the importance of each of these quotations. Record the page number in the parentheses.*

a. "He surveyed the fence, and all gladness left him [. . .]" (   ).

b. "At this dark and hopeless moment an inspiration burst upon him! Nothing less than a great, magnificent inspiration" (   ).

c. "'Like it? Well I don't see why I oughtn't to like it. Does a boy get a chance to whitewash a fence every day?'" (   ).

d. "'Now don't you see how I'm fixed? If you was to tackle this fence and anything was to happen to it—'"
   "'Oh, shucks, I'll be just as careful. Now lemme try. Say—I'll give you the core of my apple [. . .]'" (   ).

e. "And when the middle of the afternoon came, from being a poor poverty-stricken boy in the morning, Tom was literally rolling in wealth" (   ).

9. **Literary Elements**   *Look at this chapter's title and explain why you think this story is placed in this chapter. Explain in which other chapter(s) you might place this story, as relevant to the literary element(s) of that chapter.*

10. **Foreshadowing, Irony, and/or Symbolism**   *Explain examples of foreshadowing, irony, and/or symbolism in this story.*

FOLLOW-UP QUESTIONS

10 SHORT QUESTIONS

Select the __best__ answer for each.

____ 1. It is a
   a. sunny day.
   b. rainy day.
   c. cold day.

____ 2. Tom
   a. does not paint the fence at all.
   b. wants to paint the fence.
   c. does not want to paint the fence.

____ 3. Before, Tom had thought going to pump water was
   a. a chore.
   b. fun.
   c. a good escape.

____ 4. Now, Tom would rather
   a. do chores.
   b. paint the fence.
   c. go to get water.

____ 5. Ben seems to be
   a. a stranger to Tom.
   b. Tom's good friend.
   c. Tom's rival.

____ 6. Ben is
   a. piloting a riverboat.
   b. pretending to pilot a riverboat.
   c. on a riverboat.

____ 7. The boys consider riverboats to be
   a. fun and adventuresome.
   b. hard work.
   c. boring and dull.

____ 8. Tom tells Ben Aunt Polly is "particular"
   a. to scare him away.
   b. to insult him.
   c. to lure him in.

____ 9. Ben is
   a. the only painter.
   b. not the only painter.
   c. the only other boy.

____ 10. Tom
   a. tricks the other boys into painting the fence.
   b. does not trick the other boys into painting the fence.
   c. cannot trick the other boys into painting the fence.

5 SIGNIFICANT QUOTATIONS

Explain the importance of each of these quotations.

1. "Sighing he dipped his brush and passed it along the topmost plank; repeated the operation; did it again; compared the insignificant whitewashed streak with the far-reaching continent of unwhite-washed fence, and sat down on a tree-box discouraged."

2. "Bringing water from the town pump had always been hateful work in Tom's eyes, before, but now it did not strike him so."

3. " 'Say, Tom, let *me* whitewash a little.' "

4. "Tom gave up the brush with reluctance in his face but alacrity in his heart."

5. "There are wealthy gentlemen in England who drive four-horse passenger-coaches twenty or thirty miles on a daily line, in the summer, because the privilege costs them considerable money; but if they were offered wages for the service, that would turn it into work and then they would resign."

2 Comprehension Essay Questions

Use specific details and information from the story to answer these questions as completely as possible.

1. The fence is central to this story. What is the significance of the fence? Use specific details and information from the story.

2. How does Tom trick the boys? Use specific details and information from the story to support your explanation.

Discussion Questions

Be prepared to discuss these questions in class.

1. Do you think what Tom does is fair, smart, or unfair? Use specific details from the story to support your thinking?

2. When have you tricked someone? Using specific details from the story, compare and contrast your trickery with the tricks Tom plays.

Writing

Use each of these ideas for writing an essay.

1. "Whitewashing" means to paint a surface with thin, white paint. "Whitewashing" has also come to mean cleaning up someone else's mess. Compare a time you used someone to clean up your mess or a time someone used you to clean up her or his mess to Tom's trickery.

2. "Whitewashing" also means to cover unpleasant facts with denials, lies, or half-truths. Tell the story of a time you or someone you know whitewashed facts.

Further Writing

1. Tom Sawyer in this story and Dee in "Everyday Use" by Alice Walker (page 108) use ruses or pretenses to try to get what they want. Compare and contrast their manipulations and their goals.

2. Research the animal rights movement, and include a discussion of Twain's "A Dog's Tale" (available in a library), one of the most poignant and compelling pieces written that is germane to animal treatment.

The Cask of Amontillado

EDGAR ALLAN POE

PRE-READING VOCABULARY
CONTEXT

Use context clues to define these words before reading. Use a dictionary as needed.

1. Treating Jacqui, who is very smart, as if she has no brains is an *insult* to her intelligence. *Insult* means _____.

2. Because they lost the World Series, the Yankees will seek *revenge* against the Tigers. *Revenge* means _____.

3. After defeating the Tigers 21–0, the Yankees felt *avenged. Avenged* means _____.

4. The ability to identify fine things, such as art or wine, shows Matt's *connoisseurship. Connoisseurship* means _____.

5. Loretta went on the rides and ate lots of cotton candy at the *carnival. Carnival* means _____.

6. The queen stored her jewels in a secure *vault* in the palace. *Vault* means _____.

7. Either potassium or sodium combined with nitrate make a nasty smelling substance called *nitre. Nitre* means _____.

8. Giorgio lives in a magnificent *palazzo* with forty rooms surrounded by colorful gardens. *Palazzo* means _____.

9. Edith lighted the citronella *flambeaux* that were set on stands around the pool. *Flambeaux* means _____.

10. Ancient Christians buried their dead in the *catacombs'* cave-like tunnels under Rome. *Catacomb* means _____.

11. Ricki stopped at the wine store to buy a fine bottle of *Medoc* for dinner. *Medoc* means _____.

12. The *masons* built the wall, brick by brick. *Mason* means

_____.

13. To build the brick wall, the masons spread the cement between the bricks with a *trowel*. *Trowel* means _____.

14. Justin wore a large velvet *cloak* over his tuxedo for the opening night. *Cloak* means _____.

15. The prince was buried in a *crypt* under the rose garden behind the castle. *Crypt* means _____.

16. The masons working on the brick wall used *mortar* to seal the bricks together. *Mortar* means _____.

17. Lisa hid her secret diary in a little *niche* under the window seat in her room. *Niche* means _____.

18. The masons placed the bricks one layer after another, *tier* by *tier*. *Tier* means _____.

19. Christina was able to put the thread through the small *aperture* in the needle. *Aperture* means _____.

20. Because we will die one day, we are called *mortals*. *Mortal* means

_____.

PRE-READING VOCABULARY
STRUCTURAL ATTACK

Define these words by solving the parts. Use the Glossary or a dictionary as needed.

1. definitiveness
2. unredressed
3. conical
4. intermingling
5. foulness
6. unsheathing

Use context clues Poe gives you to define this word.

" 'It is this,' I answered, producing a trowel from beneath the folds of my *roquelaire*." *Roquelaire* means _____.

PRE-READING QUESTIONS

Try answering these questions as you read.

Who are the main characters in the story?

What role does Luchesi play?

Where does the story take place?

What is happening in the story?

The Cask of Amontillado

EDGAR ALLAN POE

Edgar Allan Poe was born in 1809 and orphaned at a young age. He was adopted by John Allan, a rather militaristic businessman from Richmond, Virginia. Adoption by a person of means was not uncommon and would have been fortunate for the young Poe, except that Poe's free spirit and his father's precision clashed. John Allan provided Poe with study at the University of Virginia—but Poe withdrew due to drinking problems—and then at West Point—but Poe was dismissed due to a disciplinary problem. Poe later married his very young cousin, Virginia Clemm, but the probable nonconsummation of this marriage and the early death of young Virginia contributed to Poe's idealization of both real and imagined women. His life, in fact, was one of continual disappointments. After Virginia's death, Poe sank into intermittent depressions, suffered bouts of insanity, and experienced hallucinations. Writing for many others, he wanted to publish his own magazine, but this dissolved in financial failure. He eventually died in Baltimore in 1849.

However, it is from these very problems that Poe's genius soars. He envelops the reader with his perceived worlds of the sane and the insane, the rational and macabre, with equal ease. Credited with developing the modern mystery form, Poe's every word and every action draws the reader in, mixing reality with irreality, sanity with madness. His other works include "The Pit and the Pendulum" and "The Fall of the House of Usher."

The thousand injuries of Fortunato I had borne as I best could; but when he ventured upon insult, I vowed revenge. You, who so well know the nature of my soul, will not suppose, however, that I gave utterance to a threat. *At length* I would be avenged; this was a point definitely settled—but the very definitiveness with which it was resolved, precluded the idea of risk. I must not only punish, but punish with impunity. A wrong is unredressed when retribution overtakes its redresser. It is equally unredressed when the avenger fails to make himself felt as such to him who has done the wrong.

2   It must be understood, that neither by word nor deed had I given Fortunato cause to doubt my good-will. I continued, as was my wont, to smile in his face, and he did not perceive that my smile *now* was at the thought of his immolation.

3   He had a weak point—this Fortunato—although in other regards he was a man to be respected and even feared. He prided himself on his connoisseurship in wine. Few Italians have the true virtuoso spirit. For the most part their enthusiasm is adopted to suit the time and opportunity—to practise imposture, upon the British and Austrian millionaires. In painting and gemmary Fortunato, like his countrymen, was a quack—but in the matter of old wines he was sincere. In this respect I did not differ from him materially: I was skilful in the Italian vintages myself, and bought largely whenever I could.

4   It was about dusk, one evening during the supreme madness of the carnival season, that I encountered my friend. He accosted me with excessive warmth, for he had been drinking much. The man wore motley. He had on a tight-fitting parti-striped dress, and his head was surmounted by the conical cap and bells. I was so pleased to see him, that I thought I should never have done wringing his hand.

5   I said to him: "My dear Fortunato, you are luckily met. How remarkably well you are looking to-day! But I have received a pipe of what passes for Amontillado, and I have my doubts."

6   "How?" said he. "Amontillado? A pipe? Impossible! And in the middle of the carnival!"

7   "I have my doubts," I replied; "and I was silly enough to pay the full Amontillado price without consulting you in the matter. You were not to be found, and I was fearful of losing a bargain."

8   "Amontillado!"

9   "I have my doubts."

10   "Amontillado!"

11   "And I must satisfy them."

12   "Amontillado!"

13   "As you are engaged, I am on my way to Luchesi. If any one has a critical turn, it is he. He will tell me—"

14   "Luchesi cannot tell Amontillado from Sherry."

15   "And yet some fools will have it that his taste is a match for your own."

16   "Come, let us go."

17   "Whither?"

18   "To your vaults."

19   "My friend, no; I will not impose upon your good nature. I perceive you have an engagement. Luchesi—"

20   "I have no engagement;—come."

21   "My friend, no. It is not the engagement, but the severe cold with which I perceive you are afflicted. The vaults are insufferably damp. They are encrusted with nitre."

22   "Let us go, nevertheless. The cold is merely nothing. Amontillado! You have been imposed upon. And as for Luchesi, he cannot distinguish Sherry from Amontillado."

23   Thus speaking, Fortunato possessed himself of my arm. Putting on a mask of black silk, and drawing a *roquelaire* closely about my person, I suffered him to hurry me to my palazzo.

24   There were no attendants at home; they had absconded to make merry in honor of the time. I had told them that I should not return until the morning, and had given them explicit orders not to stir from the house. These orders were sufficient, I well knew, to insure their immediate disappearance, one and all, as soon as my back was turned.

25   I took from their sconces two flambeaux, and giving one to Fortunato, bowed him through several suites of rooms to the archway that led into the vaults. I passed down a long and winding staircase, requesting him to be cautious as he followed. We came at length to the foot of the descent, and stood together on the damp ground of the catacombs of the Montresors.

26   The gait of my friend was unsteady, and the bells upon his cap jingled as he strode.

27   "The pipe?" said he.

28   "It is farther on," said I; "but observe the white webwork which gleams from these cavern walls."

29   He turned toward me, and looked into my eyes with two filmy orbs that distilled the rheum of intoxication.

30   "Nitre?" he asked, at length.

31   "Nitre," I replied. "How long have you had that cough?"

32   "Ugh! ugh! ugh!—ugh! ugh! ugh!—ugh! ugh! ugh!—ugh! ugh! ugh!—ugh! ugh! ugh!"

33   My poor friend found it impossible to reply for many minutes.

34   "It is nothing," he said, at last.

35   "Come," I said with decision, "we will go back; your health is precious. You are rich, respected, admired, beloved; you are happy, as once
I was. You are a man to be missed. For me it is no matter. We will go
back; you will be ill, and I cannot be responsible. Besides, there is
Luchesi—"

36   "Enough," he said; "the cough is a mere nothing; it will not kill
me. I shall not die of a cough."

37   "True—true," I replied; "and, indeed, I had no intention of alarm-
ing you unnecessarily; but you should use all proper caution. A draught
of this Medoc will defend us from the damps."

38   Here I knocked off the neck of a bottle which I drew from a long
row of its fellows that lay upon the mould.

39   "Drink," I said, presenting him the wine.

40   He raised it to his lips with a leer. He paused and nodded to me
familiarly, while his bells jingled.

41   "I drink," he said, "to the buried that repose around us."

42   "And I to your long life."

43   He again took my arm, and we proceeded.

44   "These vaults," he said, "are extensive."

45   "The Montresors," I replied, "were a great and numerous family."

46   "I forget your arms."

47   "A huge human foot d'or, in a field azure; the foot crushes a ser-
pent rampant whose fangs are imbedded in the heel."

48   "And the motto?"

49   "Nemo me impune lacessit."

50   "Good!" he said.

51   The wine sparkled in his eyes and the bells jingled. My own fancy
grew warm with the Medoc. We had passed through walls of piled
bones, with casks and puncheons intermingling, into the inmost
recesses of the catacombs. I paused again, and this time I made bold to
seize Fortunato by an arm above the elbow.

52   "The nitre!" I said; "see, it increases. It hangs like moss upon the
vaults. We are below the river's bed. The drops of moisture trickle
among the bones. Come, we will go back ere it is too late. Your
cough—"

53   "It is nothing," he said; "let us go on. But first, another draught of
the Medoc."

54   I broke and reached him a flagon of De Grâve. He emptied it at a
breath. His eyes flashed with a fierce light. He laughed and threw the
bottle upward with a gesticulation I did not understand.

55   I looked at him in surprise. He repeated the movement—a
grotesque one.

56   "You do not comprehend?" he said.

57   "Not I," I replied.

58   "Then you are not of the brotherhood."

59   "How?"

60   "You are not of the masons."

61   "Yes, yes," I said; "yes, yes."

62   "You? Impossible! A mason?"

63   "A mason," I replied.

64   "A sign," he said.

65   "It is this," I answered, producing a trowel from beneath the folds of my *roquelaire*.

66   "You jest," he exclaimed, recoiling a few paces. "But let us proceed to the Amontillado."

67   "Be it so," I said, replacing the tool beneath the cloak, and again offering him my arm. He leaned upon it heavily. We continued our route in search of the Amontillado. We passed through a range of low arches, descended, passed on, and descending again, arrived at a deep crypt, in which the foulness of the air caused our flambeaux rather to glow than flame.

68   At the most remote end of the crypt there appeared another less spacious. Its walls had been lined with human remains, piled to the vault overhead, in the fashion of the great catacombs of Paris. Three sides of this interior crypt were still ornamented in this manner. From the fourth the bones had been thrown down, and lay promiscuously upon the earth, forming at one point a mound of some size. Within the wall thus exposed by the displacing of the bones, we perceived a stiff interior recess, in depth about four feet, in width three, in height six or seven. It seemed to have been constructed for no especial use within itself, but formed merely the interval between two of the colossal supports of the roof of the catacombs, and was backed by one of their circumscribing walls of solid granite.

69   It was in vain that Fortunato, uplifting his dull torch, endeavored to pry into the depth of the recess. Its termination the feeble light did not enable us to see.

70   "Proceed," I said; "herein is the Amontillado. As for Luchesi—"

71   "He is an ignoramus," interrupted my friend, as he stepped unsteadily forward, while I followed immediately at his heels. In an instant he had reached the extremity of the niche, and finding his progress arrested by the rock, stood stupidly bewildered. A moment more and I had fettered him to the granite. In its surface were two iron staples, distant from each other about two feet, horizontally. From one of these depended a short chain, from the other a padlock. Throwing the links about his waist, it was but the work of a few seconds to

secure it. He was too much astounded to resist. Withdrawing the key I
stepped back from the recess.

72   "Pass your hand," I said, "over the wall; you cannot help feeling
the nitre. Indeed it is *very* damp. Once more let me *implore* you to
return. No? Then I must positively leave you. But I must first render
you all the little attentions in my power."

73   "The Amontillado!" ejaculated my friend, not yet recovered from
his astonishment.

74   "True," I replied; "the Amontillado."

75   As I said these words I busied myself among the pile of bones of
which I have before spoken. Throwing them aside, I soon uncovered a
quantity of building stone and mortar. With these materials and with the
aid of my trowel, I began vigorously to wall up the entrance of the niche.

76   I had scarcely laid the first tier of the masonry when I discovered
that the intoxication of Fortunato had in a great measure worn off. The
earliest indication I had of this was a low moaning cry from the depth
of the recess. It was *not* the cry of a drunken man. There was then a
long and obstinate silence. I laid the second tier, and the third, and the
fourth; and then I heard the furious vibrations of the chain. The noise
lasted for several minutes, during which, that I might hearken to it
with the more satisfaction, I ceased my labors and sat down upon the
bones. When at last the clanking subsided, I resumed the trowel, and
finished without interruption the fifth, the sixth, and the seventh tier.
The wall was now nearly upon a level with my breast. I again paused,
and holding the flambeaux over the mason-work, threw a few feeble
rays upon the figure within.

77   A succession of loud and shrill screams, bursting suddenly from
the throat of the chained form, seemed to thrust me violently back. For
a brief moment I hesitated—I trembled. Unsheathing my rapier, I
began to grope with it about the recess; but the thought of an instant
reassured me. I placed my hand upon the solid fabric of the catacombs,
and felt satisfied. I reapproached the wall. I replied to the yells of him
who clamored. I re-echoed—I aided—I surpassed them in volume and
in strength. I did this, and the clamorer grew still.

78   It was now midnight, and my task was drawing to a close. I had
completed the eighth, the ninth, and the tenth tier. I had finished a portion of the last and the eleventh; there remained but a single stone to
be fitted and plastered in. I struggled with its weight; I placed it par-
tially in its destined position. But now there came from out the niche a
low laugh that erected the hairs upon my head. It was succeeded by a
sad voice, which I had difficulty in recognizing as that of the noble Fortunato. The voice said—

79   "Ha! ha! ha!—he! he!—a very good joke indeed—an excellent jest. We will have many a rich laugh about it at the palazzo—he! he! he!—over our wine—he! he! he!"

80   "The Amontillado!" I said.

81   "He! he! he!—he! he! he!—yes, the Amontillado. But is it not getting late? Will not they be awaiting us at the palazzo, the Lady Fortunato and the rest? Let us be gone."

82   "Yes," I said, "let us be gone."

83   *"For the love of God, Montresor!"*

84   "Yes," I said, "for the love of God!"

85   But to these words I hearkened in vain for a reply. I grew impatient. I called aloud:

86   "Fortunato!"

87   No answer. I called again:

88   "Fortunato!"

89   No answer still. I thrust a torch through the remaining aperture and let it fall within. There came forth in return only a jingling of the bells. My heart grew sick—on account of the dampness of the catacombs. I hastened to make an end of my labor. I forced the last stone into its position; I plastered it up. Against the new masonry I re-erected the old rampart of bones. For half of a century no mortal has disturbed them. *In pace requiescat!*

The Cask of Amontillado

JOURNAL

1. **MLA Works Cited**   *Using this model, record this story here.*

   *Author's Last Name, First Name. "Title of the Story." <u>Title of the Book</u>.
   3rd ed. Ed. First Name Last Name. City: Publisher, year. Pages of
   the story.*

2. **Main Character(s)**   *Describe each main character, and explain why you
   think each is a main character.*

3. **Supporting Characters**   *Describe each supporting character, and explain why
   you think each is a supporting character.*

4. **Setting**   *Describe the setting(s) and any relevant prop(s).*

5. **Sequence** *Outline the events of the story in order.*

6. **Plot** *Tell the story in no more than three sentences.*

7. **Conflicts** *Identify and explain all the conflicts involved here.*

8. **Significant Quotations** *Explain the importance of each of these quotations. Record the page number in the parentheses.*
   a. "I must not only punish, but punish with impunity" (   ).

   b. "He [Fortunato] prided himself on his connoisseurship in wine" (   ).

   c. " 'Amontillado!' " (   ).
      " 'As you are engaged, I am on my way to Luchesi' " (   ).

d. " 'It is this,' I answered, producing a trowel from beneath the folds of my *roquelaire*" (   ).

e. " 'Ha! ha! ha!—he! he!—a very good joke indeed—an excellent jest. We will have many a rich laugh about it at the palazzo—he! he! he!—over the wine—he! he! he!' " (   ).

9. **Literary Elements**   *Look at this chapter's title and explain why you think this story is placed in this chapter. Explain in which other chapter(s) you might place this story, as relevant to the literary element(s) of that chapter.*

10. **Foreshadowing, Irony, and/or Symbolism**   *Explain examples of foreshadowing, irony, and/or symbolism in this story.*

FOLLOW-UP QUESTIONS

10 SHORT QUESTIONS

Select the <u>best</u> answer for each.

_____ 1. Montresor looks on Fortunato as
   a. a friend.
   b. an enemy.
   c. a co-worker.

_____ 2. Montresor
   a. is courteous to Fortunato.
   b. is discourteous to Fortunato.
   c. ignores Fortunato.

_____ 3. Amontillado is
   a. a wine.
   b. a pipe.
   c. a person.

_____ 4. Montresor probably
   a. works hard as a mason every day.
   b. knows little about masonry.
   c. comes from a wealthy family.

_____ 5. Fortunato is
   a. jealous of Luchesi.
   b. friendly with Luchesi.
   c. does not know Luchesi.

_____ 6. This story probably takes place in
   a. France.
   b. America.
   c. Italy.

_____ 7. The bones probably indicate
   a. more murders.
   b. a burial place.
   c. many hungry dogs.

_____ 8. Montresor uses Luchesi to
   a. scare Fortunato away.
   b. lure Fortunato on.
   c. help Fortunato.

_____ 9. Montresor
   a. has planned well.
   b. has not planned well.
   c. has no plans.

_____ 10. Montresor acts out of
   a. friendship.
   b. jealousy.
   c. revenge.

5 SIGNIFICANT QUOTATIONS

Explain the importance of each of these quotations.

1. "The thousand injuries of Fortunato I had borne as I best could; but when he ventured upon insult, I vowed revenge."

2. "He [Fortunato] prided himself on his connoisseurship in wine."

3. " 'Amontillado? A pipe? Impossible!' "

4. " 'Luchesi cannot tell Amontillado from Sherry.' "

5. "Against the new masonry I re-erected the old rampart of bones. For half a century no mortal has disturbed them."

2 Comprehension Essay Questions

Use specific details and information from the story to answer these questions as completely as possible.

1. How does the title relate to the story? Explain the significance of the title using specific details and information from the story.

2. Poe plays with our feelings for the protagonist and the antagonist. Who is the protagonist and who is the antagonist? Use specific details and information from the story.

Discussion Questions

Be prepared to discuss these questions in class.

1. How does the illustration demonstrate the story? Use specific details from the story to support your ideas.

2. Who is the protagonist and who is the antagonist in this story? How does Poe play with the reader concerning protagonist and antagonist?

Writing

Use each of these ideas for writing an essay.

1. We all have weaknesses (chocolate, being late, and so forth). Tell the story of a time one of your weaknesses got you into trouble.

2. Using specific details and information from this story, explain the shifting roles of protagonist and antagonist in the story.

Further Writing

1. Compare and contrast Montresor with the Count of Monte Cristo in The Count of Monte Cristo (available in a library or video store).

2. Research today's use of the insanity plea in criminal actions, and use Poe's story as an insightful anecdote in this study.

To Build a Fire

JACK LONDON

PRE-READING VOCABULARY
CONTEXT

Use context clues to define these words before reading. Use a dictionary as needed.

1. The freezing winds whipped across the *Yukon* area of northwest Canada. *Yukon* means _____.

2. The Apache put the soft, leather *moccasins* on his feet. *Moccasin* means _____.

3. Men who use chewing tobacco spit out a brown-colored *spittle.* *Spittle* means _____.

4. If you put ice on a sore, the pain will go away, and the area will lose all feeling and become *numb. Numb* means _____ .

5. Large and furry *huskies* are often used in teams to pull dog sleds over the snow. *Husky* means _____.

6. Things we know how to do without ever being taught are called *instincts. Instinct* means _____.

7. When Barry awoke, the sunlight and birds chirping came into his *consciousness. Consciousness* means _____.

8. Jen was *apprehensive* that she would miss the plane because she woke up so late. *Apprehensive* means _____.

9. The freezing *arctic* winds came from the North Pole and brought a large amount of snow and sleet. *Arctic* means

_____.

10. Jack felt *compelled* to put money in the bank after he wrote a large check. *Compel* means _____.

11. Tom *obeyed* the speed limit sign and slowed down to 25 mph. *Obey* means _____.

12. Since Maureen had put the steak in the freezer, it had to *thaw out* before she could cook it. *Thaw out* means _____.

13. Mary Beth *singed* the cake when she left it in the oven too long. *Singe* means _____ .

14. We have *inherited* much of our size, shape, and intelligence from our ancestors who lived before us. *Inherited* means

_____.

15. Everyone got wet when the canoe *capsized* and dumped us in the water. *Capsized* means _____.

16. When the snow on the mountain became too heavy, it all came down in a loud *avalanche*. *Avalanche* means _____.

17. With clumsy mittens on her hands, Martina *fumbled* the snowball and watched it fall to the ground. *Fumbled* means

_____.

18. The snow fell so heavily during the *blizzard* that Bernadette could not see two feet in front of her. *Blizzard* means _____.

19. Birds and worms were eating the *carcass* of the dead snake. *Carcass* means _____.

20. The clerks became *suspicious* of the new employee when money was missing and he was observed buying new clothes. *Suspicious* means _____.

Pre-reading Vocabulary
Structural Attack

Define these words by solving the parts. Use the Glossary or a dictionary as needed.

1. little-traveled
2. timberland
3. freeze-up
4. unbroken
5. hairline
6. spruce-covered
7. strangeness
8. undoubtedly
9. frailty
10. roundabout
11. immortality
12. mittened
13. warm-whiskered
14. gray-coated
15. crystalled
16. solidity
17. observant
18. candied
19. firewood
20. underbrush
21. old-timer
22. rapidity
23. lifeless
24. fire-provider
25. birchbark
26. faraway
27. food-provider

Pre-reading Questions

Try answering these questions as you read.

What is the setting?

Why is it important to build a fire?

Why can't the man build a fire?

What does the dog know?

What does the man know?

To Build a Fire

JACK LONDON

Jack London was born in San Francisco in 1876. London at first completed only elementary school as a result of his family's financial problems. He worked variously as a paperboy, a bowling alley pinsetter, a sailor (traveling as far as Japan), a hunter, and a hobo (traveling through mainland America, Canada, and Alaska). He became an avid reader, eventually completed high school, and then entered the University of California. He left after one semester and turned to writing. London died in Santa Rosa, California in 1916.

Drawing from his travels and influenced by Marx, Nietzsche, and Darwin, London continually discusses instinct and base survival in his writing. The author of many stories, The Call of the Wild remains his master work.

Day had broken cold and gray, exceedingly cold and gray, when the man turned aside from the main Yukon trail and climbed the high earth bank, where a dim and little-traveled trail led eastward through the fat spruce timberland. It was a steep bank, and he paused for breath at the top, excusing the act to himself by looking at his watch. It was nine o'clock. There was no sun nor hint of sun, though there was not a cloud in the sky. It was a clear day, and yet there seemed an intangible pall over the face of things, a subtle gloom that made the day dark, and that was due to the absence of sun. This fact did not worry the man. He was used to the lack of sun. It had been days since he had seen the sun, and he knew that a few more days must pass before that cheerful orb, due south, would just peep above the skyline and dip immediately from view.

2   The man flung a look back along the way he had come. The Yukon lay a mile wide and hidden under three feet of ice. On top of this ice were as many feet of snow. It was all pure white, rolling in gentle undulations where the ice jams of the freeze-up had formed. North and south, as far as his eye could see, it was unbroken white, save for a dark hairline that curved and twisted from around the spruce-covered island to the south, and that curved and twisted away into the north, where it disappeared behind another spruce-covered island. This dark hairline was the trail—the main trail—that led south five hundred miles to the Chilcoot Pass, Dyea, and salt water; and that led north seventy miles to Dawson, and still on to the north a thousand miles to Nulato, and finally to St. Michael on Bering Sea, a thousand miles and half a thousand more.

3   But all this—the mysterious, far-reaching hairline trail, the absence of sun from the sky, the tremendous cold, and the strangeness and weirdness of it all—made no impression on the man. It was not because he was long used to it. He was a newcomer in the land, a *chechaquo*, and this was his first winter. The trouble with him was that he was without imagination. He was quick and alert in the things of life, but only in the things, and not in the significances. Fifty degrees below zero meant eighty-odd degrees of frost. Such fact impressed him as being cold and uncomfortable, and that was all. It did not lead him to meditate upon his frailty as a creature of temperature, and upon man's frailty in general, able to live within certain narrow limits of heat and cold and from there on it did not lead him to the conjectural field of immortality and man's place in the universe. Fifty degrees below zero stood for a bite of frost that hurt and that must be guarded against by the use of mittens, ear flaps, warm moccasins, and thick socks. Fifty degrees below zero was to him just precisely fifty degrees below zero. That there should be anything more to it than that was a thought that never entered his head.

4   As he turned to go on, he spat speculatively. There was a sharp, explosive crackle that startled him. He spat again. And again, in the air, before it could fall to the snow, the spittle crackled. He knew that at fifty below spittle crackled on the snow, but this spittle had crackled in the air. Undoubtedly it was colder than fifty below—how much colder he did not know. But the temperature did not matter. He was bound for the old claim on the left fork of Henderson Creek, where the boys were

already. They had come over across the divide from the Indian Creek country, while he had come the roundabout way to take a look at the possibilities of getting out logs in the spring from the islands in the Yukon. He would be in to camp by six o'clock; a bit after dark, it was true, but the boys would be there, a fire would be going, and a hot supper would be ready. As for lunch, he passed his hand against the protruding bundle under his jacket. It was also under his shirt, wrapped up in a handkerchief and lying against the naked skin. It was the only way to keep the biscuits from freezing. He smiled agreeably to himself as he thought of those biscuits, each cut open and sopped in bacon grease, and each enclosing a generous slice of fried bacon.

5   He plunged in among the big spruce trees. The trail was faint. A foot of snow had fallen since the last sled had passed over, and he was glad he was without a sled, traveling light. In fact, he carried nothing but the lunch wrapped in the handkerchief. He was surprised, however, at the cold. It certainly was cold, he concluded, as he rubbed his numb nose and cheek bones with his mittened band. He was a warm-whiskered man, but the hair on his face did not protect the high cheek bones and the eager nose that thrust itself aggressively into the frosty air.

6   At the man's heels trotted a dog, a big native husky, the proper wolf dog, gray-coated and without any visible or temperamental difference from its brother, the wild wolf. The animal was depressed by the tremendous cold. It knew that it was no time for traveling. Its instinct told it a truer tale than was told to the man by the man's judgment. In reality, it was not merely colder than fifty below zero; it was colder than sixty below, than seventy below. It was seventy-five below zero. Since the freezing point is thirty-two above zero, it meant that one hundred and seven degrees of frost obtained. The dog did not know anything about thermometers. Possibly in the brain there was no sharp consciousness of a condition of very cold such as was in the man's brain. But the brute had its instinct. It experienced a vague but menacing apprehension that subdued it and made it slink along at the man's heels, and that made it question eagerly every unwonted movement of the man, as if expecting him to go into camp or to seek shelter somewhere and build a fire. The dog had learned fire, and it wanted fire, or else to burrow under the snow and cuddle its warmth away from the air.

7   The frozen moisture of its breathing had settled on its fur in a fine powder of frost, and especially were its jowls, muzzle, and eyelashes whitened by its crystalled breath. The man's red beard and mustache were likewise frosted, but more solidly, the deposit taking the form of ice and increasing with every warm, moist breath he exhaled. Also the man was chewing tobacco, and the muzzle of ice held his lips so rigidly

that he was unable to clean his chin when he expelled the juice. The result was that a crystal beard of the color and solidity of amber was increasing its length on his chin. If he fell down it would shatter itself, like glass, into brittle fragments. But he did not mind the appendage. It was the penalty all tobacco-chewers paid in that country, and he had been out before in two cold snaps. They had not been so cold as this, he knew, but by the spirit thermometer at Sixty Mile he knew they had been registered at fifty below and at fifty-five.

8   He held on through the level stretch of woods for several miles, crossed a wide flat of boulders, and dropped down a bank to the frozen bed of a small stream. This was Henderson Creek, and he knew he was ten miles from the forks. He looked at his watch. It was ten o'clock. He was making four miles an hour, and he calculated that he would arrive at the forks at half-past twelve. He decided to celebrate that event by eating his lunch there.

9   The dog dropped in again at his heels, with a tail drooping discouragement, as the man swung along the creek bed. The furrow of the old sled trail was plainly visible, but a dozen inches of snow covered the marks of the last runners. In a month no man had come up or down that silent creek. The man held steadily on. He was not much given to thinking, and just then particularly he had nothing to think about save that he would eat lunch at the forks and that at six o'clock he would be in camp with the boys. There was nobody to talk to; and, had there been, speech would have been impossible because of the ice muzzle on his mouth. So he continued monotonously to chew tobacco and to increase the length of his amber beard.

10   Once in a while the thought reiterated itself that it was very cold and that he had never experienced such cold. As he walked along he rubbed his cheek bones and nose with the back of his mittened hand. He did this automatically, now and again changing hands. But rub as he would, the instant he stopped his cheek bones went numb, and the following instant the end of his nose went numb. He was sure to frost his cheeks; he knew that, and experienced a pang of regret that he had not devised a nose strap of the sort Bud wore in cold snaps. Such a strap passed across the cheeks, as well, and saved them. But it didn't matter much, after all. What were frosted cheeks? A bit painful, that was all; they were never serious.

11   Empty as the man's mind was of thoughts, he was keenly observant, and he noticed the changes in the creek, the curves and bends and timber jams, and always he sharply noted where he placed his feet. Once, coming around a bend, he shied abruptly, like a startled horse, curved away from the place where he had been walking, and retreated

several paces back along the trail. The creek, he knew, was frozen clear to the bottom—no creek could contain water in that arctic winter—but he knew also that there were springs that bubbled out from the hillsides and ran along under the snow and on top of the ice of the creek. He knew that the coldest snaps never froze these springs, and he knew likewise their danger. They were traps. They hid pools of water under the snow that might be three inches deep, or three feet. Sometimes a skin of ice half an inch thick covered them, and in turn was covered by the snow. Sometimes there were alternate layers of water and ice skin, so that when one broke through he kept on breaking through for a while, sometimes wetting himself to the waist.

12   That was why he had shied in such panic. He had felt the give under his feet and heard the crackle of a snow-hidden ice skin. And to get his feet wet in such a temperature meant trouble and danger. At the very least it meant delay, for he would be forced to stop and build a fire, and under its protection to bare his feet while he dried his socks and moccasins. He stood and studied the creek bed and its banks, and decided that the flow of water came from the right. He reflected a while, rubbing his nose and cheeks, then skirted to the left, stepping gingerly and testing the footing for each step. Once clear of the danger, he took a fresh chew of tobacco and swung along at his four-mile gait.

13   In the course of the next two hours he came upon several similar traps. Usually the snow above the hidden pools had a sunken candied appearance that advertised the danger. Once again, however, he had a close call; and once, suspecting danger, he compelled the dog to go on in front. The dog did not want to go. It hung back until the man shoved it forward, and then it went quickly across the white, unbroken surface. Suddenly it broke through, floundered to one side, and got away to firmer footing. It had wet its forefeet and legs, and almost immediately the water that clung to it turned to ice. It made quick efforts to lick the ice off its legs, then dropped down in the snow and began to bite out the ice that had formed between the toes. This was a matter of instinct. To permit the ice to remain there would mean sore feet. It did not know this. It merely obeyed the mysterious prompting that arose from the deep crypts of its being. But the man knew, having achieved a judgment on the subject, and he removed the mitten from his right hand and helped tear out the ice particles. He did not expose his fingers more than a minute, and was astonished at the swift numbness that smote them. It certainly was cold. He pulled on the mitten hastily, and beat the hand savagely across his chest.

14   At twelve o'clock the day was at its brightest. Yet the sun was too far south on its winter journey to clear the horizon. The bulge of the

earth intervened between it and Henderson Creek, where the man walked under a clear sky at noon and cast no shadow. At half-past twelve, to the minute, he arrived at the forks of the creek. He was pleased at the speed he had made. If he kept it up, he would certainly be with the boys by six. He unbuttoned his jacket and shirt and drew forth his lunch. The action consumed no more than a quarter of a minute, yet in that brief moment the numbness laid hold of the exposed fingers. He did not put the mitten on, but, instead, struck the fingers a dozen sharp smashes against his leg. Then he sat down on a snow-covered log to eat. The sting that followed upon the striking of his fingers against his leg ceased so quickly that he was startled. He had had no chance to take a bite of biscuit. He struck the fingers repeatedly and returned them to the mitten, baring the other hand for the purpose of eating. He tried to take a mouthful, but the ice muzzle prevented. He had forgotten to build a fire and thaw out. He chuckled at his foolishness, and as he chuckled he noted the numbness creeping into the exposed fingers. Also he noted that the stinging which had first come to his toes when he sat down was already passing away. He wondered whether the toes were warm or numb. He moved them inside the moccasins and decided that they were numb.

15   He pulled the mitten on hurriedly and stood up. He was a bit frightened. He stamped up and down until the stinging returned into the feet. It certainly was cold, was his thought. That man from Sulphur Creek had spoken the truth when telling how cold it sometimes got in the country. And he had laughed at him at the time! That showed one must not be too sure of things.

16   There was no mistake about it, it *was* cold. He strode up and down, stamping his feet and threshing his arms, until reassured by the returning warmth. Then he got out matches and proceeded to make a fire. From the undergrowth, where high water of the previous spring had lodged a supply of seasoned twigs, he got his firewood. Working carefully from a small beginning, he soon had a roaring fire, over which he thawed the ice from his face and in the protection of which he ate his biscuits. For the moment the cold of space was outwitted. The dog took satisfaction in the fire, stretching out close enough for warmth and far enough away to escape being singed.

17   When the man had finished, he filled his pipe and took his comfortable time over a smoke. Then he pulled on his mittens, settled the ear flaps of his cap firmly about his ears, and took the creek trail up the left fork. The dog was disappointed and yearned back toward the fire. The man did not know cold. Possibly all the generations of his ancestry had been ignorant of cold, of real cold, of cold one hundred and seven

degrees below freezing point. But the dog knew; all its ancestry knew, and it had inherited the knowledge. And it knew that it was not good to walk abroad in such fearful cold. It was the time to lie snug in a hole in the snow and wait for a curtain of cloud to be drawn across the face of outer space whence this cold came. On the other hand, there was no keen intimacy between the dog and the man. The one was the toil-slave of the other, and the only caresses it had ever received were the caresses of the whiplash and of harsh and menacing throat sounds that threatened the whiplash. So the dog made no effort to communicate its apprehension to the man. It was not concerned in the welfare of the man; it was for its own sake that it yearned back toward the fire. But the man whistled, and spoke to it with the sound of whiplashes, and the dog swung in at the man's heels and followed after.

18   The man took a chew of tobacco and proceeded to start a new amber beard. Also, his moist breath quickly powdered with white his mustache, eyebrows, and lashes. There did not seem to be so many springs on the left fork of the Henderson, and for half an hour the man saw no signs of any. And then it happened. At a place where there were no signs, where the soft, unbroken snow seemed to advertise solidity beneath, the man broke through. It was not deep. He wet himself halfway to the knees before he floundered out to the firm crust.

19   He was angry, and cursed his luck aloud. He had hoped to get into camp with the boys at six o'clock, and this would delay him an hour, for he would have to build a fire and dry out his footgear. This was impera-tive at that low temperature—he knew that much; and he turned aside to the bank, which he climbed. On top, tangled in the underbrush about the trunks of several small spruce trees, was a high-water deposit of dry firewood—sticks and twigs, principally, but also larger portions of sea-soned branches and fine, dry, last year's grasses. He threw down several large pieces on top of the snow. This served for a foundation and pre-vented the young flame from drowning itself in the snow it otherwise would melt. The flame he got by touching a match to a small shred of birchbark that he took from his pocket. This burned even more readily than paper. Placing it on the foundation, he fed the young flame with wisps of dry grass and with the tiniest of dry twigs.

20   He worked slowly and carefully, keenly aware of his danger. Gradu-ally, as the flame grew stronger, he increased the size of the twigs with which he fed it. He squatted in the snow, pulling the twigs out from their entanglement in the brush and feeding them directly to the flame. He knew there must be no failure. When it is seventy-five below zero, a man must not fail in his first attempt to build a fire—that is, if his feet are wet. If his feet are dry, and he fails, he can run along the trail for half

a mile and restore his circulation. But the circulation of wet and freezing feet cannot be restored by running when it is seventy-five below. No matter how fast he runs, the wet feet will freeze the harder.

21   All this the man knew. The old-timer on Sulphur Creek had told him about it the previous fall, and now he was appreciating the advice. Already all sensation had gone out of his feet. To build a fire, he had been forced to remove his mittens, and the fingers had quickly gone numb. His pace of four miles an hour had kept his heart pumping blood to the surface of his body and to all the extremities. But the instant he stopped, the action of the pump eased down. The cold of space smote the unprotected tip of the planet, and he, being on that unprotected tip, received the full force of the blow. The blood of his body recoiled before it. The blood was alive, like the dog, and like the dog it wanted to hide away and cover itself up from the fearful cold. So long as he walked four miles an hour, he pumped that blood, willy-nilly, to the surface; but now it ebbed away and sank down into the recesses of his body. The extremities were the first to feel its absence. His wet feet froze the faster, and his exposed fingers numbed the faster, though they had not yet begun to freeze. Nose and cheeks were already freezing, while the skin of all his body chilled as it lost its blood.

22   But he was safe. Toes and nose and cheeks would be only touched by the frost, for the fire was beginning to burn with strength. He was feeding it with twigs the size of his finger. In another minute he would be able to feed it with branches the size of his wrist, and then he could remove his wet footgear, and, while it dried, he could keep his naked feet warm by the fire, rubbing them at first, of course, with snow. The fire was a success. He was safe. He remembered the advice of the old-timer on Sulphur Creek, and smiled. The old-timer had been very serious in laying down the law that no man must travel alone in the Klondike after fifty below. Well, here he was; he had had the accident; he was alone; and he had saved himself. Those old-timers were rather womanish, some of them, he thought. All a man had to do was to keep his head, and he was all right. Any man who was a man could travel alone. But it was surprising the rapidity with which his cheeks and nose were freezing. And he had not thought his fingers could go lifeless in so short a time. Lifeless they were, for he could scarcely make them move together to grip a twig, and they seemed remote from his body and from him. When he touched a twig he had to look and see whether or not he had bold of it. The wires were pretty well down between him and his finger ends.

23   All of which counted for little. There was the fire, snapping and crackling and promising life with every dancing flame. He started to untie his moccasins. They were coated with ice; the thick German socks were like sheaths of iron halfway to the knees; and the moccasin

strings were like rods of steel all twisted and knotted as by some con-
flagration. For a moment he tugged with his numb fingers, then, realizing the folly of it, he drew his sheath knife.

24   But before he could cut the strings, it happened. It was his own
fault, or, rather, his mistake. He should not have built the fire under the
spruce tree. He should have built it in the open. But it had been easier to
pull the twigs from the brush and drop them directly on the fire. Now
the tree under which he had done this carried a weight of snow on its
boughs. No wind had blown for weeks, and each bough was fully
freighted. Each time he had pulled a twig he had communicated a slight
agitation to the tree—an imperceptible agitation, so far as he was concerned, but an agitation sufficient to bring about the disaster. High up
in the tree one bough capsized its load of snow. This fell on the boughs
beneath, capsizing them. This process continued, spreading out and
involving the whole tree. It grew like an avalanche, and it descended
without warning upon the man and the fire, and the fire was blotted
out! Where it had burned was a mantle of fresh and disordered snow.

25   The man was shocked. It was as though he had just heard his own
sentence of death. For a moment he sat and stared at the spot where the
fire had been. Then he grew very calm. Perhaps the old-timer on Sulphur Creek was right. If he had only had a trail mate he would have
been in no danger now. The trail mate could have built the fire. Well, it
was up to him to build the fire over again, and this second time there
must be no failure. Even if he succeeded, he would most likely lose
some toes. His feet must be badly frozen by now, and there would be
some time before the second fire was ready.

26   Such were his thoughts, but he did not sit and think them. He was
busy all the time they were passing through his mind. He made a new
foundation for a fire, this time in the open, where no treacherous tree
could blot it out. Next he gathered dry grasses and tiny twigs from the
high-water flotsam. He could not bring his fingers together to pull
them out, but he was able to gather them by the handful. In this way he
got many rotten twigs and bits of green moss that were undesirable,
but it was the best he could do. He worked methodically, even collecting an armful of the larger branches to be used later when the fire gathered strength. And all the while the dog sat and watched him, a certain
yearning wistfulness in its eyes, for it looked upon him as the fire-
provider, and the fire was slow in coming.

27   When all was ready, the man reached in his pocket for a second
piece of birchbark. He knew the bark was there, and, though he could
not feel it with his fingers, he could hear its crisp rustling as he fumbled for it. Try as he would, he could not clutch hold of it. And all the
time, in his consciousness, was the knowledge that each instant his

feet were freezing. This thought tended to put him in a panic, but he
fought against it and kept calm. He pulled on his mittens with his
teeth, and threshed his arms back and forth, beating his hands with all
his might against his sides. He did this sitting down, and he stood up to
do it; and all the while the dog sat in the snow, its wolf brush of a tail
curled around warmly over its forefeet, its sharp wolf ears pricked forward intently as it watched the man. And the man, as he beat and
threshed his arms and hands, felt a great surge of envy as he regarded
the creature that was warm and secure in its natural covering.

28   After a while he was aware of the first faraway signals of sensation
in his beaten fingers. The faint tingling grew stronger till it evolved
into a stinging ache that was excruciating, but which the man hailed
with satisfaction. He stripped the mitten from his right hand and
fetched forth the birchbark. The exposed fingers were quickly going
numb again. Next he brought out his bunch of sulphur matches. But
the tremendous cold had already driven the life out of his fingers. In his
effort to separate one match from the others, the whole bunch fell in
the snow. He tried to pick it up out of the snow, but failed. The dead
fingers could neither touch nor clutch. He was very careful. He drove
the thought of his freezing feet, and nose, and cheeks, out of his mind,
devoting his whole soul to the matches. He watched, using the sense of
vision in place of that of touch, and when he saw his fingers on each
side the bunch, he closed them—that is, he willed to close them, for
the wires were down, and the fingers did not obey. He pulled the mitten on the right hand, and beat it fiercely against his knee. Then, with
both mittened hands, he scooped the bunch of matches, along with
much snow, into his lap. Yet he was no better off.

29   After some manipulation he managed to get the bunch between
the heels of his mittened hands. In this fashion he carried it to his
mouth. The ice crackled and snapped when by a violent effort he
opened his mouth. He drew the lower jaw in, curled the upper lip out of
the way, and scraped the bunch with his upper teeth in order to separate a match. He succeeded in getting one, which he dropped on his lap.
He was no better off. He could not pick it up. Then he devised a way.
He picked it up in his teeth and scratched it on his leg. Twenty times
he scratched before he succeeded in lighting it. As it flamed he held it
with his teeth to the birchbark. But the burning brimstone went up his
nostrils and into his lungs, causing him to cough spasmodically. The
match fell into the snow and went out.

30   The old-timer on Sulphur Creek was right, he thought in the
moment of controlled despair that ensued: after fifty below, a man
should travel with a partner. He beat his hands, but failed in exciting
any sensation. Suddenly he bared both hands, removing the mittens

with his teeth. He caught the whole bunch between the heels of his hands. His arm muscles, not being frozen, enabled him to press the hand heels tightly against the matches. Then he scratched the bunch along his leg. It flared into flame, seventy sulphur matches at once! There was no wind to blow them out. He kept his head to one side to escape the strangling fumes, and held the blazing bunch to the birch-bark. As he so held it, he became aware of sensation in his hands. His flesh was burning. He could smell it. Deep down below the surface he could feel it. The sensation developed into pain that grew acute. And still he endured it, holding the flame of the matches clumsily to the bark that would not light readily because his own burning hands were in the way, absorbing most of the flame.

31   At last when he could endure no more, he jerked his hands apart. The blazing matches fell sizzling into the snow, but the birchbark was alight. He began laying dry grasses and the tiniest twigs on the flame. He could not pick and choose, for he had to lift the fuel between the heels of his hands. Small pieces of rotten wood and green moss clung to the twigs, and he bit them off as well as he could with his teeth. He cherished the flame carefully and awkwardly. It meant life, and it must not perish. The withdrawal of blood from the surface of his body now made him shiver, and he grew more awkward. A large piece of green moss fell squarely on the little fire. He tried to poke it out with his fin-gers, but his shivering frame made him poke too far, and he disrupted the nucleus of the little fire, the burning grasses and tiny twigs separat-ing and scattering. He tried to poke them together again, but, in spite of the tenseness of the effort, his shivering got away with him, and the twigs were hopelessly scattered. Each twig gushed a puff of smoke and went out. The fire-provider had failed. As he looked apathetically about him, his eyes chanced on the dog, sitting across the ruins of the fire from him, in the snow, making restless, hunching movements, slightly lifting one forefoot and then the other, shifting its weight back and forth on them with wistful eagerness.

32   The sight of the dog put a wild idea into his head. He remembered the tale of the man, caught in a blizzard, who killed a steer and crawled inside the carcass, and so was saved. He would kill the dog and bury his hands in the warm body until the numbness went out of them. Then he could build another fire. He spoke to the dog, calling it to him; but in his voice was a strange note of fear that frightened the animal, who had never known the man to speak in such way before. Something was the matter, and its suspicious nature sensed danger—it knew not what danger, but somewhere, somehow, in its brain arose an apprehension of the man. It flattened its ears down at the sound of the man's voice, and its restless, hunching movements, and the liftings and shiftings of its

forefeet became more pronounced; but it would not come to the man. He got on his hands and knees and crawled toward the dog. This unusual posture again excited suspicion, and the animal sidled mincingly away.

33   The man sat up in the snow for a moment and struggled for calmness. Then he pulled on his mittens, by means of his teeth, and got upon his feet. He glanced down at first in order to assure himself that he was really standing up, for the absence of sensation in his feet left him unrelated to the earth. His erect position in itself started to drive the webs of suspicion from the dog's mind; and when he spoke peremptorily with the sound of whiplashes in his voice, the dog rendered its customary allegiance and came to him. As it came within reaching distance, the man lost control. His arms flashed out to the dog, and he experienced genuine surprise when he discovered that his hands could not clutch, that there was neither bend nor feeling in the fingers. He had forgotten for the moment that they were frozen and that they were freezing more and more. All this happened quickly, and before the animal could get away, he encircled its body with his arms. He sat down in the snow, and in this fashion held the dog, while it snarled and whined and struggled.

34   But it was all he could do, hold its body encircled in his arms and sit there. He realized that he could not kill the dog. There was no way to do it. With his helpless hands he could neither draw nor hold his sheath knife nor throttle the animal. He released it, and it plunged wildly away, with tail between its legs, and still snarling. It halted forty feet away and surveyed him curiously, with ears sharply pricked forward. The man looked down at his hands in order to locate them, and found them hanging on the ends of his arms. It struck him as curious that one should have to use his eyes in order to find out where his hands were. He began threshing his arms back and forth, beating the mittened hands against his sides. He did this for five minutes, violently, and his heart pumped enough blood up to the surface to put a stop to his shivering. But no sensation was aroused in the hands. He had an impression that they hung like weights on the ends of his arms, but when he tried to run the impression down, he could not find it.

35   A certain fear of death, dull and oppressive, came to him. This fear quickly became poignant as he realized that it was no longer a mere matter of freezing his fingers and toes, or of losing his hands and feet, but that it was a matter of life and death, with the chances against him. This threw him into a panic, and he turned and ran up the creek bed along the old dim trail. The dog joined in behind and kept up with him. He ran blindly, without intention, in fear such as he had never known in his life. Slowly, as he plowed and floundered through the snow, he

began to see things again,—the banks of the creek, the old timber jams, the leafless aspens, and the sky. The running made him feel better. He did not shiver. Maybe, if he ran on, his feet would thaw out; and, anyway, if he ran far enough he would reach the camp and the boys. Without doubt he would lose some fingers and toes and some of his face; but the boys would take care of him, and save the rest of him when he got there. And at the same time there was another thought in his mind that said he would never get to the camp and the boys; that it was too many miles away, that the freezing had too great a start on him, and that he would soon be stiff and dead. This thought he kept in the background and refused to consider. Sometimes it pushed itself forward and demanded to be heard, and he thrust it back and strove to think of other things.

36   It struck him as curious that he could run at all on feet so frozen that he could not feel them when they struck the earth and took the weight of his body. He seemed to himself to skim along above the surface, and to have no connection with the earth. Somewhere he had once seen a winged Mercury, and he wondered if Mercury felt as he felt when skimming over the earth.

37   His theory of running until he reached camp and the boys had one flaw in it: he lacked the endurance. Several times he stumbled, and finally he tottered, crumpled up, and fell. When he tried to rise, he failed. He must sit and rest, he decided, and next time he would merely walk and keep on going. As he sat and regained his breath, he noted that he was feeling quite warm and comfortable. He was not shivering, and it even seemed that a warm glow had come to his chest and trunk. And yet, when he touched his nose or cheeks, there was no sensation. Running would not thaw them out. Nor would it thaw out his hands and feet.

38   Then the thought came to him that the frozen portions of his body must be extending. He tried to keep this thought down, to forget it, to think of something else; he was aware of the panicky feeling that it caused, and he was afraid of the panic. But the thought asserted itself, and persisted, until it produced a vision of his body totally frozen. This was too much, and he made another wild run along the trail. Once he slowed down to a walk, but the thought of the freezing extending itself made him run again.

39   And all the time the dog ran with him, at his heels. When he fell down a second time, it curled its tail over its forefeet and sat in front of him, facing him, curiously eager and intent. The warmth and security of the animal angered him, and he cursed it till it flattened down its ears appeasingly. This time the shivering came more quickly upon the man. He was losing in his battle with the frost. It was creeping into his

body from all sides. The thought of it drove him on, but he ran no more than a hundred feet, when he staggered and pitched headlong. It was his last panic. When he had recovered his breath and control, he sat up and entertained in his mind the conception of meeting death with dignity. However, the conception did not come to him in such terms. His idea of it was that he had been making a fool of himself, running around like a chicken with its head cut off—such was the simile that occurred to him. Well, he was bound to freeze anyway, and he might as well take it decently. With this new-found peace of mind came the first glimmerings of drowsiness. A good idea, he thought, to sleep off to death. It was like taking an anesthetic. Freezing was not so bad as people thought. There were lots worse ways to die.

40   He pictured the boys finding his body next day. Suddenly he found himself with them, coming along the trail and looking for himself. And, still with them, he came around a turn in the trail and found himself lying in the snow. He did not belong with himself any more, for even then he was out of himself, standing with the boys and looking at himself in the snow. It certainly was cold, was his thought. When he got back to the States, he could tell the folks what real cold was. He drifted on from this to a vision of the old-timer on Sulphur Creek. He could see him quite clearly, warm and comfortable, and smoking a pipe.

41   "You were right, old hoss; you were right," the man mumbled to the old-timer of Sulphur Creek.

42   Then the man drowsed off into what seemed to him the most comfortable and satisfying sleep he had ever known. The dog sat facing him and waiting. The brief day drew to a close in a long, slow twilight. There were no signs of a fire to be made, and, besides, never in the dog's experience had it known a man to sit like that in the snow and make no fire. As the twilight drew on, its eager yearning for the fire mastered it, and with a great lifting and shifting of forefeet, it whined softly, then flattened its ears down in anticipation of being chidden by the man. But the man remained silent. Later, the dog whined loudly. And still later it crept close to the man and caught the scent of death. This made the animal bristle and back away. A little longer it delayed, howling under the stars that leaped and danced and shone brightly in the cold sky. Then it turned and trotted up the trail in the direction of the camp it knew, where were other food-providers and fire-providers.

To Build a Fire

JOURNAL

1. **MLA Works Cited**   *Using this model, record this story here.*

   Author's Last Name, First Name. "Title of the Story." <u>Title of the Book</u>.
   3rd ed. Ed. First Name Last Name. City: Publisher, year. Pages of
   the story.

2. **Main Character(s)**   *Describe each main character, and explain why you think each is a main character.*

3. **Supporting Characters**   *Describe each supporting character, and explain why you think each is a supporting character.*

4. **Setting**   *Describe the setting(s) and any relevant prop(s).*

5. Sequence *Outline the events of the story in order.*

6. Plot *Tell the story in no more than three sentences.*

7. Conflicts *Identify and explain all the conflicts involved here.*

8. Significant Quotations *Explain the importance of each of these quotations. Record the page number in the parentheses.*

  a. "Fifty degrees below zero was to him just precisely fifty degrees below zero. That there should be anything more to it than that was a thought that never entered his head" (   ).

  b. "Its instinct told it a truer tale than was told to the man by the man's judgment" (   ).

c. "At a place where there were no signs, where the soft, unbroken snow seemed to advertise solidity beneath, the man broke through" (   ).

d. "Each time he had pulled a twig he had communicated a slight agitation to the tree—an imperceptible agitation, so far as he was concerned, but an agitation sufficient to bring about the disaster" (   ).

e. "And still later it crept close to the man and caught the scent of death" (   ).

9. **Literary Elements**   *Look at this chapter's title and explain why you think this story is placed in this chapter. Explain in which other chapter(s) you might place this story, as relevant to the literary element(s) of that chapter.*

10. **Foreshadowing, Irony, and or Symbolism**   *Explain examples of foreshadowing, irony, and/or symbolism in this story.*

FOLLOW-UP QUESTIONS

10 SHORT QUESTIONS

Select the <u>best</u> answer for each.

____ 1. The story is set in
   a. eastern North America.
   b. northern North America.
   c. Africa.

____ 2. The man stays
   a. in the fields.
   b. away from the water.
   c. close to the water.

____ 3. The man is looking for
   a. logging routes.
   b. the creek.
   c. the path.

____ 4. The dog is
   a. happy to be out in this weather.
   b. unhappy to be out in this weather.
   c. unconcerned about being out in this weather.

____ 5. The dog is
   a. happy to leave the fire.
   b. unhappy to leave the fire.
   c. unconcerned about leaving the fire.

____ 6. The one who knows that it is too cold to be out in this weather is
   a. the dog.
   b. the man.
   c. the other campers.

____ 7. The man does
   a. not meet the old-timer.
   b. listen well to the old-timer.
   c. not listen well to the old-timer.

____ 8. The man builds the second fire
   a. too close to the spruce tree.
   b. far away from the spruce tree.
   c. too close to the creek.

____ 9. The man
   a. tries to help the dog.
   b. leaves the dog alone.
   c. wants to kill the dog.

____ 10. The one who probably makes it back to camp is
   a. the man.
   b. the dog.
   c. the old-timer.

5 SIGNIFICANT QUOTATIONS

Explain the importance of each of these quotations.

1. "It [fifty degrees below zero] did not lead him to meditate upon his frailty as a creature of temperature, and upon man's frailty in general [. . .]."

2. "The animal was depressed by the tremendous cold. It knew that it was no time for traveling."

3. "And then it happened. [. . .]. He wet himself halfway to the knees before he floundered out to the firm crust."

4. "But before he could cut the strings, it happened. [. . .]. He should not have built the fire under the spruce tree."

5. "Then it turned and trotted up the trail in the direction of the camp it knew [. . .]."

2 Comprehension Essay Questions

Use specific details and information from the story to answer these questions as completely as possible.

1. How does the title relate to the story? Explain the significance of the title using specific details and information from the story.

2. London seems to respect the dog's natural knowledge more than the learned knowledge of the man. How does he present this? Use specific details and information from the story.

Discussion Questions

Be prepared to discuss these questions in class.

1. How does the illustration demonstrate this story? Use specific details from the story to support your ideas.

2. Are you more sympathetic with the man or with the dog? Explain your feelings.

Writing

Use each of these ideas for writing an essay.

1. Write a narrative essay about a place in nature that has outwitted you or someone you know.

2. Write a narrative essay about a time that a pet or another animal has been wiser than you.

Further Writing

1. Read the Tao Te Ching (available in a library) to learn about the Eastern view of harmony with nature. London's sense of harmony with nature is quite Eastern. Compare what you learned in this story with what you learn from the Tao.

2. Like London, Ray Bradbury questions the assumed intelligence of man's knowledge. Compare human intelligence in this story with that in Bradbury's "There Will Come Soft Rains" (page 93).

Notes

CHAPTER 3

Plot and Foreshadowing

A story is based around a simple skeleton of events called a **plot**. Around this basic plot, a logical order of events or **sequence** occurs that builds tension or, in mysteries, suspense. In stories we call all the events in the sequence a **story line**.

Have you ever gone to the movies and watched the end credits roll while you were still waiting for the movie to get going? You looked at the person sitting next to you, felt cheated, and asked "What happened?" What happened is that somewhere along the line, the storyteller failed.

In a well-written story, one event logically leads to another event, and then to another, and so on, so that each word and action counts and builds tension that carries your interest. The tension peaks at the **climax** and then resolves in the **dénouement**. When any of these pieces is missing, poorly developed, or unbelievable, we are disappointed. (Movie sequels, in fact, purposely stop at the climax and before the dénouement so that we will return for the next episode.)

Each story in this chapter depends on the flow of events in the story. Nathalie sets out to control the events in "The Kiss" while the narrator seems overwhelmed by the events in "Salvation." Foreshadowing plays a key role in "Wine on the Desert." Then, human decisions shape the events in both "The Last Leaf" and "The Lady or the Tiger?"

Foreshadowing is a technique some authors use to help explain or predict events to come. The author may sprinkle information or hints throughout the story to help predict actions that are yet to happen. Edgar Allan Poe is a master at foreshadowing. In his stories, there are hints along the way, although readers almost always miss the clues on the first reading and are astonished at the endings. After reading the stories in this chapter, look back and notice that each story has hints along the way that help predict each unsettling ending.

The Kiss

Kate Chopin

Pre-reading Vocabulary
Context

Use context clues to define these words before reading. Use a dictionary as needed.

1. Little Allison gave her brother, Jacob, a *kiss* on his cheek to thank him for giving her a new Barbie doll. *Kiss* means _____.

2. When the sun went down, Michelle lit many candles that threw dark but interesting *shadows* on the walls. *Shadow* means
   _____.

3. George found it very hard to read his reports in poor lighting, because nothing was clear in the dark *obscurity*. *Obscurity* means
   _____.

4. Robert and Krystil are *ardent* readers and go to Borders, Barnes and Noble, or the library every chance they get. *Ardent*
   means _____.

5. Laura and Dave are constant *companions*, going everywhere together and doing everything together. *Companion* means
   _____.

6. Jose is very open and honest and is quite *guileless*, so he does not understand when people try to plan and scheme. *Guileless* means
   _____.

7. John is *enormously* talented and can draw anything to look lifelike, from animals to people to scenery. *Enormous* means
   _____.

8. To entertain guests, Teddy planned a lovely *reception* at a country club overlooking a golf course. *Reception* means

_____.

9. Alice and Tom still enjoy *lingering* memories of their trip to Hawaii every time they look back over the trip's pictures. *Lingering* means

_____.

10. Missy had some *confusion* over which room to go to for specific courses, so she got out her course schedule. *Confusion* means

_____.

11. When the professor called on her, Clarice was so surprised she stuttered and *stammered* and did not know what to say. *Stammer* means _____.

12. Renée found the movie very *comical* and still laughs whenever she thinks about it. *Comical* means _____.

13. Losing someone or something you are close to can bring real and sorrowful *misery*. *Misery* means _____.

14. Lisa called Aley back instead of Ali, because the phone message was not clear and she *misinterpreted* the name. *Misinterpret* means

_____.

15. Dressed in turquoise silk with aquamarines for jewels, Margaret looked *radiant* at her daughter's wedding. *Radiant* means _____.

16. Dodee and Rich felt *triumphant* when they won the bid on the new house they wanted to buy so badly. *Triumphant* means

_____.

17. Ashley and Caitlin *blush* with rosy red cheeks whenever they run around and get warm. *Blush* means _____.

18. Mark was so *insolent* and nasty to his mother that I would have grounded him for a month. *Insolent* means _____.

19. Playing chess, Carrie and Reid are able to plan and control every move and are accomplished *chess players*. *Chess players* means

_____.

20. Bob, Geri, and Anthony always thank people for helping them and are never *ungrateful* to anyone. *Ungrateful* means

_____.

PRE-READING VOCABULARY STRUCTURAL ATTACK

Define these words by solving the parts. Use the Glossary or a dictionary as needed.

1. uncertain
2. overtaken
3. newcomer
4. angrily
5. self-justification
6. unavoidable
7. uncomfortable
8. misinterpreted
9. unreasonable

PRE-READING QUESTIONS

Try answering these questions as you read.

What does Mr. Harvy do?

What does Miss Nathalie do?

What does Mr. Brantain do?

The Kiss

Kate Chopin

Kate O'Flaherty Chopin was born in St. Louis, Missouri in 1851 to an affluent family. Although her father died when she was young, her widowed mother gave young Kate a taste of female independence. In 1870 Kate married Oscar Chopin and moved to New Orleans and then Natchitoches Parish. Here she met the Creoles, Acadians, and African Americans she would later write about. However, Oscar died in 1882, and by 1884 she sold the plantation, gathered her five children, and returned home to St. Louis where she began to write for popular women's magazines. Influenced noticeably by Guy de Maupassant's sense of irony and Henrik Ibsen's social comment, Chopin wrote stories, often touched with rich symbols and images of nature, that question societal assumptions and dictates. The Awakening remains her masterwork, although stories such as "Desiree's Baby" and "The Kiss" offer Chopin at her most terse. Chopin died in 1904.

It was still quite light out of doors, but inside with the curtains drawn and the smouldering fire sending out a dim, uncertain glow, the room was full of deep shadows.

2   Brantain sat in one of these shadows; it had overtaken him and he did not mind. The obscurity lent him courage to keep his eyes fastened as ardently as he looked upon the girl who sat in the firelight.

3   She was very handsome, with a certain fine, rich coloring that belongs to the healthy brune type. She was quite composed, as she idly stroked the satiny coat of the cat that lay curled in her lap, and she occasionally sent a slow glance into the shadow where her companion sat. They were talking low, of indifferent things which plainly were not the things that occupied their thoughts. She knew that he loved her—a frank, blustering fellow without guile enough to conceal his

feelings, and no desire to do so. For two weeks past he had sought her society eagerly and persistently. She was confidently waiting for him to declare himself and she meant to accept him. The rather insignificant and unattractive Brantain was enormously rich; and she liked and required the entourage which wealth could give her.

4   During one of the pauses between their talk of the last tea and the next reception the door opened and a young man entered whom Brantain knew quite well. The girl turned her face toward him. A stride or two brought him to her side, and bending over her chair—before she could suspect his intention, for she did not realize that he had not seen her visitor—he pressed an ardent, lingering kiss upon her lips.

5   Brantain slowly arose; so did the girl arise, but quickly, and the newcomer stood between them, a little amusement and some defiance struggling with the confusion in his face.

6   "I believe," stammered Brantain, "I see that I have stayed too long. I—I had no idea—that is, I must wish you good-by." He was clutching his hat with both hands, and probably did not perceive that she was extending her hand to him, her presence of mind had not completely deserted her; but she could not have trusted herself to speak.

7   "Hang me if I saw him sitting there, Nattie! I know it's deuced awkward for you. But I hope you'll forgive me this once—this very first break. Why, what's the matter?"

8   "Don't touch me; don't come near me," she returned angrily. "What do you mean by entering the house without ringing?"

9   "I came in with your brother, as I often do," he answered coldly, in self-justification. "We came in the side way. He went upstairs and I came in here hoping to find you. The explanation is simple enough and ought to satisfy you that the misadventure was unavoidable. But do say that you forgive me, Nathalie," he entreated, softening.

10   "Forgive you! You don't know what you are talking about. Let me pass. It depends upon—a good deal whether I forgive you."

11   At that next reception which she and Brantain had been talking about she approached the young man with a delicious frankness of manner when she saw him there.

12   "Will you let me speak to you a moment or two, Mr. Brantain?" she asked with an engaging but perturbed smile. He seemed extremely unhappy; but when she took his arm and walked away with him, seeking a retired corner, a ray of hope mingled with the almost comical misery of his expression. She was apparently very outspoken.

13   "Perhaps I should not have sought this interview, Mr. Brantain; but—but, oh, I have been very uncomfortable, almost miserable since that little encounter the other afternoon. When I thought how you might have misinterpreted it, and believed things"—hope was plainly

gaining the ascendancy over misery in Brantain's round, guileless face—"of course, I know it is nothing to you, but for my own sake I do want you to understand that Mr. Harvy is an intimate friend of long standing. Why, we have always been like cousins—like brother and sister, I may say. He is my brother's most intimate associate and often fancies that he is entitled to the same privileges as the family. Oh, I know it is absurd, uncalled for, to tell you this; undignified even," she was almost weeping, "but it makes so much difference to me what you think of—me." Her voice had grown very low and agitated. The misery had all disappeared from Brantain's face.

14   "Then you do really care what I think, Miss Nathalie? May I call you Miss Nathalie?" They turned into a long, dim corridor that was lined on either side with tall, graceful plants. They walked slowly to the very end of it. When they turned to retrace their steps Brantain's face was radiant and hers was triumphant.

15   Harvy was among the guests at the wedding; and he sought her out in a rare moment when she stood alone.

16   "Your husband," he said, smiling, "has sent me over to kiss you."

17   A quick blush suffused her face and round polished throat. "I suppose it's natural for a man to feel and act generously on an occasion of this kind. He tells me he doesn't want his marriage to interrupt wholly that pleasant intimacy which has existed between you and me. I don't know what you've been telling him," with an insolent smile, "but he has sent me here to kiss you."

18   She felt like a chess player who, by the clever handling of his pieces, sees the game taking the course intended. Her eyes were bright and tender with a smile as they glanced up into his; and her lips looked hungry for the kiss which they invited.

19   "But, you know," he went on quietly, "I didn't tell him so, it would have seemed ungrateful, but I can tell you. I've stopped kissing women; it's dangerous."

20   Well, she had Brantain and his million left. A person can't have everything in this world; and it was a little unreasonable of her to expect it.

The Kiss

JOURNAL

1. **MLA Works Cited**   *Using this model, record this story here.*

   Author's Last Name, First Name. "Title of the Story." Title of the Book. 3rd ed. Ed. First Name Last Name. City: Publisher, year. Pages of the story.

2. **Main Character(s)**   *Describe each main character, and explain why you think each is a main character.*

3. **Supporting Characters**   *Describe each supporting character, and explain why you think each is a supporting character.*

4. **Setting**   *Describe the setting(s) and any relevant prop(s).*

5. **Sequence**   *Outline the events of the story in order.*

6. **Plot**   *Tell the story in no more than two sentences.*

7. **Conflicts**   *Identify and explain all the conflicts involved here.*

8. **Significant Quotations**   *Explain the importance of each of these quotations. Record the page number in the parentheses.*

  a. "Brantain sat in one of those shadows; it had overtaken him and he did not mind" (   ).

  b. "A stride or two brought him to her side, and bending over her chair—before she could suspect his intention, for she did not realize that he had not seen her visitor—he pressed an ardent, lingering kiss upon her lips" (   ).

  c. " 'Don't touch me; don't come near me,' she returned angrily" (   ).

  d. " 'Why, we have always been like cousins—like brother and sister' " (   ).

  e. "She felt like a chess player who, by the clever handling of his pieces, sees the game taking the course intended" (   ).

9. **Literary Elements**   *Look at this chapter's title and explain why you think this story is placed in this chapter. Explain in which other chapter(s) you might place this story, as relevant to the literary element(s) of that chapter.*

10. **Foreshadowing, Irony, and/or Symbolism**   *Explain examples of foreshadowing, irony, and/or symbolism in this story.*

FOLLOW-UP QUESTIONS

10 SHORT QUESTIONS

Select the <u>best</u> answer for each.

_____ 1. Nathalie
   a. knows Brantain is in the shadows.
   b. does not know Brantain is seated in the shadows.
   c. has not yet met Brantain.

_____ 2. Nathalie
   a. knows Brantain is rich.
   b. has no idea of Brantain's wealth.
   c. does not care about Brantain's wealth.

_____ 3. At that moment, Nathalie
   a. expects Harvy to kiss her.
   b. is happy Harvy kisses her.
   c. is caught off guard by the kiss.

_____ 4. Brantain
   a. is upset by the kiss.
   b. does not see the kiss.
   c. does not care about the kiss.

_____ 5. Harvy
   a. knows Brantain is there.
   b. does not know Brantain is there.
   c. does not care if Brantain is there.

_____ 6. Harvy kissing Nathalie
   a. does not upset Brantain.
   b. probably has never happened before.
   c. probably has happened before.

_____ 7. Brantain
   a. stays.
   b. leaves.
   c. is not there.

_____ 8. Later, Nathalie
   a. says she loves Harvy.
   b. ignores the kiss.
   c. blames the kiss on Harvy.

_____ 9. Ultimately, Brantain
   a. leaves Nathalie.
   b. marries Nathalie.
   c. shoots Harvy.

_____ 10. Ultimately, Nathalie seems
   a. to love Brantain deeply.
   b. to want to marry Harvy desperately.
   c. to have wanted both love and money.

5 SIGNIFICANT QUOTATIONS

Explain the importance of each of these quotations.

1. "The obscurity lent him courage to keep his eyes fastened as ardently as he liked upon the girl who sat in the firelight."

2. "A stride or two brought him to her side; and bending over her chair—before she could suspect his intention, for she did not realize that he had not seen her visitor—he pressed an ardent, lingering kiss upon her lips."

3. " 'Hang me if I saw him sitting there, Nattie! I know it's deuced awkward for you.' "

4. " 'When I thought how you might have misinterpreted it, and believed things—[. . .].' "

5. "Her eyes were bright and tender with a smile as they glanced up into his; and her lips looked hungry for the kiss which they invited."

2 COMPREHENSION ESSAY QUESTIONS

Use specific details and information from the story to answer these questions as completely as possible.

1. How does the title relate to the story? Use specific details and information from the story to substantiate your answer.

2. What roles do the settings play in this story? Use specific details and information from the story to substantiate your answers.

DISCUSSION QUESTIONS

Be prepared to discuss these questions in class.

1. How do you feel about Nathalie? Brantain? Harvy?

2. Who is the protagonist here? The antagonist?

WRITING

Use each of these ideas for writing an essay.

1. There is certainly a good deal of deception and manipulation going on in this story. Think of a time you or someone you know deceived or manipulated someone else. Describe the deception or manipulation and the consequences of that behavior.

2. There is also a good deal of insincerity in this story. Describe a time you or someone you know was fooled by someone else's insincerity.

Further Writing

1. Read "The Story of an Hour" by Kate Chopin (page 261) and compare Nathalie with Louise Mallard and Brantain with Brently Mallard.

2. Read "An Embarrassing Position" by Kate Chopin (available in a library) and compare Nathalie with Eva Artless and Brantain with Willis Parkham.

Salvation

LANGSTON HUGHES

PRE-READING VOCABULARY
CONTEXT

Use context clues to define these words before reading. Use a dictionary as needed.

1. Stealing, telling lies, harming others, and committing murder are all considered very serious *sins*. *Sin* means _____.

2. Nick enjoyed the animated *revival meeting* that included lively music and spirited prayer. *Revival meeting* means _____.

3. After becoming a minister, Brian was often the *preacher* in the church on Sunday morning. *Preacher* means _____.

4. When he feels he needs strength, Roger is often found *praying* to St. Anthony to help him. *Praying* means _____.

5. In the Christian religion, *Jesus* is considered the savior of all humankind. *Jesus* means _____.

6. At the funeral, the children of the person who died were the saddest *mourners*. *Mourner* means _____.

7. Kind and innocent people are often considered *lambs* because *lambs* are gentle and helpless animals. *Lamb* means _____.

8. Many religions believe that the body of a person dies here on Earth, but the *soul* of that person lives on after death. *Soul* means

    _____.

9. Carol worships *God* the almighty Father and Creator every time she goes to church. *God* means _____.

10. When Evelyn walked in the church, she saw the beautiful marble *altar* at the front of the church. *Altar* means _____.

11. Akim went through training and became a *deacon* so that he could help the minister with Sunday services. *Deacon* means

    _____.

12. When everyone left and there was no one else in sight, Letisha realized that she was totally *alone*. *Alone* means _____.

13. When everyone arrived at church, the minister then began the ceremony and addressed the whole *congregation*. *Congregation* means

    _____.

14. When the airplane was late, Barbara and Sarah ended up *waiting* for another plane to arrive. *Waiting* means _____.

15. After Nala lied to her mother, Nala felt terribly *ashamed* and finally told the truth to get rid of her guilt. *Ashamed* means

    _____.

16. Nala realized that telling the truth was much better than *lying*, because *lying* only makes things worse. *Lying* means

    _____.

17. Ethan studied long and hard to become a good *minister* so that he could lead his own church. *Minister* means _____.

18. When the queen entered the room, everyone became *hushed* and there was not a sound in the room. *Hushed* means _____.

19. At the end of the prayer service, the congregation all said "*Amen*," signifying they all agreed. *Amen* means _____.

20. In Christianity, God is the Creator, the Son is the Savior, and the *Holy Ghost* is the Spirit. *Holy Ghost* means _____.

PRE-READING VOCABULARY
STRUCTURAL ATTACK

Define these words by solving the parts. Use the Glossary or a dictionary as needed.

1. hardened
2. sinner
3. rhythmical
4. jet-black
5. work-gnarled
6. proudly
7. rejoicing
8. grinning
9. joyous
10. lied
11. deceived
12. rejoicing

PRE-READING QUESTIONS

Try answering these questions as you read.

Who is the narrator?

Who is Westley?

Where are they?

What are they supposed to do?

Salvation

LANGSTON HUGHES

Langston Hughes was born in Joplin, Missouri in 1902. After his parents' separation, he spent his early childhood with his grandmother in Lawrence, Kansas. His grandmother gave him a positive outlook on his African American heritage and on life through her stories filled with characters who triumphed over life's problems with zeal and determination. At twelve, he moved back with his mother and lived in Lincoln, Illinois. Later, he served as a crewman on freighters and traveled to Africa, Holland, and Paris. He returned to Washington, D. C. and then moved to New York City. Sharing the same patron with Zora Neale Hurston, he attended Columbia University and eventually became a central figure in the Harlem Renaissance. He died in 1967.

Hughes enjoyed a fruitful writing career. His writings reflect the rhythms of Harlem and the positive attitudes of his grandmother. His poems and short stories are available in many collections.

I was saved from sin when I was going on thirteen. But not really saved. It happened like this. There was a big revival at my Auntie Reed's church. Every night for weeks there had been much preaching, singing, praying, and shouting, some very hardened sinners had been brought to Christ, and the membership of the church had grown by leaps and bounds. Then just before the revival ended, they held a special meeting for children, "to bring the young lambs to the fold." My aunt spoke of it for days ahead. That night I was escorted to the front row and placed on the mourners' bench with all the other young sinners, who had not yet been brought to Jesus.

2   My aunt told me that when you were saved you saw a light, and something happened to you inside! And Jesus came into your life! And God was with you from then on! She said you could see and hear and feel Jesus in your soul. I believed her. I had heard a great many old people say the same thing and it seemed to me they ought to know. So I sat there calmly in the hot, crowded church, waiting for Jesus to come to me.

3   The preacher preached a wonderful rhythmical sermon, all moans and shouts and lonely cries and dire pictures of hell, and then he sang a song about the ninety and nine safe in the fold, but one little lamb was left out in the cold. Then he said: "Won't you come? Won't you come to Jesus? Young lambs, won't you come?" And he held out his arms to all us young sinners there on the mourners' bench. And the little girls cried. And some of them jumped up and went to Jesus right away. But most of us just sat there.

4   A great many old people came and knelt around us and prayed, old women with jet-black faces and braided hair, old men with work-gnarled hands. And the church sang a song about the lower lights are burning, some poor sinners to be saved. And the whole building rocked with prayer and song.

5   Still I kept waiting to *see* Jesus.

6   Finally all the young people had gone to the altar and were saved, but one boy and me. He was a rounder's son named Westley. Westley and I were surrounded by sisters and deacons praying. It was very hot in the church, and getting late now. Finally Westley said to me in a whisper: "God damn! I'm tired o' sitting here. Let's get up and be saved." So he got up and was saved.

7   Then I was left all alone on the mourners' bench. My aunt came and knelt at my knees and cried, while prayers and songs swirled all around me in the little church. The whole congregation prayed for me alone, in a mighty wail of moans and voices. And I kept waiting serenely for Jesus, waiting, waiting—but he didn't come. I wanted to see him, but nothing happened to me. Nothing! I wanted something to happen to me, but nothing happened.

8   I heard the songs and the minister saying: "Why don't you come? My dear child, why don't you come to Jesus? Jesus is waiting for you. He wants you. Why don't you come? Sister Reed, what is this child's name?"

9   "Langston," my aunt sobbed.

10   "Langston, why don't you come? Why don't you come and be saved? Oh, Lamb of God! Why don't you come?"

11   Now it was really getting late. I began to be ashamed of myself, holding everything up so long. I began to wonder what God thought about Westley, who certainly hadn't seen Jesus either, but who was now sitting proudly on the platform, swinging his knickerbockered legs and grinning down at me, surrounded by deacons and old women on their knees praying. God had not struck Westley dead for taking his name in vain or for lying in the temple. So I decided that maybe to save further trouble, I'd better lie, too, and say that Jesus had come, and get up and be saved.

12   So I got up.

13   Suddenly the whole room broke into a sea of shouting, as they saw me rise. Waves of rejoicing swept the place. Women leaped in the air. My aunt threw her arms around me. The minister took me by the hand and led me to the platform.

14   When things quieted down, in a hushed silence, punctuated by a few ecstatic "Amens," all the new young lambs were blessed in the name of God. Then joyous singing filled the room.

15   That night, for the last time in my life but one—for I was a big boy twelve years old—I cried. I cried, in bed alone, and couldn't stop. I buried my head under the quilts, but my aunt heard me. She woke up and told my uncle I was crying because the Holy Ghost had come into my life, and because I had seen Jesus. But I was really crying because I couldn't bear to tell her that I had lied, that I had deceived everybody in church, that I hadn't seen Jesus, and that now I didn't believe there was a Jesus any more, since he didn't come to help me.

Salvation

Journal

1. MLA Works Cited   *Using this model, record this story here.*

*Author's Last Name, First Name. "Title of the Story." <u>Title of the Book</u>.
3rd ed. Ed. First Name Last Name. City: Publisher, year. Pages of
the story.*

2. Main Character(s)   *Describe each main character, and explain why you think each is a main character.*

3. Supporting Characters   *Describe each supporting character, and explain why you think each is a supporting character.*

4. Setting   *Describe the setting(s) and any relevant prop(s).*

5. Sequence   *Outline the events of the story in order.*

6. Plot   *Tell the story in no more than two sentences.*

7. Conflicts   *Identify and explain all the conflicts involved here.*

8. Significant Quotations   *Explain the importance of each of these quotations. Record the page number in the parentheses.*

a. "There was a big revival meeting at my Auntie Reed's church" (   ).

b. "My aunt told me that when you were saved you saw a light, and something happened to you inside!" (   ).

c. "Then he said: 'Won't you come? Won't you come to Jesus?' " (   ).

d. "Finally all the young people had gone to the altar and were saved [. . .]" (   ).

e. "Waves of rejoicing swept the place" (   ).

9. **Literary Elements**   *Look at this chapter's title and explain why you think this story is placed in this chapter. Explain in which other chapter(s) you might place this story, as relevant to the literary element(s) of that chapter.*

10. **Foreshadowing, Irony, and/or Symbolism**   *Explain examples of foreshadowing, irony, and/or symbolism in this story.*

FOLLOW-UP QUESTIONS

10 SHORT QUESTIONS

Select the <u>best</u> answer for each.

_____ 1. The narrator and the author are probably
   a. different people.
   b. relatives.
   c. the same person.

_____ 2. This occasion is probably
   a. a religious ceremony.
   b. a school graduation.
   c. a birthday party.

_____ 3. The narrator probably lives with
   a. his parents.
   b. Westley.
   c. his aunt.

_____ 4. In this story, sinners need
   a. to stay the same.
   b. to change.
   c. to sing.

_____ 5. narrator feels he needs
   a. to hear God.
   b. to see God.
   c. to feel God.

_____ 6. Compared to the girls, the boys
   a. take longer.
   b. take less time.
   c. take the same amount of time.

_____ 7. "Lambs" refers to
   a. the children to be saved.
   b. the older people.
   c. the minister.

_____ 8. The ceremony is generally
   a. very quiet.
   b. very active.
   c. very reserved.

_____ 9. In the end, Westley
   a. does see God.
   b. does feel God.
   c. lies about seeing God.

_____ 10. In the end, the narrator
   a. does see God.
   b. does feel God.
   c. lies about seeing God.

5 SIGNIFICANT QUOTATIONS

Explain the importance of each of these quotations.

1. "That night I was escorted to the front row and placed on the mourners' bench with all the other young sinners, who had not yet been brought to Jesus."

2. "She said you could see and hear and feel Jesus in your soul. I believed her."

3. "Westley and I were surrounded by sisters and deacons praying."

4. "Suddenly the whole room broke into a sea of shouting, as they saw me rise."

5. "That night, for the last time in my life but one—for I was a big boy twelve years old—I cried."

2 COMPREHENSION ESSAY QUESTIONS

Use specific details and information from the story to answer these questions as completely as possible.

1. How would you describe the narrator's experience? Use specific details and information from the story to support your answer.

2. What significant roles do the setting and the supporting characters play? Use specific details and information from the story to support your answer.

DISCUSSION QUESTIONS

Be prepared to discuss these questions in class.

1. When have you told a lie to get yourself out of a difficult position? How is your experience similar to or different from the narrator's experience?

2. What are the ironies in this story? Use specific details from the story to support your thinking.

WRITING

Use each of these ideas for writing an essay.

1. Discuss a time when you have been expected to do more—or less—than you could do, and discuss the results of that unmet expectation.

2. Discuss a spiritual experience you have had or someone you know has had, and discuss the results of that experience.

Further Writing

1. Research evangelistic religions and the impact of congregations and rituals on their members' conduct and beliefs.

2. Research religious passage rites among either mainstream and/or tribal religions.

Wine on the Desert

MAX BRAND

PRE-READING VOCABULARY CONTEXT

Use context clues to define these words before reading. Use a dictionary as needed.

1. Alice occasionally enjoys a glass of white *wine* made from the grapes grown in Napa Valley. *Wine* means _____.

2. When Angela went to Arizona, all the sand and hot weather reminded her of the desert. *Desert* means _____.

3. When Heather wanted to enforce the law, she became a county *sheriff* to investigate crimes and uphold the law. *Sheriff* means

   _____.

4. Anna joined a *posse* of people to help Sheriff Heather investigate and pursue criminals. *Posse* means _____.

5. Debbie became interested in wines and decided to buy a *vineyard* so that she could grow her own grapes. *Vineyard* means

   _____.

6. Dan bought several large metal *tanks* to hold water for the sprinkling system in his yard. *Tank* means _____.

7. When it did not rain for days and days, Gert had to water her plants during the *drought*. *Drought* means _____.

8. After running the mile and sweating a lot, Joseph was very dry and *thirsty* and just wanted a drink of water. *Thirsty* means

   _____.

9. In order to get a drink of water out of the large open container on the ranch, Anthony used a ladle or *dipper*. *Dipper* means

_____.

10. To go duck hunting, Wilson bought a long *Winchester rifle* that took large bullets and was three feet long. *Winchester rifle* means

_____.

11. In order to learn how to use a gun, Sallie bought a small *Colt revolver* and went to practice at a firing range. *Colt revolver* means

_____.

12. Santi found the water in the tub had *leaked* out through a large hole in the bottom of the tub. *Leak* means _____.

13. When he went camping, Patrick took a small *canteen* filled with water that he carried in his backpack. *Canteen* means

_____.

14. To carry the new gun that she was given by the sheriff, Georgiana bought a *holster* that she belted around her waist. *Holster* means

_____.

15. Jennifer is very afraid of loud thunder and lives in *terror* of a thunderstorm coming when she is alone. *Terror* means

_____.

16. After Zachary was woken up too early, he *staggered* back and forth around the room until he woke up. *Stagger* means

_____.

17. When Mark lost his wallet and could not remember where anything was, he thought he was losing his mind and going *mad*. *Mad* means

_____.

18. When Lucille has lunch, she eats very slowly and is always careful to *swallow* her food slowly. *Swallow* means _____.

19. When Carl ate his dinner too fast, he swallowed too fast and nearly *choked* on a piece of meat. *Choke* means _____.

20. MaryBeth loves the *still* of the night when everything is so quiet and she can hear a single drop of rain. *Still* means _____.

PRE-READING VOCABULARY
STRUCTURAL ATTACK

Define these words by solving the parts. Use a dictionary as needed.

1. dryness
2. windmill
3. accounted
4. darkened
5. unstirred
6. reddish
7. powdered
8. flowering
9. sweetness
10. coolness
11. wooden
12. stiffness
13. sunset
14. loosening
15. fifteen-shot
16. semicircle
17. dogtrot
18. useless
19. heartily
20. uncorked
21. lukewarm
22. horribly
23. thundering

PRE-READING QUESTIONS

Try answering these questions as you read.

Who is Durante?

Who is Tony?

Where are they?

What happens to Tony's father? Tony? Durante?

Wine on the Desert

Max Brand

Max Brand was born Frederick Shiller Faust in Seattle in 1892. He learned his love of reading from his mother and, after his mother died when he was only eight and his father died five years later, Faust lived with different relatives and then attended the University of California at Berkeley. Creativity and self-defeat began to emerge as themes in Faust's life. At Berkeley, he became a literary star but failed to receive his degree due to his own vitriolic radicalism. He wanted to become an esteemed epic poet, but instead he made a fortune as a narrative western, detective story, and screenplay writer. He wanted to join the World War I effort but deserted. He joined the World War II effort as a war correspondent but was killed on the first day of hostilities at Santa Maria Infante.

Faust was a prolific writer, writing an estimated 30 million words under various pennames. His most renowned works are <u>Destry Rides Again</u>, <u>Singing Guns</u>, and the <u>Dr. Kildare</u> series. His other works appear in many collections. His works can be found in libraries and in video stores.

There was no hurry, except for the thirst, like clotted salt, in the back of his throat, and Durante rode on slowly, rather enjoying the last moments of dryness before he reached the cold water in Tony's house. There was really no hurry at all. He had almost twenty-four hours' head start, for they would not find his dead man until this morning. After that, there would be perhaps several hours of delay before the sheriff gathered a sufficient posse and started on his trail. Or perhaps the sheriff would be fool enough to come alone.

2   Durante had been able to see the wheel and fan of Tony's windmill for more than an hour, but he could not make out the ten acres of the vineyard until he had topped the last rise, for the vines had been planted in a hollow. The lowness of the ground, Tony used to say, accounted for the water that gathered in the well during the wet season. The rains sank through the desert sand, through the gravels beneath, and gathered in a bowl of clay hardpan far below. In the middle of the rainless season the well ran dry, but long before that, Tony had every drop of the water pumped up into a score of tanks made of cheap corrugated iron. Slender pipe lines carried the water from the tanks to the vines and from time to time let them sip enough life to keep them until the winter darkened overhead suddenly, one November day, and the rain came down, and all the earth made a great hushing sound as it drank. Durante had heard that whisper of drinking when he was here before, but he never had seen the place in the middle of the long drought.

3   The windmill looked like a sacred emblem to Durante, and the twenty stodgy, tar-painted tanks blessed his eyes; but a heavy sweat broke out at once from his body. For the air of the hollow, unstirred by wind, was hot and still as a bowl of soup—a reddish soup. The vines were powdered with thin red dust also. They were wretched, dying things to look at, for the grapes had been gathered, the new wine had been made, and now the leaves hung in ragged tatters.

4   Durante rode up to the squat adobe house and right through the entrance into the patio. A flowering vine clothed three sides of the little court. Durante did not know the name of the plant, but it had large white blossoms with golden hearts that poured sweetness on the air. Durante hated the sweetness. It made him more thirsty.

5   He threw the reins of his mule and strode into the house. The water cooler stood in the hall outside the kitchen. There were two jars made of a porous stone, very ancient things, and the liquid which distilled through the pores kept the contents cool. The jar on the left held water; that on the right contained wine. There was a big tin dipper hanging on a peg beside each jar. Durante tossed off the cover of the vase on the left and plunged it in until the delicious coolness closed well above his wrist.

6   "Hey, Tony," he called. Out of his dusty throat the cry was a mere groaning. He drank and called again, clearly, "Tony!"

7   A voice pealed from the distance.

8   Durante, pouring down the second dipper of water, smelled the alkali dust which had shaken off his own clothes. It seemed to him that heat was radiating like light from his clothes, from his body, and the cool dimness of the house was soaking it up. He heard the wooden leg of Tony bumping on the ground, and Durante grinned. Then Tony came in with that hitch and side swing with which he accommodated the stiffness of his artificial leg. His brown face shone with sweat as though a special ray of light were focused on it.

9   "Ah, Dick!" he said. "Good old Dick! How long since you came last! Wouldn't Julia be glad! Wouldn't she be glad!"

10   "Ain't she here?" asked Durante, jerking his head suddenly away from the dripping dipper.

11   "She's away at Nogales," said Tony. "It gets so hot. I said, 'You go up to Nogales, Julia, where the wind don't forget to blow.' She cried, but I made her go."

12   "Did she cry?" asked Durante.

13   "Julia. . . that's a good girl," said Tony.

14   "Yeah. You wouldn't throw some water into that mule of mine, would you, Tony?"

15   Tony went out, with his wooden leg clumping loud on the wooden floor, softly in the patio dust. Durante found the hammock in the corner of the patio. He lay down in it and watched the color of sunset flush the mists of desert dust that rose to the zenith. The water was soaking through his body. Hunger began, and then the rattling of pans in the kitchen and the cheerful cry of Tony's voice:

16   "What you want, Dick? I got some pork. You don't want pork? I'll make you some good Mexican beans. Hot. I have plenty of good wine for you, Dick. Tortillas. Even Julia can't make tortillas like me. And what about a nice young rabbit?"

17   "All blowed full of buckshot?" growled Durante.

18   "No, no. I kill them with the rifle."

19   "You kill rabbits with a rifle?" repeated Durante, with a quick interest.

20   "It's the only gun I have," said Tony. "If I catch them in the sights, they are dead. A wooden leg cannot walk very far. I must kill them quick. You see? They come close to the house about sunrise and flop their ears. I shoot through the head."

21   "Yeah? Yeah?" muttered Durante. "Through the head?" He relaxed, scowling. He passed his hand over his face, over his head.

22   Then Tony began to bring the food out into the patio and lay it on a small wooden table. A lantern hanging against the wall of the house included the table in a dim half-circle of light. They sat there and ate. Tony had scrubbed himself for the meal. His hair was soaked in water and sleeked back over his round skull. A man in the desert might be willing to pay five dollars for as much water as went to the soaking of that hair.

23   Everything was good. Tony knew how to cook, and he knew how to keep the glasses filled with wine.

24   "This is old wine. This is my father's wine. Eleven years old," said Tony. "You look at the light through it. You see that brown in the red? That's the soft that time puts in good wine, my father always said."

25   "What killed your father?" asked Durante.

26   Tony lifted his hand as though he were listening or as though he were pointing out a thought.

27   "The desert killed him. I found his mule. It was dead, too. There was a leak in the canteen. My father was only five miles away when the buzzards showed him to me."

28   "Five miles? Just an hour...Good Lord!" said Durante. He stared with big eyes. "Just dropped down and died?" he asked.

29   "No," said Tony. "When you die of thirst, you always die just one way. First you tear off your shirt, then your undershirt. That's to be cooler.... And the sun comes and cooks your bare skin. And then you think...there is water everywhere, if you dig down far enough. You begin to dig. The dust comes up your nose. You start screaming. You break your nails in the sand. You wear the flesh off the tips of your fingers, to the bone." He took a quick swallow of wine.

30   "Unless you seen a man die of thirst, how d'you know they start screaming?" asked Durante.

31   "They got a screaming look when you find them," said Tony. "Take some more wine. The desert never can get to you here. My father showed me the way to keep the desert away from the hollow. We live pretty good here. No?"

32   "Yeah," said Durante, loosening his shirt collar. "Yeah, pretty good."

33   Afterward he slept well in the hammock until the report of a rifle waked him and he saw the color of dawn in the sky. It was such a great, round bowl that for a moment he felt as though he were above, looking down into it.

34   He got up and saw Tony coming in holding a rabbit by the ears, the rifle in his other hand.

35   "You see?" said Tony. "Breakfast came and called on us!" He laughed.

36   Durante examined the rabbit with care. It was nice and fat and it had been shot through the head—through the middle of the head. Such a shudder went down the back of Durante that he washed gingerly before breakfast. He felt that his blood was cooled for the entire day.

37   It was a good breakfast, too, with flapjacks and stewed rabbit with green peppers, and a quart of strong coffee. Before they had finished, the sun struck through the east window and started them sweating.

38   "Gimme a look at that rifle of yours, Tony, will you?" Durante asked.

39   "You take a look at my rifle, but don't you steal the luck that's in it," laughed Tony. He brought the fifteen-shot Winchester.

40   "Loaded right to the brim?" asked Durante.

41   "I always load it full the minute I get back home," said Tony.

42   "Tony, come outside with me," commanded Durante.

43   They went out from the house. The sun turned the sweat of Durante to hot water and then dried his skin so that his clothes felt transparent. "Tony, I gotta be mean," said Durante. "Stand right there where I can see you. Don't try to get close. Now listen. The sheriff's gunna be along this trail sometime today, looking for me. He'll load up himself and all his gang with water out of your tanks. Then he'll follow my sign across the desert. Get me? He'll follow if he finds water on the place. But he's not gunna find water."

44   "What you done, poor Dick?" said Tony. "Now look, I could hide you in the old wine cellar where nobody—"

45   "The sheriff's not gunna find water," said Durante. "It's gunna be like this."

46   He put the rifle to his shoulder, aimed, fired. The shot struck the base of the nearest tank, ranging down through the bottom. A semicircle of darkness began to stain the soil near the edge of the iron wall.

47   Tony fell on his knees. "No, no, Dick! Good Dick!" he said. "Look! All the vineyard. It will die. It will turn into old, dead wood, Dick…"

48   "Shut your face," said Durante. "Now I've started, I kinda like the job."

49   Tony fell on his face and put his hands over his ears. Durante drilled a bullet hole through the tanks, one after another. Afterward, he leaned on the rifle.

50   "Take my canteen and go in and fill it with water out of the cooling jar," he said, "Snap to it, Tony!"

51   Tony got up. He raised the canteen and looked around him, not at the tanks from which the water was pouring so that the noise of the earth drinking was audible, but at the rows of his vineyard. Then he went into the house.

52   Durante mounted his mule. He shifted the rifle to his left hand and drew out the heavy Colt from its holster. Tony came dragging back to him, his head down. Durante watched Tony with a careful revolver, but he gave up the canteen without lifting his eyes.

53   "The trouble with you, Tony," said Durante, "is you're yellow. I'd of fought a tribe of wildcats with my bare hands before I'd let 'em do what I'm doin' to you. But you sit back and take it."

54   Tony did not seem to hear. He stretched out his hands to the vines. "Will you let them all die?" he asked.

55   Durante shrugged his shoulders. He shook the canteen to make sure that it was full. It was so brimming that there was hardly room for the liquid to make a sloshing sound. Then he turned the mule and kicked it into a dogtrot. Half a mile from the house of Tony, he threw the empty rifle to the ground. There was no sense packing that useless weight, and Tony with his peg leg would hardly come this far.

56   Durante looked back, a mile or so later, and saw the little image of Tony picking up the rifle from the dust, then staring earnestly after his guest. Durante remembered the neat little hole clipped through the head of the rabbit. Wherever he went, his trail never could return again to the vineyard in the desert. But then, commencing to picture to himself the arrival of the sweating sheriff and his posse at the house of Tony, Durante laughed heartily.

57   The sheriff's posse could get plenty of wine, of course, but without water a man could not hope to make the desert voyage, even with a mule or a horse to help him on the way. Durante patted the full, rounding side of his canteen. He might even now begin with the first sip but it was a luxury to postpone pleasure until desire became greater.

58   He raised his eyes along the trail. Close by, it was merely dotted with occasional bones. But distance joined the dots into an unbroken chalk line which wavered with a strange leisure across the Apache Desert, pointing toward the cool blue promise of the mountains. The next morning he would be among them.

59   A coyote whisked out of a gully and ran like a gray puff of dust on the wind. His tongue hung out like a little red rag from the side of his mouth, and suddenly Durante was dry to the marrow. He uncorked and lifted his canteen. It had a slightly sour smell; perhaps the sacking which covered it had grown a trifle old. And then he poured a great mouthful of lukewarm liquid. He had swallowed it before his senses could give him warning.

60   It was wine!

61   He looked first of all toward the mountains. They were as calmly blue, as distant as when he had started that morning. Twenty-four hours not on water, but on wine!

62 "I deserve it," said Durante. "I trusted him to fill the canteen. I deserve it. Curse him!" With a mighty resolution, he quieted the panic in his soul. He would not touch the stuff until noon. Then he would take one discreet sip. He would win through.

63 Hours went by. He looked at his watch and found it was only ten o'clock. And he had thought that it was on the verge of noon! He uncorked the wine and drank freely and, corking the canteen, felt almost as though he needed a drink of water more than before. He sloshed the contents of the canteen. Already it was horribly light.

64 Once, he turned the mule and considered the return trip. But he could remember the head of the rabbit too clearly, drilled right through the center. The vineyard, the rows of old twisted, gnarled little trunks with the bark peeling off...every vine was to Tony like a human life. And Durante had condemned them all to death!

65 He faced the blue of the mountains again. His heart raced in his breast with terror. Perhaps it was fear and not the suction of that dry and deadly air that made his tongue cleave to the roof of his mouth.

66 The day grew old. Nausea began to work in his stomach, nausea alternating with sharp pains. When he looked down, he saw that there was blood on his boots. He had been spurring the mule until the red ran down from its flanks. It went with a curious stagger, like a rocking horse with a broken rocker. Durante grew aware that he had been keeping the mule at a gallop for a long time. He pulled it to a halt. It stood with wide-braced legs. Its head was down. When he leaned from the saddle, he saw that its mouth was open.

67 "It's gunna die," said Durante. "It's gunna die....What a fool I been...."

68 The mule did not die until after sunset. Durante left everything except his revolver. He packed the weight of that for an hour and discarded it, in turn. His knees were growing weak. When he looked up at the stars, they shone white and clear for a moment only, and then whirled into little racing circles and scrawls of red.

69 He lay down. He kept his eyes closed and waited for the shaking to go out of his body, but it would not stop. And every breath of darkness was like an inhalation of black dust. He got up and went on, staggering. Sometimes he found himself running.

70 Before you die of thirst, you go mad. He kept remembering that. His tongue had swollen big. Before it choked him, if he lanced it with his knife the blood would help him; he would be able to swallow. Then he remembered that the taste of blood is salty.

71 Once, in his boyhood, he had ridden through a pass with his father and they had looked down on the sapphire of a mountain lake, a hundred thousand million tons of water as cold as snow....

72   When he looked up, now, there were no stars; and this frightened him terribly. He never had seen a desert night so dark. His eyes were failing; he was being blinded. When the morning came, he would not be able to see the mountains, and he would walk around and around in a circle until he dropped and died.

73   No stars, no wind; the air as still as the water of a stale pool, and he in the dregs at the bottom....

74   He seized his shirt at the throat and tore it away so that it hung in two rags from his hips.

75   He could see the earth only well enough to stumble on the rocks. But there were no stars in the heavens. He was blind. He had no more hope than a rat in a well. Ah, but devils know how to put poison in wine that will steal all the senses or any one of them. And Tony had chosen to blind Durante.

76   He heard a sound like water. It was the swishing of the soft, deep sand through which he was treading—sand so soft that a man could dig it away with his bare hands....

77   Afterward, after many hours, out of the blind face of that sky the rain began to fall. It made first a whispering and then a delicate murmur like voices conversing, but after that, just at the dawn, it roared like the hoofs of ten thousand charging horses. Even through that thundering confusion the big birds with naked heads and red, raw necks found their way down to one place in the Apache Desert.

Wine on the Desert

Journal

1. **MLA Works Cited**   *Using this model, record this story here.*

   Author's Last Name, First Name. "Title of the Story." <u>Title of the Book</u>. 3rd ed. Ed. First Name Last Name. City: Publisher, year. Pages of the story.

2. **Main Character(s)**   *Describe each main character, and explain why you think each is a main character.*

3. **Supporting Characters**   *Describe each supporting character, and explain why you think each is a supporting character.*

4. **Setting**   *Describe the setting(s) and any relevant prop(s).*

5. **Sequence**   *Outline the events of the story in order.*

6. **Plot**   *Tell the story in no more than two sentences.*

7. **Conflicts**   *Identify and explain all the conflicts involved here.*

8. **Significant Quotations**   *Explain the importance of each of these quotations. Record the page number in the parentheses.*

   a. "He had almost twenty-four hours' head start, for they would not find his dead man until this morning" (   ).

   b. "In the middle of the rainless season the well ran dry, but long before that, Tony had every drop of the water pumped up into a score of tanks made of cheap corrugated iron" (   ).

c. "A man in the desert might be willing to pay five dollars for as much water as went to the soaking of that hair" (   ).

d. "Durante drilled a bullet hole through the tanks, one after another" (   ).

e. "He heard a sound like water. It was the swishing of the soft, deep sand through which he was treading—[. . .]" (   ).

9. **Literary Elements**   *Look at this chapter's title and explain why you think this story is placed in this chapter. Explain in which other chapter(s) you might place this story, as relevant to the literary element(s) of that chapter.*

10. **Foreshadowing, Irony, and/or Symbolism**   *Explain examples of foreshadowing, irony, and/or symbolism in this story.*

Follow-up Questions

10 Short Questions

Select the best answer for each.

____ 1. Durante probably has
   a. seen a man killed.
   b. killed a man.
   c. saved a man.

____ 2. Durante is wanted by
   a. the sheriff.
   b. Julia.
   c. Tony.

____ 3. Tony needs the tanks
   a. to store water.
   b. to store wine.
   c. to cool the windmill.

____ 4. Tony needs the water
   a. to water the vineyard.
   b. to survive.
   c. both a. and b.

____ 5. The story of Tony's father
   a. sets up the steps in dying from thirst.
   b. proves one can survive without water.
   c. is irrelevant to the story.

____ 6. Tony and Durante
   a. are joined by Julia.
   b. are alone.
   c. are longtime enemies.

____ 7. At Tony's house, Durante
   a. saves water.
   b. does not use water.
   c. wastes water.

____ 8. For filling Durante's canteen, Tony
   a. gives Durante enough water.
   b. gives Durante wine.
   c. lets Durante fill the canteen.

____ 9. After the canteen is filled,
   a. Durante takes off into the desert.
   b. Tony takes off into the desert.
   c. the sheriff arrests Durante.

____ 10. In the end,
   a. Durante is arrested.
   b. Tony is arrested.
   c. Durante dies.

5 Significant Quotations

Explain the importance of each of these quotations.

1. "After that, there would be perhaps several hours of delay before the sheriff gathered a sufficient posse and started on his trail."

2. "The windmill looked like a sacred emblem to Durante, and the twenty stodgy, tarpainted tanks blessed his eyes [. . .]."

3. " 'What killed your father?' asked Durante."

4. "It was wine!"

5. "He seized his shirt at the throat and tore it away so that it hung in two rags from his hips."

2 COMPREHENSION ESSAY QUESTIONS

Use specific details and information from the story to answers these as completely as possible.

1. How does the story of Tony's father foreshadow this story? Use specific details and information from the story to support your answer.

2. What is the central irony in this story? Use specific details and information from the story to support your answer.

DISCUSSION QUESTIONS

Be prepared to discuss these in class.

1. How many ironies do you find in this story? Use specific details and information from the story to support your ideas.

2. Who do you think the protagonist and/or the antagonist is in this story? Use specific details and information from the story to support your thinking.

WRITING

Use each of these ideas for writing an essay.

1. This story is largely about friendship. Using specific examples, present instances that demonstrate a good friendship you have, or a bad one.

2. Water is essential to all of us for survival. Tony uses various machines—the tanks, the pumps, and so forth—to survive. Tell about one or two machines that you feel—seriously or humorously—you need to survive.

Further Writing

1. Alcohol drains the body fluids. Research the effects of alcohol on exercise and on bodily functions generally.

2. Compare and contrast the characters in this story to the characters in "The Cask of Amontillado" by Edgar Allan Poe (page 154).

The Last Leaf

O. Henry

PRE-READING VOCABULARY
CONTEXT

Use context clues to define these words before reading. Use a dictionary as needed.

1. The large oak tree in our backyard offered much welcome shade in the summer because of the many *leaves* on its branches. *Leaf* means

    _____.

2. The *artist* took out his brushes and paints and sat down to paint a beautiful picture of the sunset. *Artist* means _____.

3. When beings settle together joined by a common interest, be they ants or humans, we may call the settlement a *colony*. *Colony* means

    _____.

4. In order to keep all his paints and brushes and easels in one place, the artist rented a one-room *studio* to work in. *Studio* means

    _____.

5. When Suraj got a bad cough and was very sick with *pneumonia*, the doctor feared his lungs would become permanently scarred. *Pneumonia* means _____.

6. When the disease *smote* the whole town, each person became a victim *smitten* with the disease. *Smote* and *smite* mean _____.

7. When Reid hurt his *finger* playing his guitar, he called the doctor to find out how to cure his *finger*. *Finger* means _____.

8. Dodee and Rich planted an *ivy vine* by an empty part of their fence, so the vine could grow up the fence. *Ivy vine* means _____ .

9. Ashley is so pretty that the photographer suggested that her mother check into finding out if Ashley could become a *model. Model* means

   _____.

10. The greatest work of the artist, his *masterpiece*, now hangs by itself with importance in the Metropolitan Museum. *Masterpiece* means

    _____.

11. When Jerry wanted a big dog for protection at home, he got a large *mastiff* that protected all at home. *Mastiff* means

    _____.

12. After Keith left the food outside in the heat and rain, our meal was reduced to *dissolution* and *decay. Dissolution* and *decay* mean

    _____.

13. Carol wanted to cover her windows for privacy, so she had a *shade* hung at every window that she could raise or lower when she wanted. *Shade* means _____.

14. When Santi broke the vase, he used glue to get the broken pieces to *cling* together. *Cling* means _____.

15. Wilson is a very honest person and knows that it is a *sin* against the Ten Commandments to tell a lie. *Sin* means _____.

16. When Laura was ready to have her baby, Dave drove her to the *hospital* where the doctors and nurses were waiting to help her. *Hospital* means _____.

17. When Evelyn came home from vacation, her plants, which had needed water, had all shriveled up and *died. Die* means _____.

18. In order to walk the dog at night, Jacob lit the candle in the *lantern* and carried the *lantern* to light the path. *Lantern* means

    _____.

19. To replace the bulb in the light way up in the ceiling, Alice had to get the *ladder* out and climb step by step to the top. *Ladder* means

_____.

20. Karen wanted to paint flowers so she took out a board and dotted colors of pink, yellow, and green on her *palette*. *Palette* means

_____.

PRE-READING VOCABULARY
STRUCTURAL ATTACK

Define these words by solving the parts. Use the Glossary or a dictionary as needed.

1. successful	23. weaker
2. valuable	24. idiotic
3. possibility	25. imagining
4. collector	26. foolishness
5. traversing	27. dunderhead
6. icy	28. fearfully
7. ravager	29. persistently
8. bedstead	30. upturned
9. clinical	31. wearily
10. thermometer	32. livelong
11. curative	33. lonesomest
12. horseshow	34. mysterious
13. monocle	35. merciless
14. backward	36. hallway
15. gnarled	37. comfortable
16. decoyed	38. contentedly
17. nonsense	39. useless
18. goosey	40. woollen
19. fallen	41. helpless
20. painter	42. dreadful
21. professional	43. scattered
22. softness	44. fluttered

PRE-READING QUESTIONS

Try answering these questions as you read.

What happens to Johnsy?

What does the doctor say?

What does Behrman do?

The Last Leaf

The Pathetic Story of Two Girl Artists in Old New York and a Gray-Haired Failure Who Made Successful Sacrifice at the End.

O. Henry

William Sydney Porter was born in 1862 to an educated and comfortable family living in Greensboro, North Carolina, and he grew up in the Reconstruction South. As a result of his mother's early death and his father's alcoholism, he was raised by his aunt, who gave him a love for narration. Like his father, he became a pharmacist's apprentice, and although he did not like the work, his uncle's drugstore provided him with a good vantage point from which to observe the townspeople. In 1882 he married Athol Estes Roach, settled into work at the National Bank of Texas, and bought a printing press to publish his stories in the short-lived <u>The Rolling Stone</u>. He was charged and cleared of embezzlement—a charge he consistently denied. Later, faced with retrial, he fled to New Orleans and then to Honduras, all the while observing others. Returning to Texas because of his wife's failing health and subsequent death, he was retried and sent to the Ohio state penitentiary, where he served three years of a five-year sentence. Although it was a dark period in his life, he was again observing and, perhaps, gained his compassion for the underdog, as well as the pen name "O. Henry." In 1902 he moved to New York City to produce weekly stories for the <u>New York Sunday World,</u> and at the turn of the century and amid the streets of New York that were largely filled with immigrants, he found endless stock for his stories. O. Henry died in 1910.

His stories are marked by concise characterizations, concern for working women and the poor, adroit wit, and succinct irony. His many stories and selected sketches are largely based on kernels from his real-life observations and are available in many collections.

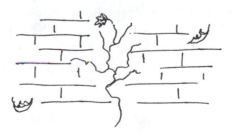

In a little district west of Washington Square the streets have run crazy and broken themselves into small strips called "places." These "places" make strange angles and curves. One street crosses itself a time or two. An artist once discovered a valuable possibility in this street. Suppose a collector with a bill for paints, paper and canvas should, in traversing this route, suddenly meet himself coming back, without a cent having been paid on account!

2   So, to quaint old Greenwich Village the art people soon came prowl-ing, hunting for north windows and eighteenth-century gables and Dutch attics and low rents. Then they imported some pewter mugs and a chafing dish or two from Sixth avenue, and become a "colony."

3   At the top of a squatty, three-story brick Sue and Johnsy had their studio. "Johnsy" was familiar for Joanna. One was from Maine; the other from California. They had met at the table d'hote of an Eighth street "Delmonico's," and found their tastes in art, chicory salad and bishop sleeves so congenial that the joint studio resulted.

4   That was in May. In November a cold, unseen stranger, whom the doctors called Pneumonia, stalked about the colony, touching one here and there with his icy finger. Over on the east side this ravager strode boldly, smiting his victims by scores, but his feet trod slowly through the maze of the narrow and moss-grown "places."

5   Mr. Pneumonia was not what you would call a chivalric old gentle-man. A mite of a little woman with blood thinned by California zephyrs was hardly fair game for the red-fisted, short-breathed old duffer. But Johnsy he smote; and she lay, scarcely moving, on her painted iron bedstead, looking through the small Dutch window-panes at the blank side of the next brick house.

6   One morning the busy doctor invited Sue into the hallway with a shaggy, gray eyebrow.

7   "She has one chance in—let us say, ten," he said, as he shook down the mercury in his clinical thermometer. "And that chance is for her to want to live. This way people have of lining-up on the side of the undertaker makes the entire pharmacopeia look silly. Your little lady has made up her mind that she's not going to get well. Has she any-thing on her mind?"

8   "She—she wanted to paint the Bay of Naples some day," said Sue.

9   "Paint?—bosh! Has she anything on her mind worth thinking about twice—a man, for instance?"

10   "A man?" said Sue, with a twang in her voice. "Is a man worth—but, no, doctor; there is nothing of the kind."

11   "Well, it is the weakness, then," said the doctor. "I will do all that science, so far as it may filter through my efforts, can accomplish. But whenever my patient begins to count the carriages in her funeral pro-cession I subtract 50 per cent from the curative power of medicines. If you will get her to ask one question about the new winter styles in cloak sleeves I will promise you a one-in-five chance for her, instead of one in ten."

12   After the doctor had gone Sue went into the workroom and cried a Japanese napkin to a pulp. Then she swaggered into Johnsy's room with her drawing board, whistling ragtime.

13   Johnsy, lay, scarcely making a ripple under the bedclothes, with her face toward the window. Sue stopped whistling, thinking she was asleep.

14   She arranged her board and began a pen-and-ink drawing to illustrate a magazine story. Young artists must pave their way to Art by drawing pictures for magazine stories that young authors write to pave their way to Literature.

15   As Sue was sketching a pair of elegant horseshow riding trousers and a monocle on the figure of the hero, an Idaho cowboy, she heard a low sound, several times repeated. She went quickly to the bedside.

16   Johnsy's eyes were open wide. She was looking out the window and counting—counting backward.

17   "Twelve," she said, and a little later "eleven;" and then "ten," and "nine;" and then "eight" and "seven" almost together.

18   Sue looked solicitously out of the window. What was there to count? There was only a bare, dreary yard to be seen, and the blank side of the brick house forty feet away. An old, old ivy vine, gnarled and decayed at the roots, climbed half way up the brick wall. The cold breath of autumn had stricken its leaves from the vine until its skeleton branches clung, almost bare, to the crumbling bricks.

19   "What is it, dear?" asked Sue.

20   "Six," said Johnsy, in almost a whisper. "They're falling faster now. Three days ago there were almost a hundred. It made my head ache to count them. But now it's easy. There goes another one. There are only five left now."

21   "Five what, dear. Tell your Sudie."

22   "Leaves. On the ivy vine. When the last one falls I must go, too. I've known that for three days. Didn't the doctor tell you?"

23   "Oh, I never heard of such nonsense," complained Sue, with magnificent scorn. "What have old ivy leaves to do with your getting well? And you used to love that vine so, you naughty girl. Don't be a goosey. Why, the doctor told me this morning that your chances for getting well real soon were—let's see exactly what he said—he said the chances were ten to one! Why, that's almost as good a chance as we have in New York when we ride on the street cars or walk past a new building. Try to take some broth now, and let Sudie go back to her drawing, so she can sell the editor man with it, and buy port wine for her sick child, and pork chops for her greedy self."

24   "You needn't get any more wine," said Johnsy, keeping her eyes fixed out the window. "There goes another. No, I don't want any broth. That leaves just four. I want to see the last one fall before it gets dark. Then I'll go, too."

25   "Johnsy, dear," said Sue, bending over her, "will you promise me to keep your eyes closed, and not look out the window until I am done

working? I must hand those drawings in by to-morrow. I need the light, or I would draw the shade down."

26   "Couldn't you draw in the other room?" asked Johnsy, coldly.

27   "I'd rather be here by you," said Sue. "Besides, I don't want you to keep looking at those silly ivy leaves."

28   "Tell me as soon as you have finished," said Johnsy, closing her eyes, and lying white and still as a fallen statue, "because I want to see the last one fall. I'm tired of waiting. I'm tired of thinking. I want to turn loose my hold on everything, and go sailing down, down, just like one of those poor, tired leaves."

29   "Try to sleep," said Sue. "I must call Behrman up to be my model for the old hermit miner. I'll not be gone a minute. Don't try to move 'till I come back."

30   Old Behrman was a painter who lived on the ground floor beneath them. He was past sixty and had a Michael Angelo's Moses beard curling down from the head of a satyr along the body of an imp. Behrman was a failure in art. Forty years he had wielded the brush without getting near enough to touch the hem of his Mistress's robe. He had been always about to paint a masterpiece, but had never yet begun it. For several years he had painted nothing except now and then a daub in the line of commerce or advertising. He earned a little by serving as a model to those young artists in the colony who could not pay the price of a professional. He drank gin to excess, and still talked of his coming masterpiece. For the rest he was a fierce little old man, who scoffed terribly at softness in any one, and who regarded himself as especial mastiff-in-waiting to protect the two young artists in the studio above.

31   Sue found Behrman smelling strongly of juniper berries in his dimly lighted den below. In one corner was a blank canvas on an easel that had been waiting there for twenty-five years to receive the first line of the masterpiece. She told him of Johnsy's fancy, and how she feared she would, indeed, light and fragile as a leaf herself, float away when her slight hold upon the world grew weaker.

32   Old Behrman, with his red eyes plainly streaming, shouted his contempt and derision for such idiotic imaginings.

33   "Vass!" he cried. "Is dere people in de world mit der foolishness to die because leafs dey drop off from a confounded vine? I haf not heard of such a thing. No, I will not bose as a model for your fool hermit-dunderhead. Vy do you allow dot silly pusiness to come in der prain of her? Ach, dot poor leetle Miss Johnsy."

34   "She is very ill and weak," said Sue, "and the fever has left her mind morbid and full of strange fancies. Very well, Mr. Behrman, if you do not care to pose for me, you needn't. But I think you are a horrid old—old flibbertigibbet."

35   "You are just like a woman!" yelled Behrman. "Who said I vill not bose? Go on. I come mit you. For half an hour I haf peen trying to say dot I am ready to bose. Gott! dis is not any blace in which one so schones at Miss Yohnsy shall lie sick. Some day I vill baint a master-piece, and ve shall all go away. Gott! yes."

36   Johnsy was sleeping when they went upstairs. Sue pulled the shade down to the window-sill, and motioned Behrman into the other room. In there they peered out the window fearfully at the ivy vine. Then they looked at each other for a moment without speaking. A persist-ent, cold rain was falling, mingled with snow. Behrman, in his old blue shirt, took his seat as the hermit-miner on an upturned kettle for a rock.

37   When Sue awoke from an hour's sleep the next morning she found Johnsy with dull, wide-open eyes staring at the drawn green shade.

38   "Pull it up; I want to see," she ordered, in a whisper.

39   Wearily she obeyed.

40   But, lo! after the beating rain and fierce gusts of wind that had endured through the livelong night, there yet stood out against the brick wall one ivy leaf. It was the last on the vine. Still dark green near its stem, but with its serrated edges tinted with the yellow of dissolu-tion and decay, it hung bravely from a branch some twenty feet above the ground.

41   "It is the last one," said Johnsy. "I thought it would surely fall during the night. I heard the wind. It will fall to-day, and I shall die at the same time."

42   "Dear, dear!" said Sue, leaning her worn face down to the pillow, "think of me, if you won't think of yourself. What would I do?"

43   But Johnsy did not answer. The lonesomest thing in all the world is a soul when it is making ready to go on its mysterious, far journey. The fancy seemed to possess her more strongly as one by one the ties that bound her to friendship and to earth were loosed.

44   The day wore away, and even through the twilight they could see the lone ivy leaf clinging to its stem against the wall. And then, with the coming of the night the north wind was again loosed, while the rain still beat against the windows and pattered down from the low Dutch eaves.

45   When it was light enough Johnsy, the merciless, commanded that the shade be raised.

46   The ivy leaf was still there.

47   Johnsy lay for a long time looking at it. And then she called to Sue, who was stirring her chicken broth over the gas stove.

48   "I've been a bad girl, Sudie," said Johnsy. "Something has made the last leaf stay there to show me how wicked I was. It is a sin to want to

die. You may bring me a little broth now, and some milk with a little port in it, and—no; bring me a hand-mirror first; and then pack some pillows about me, and I will sit up and watch you cook."

49   An hour later she said:

50   "Sudie, some day I hope to paint the Bay of Naples."

51   The doctor came in the afternoon, and Sue had an excuse to go into the hallway as he left.

52   "Even chances," said the doctor, taking Sue's thin, shaking hand in his. "With good nursing you'll win. And now I must see another case I have downstairs. Behrman, his name is—some kind of an artist, I believe. Pneumonia, too. He is an old, weak man, and the attack is acute. There is no hope for him; but he goes to the hospital to-day to be made more comfortable."

53   The next day the doctor said to Sue: "She's out of danger. You've won. Nutrition and care now—that's all."

54   And that afternoon Sue came to the bed where Johnsy lay, contentedly knitting a very blue and very useless woollen shoulder scarf, and put one arm around her, pillows and all.

55   "I have something to tell you, white mouse," she said. "Mr. Behrman died of pneumonia to-day in the hospital. He was ill only two days. The janitor found him on the morning of the first day in his room downstairs helpless with pain. His shoes and clothing were wet through and icy cold. They couldn't imagine where he had been on such a dreadful night. And then they found a lantern, still lighted, and a ladder that had been dragged from its place, and some scattered brushes, and a palette with green and yellow colors mixed on it, and—look out the window, dear, at the last ivy leaf on the wall. Didn't you wonder why it never fluttered or moved when the wind blew? Ah, darling, it's Behrman's masterpiece—he painted it there the night that the last leaf fell."

The Last Leaf

JOURNAL

1. **MLA Works Cited** *Using this model, record this story here.*

   Author's Last Name, First Name. "Title of the Story." <u>Title of the Book</u>. 3rd ed. Ed. First Name Last Name. City: Publisher, year. Pages of the story.

2. **Main Character(s)** *Describe each main character, and explain why you think each is a main character.*

3. **Supporting Characters** *Describe each supporting character, and explain why you think each is a supporting character.*

4. **Setting** *Describe the setting(s) and any relevant prop(s).*

5. Sequence *Outline the events of the story in order.*

6. Plot *Tell the story in no more than two sentences.*

7. Conflicts *Identify and explain all the conflicts involved here.*

8. Significant Quotations *Explain the importance of each of these quotations. Record the page number in the parentheses.*

   a. "In November a cold, unseen stranger, whom the doctors called Pneumonia, stalked about the colony, touching one here and there with his icy finger" (   ).

   b. " 'Your little lady had made up her mind that she's not going to get well' " (   ).

   c. " 'I want to see the last one fall before it gets dark. Then I'll go, too' " (   ).

d. " 'Something has made the last leaf stay there to show me how wicked I was' " (   ).

e. " 'They couldn't imagine where he had been on that dreadful night' " (   ).

9. **Literary Elements**   *Look at this chapter's title and explain why you think this story is placed in this chapter. Explain in which other chapter(s) you might place this story, as relevant to the literary element(s) of that chapter.*

10. **Foreshadowing, Irony, and/or Symbolism**   *Explain examples of foreshadowing, irony, and/or symbolism in this story.*

FOLLOW-UP QUESTIONS

10 SHORT QUESTIONS

Select the <u>best</u> answer for each.

_____ 1. Johnsy and Sudie's artistry is
   a. writing.
   b. drawing and painting.
   c. nursing.

_____ 2. The "colony" they live in has other
   a. writers.
   b. artists.
   c. nurses.

_____ 3. Johnsy catches
   a. the flu.
   b. a cold.
   c. pneumonia.

_____ 4. At first, the doctor feels Johnsy has
   a. a poor chance to survive.
   b. a good chance to survive.
   c. no chance to survive.

_____ 5. Johnsy says when the last leaf falls
   a. she will paint again.
   b. she will be better.
   c. she will die.

_____ 6. Behrman is
   a. a young man.
   b. an old man.
   c. their father.

_____ 7. The last leaf appears
   a. not to fall.
   b. to fall early.
   c. to fall late.

_____ 8. As the last leaf seems to remain, the doctor feels
   a. Johnsy will die.
   b. Johnsy will fail.
   c. Johnsy will live.

_____ 9. In the end, Behrman
   a. paints the last leaf.
   b. dies.
   c. both a. and b.

_____ 10. In the end, Johnsy survives because
   a. Behrman's leaf never falls.
   b. the real leaf never falls.
   c. the weather gets warmer.

5 SIGNIFICANT QUOTATIONS

Explain the importance of each of these quotations.

1. "But Johnsy he [pneumonia] smote [. . .]."

2. " 'She has one chance in—let us say, ten,' he said, as he shook down the mercury in his clinical thermometer."

3. " 'When the last one falls, I must go, too. I've known that for three days.' "

4. " 'Even chances,' said the doctor, taking Sue's thin, shaking hand in his. 'With good nursing you'll win. And now I must see another case I have downstairs.' "

5. " 'Ah, darling, it's Behrman's masterpiece—he painted it there the night that the last leaf fell.' "

2 Comprehension Essay Questions

Use specific details and information from the story to answer these questions as completely as possible.

1. How would Behrman tell this story? Use specific details and information from the story to support your thinking.

2. Why did O. Henry name this "The Last Leaf"? Use specific details and information to support your answer.

Discussion Questions

Be prepared to discuss these questions in class.

1. What humor can you find in this story?

2. What ironies are in this story?

Writing

Use each of these ideas for writing an essay.

1. The core of this story is about overcoming a difficulty, here a disease. Using concrete descriptions, write about a difficulty you have had to overcome and about what you gained from this process.

2. We learn that Johnsy and Sudie are great friends through their conversations and their actions. Think of a friend and describe that friend using only conversation and examples of specific actions. You may want to focus on a specific trait—selfishness or generosity, cleanliness or sloppiness, or so forth—and use conversation and specific actions to demonstrate that trait.

Further Writing

1. Pneumonia, either bacterial or viral, is still a very serious disease that was once usually fatal. Research today's concerns about and the treatment history of both bacterial and viral pneumonia.

2. Greenwich Village in downtown New York City, the setting for "The Last Leaf," was once a place for poor artists, but today it consists of some of the most expensive real estate in the world. Research the history of Greenwich Village and nearby TriBeCa.

The Lady or the Tiger?

FRANK STOCKTON

PRE-READING VOCABULARY
CONTEXT

Use context clues to define these words before reading. Use a dictionary as needed.

1. A person who acts uncivilized or cruel is *barbaric. Barbaric* means

   _____.

2. Carlos took a *fancy* to golf, and now he buys golf magazines and plays golf every chance he gets. *Fancy* means _____.

3. Mothers have the *authority* to ground their children. *Authority* means _____.

4. Steve shows great *valor* in standing up for what he believes, even when others disagree. *Valor* means _____.

5. In Roman times, *gladiators* fought brave battles. *Gladiator* means

   _____.

6. The lecture will take place in the large *amphitheatre* that seats several thousand. *Amphitheatre* means _____.

7. *Virtue* and pureness of heart are qualities rarely found in a material world. *Virtue* means _____.

8. The judge was *impartial* to each person and never took sides unfairly. *Impartial* means _____.

9. The criminal was *accused* of robbing the bank after police saw his face on the bank video. *Accused* means _____.

10. The actors took their show on the road and always played to large *audiences. Audience* means _____.

11. When Marna and Buzz decided to get married, they invited their favorite people to their *wedding*. *Wedding* means

    _____.

12. The hungry children *devoured* the chocolate cake in minutes. *Devour* means _____.

13. Nala showed good *judgment* when she chose staying in school and not dropping out. *Judgment* means _____.

14. When Jay sued his neighbor, they went to court to have the lawsuit decided in a *trial*. *Trial* means _____.

15. The young *courtiers* living in the king's castle enjoyed an easy life of hunting and feasting. *Courtier* means _____.

16. In America, everyone assumes that he or she can improve his or her *station* in life through hard work. *Station* means

    _____.

17. The Seymours trimmed their double front *portals* in pine rope and twinkling lights. *Portal* means _____.

18. The lovely *damsel* enjoyed arranging roses and hosting lovely tea parties. *Damsel* means _____.

19. Phyllis was overcome with *jealousy* when her neighbor's garden looked better than hers. *Jealousy* means _____.

20. Geri *anguished* over which carpet to chose, because she would have to live with it for a long time. *Anguished* means

    _____.

PRE-READING VOCABULARY
STRUCTURAL ATTACK

Define these words by solving the parts. Use the Glossary or a dictionary as needed.

1. olden
2. progressive
3. irresistible
4. manly
5. beastly
6. encircling
7. incorruptible
8. idealism
9. aforementioned
10. fiercest
11. downcast
12. chorister
13. slightest
14. uncertainty
15. unfairness
16. humanity
17. fairness
18. exceedingly
19. relentless
20. admittance
21. possessed
22. curtained
23. unimportant
24. lookers-on
25. immovably
26. hot-blooded
27. oftener
28. recovered
29. futurity

PRE-READING QUESTIONS

Try answering these questions as you read.

What is the point of the amphitheatre?

What happens to the courtier?

How does the princess feel about the maiden?

What does the princess do?

The Lady or the Tiger?

FRANK STOCKTON

Frank Stockton was born in Philadelphia, Pennsylvania in 1834. After attending school in Philadelphia, he became a wood engraver. He wrote children's stories from 1867 until 1881, when he turned to writing adult stories. With a flair for fantasy and even for some primitive science fiction, "The Lady or the Tiger?" remains his most enduring piece. Stockton died in 1902.

In the very olden time, there lived a semi-barbaric king, whose ideas, though somewhat polished and sharpened by the progressiveness of distant Latin neighbors, were still large, florid, and untrammelled, as became the half of him which was barbaric. He was a man of exuberant fancy, and, withal, of an authority so irresistible that, at his will, he turned his varied fancies into facts. He was greatly given to self-communing; and, when he and himself agreed upon any thing, the thing was done. When every member of his domestic and political systems moved smoothly in its appointed course, his nature was bland and genial; but whenever there was a little hitch, and some of his orbs got out of their orbits, he was blander and more genial still, for nothing pleased him so much as to make the crooked straight, and crush down uneven places.

2   Among the borrowed notions by which his barbarism had become semified was that of the public arena, in which, by exhibitions of manly and beastly valor, the minds of his subjects were refined and cultured.

3   But even here the exuberant and barbaric fancy asserted itself. The arena of the king was built, not to give the people an opportunity of hearing the rhapsodies of dying gladiators, nor to enable them to view the inevitable conclusion of a conflict between religious opinions and hungry jaws, but for purposes far better adapted to widen and develop the mental energies of the people. This vast amphitheatre, with its encircling galleries, its mysterious vaults, and its unseen passages, was an agent of poetic justice, in which crime was punished, or virtue rewarded, by the decrees of an impartial and incorruptible chance.

4   When a subject was accused of a crime of sufficient importance to interest the king, public notice was given that on an appointed day the fate of the accused person would be decided in the king's arena—a structure which well deserved its name; for, although its form and plan were borrowed from afar, its purpose emanated solely from the brain of this man, who, every barleycorn a king, knew no tradition to which he

owed more allegiance than pleased his fancy, and who ingrafted on every adopted form of human thought and action the rich growth of his barbaric idealism.

5   When all the people had assembled in the galleries, and the king, surrounded by his court, sat high up on his throne of royal state on one side of the arena, he gave a signal, a door beneath him opened, and the accused subject stepped out into the amphitheatre. Directly opposite him, on the other side of the enclosed space, were two doors exactly alike and side by side. It was the duty and the privilege of the person on trial, to walk directly to these doors and open one of them. He could open either door he pleased: he was subject to no guidance or influence but that of the aforementioned impartial and incorruptible chance. If he opened the one, there came out of it a hungry tiger, the fiercest and most cruel that could be procured, which immediately sprang upon him, and tore him to pieces, as a punishment for his guilt. The moment that the case of the criminal was thus decided, doleful iron bells were clanged, great wails went up from the hired mourners posted on the outer rim of the arena, and the vast audience, with bowed heads and downcast hearts, wended slowly their homeward way, mourning greatly that one so young and fair, or so old and respected, should have merited so dire a fate.

6   But, if the accused person opened the other door, there came forth from it a lady, the most suitable to his years and station that his majesty could select among his fair subjects; and to this lady he was immediately married, as a reward of his innocence. It mattered not that he might already possess a wife and family, or that his affections might be engaged upon an object of his own selection: the king allowed no such subordinate arrangements to interfere with his great scheme of retribution and reward. The exercises, as in the other instance, took place immediately, and in the arena. Another door opened beneath the king, and a priest, followed by a band of choristers, and dancing maidens blowing joyous airs on golden horns and treading an epithalamic measure, advanced to where the pair stood, side by side; and the wedding was promptly and cheerily solemnized. Then the gay brass bells rang forth their merry peals, the people shouted glad hurrahs, and the innocent man, preceded by children strewing flowers on his path, led his bride to his home.

7   This was the king's semi-barbaric method of administering justice. Its perfect fairness is obvious. The criminal could not know out of which door would come the lady: he opened either he pleased, without having the slightest idea whether, in the next instant, he was to be devoured or married. On some occasions the tiger came out of one door, and on some out of the other. The decisions of this tribunal were

not only fair, they were positively determinate: the accused person was instantly punished if he found himself guilty; and, if innocent, he was rewarded on the spot, whether he liked it or not. There was no escape from the judgments of the king's arena.

8   The institution was a very popular one. When the people gathered together on one of the great trial days, they never knew whether they were to witness a bloody slaughter or a hilarious wedding. This element of uncertainty lent an interest to the occasion which it could not otherwise have attained. Thus, the masses were entertained and pleased, and the thinking part of the community could bring no charge of unfairness against this plan; for did not the accused person have the whole matter in his own hands?

9   This semi-barbaric king had a daughter as blooming as his most florid fancies, and with a soul as fervent and imperious as his own. As is usual in such cases, she was the apple of his eye, and was loved by him above all humanity. Among his courtiers was a young man of that fineness of blood and lowness of station common to the conventional heroes of romance who love royal maidens. This royal maiden was well satisfied with her lover, for he was handsome and brave to a degree unsurpassed in all this kingdom; and she loved him with an ardor that had enough of barbarism in it to make it exceedingly warm and strong. This love affair moved on happily for many months, until one day the king happened to discover its existence. He did not hesitate nor waver in regard to his duty in the premises. The youth was immediately cast into prison, and a day was appointed for his trial in the king's arena. This, of course, was an especially important occasion; and his majesty, as well as all the people, was greatly interested in the workings and development of this trial. Never before had such a case occurred; never before had a subject dared to love the daughter of a king. In after-years such things became commonplace enough; but then they were, in no slight degree, novel and startling.

10   The tiger-cages of the kingdom were searched for the most savage and relentless beasts, from which the fiercest monster might be selected for the arena; and the ranks of maiden youth and beauty throughout the land were carefully surveyed by competent judges, in order that the young man might have a fitting bride in case fate did not determine for him a different destiny. Of course, everybody knew that the deed with which the accused was charged had been done. He had loved the princess, and neither he, she, nor any one else thought of denying the fact; but the king would not think of allowing any fact of this kind to interfere with the workings of the tribunal, in which he took such great delight and satisfaction. No matter how the affair turned out, the youth would be disposed of; and the king would take

an aesthetic pleasure in watching the course of events, which would determine whether or not the young man had done wrong in allowing himself to love the princess.

11   The appointed day arrived. From far and near the people gathered, and thronged the great galleries of the arena; and crowds, unable to gain admittance, massed themselves against its outside walls. The king and his court were in their places, opposite the twin doors—those fateful portals, so terrible in their similarity.

12   All was ready. The signal was given. A door beneath the royal party opened, and the lover of the princess walked into the arena. Tall, beautiful, fair, his appearance was greeted with a low hum of admiration and anxiety. Half the audience had not known so grand a youth had lived among them. No wonder the princess loved him! What a terrible thing for him to be there!

13   As the youth advanced into the arena, he turned, as the custom was, to bow to the king: but he did not think at all of that royal personage; his eyes were fixed upon the princess, who sat to the right of her father. Had it not been for the moiety of barbarism in her nature, it is probable that lady would not have been there; but her intense and fervid soul would not allow her to be absent on an occasion in which she was so terribly interested. From the moment that the decree had gone forth, that her lover should decide his fate in the king's arena, she had thought of nothing, night or day, but this great event and the various subjects connected with it. Possessed of more power, influence, and force of character than any one who had ever before been interested in such a case, she had done what no other person had done—she had possessed herself of the secret of the doors. She knew in which of the two rooms, that lay behind those doors, stood the cage of the tiger, with its open front, and in which waited the lady. Through these thick doors, heavily curtained with skins on the inside, it was impossible that any noise or suggestion should come from within to the person who should approach to raise the latch of one of them; but gold, and the power of a woman's will, had brought the secret to the princess.

14   And not only did she know in which room stood the lady ready to emerge, all blushing and radiant, should her door be opened, but she knew who the lady was. It was one of the fairest and loveliest of the damsels of the court who had been selected as the reward of the accused youth, should he be proved innocent of the crime of aspiring to one so far above him; and the princess hated her. Often had she seen, or imagined that she had seen, this fair creature throwing glances of admiration upon the person of her lover, and sometimes she thought these glances were perceived and even returned. Now and then she had seen them talking together; it was but for a moment or two, but much

can be said in a brief space; it may have been on most unimportant topics, but how could she know that? The girl was lovely, but she had dared to raise her eyes to the loved one of the princess; and, with all the intensity of the savage blood transmitted to her through long lines of wholly barbaric ancestors, she hated the woman who blushed and trembled behind that silent door.

15   When her lover turned and looked at her, and his eye met hers as she sat there paler and whiter than any one in the vast ocean of anxious faces about her, he saw, by that power of quick perception which is given to those whose souls are one, that she knew behind which door crouched the tiger, and behind which stood the lady. He had expected her to know it. He understood her nature, and his soul was assured that she would never rest until she had made plain to herself this thing, hidden to all other lookers-on, even to the king. The only hope for the youth in which there was any element of certainty was based upon the success of the princess in discovering the mystery; and the moment he looked upon her, he saw she had succeeded, as in his soul he knew she would succeed.

16   Then it was that his quick and anxious glance asked the question: "Which?" It was as plain to her as if he shouted it from where he stood. There was not an instant to be lost. The question was asked in a flash; it must be answered in another.

17   Her right arm lay on the cushioned parapet before her. She raised her hand, and made a slight, quick movement toward the right. No one but her lover saw her. Every eye but his was fixed on the man in the arena.

18   He turned, and with a firm and rapid step he walked across the empty space. Every heart stopped beating, every breath was held, every eye was fixed immovably upon that man. Without the slightest hesitation, he went to the door on the right, and opened it.

19   Now, the point of the story is this: Did the tiger come out of that door, or did the lady?

20   The more we reflect upon this question, the harder it is to answer. It involves a study of the human heart which leads us through devious mazes of passion, out of which it is difficult to find our way. Think of it, fair reader, not as if the decision of the question depended upon yourself, but upon that hot-blooded, semi-barbaric princess, her soul at a white heat beneath the combined fires of despair and jealousy. She had lost him, but who should have him?

21   How often, in her waking hours and in her dreams, had she started in wild horror, and covered her face with her hands as she thought of her lover opening the door on the other side of which waited the cruel fangs of the tiger!

22   But how much oftener had she seen him at the other door! How in her grievous reveries had she gnashed her teeth, and torn her hair, when she saw his start of rapturous delight as he opened the door of the lady! How her soul had burned in agony when she had seen him rush to meet that woman, with her flushing cheek and sparkling eye of triumph; when she had seen him lead her forth, his whole frame kindled with the joy of recovered life; when she had heard the glad shouts from the multitude, and the wild ringing of the happy bells; when she had seen the priest, with his joyous followers, advance to the couple, and make them man and wife before her very eyes; and when she had seen them walk away together upon their path of flowers, followed by the tremendous shouts of the hilarious multitude, in which her one despairing shriek was lost and drowned!

23   Would it not be better for him to die at once, and go to wait for her in the blessed regions of semi-barbaric futurity?

24   And yet, that awful tiger, those shrieks, that blood!

25   Her decision had been indicated in an instant, but it had been made after days and nights of anguished deliberation. She had known she would be asked, she had decided what she would answer, and, without the slightest hesitation, she had moved her hand to the right.

26   The question of her decision is one not to be lightly considered, and it is not for me to presume to set myself up as the one person able to answer it. And so I leave it with all of you: Which came out of the opened door—the lady, or the tiger?

The Lady or the Tiger?

JOURNAL

1. **MLA Works Cited**   *Using this model, record this story here.*

   Author's Last Name, First Name. "Title of the Story." <u>Title of the Book</u>.
   3rd ed. Ed. First Name Last Name. City: Publisher, year. Pages of
   the story.

2. **Main Character(s)**   *Describe each main character, and explain why you*
   think each is a main character.

3. **Supporting Characters**   *Describe each supporting character, and explain why*
   you think each is a supporting character.

4. **Setting**   *Describe the setting(s) and any relevant prop(s).*

5. Sequence   *Outline the events of the story in order.*

6. Plot   *Tell the story in no more than three sentences.*

7. Conflicts   *Identify and explain all the conflicts involved here.*

8. Significant Quotations   *Explain the importance of each of these quotations. Record the page number in the parentheses.*

   a. "Among the borrowed notions by which his barbarism had become semi-fied was that of the public arena [. . .]" ( ).

   b. "It was the duty and the privilege of the person on trial, to walk directly to these doors and open one of them" ( ).

   c. "Among his courtiers was a young man of that fineness of blood and low-ness of station common to the conventional heroes of romance who love royal maidens" ( ).

d. "The girl was lovely, but she had dared to raise her eyes to the loved one of the princess [. . .]" (   ).

e. "Then it was that his quick and anxious glance asked the question: 'Which?' " (   ).

9. **Literary Elements**   *Look at this chapter's title and explain why you think this story is placed in this chapter. Explain in which other chapter(s) you might place this story, as relevant to the literary element(s) of that chapter.*

10. **Foreshadowing, Irony, and/or Symbolism**   *Explain examples of foreshadowing, irony, and/or symbolism in this story.*

FOLLOW-UP QUESTIONS

10 SHORT QUESTIONS

*Select the **best** answer for each.*

_____ 1. The king seems
   a. brutal.
   b. kind.
   c. fair.

_____ 2. The king feels the justice of the arena is
   a. kind.
   b. barbaric.
   c. fair.

_____ 3. The princess is
   a. quiet.
   b. serene.
   c. passionate.

_____ 4. The princess loves
   a. a royal man.
   b. a non-royal man.
   c. an acceptable man.

_____ 5. The king is
   a. happy with the princess's choice.
   b. unconcerned about the princess's choice.
   c. outraged at the princess's choice.

_____ 6. The king will
   a. let the princess marry her lover.
   b. not let the princess marry her lover.
   c. think about letting the princess marry her lover.

_____ 7. The princess
   a. knows which door the maiden is behind.
   b. does not know which door the maiden is behind.
   c. does not know which door the tiger is behind.

_____ 8. The princess probably learned what she does know about the doors
   a. through a teacher.
   b. through bribery.
   c. through the king.

_____ 9. The princess
   a. is jealous of the maiden.
   b. is not jealous of the maiden.
   c. does not know of the maiden.

_____ 10. The princess
   a. can bear to see her lover torn apart.
   b. cannot bear to see her lover torn apart.
   c. does not care if her lover is torn apart.

5 SIGNIFICANT QUOTATIONS

Explain the importance of each of these quotations.

1. "This vast amphitheatre [...] was an agent of poetic justice, in which crime was punished, or virtue rewarded, by the decrees of an impartial and incorruptible chance."

2. "If he opened the one, there came out of it a hungry tiger [. . .].
   "But, if the accused person opened the other door [. . .]."

3. "This royal maiden was well satisfied with her lover [. . .]."

4. "It was one of the fairest and loveliest damsels of the court [. . .] and the princess hated her."

5. "Without the slightest hesitation, he went to the door on the right, and opened it."

2 COMPREHENSION ESSAY QUESTIONS

Use specific details and information from the story to answer these questions as completely as possible.

1. What is the king's justice system and how does it relate to the courtier? Use specific details and information from the story to support your explanation.

2. What is the maiden's role in the story? Use specific details and information from the story to support your explanation.

DISCUSSION QUESTIONS

Be prepared to discuss these questions in class.

1. What is the importance of social class in this story? How is this importance similar or different from your own community?

2. For which character do you feel the most sympathy? The least sympathy? Why?

WRITING

Use each of these ideas for writing an essay.

1. Write an ending to "The Lady or the Tiger?" Explain your ending, and include references from the story to support your logic.

2. Tell the story of a difficult choice you have had to make. Explain the circumstances and consequences of your choice.

Further Writing

1. Read Ernest Hemingway's "The Short, Happy Life of Francis Macomber" (available in a library), and compare Margot's choice with that of the princess in this story.

2. Read William Shakespeare's <u>Romeo and Juliet</u> (available in a library) or watch <u>Romeo and Juliet</u> or <u>West Side Story</u> (available in a video store) and compare Juliet's and/or Maria's choices with the princess's choices.

Notes

CHAPTER 4

Irony

Irony is found in the difference between what *is* and what *should be*. Irony may be bitter—you work and work, and someone new, who has done nothing, arrives at your job and gets the promotion you deserve. Irony may be humorous—you wake up late and race around knowing you will be late for class, only to get to school and find out that your class has been canceled. Irony may even be providential—you sleep in and miss your bus, only to find out that the bus has been in an accident and you are still safe at home. Think of ironies as unexpected twists in time, places, or events.

A story by O. Henry is a good example of irony. In the story, a gentleman treats a poor man to a Thanksgiving feast. In the end, both men end up in the hospital. The reader finds out that the poor man has had a big dinner before this second feast and is overfed. Meanwhile, the proud gentleman has spent his money on feeding this poor man who does not need more food, and the gentleman is underfed. The irony, of course, is that the man who does not need the food is fed, while the man who does need the food goes hungry.

The stories in this chapter focus on irony. Kate Chopin's "The Story of an Hour" turns marital assumptions upside down. Then the American master, O. Henry, presents touching and even bittersweet irony in "Gifts of the Magi" and, later, humorous inversion in "The Ransom of Red Chief." Dorothy Parker infuriates the reader in "The Wonderful Old Gentleman." And last, but certainly not least, Zora Neale Hurston's ironic twist satisfies the reader's sense of justice in "Sweat."

Enjoy the twists here, and reflect on the ironies you have read in other stories—and on those you have experienced in your own life.

The Story of an Hour

KATE CHOPIN

PRE-READING VOCABULARY
CONTEXT

Use context clues to define these words before reading. Use a dictionary as needed.

1. Kara was *afflicted* with headaches that caused her constant pain.
   Afflicted means _____.

2. The horrible earthquake caused a major *disaster*, with gas explosions and buildings collapsing, that resulted in injuries and deaths.
   Disaster means _____.

3. Before there were telephones, in order to send news to his family Sung Yu had to go to an office and send a *telegram*. *Telegram* means

   _____.

4. Vernie tried to *hasten* Stephanie so that she could get to school on time. *Hasten* means _____.

5. After the children lost their beloved dog, they suffered much *grief* and cried for days. *Grief* means _____.

6. The little leaves were all *aquiver* as the breeze blew through the tree.
   Aquiver means _____.

7. Some people are never allowed to laugh; they suffer severe *repression* when they see something funny. *Repression* means

   _____.

8. When Rob did not understand the directions, his face became *vacant* and without expression. *Vacant* means _____.

9. The puppy had a *keen* sense of smell and could scent a hamburger a mile away. *Keen* means _____.

10. Blood *pulses* through our veins with a steady beat. *Pulse* means
_____.

11. The king held the most *exalted* position in the realm. *Exalted* means _____.

12. In the Macy's *procession*, colorful floats followed one after another after another. *Procession* means _____.

13. The host opened the door and warmly *welcomed* each guest as he or she arrived. *Welcome* means _____.

14. Without thinking about it, Kirk followed his *impulse* and suddenly bet all his chips on red. *Impulse* means _____.

15. When Bill thinks he is right, he answers with enough confidence and *self-assertion* to convince others he is correct. *Self-assertion* means _____.

16. Nancy *implored* the builder to start her deck as soon as possible before the rains came. *Implore* means _____.

17. A substance that can change base metals into gold, that can make one live forever, or that allows one to taste the very best of life is called an *elixir*. *Elixir* means _____.

18. Daren *shuddered* at the thought of having to take another algebra test. *Shudder* means _____.

19. The Cougars yelled, screamed, and jumped in *triumph* when they won the game. *Triumph* means _____.

20. Margaret was absolutely *amazed* when she won the ten-million-dollar lottery. *Amazed* means _____.

PRE-READING VOCABULARY
STRUCTURAL ATTACK

Define these words by solving the parts. Use the Glossary or a dictionary as needed.

1. inability
2. bespoke
3. fearfully
4. powerless
5. fellow-creatures

6. illumination
7. keyhole
8. feverish
9. latchkey
10. travel-stained

PRE-READING QUESTIONS

Try answering these questions as you read.

What happens to Mr. Mallard?

How does Mrs. Mallard feel?

What happens to Mrs. Mallard?

What is ironic in the story?

The Story of an Hour

KATE CHOPIN

> **Kate O'Flaherty Chopin** was born in St. Louis, Missouri in 1851 to an affluent family. Although her father died when she was young, her widowed mother gave young Kate a taste of female independence. In 1870 Kate married Oscar Chopin and moved to New Orleans and then Natchitoches Parish. Here she met the Creoles, Acadians, and African Americans she would later write about. However Oscar died in 1882, and by 1884 she sold the plantation, gathered her five children, and returned home to St. Louis where she began to write for popular women's magazines. Influenced noticeably by Guy de Maupassant's sense of irony and Henrik Ibsen's social comment, Chopin wrote stories, often touched with rich symbols and images of nature, that question societal assumptions and dictates. <u>The Awakening</u> remains her masterwork, although stories such as "Desiree's Baby" and "The Kiss" offer Chopin at her most terse. Chopin died in 1904.

K nowing that Mrs. Mallard was afflicted with a heart trouble, great care was taken to break to her as gently as possible the news of her husband's death.

2   It was her sister Josephine who told her, in broken sentences; veiled hints that revealed in half concealing. Her husband's friend Richards was there, too, near her. It was he who had been in the news-paper office when intelligence of the railroad disaster was received, with Brently Mallard's name leading the list of "killed." He had only taken the time to assure himself of its truth by a second telegram, and had hastened to forestall any less careful, less tender friend in bearing the sad message.

3   She did not hear the story as many women have heard the same, with a paralyzed inability to accept its significance. She wept at once, with sudden, wild abandonment, in her sister's arms. When the storm of grief had spent itself she went away to her room alone. She would have no one follow her.

4   There stood, facing the open window, a comfortable, roomy armchair. Into this she sank, pressed down by a physical exhaustion that haunted her body and seemed to reach into her soul.

5   She could see in the open square before her house the tops of trees that were all aquiver with the new spring life. The delicious breath of rain was in the air. In the street below a peddler was crying his wares. The notes of a distant song which some one was singing reached her faintly, and countless sparrows were twittering in the eaves.

6   There were patches of blue sky showing here and there through the clouds that had met and piled one above the other in the west facing her window.

7   She sat with her head thrown back upon the cushion of the chair, quite motionless, except when a sob came up into her throat and shook her, as a child who has cried itself to sleep continues to sob in its dreams.

8   She was young, with a fair, calm face, whose lines bespoke repression and even a certain strength. But now there was a dull stare in her eyes, whose gaze was fixed away off yonder on one of those patches of blue sky. It was not a glance of reflection, but rather indicated a suspension of intelligent thought.

9   There was something coming to her and she was waiting for it, fearfully. What was it? She did not know; it was too subtle and elusive to name. But she felt it, creeping out of the sky, reaching toward her through the sounds, the scents, the color that filled the air.

10   Now her bosom rose and fell tumultuously. She was beginning to recognize this thing that was approaching to possess her, and she was striving to beat it back with her will—as powerless as her two white slender hands would have been.

11   When she abandoned herself a little whispered word escaped her slightly parted lips. She said it over and over under her breath: "free, free, free!" The vacant stare and the look of terror that had followed it went from her eyes. They stayed keen and bright. Her pulses beat fast, and the coursing blood warmed and relaxed every inch of her body.

12   She did not stop to ask if it were or were not a monstrous joy that held her. A clear and exalted perception enabled her to dismiss the suggestion as trivial.

13   She knew that she would weep again when she saw the kind, tender hands folded in death; the face that had never looked save with love

upon her, fixed and gray and dead. But she saw beyond that bitter moment a long procession of years to come that would belong to her absolutely. And she opened and spread her arms out to them in welcome.

14   There would be no one to live for her during those coming years; she would live for herself. There would be no powerful will bending hers in that blind persistence with which men and women believe they have a right to impose a private will upon a fellow-creature. A kind intention or a cruel intention made the act seem no less a crime as she looked upon it in that brief moment of illumination.

15   And yet she had loved him—sometimes. Often she had not. What did it matter! What could love, the unsolved mystery, count for in the face of this possession of self-assertion which she suddenly recognized as the strongest impulse of her being!

16   "Free! Body and soul free!" she kept whispering.

17   Josephine was kneeling before the closed door with her lips to the keyhole, imploring for admission. "Louise, open the door! I beg; open the door—you will make yourself ill. What are you doing, Louise? For heaven's sake open the door."

18   "Go away. I am not making myself ill." No; she was drinking in a very elixir of life through that open window.

19   Her fancy was running riot along those days ahead of her. Spring days, and summer days, and all sorts of days that would be her own. She breathed a quick prayer that life might be long. It was only yesterday she had thought with a shudder that life might be long.

20   She arose at length and opened the door to her sister's importunities. There was a feverish triumph in her eyes, and she carried herself unwittingly like a goddess of Victory. She clasped her sister's waist, and together they descended the stairs. Richards stood waiting for them at the bottom.

21   Someone was opening the front door with a latchkey. It was Brently Mallard who entered, a little travel-stained, composedly carrying his grip-sack and umbrella. He had been far from the scene of the accident, and did not even know there had been one. He stood amazed at Josephine's piercing cry; at Richards' quick motion to screen him from the view of his wife.

22   But Richards was too late.

23   When the doctors came they said she had died of heart disease—of joy that kills.

The Story of an Hour

JOURNAL

1. **MLA Works Cited**   *Using this model, record this story here.*

   *Author's Last Name, First Name. "Title of the Story." <u>Title of the Book</u>.
   3rd ed. Ed. First Name Last Name. City: Publisher, year. Pages of
   the story.*

2. **Main Character(s)**   *Describe each main character, and explain why you
   think each is a main character.*

3. **Supporting Characters**   *Describe each supporting character, and explain why
   you think each is a supporting character.*

4. **Setting**   *Describe the setting(s) and any relevant prop(s).*

5. **Sequence**   *Outline the events of the story in order.*

6. **Plot**   *Tell the story in no more than two sentences.*

7. **Conflicts**   *Identify and explain all the conflicts involved here.*

8. **Significant Quotations**   *Explain the importance of each of these quotations. Record the page number in the parentheses.*

   a. "Knowing that Mrs. Mallard was afflicted with a heart trouble, great care was taken to break to her as gently as possible the news of her husband's death" (   ).

   b. "When the storm of grief had spent itself she went away to her room alone" (   ).

c. "She could see in the open square before her house the tops of trees that were all aquiver with the new spring life" (   ).

d. "When she abandoned herself a little whispered word escaped her slightly parted lips. She said it over and over under her breath: 'free, free, free!' " (   ).

e. "Someone was opening the door with a latchkey" (   ).

9. **Literary Elements**   *Look at this chapter's title and explain why you think this story is placed in this chapter. Explain in which other chapter(s) you might place this story, as relevant to the literary element(s) of that chapter.*

10. **Foreshadowing, Irony, and/or Symbolism**   *Explain examples of foreshadowing, irony, and/or symbolism in this story.*

FOLLOW-UP QUESTIONS

10 SHORT QUESTIONS

*Select the **best** answer for each.*

____ 1. The person to first hear the news of the accident is
a. Mrs. Mallard.
b. Josephine.
c. Richards.

____ 2. S/he hears the news
a. at the railroad station.
b. at the newspaper office.
c. at home.

____ 3. Josephine and Richards are at the Mallard house
a. to awaken Mrs. Mallard.
b. to have lunch with Mrs. Mallard.
c. to tell Mrs. Mallard about the accident.

____ 4. Mrs. Mallard is immediately
a. overwhelmed.
b. overjoyed.
c. unimpressed.

____ 5. Mrs. Mallard
a. goes to her room.
b. stays with her sister.
c. makes lunch.

____ 6. Mrs. Mallard slowly
a. cries.
b. faints.
c. whispers "free."

____ 7. Mrs. Mallard
a. always loved Brently Mallard.
b. did not always love Brently Mallard.
c. was looking forward to Brently Mallard's return.

____ 8. Brently Mallard
a. was at home all the time.
b. was in the accident.
c. was not in the accident.

____ 9. Brently Mallard
a. does come home.
b. does not come home.
c. is dead.

____ 10. Mrs. Mallard is
a. delighted by his return.
b. unmoved by his return.
c. destroyed by his return.

5 SIGNIFICANT QUOTATIONS

Explain the importance of each of these quotations.

1. "Knowing that Mrs. Mallard was afflicted with a heart condition, great care was taken to break to her as gently as possible the news of her husband's death."

2. "She wept at once, with sudden, wild abandonment, in her sister's arms."

3. "There was something coming to her and she was waiting for it, fearfully."

4. "She breathed a quick prayer that life might be long. It was only yesterday she had thought with a shudder that life might be long."

5. "When the doctors came they said she had died of heart disease—of joy that kills."

2 COMPREHENSION ESSAY QUESTIONS

Use specific details and information from the story to answer these questions as completely as possible.

1. How does the title relate to the story? Explain the significance of the title using specific details and information from the story.

2. What does the phrase "of joy that kills" mean? Use specific details and information from the story in your explanation.

DISCUSSION QUESTIONS

Be prepared to discuss these questions in class.

1. What does this story tell you about assumptions concerning husbands and wives? Use specific details from the story to support your ideas.

2. For which character do you feel more sympathy? Why?

WRITING

Use each of these ideas for writing an essay.

1. We have all tried to cover up our feelings at one time or another. Tell the story of a time you or someone you know used pleasure or sorrow to cover up real feelings about a situation or event. Pay special attention in your narrative to the reactions of others.

2. We have all made mistakes about how we think others feel. Sometimes these misunderstandings are quite humorous. Describe a time when you or someone you know assumed the wrong thing about someone else's feelings.

Further Writing

1. Discuss the similarities between Mrs. Mallard in this story and Calixta in Kate Chopin's "The Storm" (available in a library).

2. Discuss the similarities between Mrs. Mallard in this story and Nathalie in Kate Chopin's "The Kiss" (page 193).

3. Discuss the similarities between Mrs. Mallard in this story and Mrs. Alving in Henrik Ibsen's Ghosts (available in a library).

Gifts of the Magi

O. HENRY

PRE-READING VOCABULARY
CONTEXT

Use context clues to define these words before reading. Use a dictionary as needed.

1. Sam was always cheap and never paid for anything he didn't have to, as a result of his *parsimony*. *Parsimony* means

   _____.

2. Rajan would never live in a *shabby* little shack and always demands the best in life. *Shabby* means _____.

3. Patricia owns and maintains her home and is truly the *mistress* of her house. *Mistress* means _____.

4. Laura likes only the very fine and beautiful—the most *sterling*—things in life. *Sterling* means _____.

5. Baby Alex has many *possessions*, including toys, books, trains, beautiful clothes, and a sun-filled room. *Possession* means

   _____.

6. At Niagara Falls, the water comes *cascading* down the falls at the rate of thousands of gallons each minute. *Cascading* means

   _____.

7. Cy went *ransacking* through his closet trying to find his favorite fraternity T-shirt that was lost. *Ransack* means

   _____.

8. Ted attached a *fob chain* to his pocket watch so that it would hang out of his vest pocket for all to see. *Fob chain* means

   _____.

9. The town suffered the *ravages* of war with burned-down buildings and blown-apart streets. *Ravage* means _____.

10. In past times, being a dancer in a line as a *chorus girl* was looked on as a lowly job only for loose women. *Chorus girl* means

_____.

11. Sundeep was *terrified* of snakes and would faint at the sight of one. *Terrified* means _____.

12. Bernie has the most *peculiar* laugh and no one else in the world can laugh the way he does. *Peculiar* means _____.

13. The men who came to visit baby Jesus and who brought precious gifts were considered to be wise and were called the *magi*. *Magi* means

_____.

14. George was *ecstatic* when his name was called as the winner of the lottery. *Ecstatic* means _____.

15. Stu became *hysterical* and had to be calmed down when he learned his cat had suddenly died. *Hysterical* means _____.

16. After Lori took the medicine, her headache *vanished* and she felt fine. *Vanish* means _____.

17. Trish loves hot fudge sundaes and absolutely *craves* one when she hasn't had one in a long time. *Crave* means _____.

18. Nicole had wonderfully thick hair, and she took very special care of her beautiful *tresses*. *Tress* means _____.

19. The newborn Jesus may be referred to as the *Babe in the manger*. *Babe in the manger* means _____.

20. Simon *sacrificed* his free time to help teach the students how to write poetry. *Sacrifice* means _____.

PRE-READING VOCABULARY
STRUCTURAL ATTACK

Define these words by solving the parts. Use the Glossary or a dictionary as needed.

1. bulldozing
2. predominating
3. subsiding
4. furnished
5. blurred
6. airshaft
7. rippling
8. nervously
9. ornamentation
10. close-lying
11. critically
12. overcoat
13. immovable
14. fixedly
15. laboriously
16. mathematician
17. illumination
18. necessitating
19. lamely

PRE-READING QUESTIONS

Try answering these questions as you read.

What does Della sell?

What does Della buy?

What does Jim sell?

What does Jim buy?

What is ironic in the story?

Gifts of the Magi

O. HENRY

William Sydney Porter was born in 1862 to an educated and comfortable family living in Greensboro, North Carolina, and he grew up in the Reconstruction South. As a result of his mother's early death and his father's alcoholism, he was raised by his aunt, who gave him a love for narration. Like his father, he became a pharmacist's apprentice, and although he did not like the work, his uncle's drugstore provided him with a good vantage point from which to observe the townspeople. In 1882 he married Athol Estes Roach, settled into work at the National Bank of Texas, and bought a printing press to publish his stories in the short-lived <u>The Rolling Stone</u>. He was charged and cleared of embezzlement—a charge he consistently denied. Later, faced with retrial, he fled to New Orleans and then to Honduras, all the while observing others. Returning to Texas because of his wife's failing health and subsequent death, he was retried and sent to the Ohio state penitentiary, where he served three years of a five-year sentence. Although it was a dark period in his life, he was again observing and, perhaps, gained his compassion for the underdog, as well as the pen name "O. Henry." In 1902 he moved to New York City to produce weekly stories for the <u>New York Sunday World,</u> and at the turn of the century and amid the streets of New York that were largely filled with immigrants, he found endless stock for his stories. O. Henry died in 1910.

His stories are marked by concise characterizations, concern for working women and the poor, adroit wit, and succinct irony. His many stories and selected sketches are largely based on kernels from his real-life observations and are available in many collections.

One dollar and eighty-seven cents. That was all. And 60 cents of it was in pennies. Pennies saved one and two at a time by bulldozing the grocer and the vegetable man and the butcher until one's cheeks burned with the silent imputation of parsimony that such close dealing implied. Three times Della counted it. One dollar and eighty-seven cents. And the next day would be Christmas.

2   There was clearly nothing to do but flop down on the shabby little couch and howl. So Della did it. Which instigates the moral reflection that life is made up of sobs, sniffles and smiles, with sniffles predominating.

3   While the mistress of the home is gradually subsiding from the first stage to the second, take a look at the home. A furnished flat at $8 per week. It did not exactly beggar description, but it certainly had that word on the lookout for the mendicancy squad.

4   In the vestibule below belonged to this flat a letter-box into which no letter would go, and an electric button from which no mortal finger could coax a ring. Also appertaining thereunto was a card bearing the name "Mr. James Dillingham Young."

5   The "Dillingham" had been flung to the breeze during a former period of prosperity when its possessor was being paid $30 per week. Now, when the income was shrunk to $20, the letters of "Dillingham" looked blurred, as though they were thinking seriously of contracting to a modest and unassuming D. But whenever Mr. James Dillingham Young came home and reached his flat above he was called "Jim" and greatly hugged by Mrs. James Dillingham Young, already introduced to you as Della. Which is all very good.

6   Della finished her cry and attended to her cheeks with the powder rag. She stood by the window and looked out dully at a gray cat walking a gray fence in a gray backyard. Tomorrow would be Christmas Day, and she had only $1.87 with which to buy Jim a present. She had been saving every penny she could for months, with this result. Twenty dollars a week doesn't go far. Expenses had been greater than she had calculated. They always are. Only $1.87 to buy a present for Jim. Her Jim. Many a happy hour she had spent planning for something nice for him. Something fine and rare and sterling—something just a little bit near to being worthy of the honor of being owned by Jim.

7   There was a pier-glass between the windows of the room. Perhaps you have seen a pier-glass in an $8 flat. A very thin and very agile person may, by observing his reflection in a rapid sequence of longitudinal strips, obtain a fairly accurate conception of his looks. Della, being slender, had mastered the art.

8   Suddenly she whirled from the window and stood before the glass. Her eyes were shining brilliantly, but her face had lost its color within twenty seconds. Rapidly she pulled down her hair and let it fall to its full length.

9   Now, there were two possessions of the James Dillingham Youngs in which they both took a mighty pride. One was Jim's gold watch that had been his father's and his grandfather's. The other was Della's hair. Had the Queen of Sheba lived in the flat across the airshaft Della would

have let her hair hang out the window some day to dry and mocked at Her Majesty's jewels and gifts. Had King Solomon been the janitor, with all his treasures piled up in the basement, Jim would have pulled out his watch every time he passed, just to see him pluck at his beard from envy.

10   So now Della's beautiful hair fell about her, rippling and shining like a cascade of brown waters. It reached below her knee and made itself almost a garment for her. And then she did it up again nervously and quickly. Once she faltered for a minute and stood still while a tear or two splashed on the worn red carpet.

11   On went her old brown jacket; on went her old brown hat. With a whirl of skirts and with the brilliant sparkle still in her eyes, she fluttered out the door and down the stairs to the street.

12   Where she stopped the sign read: "Mme. Sofronie. Hair Goods of All Kinds." One flight up Della ran, and collected herself, panting, before Madame, large, too white, chilly and hardly looking the "Sofronie."

13   "Will you buy my hair?" asked Della.

14   "I buy hair," said Madame. "Take yer hat off and let's have a sight at the looks of it."

15   Down rippled the brown cascade.

16   "Twenty dollars," said Madame, lifting the mass with a practised hand.

17   "Give it to me quick," said Della.

18   Oh, and the next two hours tripped by on rosy wings. Forget the hashed metaphor. She was ransacking the stores for Jim's present.

19   She found it at last. It surely had been made for Jim and no one else. There was none other like it in any of the stores, and she had turned all of them inside out. It was a platinum fob chain simple and chaste in design, properly proclaiming its value by substance alone and not by meretricious ornamentation—as all good things should do. It was even worthy of The Watch. As soon as she saw it she knew that it must be Jim's. It was like him. Quietness and value—the description applied to both. Twenty-one dollars they took from her for it, and she hurried home with the 87 cents. With that chain on his watch Jim might be properly anxious about the time in any company. Grand as the watch was, he sometimes looked at it on the sly on account of the old leather strap that he used in place of a chain.

20   When Della reached home her intoxication gave way a little to prudence and reason. She got out her curling irons and lighted the gas and went to work repairing the ravages made by generosity added to love. Which is always a tremendous task, dear friends—a mammoth task.

21   Within forty minutes her head was covered with tiny, close-lying curls that made her look wonderfully like a truant schoolboy. She looked at her reflection in the mirror long, carefully and critically.

22   "If Jim doesn't kill me," she said to herself, "before he takes a second look at me, he'll say I look like a Coney Island chorus girl. But what could I do—oh, what could I do with a dollar and eighty-seven cents!"

23   At 7 o'clock the coffee was made and the frying pan was on the back of the stove hot and ready to cook the chops.

24   Jim was never late. Della doubled the fob chain in her hand and sat on the corner of the table near the door that he always entered. Then she heard his step on the stair away down on the first flight, and she turned white for just a moment. She had a habit of saying little silent prayers about the simplest everyday things, and now she whispered: "Please, God, make him think I am still pretty."

25   The door opened and Jim stepped in and closed it. He looked thin and very serious. Poor fellow, he was only twenty-two—and to be burdened with a family! He needed a new overcoat and he was without gloves.

26   Jim stopped inside the door, as immovable as a setter at the scent of quail. His eyes were fixed upon Della, and there was an expression in them that she could not read, and it terrified her. It was not anger, nor surprise, nor disapproval, nor horror, nor any of the sentiments that she had been prepared for. He simply stared at her fixedly with that peculiar expression on his face.

27   Della wriggled off the table and went for him.

28   "Jim, darling," she cried, "don't look at me that way. I had my hair cut off and sold it because I couldn't have lived through Christmas without giving you a present. It'll grow again—you won't mind, will you? I just had to do it. My hair grows awfully fast. Say 'Merry Christmas!' Jim, and let's be happy. You don't know what a nice—what a beautiful, nice gift I've got for you."

29   "You've cut off your hair?" asked Jim, laboriously, as if he had not arrived at that patent fact yet even after the hardest mental labor.

30   "Cut it off and sold it," said Della. "Don't you like me just as well, anyhow? I'm me without my hair, ain't I?"

31   Jim looked about the room curiously.

32   "You say your hair is gone?" he said, with an air almost of idiocy.

33   "You needn't look for it," said Della. "It's sold, I tell you—sold and gone too. It's Christmas Eve, boy. Be good to me, for it went for you. Maybe the hairs of my head were numbered," she went on with a sudden serious sweetness, "but nobody could ever count my love for you. Shall I put the chops on, Jim?"

34   Out of his trance Jim seemed to quickly wake. He enfolded his Della. For ten seconds let us regard with discreet scrutiny some inconsequential object in the other direction. Eight dollars a week or a million a year—what is the difference? A mathematician or a wit would

give you the wrong answer. The magi brought valuable gifts, but that was not among them. This dark assertion will be illuminated later on.

35   Jim drew a package from his overcoat pocket and threw it upon the table.

36   "Don't make any mistake, Dell," he said, "about me. I don't think there's anything in the way of a haircut or a shave or a shampoo that could make me like my girl any less. But if you'll unwrap that package you may see why you had me going awhile at first."

37   White fingers and nimble tore at the string and paper. And then an ecstatic scream of joy; and then, alas! a quick feminine change to hysterical tears and wails, necessitating the immediate employment of all the comforting powers of the lord of the flat.

38   For there lay The Combs—the set of combs, side and back, that Della had worshipped for long in a Broadway window. Beautiful combs, pure tortoise shell, with jewelled rims—just the shade to wear in the beautiful vanished hair. They were expensive combs, she knew, and her heart had simply craved and yearned over them without the least hope of possession. And now, they were hers, but the tresses that should have adorned the coveted adornments were gone.

39   But she hugged them to her bosom, and at length she was able to look up with dim eyes and a smile and say: "My hair grows so fast, Jim!"

40   And then Della leaped up like a little singed cat and cried, "Oh, oh!"

41   Jim had not yet seen his beautiful present. She held it out to him eagerly upon her open palm. The dull, precious metal seemed to flash with a reflection of her bright and ardent spirit.

42   "Isn't it a dandy, Jim? I hunted all over town to find it. You'll have to look at the time a hundred times a day now. Give me your watch. I want to see how it looks on it."

43   Instead of obeying, Jim tumbled down on the couch and put his hands under the back of his head and smiled.

44   "Dell," said he, "let's put our Christmas presents away and keep 'em a while. They're too nice to use just at present. I sold the watch to get the money to buy your combs. And now suppose you put the chops on."

45   The magi, as you know, were wise men—wonderfully wise men—who brought gifts to the Babe in the manger. They invented the art of giving Christmas gifts. Being wise, their gifts were no doubt wise ones, possibly bearing the privilege of exchange in case of duplication. And here I have lamely related to you the uneventful chronicle of two foolish children in a flat who most unwisely sacrificed for each other the greatest treasures of their house. But in a last word to the wise of these days let it be said that of all who give gifts these two were of the wisest. Of all who give and receive gifts, such as they are the wisest. Everywhere they are the wisest. They are the magi.

Gifts of the Magi

JOURNAL

1. **MLA Works Cited**   *Using this model, record this story here.*

   Author's Last Name, First Name. "Title of the Story." <u>Title of the Book</u>.
   3rd ed. Ed. First Name Last Name. City: Publisher, year. Pages of
   the story.

2. **Main Character(s)**   *Describe each main character, and explain why you think each is a main character.*

3. **Supporting Characters**   *Describe each supporting character, and explain why you think each is a supporting character.*

4. **Setting**   *Describe the setting(s) and any relevant prop(s).*

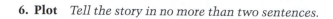

5. Sequence   *Outline the events of the story in order.*

6. Plot   *Tell the story in no more than two sentences.*

7. Conflicts   *Identify and explain all the conflicts involved here.*

8. Significant Quotations   *Explain the importance of each of these quotations. Record the page number in the parentheses.*

   a. "Tomorrow would be Christmas Day, and she had only $1.87 with which to buy Jim a present" (   ).

   b. "One was Jim's gold watch that had been his father's and his grandfather's. The other was Della's hair" (   ).

c. " 'Will you buy my hair?' asked Della" (   ).

d. "For there lay The Combs—the set of combs, side and back, that Della had worshipped for long in a Broadway window" (   ).

e. " 'Dell,' he said, 'let's put our Christmas presents away and keep 'em for a while' " (   ).

9. **Literary Elements**   *Look at this chapter's title and explain why you think this story is placed in this chapter. Explain in which other chapter(s) you might place this story, as relevant to the literary element(s) of that chapter.*

10. **Foreshadowing, Irony, and/or Symbolism**   *Explain examples of foreshadowing, irony, and/or symbolism in this story.*

FOLLOW-UP QUESTIONS

10 SHORT QUESTIONS

Select the <u>best</u> answer for each.

____ 1. This story is set in
a. Boston.
b. Dallas.
c. New York.

____ 2. The Youngs are
a. rich.
b. poor.
c. middle class.

____ 3. Della's most prized possession is her
a. apartment.
b. hair.
c. watch.

____ 4. Jim's most prized possession is his
a. apartment.
b. hair.
c. watch.

____ 5. Della wants to
a. sell her hair.
b. pawn Jim's watch.
c. purchase the combs.

____ 6. Della wants to
a. buy the combs.
b. buy Jim's watch.
c. buy Jim a fob chain.

____ 7. Jim wants to
a. sell Della's hair.
b. sell his watch.
c. purchase the fob chain.

____ 8. Jim wants to
a. buy the combs.
b. buy the watch.
c. buy the fob chain.

____ 9. The gifts are for
a. Della's birthday.
b. Jim's birthday.
c. Christmas.

____ 10. Their celebration
a. is ruined because of the gifts.
b. is not ruined because of the gifts.
c. is ruined by their losses.

5 SIGNIFICANT QUOTATIONS

Explain the importance of each of these quotations.

1. "One dollar and eighty-seven cents. That was all."

2. "Now, there were two possessions of the James Dillingham Youngs in which they both took a mighty pride."

3. " 'I buy hair,' said Madame."

4. "And now, they were hers, but the tresses that should have adorned the coveted adornments were gone."

5. " 'Dell,' he said, 'let's put our Christmas presents away and keep 'em a while.' "

2 Comprehension Essay Questions

Use specific details and information from the story to answer these questions as completely as possible.

1. What are the ironies in this story? Use specific details and information from the story.

2. "Magi" has come to imply "wise men." What is ironic about this title? Use specific details and information from the story.

Discussion Questions

Be prepared to discuss these questions in class.

1. Do you feel more disappointed for Della or for Jim? Why?

2. Do you think they communicate and understand each other too well or too poorly? Use specific details from the story to explain your thinking.

Writing

Use each of these ideas for writing an essay.

1. Tell the story of a purchase that you or someone you know worked or saved long and hard for and that turned out not to be worth the effort.

2. Tell the story of an ironic twist in your life or in the life of someone you know.

Further Writing

1. "Gifts of the Magi" is classic O. Henry. Compare the irony in this story to the irony centered on an object in Guy de Maupassant's "The Necklace" (available in a library).

2. Compare the irony of these gifts with the irony of the inheritance in Dorothy Parker's "The Wonderful Old Gentleman" (page 285).

The Wonderful Old Gentleman

DOROTHY PARKER

PRE-READING VOCABULARY
CONTEXT

Use context clues to define these words before reading. Use a dictionary as needed.

1. The children put everything scary they could think of into the haunted house so that it would be a *chamber of horrors. Chamber of horrors* means _____.

2. Josette wanted to see the beautiful paintings in person, so she went to the *museum. Museum* means _____.

3. The hungry tiger was *savage* as it ripped apart the raw meat thrown to it. *Savage* means _____.

4. The ugly statue, with its hanging tongue and ragged claws, was *grotesque. Grotesque* means _____.

5. Meredith *married well* when she wed the multimillionaire who offered her a life of ease and comfort. *Married well* means

    _____.

6. When the clerk left to find a new job, her boss Pam wrote her a very nice *reference. Reference* means _____.

7. Leah took the white cotton *handkerchief* trimmed in lace from her purse to wipe her tears. *Handkerchief* means _____.

8. Lena wore the beautiful *crepe de Chine* gown with her topaz and amethyst jewelry. *Crepe de Chine* means _____.

9. Theo's coat was all *rumpled* and wrinkled after he slept in it all night on the train. *Rumpled* means _____.

10. Eli was absolutely *distraught* when he found out that his favorite team, the Tigers, had lost the championship. *Distraught* means

_____.

11. Sallie bought a very expensive *Persian rug* to lay in the middle of the foyer floor. *Persian rug* means _____.

12. Gert needed to hire several *servants* to cook and clean when she bought the forty-room mansion. *Servant* means

_____.

13. When Danny went away to school, he had to pay five hundred dollars a month *board* money for his room and food. *Board* means

_____.

14. When Renée was kinder to one child than to the other, she was definitely showing her *favoritism*. *Favoritism* means

_____.

15. Angela chose to ride in the limousine with the *chauffeur* driving rather than take her own car. *Chauffeur* means

_____.

16. When the company was hiring typists and filers, Jay found a *clerical* summer job. *Clerical* means _____.

17. After spending all of his mom's money and then going to jail for robbery, Paul became the *black sheep* of the family. *Black sheep* means _____.

18. Bob stated clearly in his *will* that all his money would go to his children when he died. *Will* means _____.

19. Scott found all the noise and confusion around him very *disturbing*. *Disturbing* means _____.

20. The family *passionately* loved their little dog and were beside themselves when she died. *Passionate* means _____.

PRE-READING VOCABULARY
STRUCTURAL ATTACK

Define these words by solving the parts. Use the Glossary or a dictionary as needed.

1. living-room
2. discomfort
3. wedding-present
4. transforming
5. high-ceilinged
6. woodwork
7. unavoidable
8. eyeless
9. earthy
10. center-table
11. blameless
12. shoulder-muscles
13. bronze-colored
14. curly-headed
15. realistically
16. steel-engraving
17. chariot-race
18. maddened
19. grave-like
20. hopelessly
21. casualness
22. upright
23. ash-receiver
24. nervousness
25. unconscious
26. necessitating
27. untidiness
28. painstakingly
29. forefinger
30. storm-window
31. light-fixture
32. guest-room
33. fair-mindedness
34. lovelier
35. liveliness
36. seaman
37. housekeeper
38. kindliest
39. shakily

PRE-READING QUESTIONS

Try answering these questions as you read.

Who is the Old Gentleman?

What is Mrs. Bain like? Mrs. Whittaker?

What does the Old Gentleman do to Mrs. Bain? Mrs. Whittaker?

Who really cares about the Old Gentleman?

What is ironic in this story?

The Wonderful Old Gentleman

DOROTHY PARKER

Dorothy Rothschild Parker was born in 1893 to a well-to-do Jewish father and a Protestant mother. She grew up in New York City. With her mother dying shortly after Parker was born, Parker grew to resent her strict father and what she perceived as her mixed heritage. She was part of the Manhattan scene, first as a writer for <u>Vogue</u>, then as a critic for <u>Vanity Fair</u>, and then as a writer for the <u>New Yorker</u>. With her second husband, Alan Campbell, she moved to California and wrote the script for the 1937 film, <u>A Star is Born</u>. Holding long-time family resentments, developing cynical views on relationships, and having an interest in liberal politics, Parker led a rather unsettled life. Her writing offers concise and often bitterly ironic support for sincere women, while it often abrades superficial women and men in general. Her many short stories appear in several collections. Parker died in 1967.

I f the Bains had striven for years, they could have been no more successful in making their living-room into a small but admirably complete museum of objects suggesting strain, discomfort, or the tomb. Yet they had never even tried for the effect. Some of the articles that the room contained were wedding-presents; some had been put in from time to time as substitutes as their predecessors succumbed to age and wear; a few had been brought along by the Old Gentleman when he had come to make his home with the Bains some five years before.

2   It was curious how perfectly they all fitted into the general scheme. It was as if they had all been selected by a single enthusiast to whom time was but little object, so long as he could achieve the eventual result of transforming the Bain living-room into a home chamber of horrors, modified a bit for family use.

3   It was a high-ceilinged room, with heavy, dark old woodwork, that brought long and unavoidable thoughts of silver handles and weaving worms. The paper was the color of stale mustard. Its design, once a dashing affair of a darker tone splashed with twinkling gold, had faded into lines and smears that resolved themselves, before the eyes of the sensitive, into hordes of battered heads and tortured profiles, some eyeless, some with clotted gashes for mouths.

4   The furniture was dark and cumbersome and subject to painful creakings—sudden, sharp creaks that seemed to be wrung from its brave silence only when it could bear no more. A close, earthy smell came from its dulled tapestry cushions, and try as Mrs. Bain might, furry gray dust accumulated in the crevices.

5   The center-table was upheld by the perpetually strained arms of three carved figures, insistently female to the waist, then trailing discreetly off into a confusion of scrolls and scales. Upon it rested a row of blameless books, kept in place at the ends by the straining shoulder-muscles of two bronze-colored plaster elephants, forever pushing at their tedious toil.

6   On the heavily carved mantel was a gayly colored figure of a curly-headed peasant boy, ingeniously made so that he sat on the shelf and dangled one leg over. He was in the eternal act of removing a thorn from his chubby foot, his round face realistically wrinkled with the cruel pain. Just above him hung a steel-engraving of a chariot-race, the dust flying, the chariots careening wildly, the drivers ferociously lashing their maddened horses, the horses themselves caught by the artist the moment before their hearts burst, and they dropped in their traces.

7   The opposite wall was devoted to the religious in art; a steel-engraving of the Crucifixion, lavish of ghastly detail; a sepia-print of the martyrdom of Saint Sebastian, the cords cutting deep into the arms writhing from the stake, arrows bristling in the thick, soft-looking body; a water-color copy of a "Mother of Sorrows," the agonized eyes raised to a cold heaven, great, bitter tears forever on the wan cheeks, paler for the grave-like draperies that wrapped the head.

8   Beneath the windows hung a painting in oil of two lost sheep, huddled hopelessly together in the midst of a wild blizzard. This was one of the Old Gentleman's contributions to the room. Mrs. Bain was wont to observe of it that the frame was worth she didn't know how much.

9   The wall-space beside the door was reserved for a bit of modern art that had once caught Mr. Bain's eye in a stationer's window—a colored print, showing a railroad-crossing, with a train flying relentlessly toward it, and a low, red automobile trying to dash across the track before the iron terror shattered it into eternity. Nervous visitors who were given chairs facing this scene usually made opportunity to change their seats before they could give their whole minds to the conversation.

10   The ornaments, placed with careful casualness on the table and the upright piano, included a small gilt lion of Lucerne, a little, chipped, plaster Laocoön, and a savage china kitten eternally about to pounce upon a plump and helpless china mouse. This last had been one of the Old Gentleman's own wedding-gifts. Mrs. Bain explained, in tones low with awe, that it was very old.

11   The ash-receivers, of Oriental manufacture, were in the form of grotesque heads, tufted with bits of gray human hair, and given bulging, dead, glassy eyes and mouths stretched into great gapes, into which those who had the heart for it might flick their ashes. Thus the smallest details of the room kept loyally to the spirit of the thing, and carried on the effect.

12   But the three people now sitting in the Bains' living-room were not in the least oppressed by the decorative scheme. Two of them, Mr. and Mrs. Bain, not only had had twenty-eight years of the room to accustom themselves to it, but had been stanch admirers of it from the first. And no surroundings, however morbid, could close in on the aristocratic calm of Mrs. Bain's sister, Mrs. Whittaker.

13   She graciously patronized the very chair she now sat in, smiled kindly on the glass of cider she held in her hand. The Bains were poor, and Mrs. Whittaker had, as it is ingenuously called, married well, and none of them ever lost sight of these facts.

14   But Mrs. Whittaker's attitude of kindly tolerance was not confined to her less fortunate relatives. It extended to friends of her youth, working people, the arts, politics, the United States in general, and God, Who had always supplied her with the best of service. She could have given Him an excellent reference at any time.

15   The three people sat with a comfortable look of spending the evening. There was an air of expectancy about them, a not unpleasant little nervousness, as of those who wait for a curtain to rise. Mrs. Bain

had brought in cider in the best tumblers, and had served some of her nut cookies in the plate painted by hand with clusters of cherries—the plate she had used for sandwiches when, several years ago, her card club had met at her house.

16   She had thought it over a little tonight, before she lifted out the cherry plate, then quickly decided and resolutely heaped it with cookies. After all, it was an occasion—formal, perhaps, but still an occasion. The Old Gentleman was dying upstairs. At five o'clock that afternoon the doctor had said that it would be a surprise to him if the Old Gentleman lasted till the middle of the night—a big surprise, he had augmented.

17   There was no need for them to gather at the Old Gentleman's bedside. He would not have known any of them. In fact, he had not known them for almost a year, addressing them by wrong names and asking them grave, courteous questions about the health of husbands or wives or children who belonged to other branches of the family. And he was quite unconscious now.

18   Miss Chester, the nurse who had been with him since "this last stroke," as Mrs. Bain importantly called it, was entirely competent to attend and watch him. She had promised to call them if, in her tactful words, she saw any signs.

19   So the Old Gentleman's daughters and son-in-law waited in the warm living-room, and sipped their cider, and conversed in low, polite tones.

20   Mrs. Bain cried a little in pauses in the conversation. She had always cried easily and often. Yet, in spite of her years of practice, she did not do it well. Her eyelids grew pink and sticky, and her nose gave her no little trouble, necessitating almost constant sniffling. She sniffled loudly and conscientiously, and frequently removed her pince-nez to wipe her eyes with a crumpled handkerchief, gray with damp.

21   Mrs. Whittaker, too, bore a handkerchief, but she appeared to be holding it in waiting. She was dressed, in compliment to the occasion, in her black crepe de Chine, and she had left her lapis-lazuli pin, her olivine bracelet, and her topaz and amethyst rings at home in her bureau drawer, retaining only her lorgnette on its gold chain, in case there should be any reading to be done.

22   Mrs. Whittaker's dress was always studiously suited to its occasion; thus, her bearing had always that calm that only the correctly attired may enjoy. She was an authority on where to place monograms on linen, how to instruct working folk, and what to say in letters of condolence. The word "lady" figured largely in her conversation. Blood, she often predicted, would tell.

23   Mrs. Bain wore a rumpled white shirt-waist and the old blue skirt she saved for "around the kitchen." There had been time to change, after she had telephoned the doctor's verdict to her sister, but she had not been quite sure whether it was the thing to do. She had thought that Mrs. Whittaker might expect her to display a little distraught untidiness at a time like this; might even go in for it in a mild way herself.

24   Now Mrs. Bain looked at her sister's elaborately curled, painstakingly brown coiffure, and, nervously patted her own straggling hair, gray at the front, with strands of almost lime-color in the little twist at the back. Her eyelids grew wet and sticky again, and she hung her glasses over one forefinger while she applied the damp handkerchief. After all, she reminded herself and the others, it was her poor father.

25   Oh, but it was really the best thing, Mrs. Whittaker explained in her gentle, patient voice.

26   "You wouldn't want to see father go on like this," she pointed out. Mr. Bain echoed her, as if struck with the idea. Mrs. Bain had nothing to reply to them. No, she wouldn't want to see the Old Gentleman go on like this.

27   Five years before, Mrs. Whittaker had decided that the Old Gentleman was getting too old to live alone with only old Annie to cook for him and look after him. It was only a question of a little time before it "wouldn't have looked right," his living alone, when he had his children to take care of him. Mrs. Whittaker always stopped things before they got to the stage where they didn't look right. So he had come to live with the Bains.

28   Some of his furniture had been sold; a few things, such as his silver, his tall clock, and the Persian rug he had bought at the Exposition, Mrs. Whittaker had found room for in her own house; and some he brought with him to the Bains'.

29   Mrs. Whittaker's house was much larger than her sister's, and she had three servants and no children. But, as she told her friends, she had held back and let Allie and Lewis have the Old Gentleman.

30   "You see," she explained, dropping her voice to the tones reserved for not very pretty subjects, "Allie and Lewis are—well, they haven't a great deal."

31   So it was gathered that the Old Gentleman would do big things for the Bains when he came to live with them. Not exactly by paying board—it is a little too much to ask your father to pay for his food and lodging, as if he were a stranger. But, as Mrs. Whittaker suggested, he could do a great deal in the way of buying needed things for the house and keeping everything going.

32   And the Old Gentleman did contribute to the Bain household. He bought an electric heater and an electric fan, new curtains, storm-

windows, and light-fixtures, all for his bedroom; and had a nice little bathroom for his personal use made out of the small guest-room adjoining it.

33   He shopped for days until he found a coffee-cup large enough for his taste; he bought several large ash-trays, and a dozen extra-size bath-towels, that Mrs. Bain marked with his initials. And every Christmas and birthday he gave Mrs. Bain a round, new, shining ten-dollar gold piece. Of course, he presented gold pieces to Mrs. Whittaker, too, on like appropriate occasions. The Old Gentleman prided himself always on his fair-mindedness. He often said that he was not one to show any favoritism.

34   Mrs. Whittaker was Cordelia-like to her father during his declining years. She came to see him several times a month, bringing him jelly or potted hyacinths. Sometimes she sent her car and chauffeur for him, so that he might take an easy drive through the town, and Mrs. Bain might be afforded a chance to drop her cooking and accompany him. When Mrs. Whittaker was away on trips with her husband, she almost never neglected to send her father picture post-cards of various points of interest.

35   The Old Gentleman appreciated her affection, and took pride in her. He enjoyed being told that she was like him.

36   "That Hattie," he used to tell Mrs. Bain, "she's a fine woman—a fine woman."

37   As soon as she had heard that the Old Gentleman was dying Mrs. Whittaker had come right over, stopping only to change her dress and have her dinner. Her husband was away in the woods with some men, fishing. She explained to the Bains that there was no use in disturbing him—it would have been impossible for him to get back that night. As soon as—well, if anything happened she would telegraph him, and he could return in time for the funeral.

38   Mrs. Bain was sorry that he was away. She liked her ruddy, jovial, loud-voiced brother-in-law.

39   "It's too bad that Clint couldn't be here," she said, as she had said several times before. "He's so fond of cider," she added.

40   "Father," said Mrs. Whittaker, "was always very fond of Clint." Already the Old Gentleman had slipped into the past tense.

41   "Everybody likes Clint," Mr. Bain stated.

42   He was included in the "everybody." The last time he had failed in business, Clint had given him the clerical position he had since held over at the brush works. It was pretty generally understood that this had been brought about through Mrs. Whittaker's intervention, but still they were Clint's brush works, and it was Clint who paid him his salary. And forty dollars a week is indubitably forty dollars a week.

43   "I hope he'll be sure and be here in time for the funeral," said Mrs. Bain. "It will be Wednesday morning, I suppose, Hat?"

44   Mrs. Whittaker nodded.

45   "Or perhaps around two o'clock Wednesday afternoon," she amended. "I always think that's a nice time. Father has his frock coat, Allie?"

46   "Oh, yes," Mrs. Bain said eagerly. "And it's all clean and lovely. He has everything. Hattie, I noticed the other day at Mr. Newton's funeral they had more of a blue necktie on him, so I suppose they're wearing them—Mollie Newton always has everything just so. But I don't know—"

47   "I think," said Mrs. Whittaker firmly, "that there is nothing lovelier than black for an old gentleman."

48   "Poor Old Gentleman," said Mr. Bain, shaking his head. "He would have been eighty-five if he just could have lived till next September. Well, I suppose it's all for the best."

49   He took a small draft of cider and another cookie.

50   "A wonderful, wonderful life," summarized Mrs. Whittaker. "And a wonderful, wonderful old gentleman.

51   "Well, I should say so," said Mrs. Bain. "Why, up to the last year he was as interested in everything! It was, 'Allie, how much do you have to give for your eggs now?' and 'Allie, why don't you change your butcher? —this one's robbing you,' and 'Allie, who was that you were talking to on the telephone?' all day long! Everybody used to speak of it."

52   "And he used to come to the table right up to this stroke," Mr. Bain related, chuckling reminiscently. "My, he used to raise Cain when Allie didn't cut up his meat fast enough to suit him. Always had a temper, I'll tell you, the Old Gentleman did. Wouldn't stand for us having anybody in to meals—he didn't like that worth a cent. Eighty-four years old, and sitting right up there at the table with us!"

53   They vied in telling instances of the Old Gentleman's intelligence and liveliness, as parents cap one another's anecdotes of precocious children.

54   "It's only the past year that he had to be helped up- and downstairs," said Mrs. Bain. "Walked up-stairs all by himself, and more than eighty years old!"

55   Mrs. Whittaker was amused.

56   "I remember you said that once when Clint was here," she remarked, "and Clint said, 'Well, if you can't walk up-stairs by the time you're eighty, when are you going to learn?'"

57   Mrs. Bain smiled politely, because her brother-in-law had said it. Otherwise she would have been shocked and wounded.

58   "Yes, sir," said Mr. Bain. "Wonderful."

59   "The only thing I could have wished," Mrs. Bain said, after a pause—"I could have wished he'd been a little different about Paul. Somehow I've never felt quite right since Paul went into the navy."

60   Mrs. Whittaker's voice fell into the key used for the subject that has been gone over and over and over again.

61   "Now, Allie," she said, "you know yourself that was the best thing that could have happened. Father told you that himself, often and often. Paul was young, and he wanted to have all his young friends running in and out of the house, banging doors and making all sorts of racket, and it would have been a terrible nuisance for father. You must realize that father was more than eighty years old, Allie."

62   "Yes, I know," Mrs. Bain said. Her eyes went to the photograph of her son in his seaman's uniform, and she sighed.

63   "And besides," Mrs. Whittaker pointed out triumphantly, "now that Miss Chester's here in Paul's room, there wouldn't have been any room for him. So you see!"

64   There was rather a long pause. Then Mrs. Bain edged toward the other thing that had been weighing upon her.

65   "Hattie," she said, "I suppose—I suppose we'd ought to let Matt know?"

66   "I shouldn't," said Mrs. Whittaker composedly. She always took great pains with her "shall's" and "will's." "I only hope that he doesn't see it in the papers in time to come on for the funeral. If you want to have your brother turn up drunk at the services, Allie, *I* don't."

67   "But I thought he'd straightened up," said Mr. Bain. "Thought he was all right since he got married."

68   "Yes, I know, I know, Lewis," Mrs. Whittaker said wearily. "I've heard all about that. All I say is, *I* know what Matt is."

69   "John Loomis was telling me," reported Mr. Bain, "he was going through Akron, and he stopped off to see Matt. Said they had a nice little place, and he seemed to be getting along fine. Said she seemed like a crackerjack housekeeper."

70   Mrs. Whittaker smiled.

71   "Yes," she said, "John Loomis and Matt were always two of a kind—you couldn't believe a word either of them said. Probably she did seem to be a good housekeeper. I've no doubt she acted the part very well. Matt never made any bones of the fact that she was on the stage once, for almost a year. Excuse me from having that woman come to father's funeral. If you want to know what *I* think, *I* think that Matt marrying a woman like that had a good deal to do with hastening father's death."

72   The Bains sat in awe.

73   "And after all father did for Matt, too," added Mrs. Whittaker, her voice shaken.

74   "Well, I should think so," Mr. Bain was glad to agree.

75   "I remember how the Old Gentleman used to try and help Matt get along. He'd go down, like it was to Mr. Fuller, that time Matt was working at the bank, and he'd explain to him, 'Now, Mr. Fuller,' he'd say, 'I don't know whether you know it, but this son of mine has always been what you might call the black sheep of the family. He's been kind of a drinker,' he'd say, 'and he's got himself into trouble a couple of times, and if you'd just keep an eye on him, so's to see he keeps straight, it'd be a favor to me.'

76   "Mr. Fuller told me about it himself. Said it was wonderful the way the Old Gentleman came right out and talked just as frankly to him. Said *he'd* never had any idea Matt was that way—wanted to hear all about it."

77   Mrs. Whittaker nodded sadly.

78   "Oh, I know," she said. "Time and again father would do that. And then, as like as not, Matt would get one of sulky fits, and not turn up at his work."

79   "And when Matt would be out of work," Mrs. Bain said, "the way father'd hand him out his car-fare, and I don't know what all! When Matt was a grown man, going on thirty years old, father would take him down to Newins & Malley's and buy him a whole new outfit— pick out everything himself. He always used to say Matt was the kind that would get cheated out of his eye-teeth if he went into a store alone."

80   "My, father hated to see anybody make a fool of themselves about money," Mrs. Whittaker commented. "Remember how he always used to say, 'Anybody can make money, but it takes a wise man to keep it'?"

81   "I suppose he must be a pretty rich man," Mr. Bain said, abruptly restoring the Old Gentleman to the present.

82   "Oh—rich!" Mrs. Whittaker's smile was at its kindliest. "But he managed his affairs very well, father did, right up to the last. Everything is in splendid shape, Clint says."

83   "He showed you the will, didn't he, Hat?" asked Mrs. Bain, forming bits of her sleeve into little plaits between her thin, hard fingers.

84   "Yes," said her sister. "Yes, he did. He showed me the will. A little over a year ago, I think it was, wasn't it? You know, just before he started to fail, that time."

85   She took a small bite of cooky.

86   "*Awfully* good," she said. She broke into a little bubbly laugh, the laugh she used at teas and wedding receptions and fairly formal din-

ners. "You know," she went on, as one sharing a good story, "he's gone and left all that old money to me. 'Why, Father!' I said, as soon as I'd read that part. But it seems he'd gotten some sort of idea in his head that Clint and I would be able to take care of it better than anybody else, and you know what father was, once he made up that mind of his. You can just imagine how *I* felt. I couldn't say a thing."

87   She laughed again, shaking her head in amused bewilderment.

88   "Oh, and Allie," she said, "he's left you all the furniture he brought here with him, and all the things he bought since he came. And Lewis is to have his set of Thackeray. And that money he lent Lewis, to try and tide him over in the hardware business that time—that's to be regarded as a gift."

89   She sat back and looked at them, smiling.

90   "Lewis paid back most all of that money father lent him that time," Mrs. Bain said. "There was only about two hundred dollars more, and then he would have had it all paid up."

91   "That's to be regarded as a gift," insisted Mrs. Whittaker. She leaned over and patted her brother-in-law's arm. "Father always liked you, Lewis," she said softly.

92   "Poor Old Gentleman," murmured Mr. Bain.

93   "Did it—did it say anything about Matt?" asked Mrs. Bain.

94   "Oh, Allie!" Mrs. Whittaker gently reproved her. "When you think of all the money father spent and spent on Matt, it seems to me he did more than enough—more than enough. And then when Matt went way off there to live, and married that woman, and never a word about it— father hearing it all through strangers—well, I don't think any of us realize how it hurt father. He never said much about it, but I don't think he ever got over it. I'm always so thankful that poor dear mother didn't live to see how Matt turned out."

95   "Poor mother," said Mrs. Bain shakily, and brought the grayish handkerchief into action once more. "I can hear her now, just as plain. 'Now, children,' she used to say, 'do for goodness' sake let's all try and keep your father in a good humor.' If I've heard her say it once, I've heard her say it a hundred times. Remember, Hat?"

96   "Do I remember!" said Mrs. Whittaker. "And do you remember how they used to play whist, and how furious father used to get when he lost?"

97   "Yes," Mrs. Bain cried excitedly, "and how mother used to have to cheat, so as to be sure and not win from him? She got so she used to be able to do it just as well!"

98   They laughed softly, filled with memories of the gone days. A pleasant, thoughtful silence fell around them.

99   Mrs. Bain patted a yawn to extinction, and looked at the clock.

100   "Ten minutes to eleven," she said. "Goodness, I had no idea it was anywhere near so late. I wish—" She stopped just in time, crimson at what her wish would have been.

101   "You see, Lew and I have got in the way of going to bed early," she explained. "Father slept so light, we couldn't have people in like we used to before he came here, to play a little bridge or anything, on account of disturbing him. And if we wanted to go to the movies or anywhere, he'd go on so about being left alone that we just kind of gave up going."

102   "Oh, the Old Gentleman always let you know what he wanted," said Mr. Bain, smiling. "He was a wonder, *I'll* tell you. Nearly eighty-five years old!"

103   "Think of it," said Mrs. Whittaker.

104   A door clicked open above them, and feet ran quickly and not lightly down the stairs. Miss Chester burst into the room.

105   "Oh, Mrs. Bain!" she cried. "Oh, the Old Gentleman! Oh, he's gone! I noticed him kind of stirring and whimpering a little, and he seemed to be trying to make motions at his warm milk, like as if he wanted some. So I put the cup up to his mouth, and he sort of fell over, and just like that he was gone, and the milk all over him."

106   Mrs. Bain instantly collapsed into passionate weeping. Her husband put his arm tenderly about her, and murmured a series of "Now-now's."

107   Mrs. Whittaker rose, set her cider-glass carefully on the table, shook out her handkerchief, and moved toward the door.

108   "A lovely death," she pronounced. "A wonderful, wonderful life, and now a beautiful, peaceful death. Oh, it's the best thing, Allie; it's the best thing."

109   "Oh, it is, Mrs. Bain; it's the best thing," Miss Chester said earnestly. "It's really a blessing. That's what it is."

110   Among them they got Mrs. Bain up the stairs.

The Wonderful Old Gentleman

JOURNAL

1. **MLA Works Cited**   *Using this model, record this story here.*

   Author's Last Name, First Name. "Title of the Story." <u>Title of the Book</u>. 3rd ed. Ed. First Name Last Name. City: Publisher, year. Pages of the story.

2. **Main Character(s)**   *Describe each main character, and explain why you think each is a main character.*

3. **Supporting Characters**   *Describe each supporting character, and explain why you think each is a supporting character.*

4. **Setting**   *Describe the setting(s) and any relevant prop(s).*

5. Sequence   *Outline the events of the story in order.*

6. Plot   *Tell the story in no more than two sentences.*

7. Conflicts   *Identify and explain all the conflicts involved here.*

8. Significant Quotations   *Explain the importance of each of these quotations. Record the page number in the parentheses.*

a. "Mrs. Whittaker, too, bore a handkerchief, but she appeared to be holding it in waiting" (   ).

b. "Mrs. Whittaker's house was much larger than her sister's, and she had three servants and no children. But, as she told her friends, she had held back and let Allie and Lewis have the Old Gentleman" (   ).

c. " 'And besides,' Mrs. Whittaker pointed out triumphantly, 'now that Miss Chester's here in Paul's room, there wouldn't have been any room for him' " (   ).

d. " 'Mr. Fuller told me about it himself. [. . .]. Said *he'd* never had any idea Matt was that way—wanted to hear all about it' " (   ).

e. " 'You know,' she went on, as one sharing a good story, 'he's gone and left all that old money to me' " (   ).

9. **Literary Elements**   *Look at this chapter's title and explain why you think this story is placed in this chapter. Explain in which other chapter(s) you might place this story, as relevant to the literary element(s) of that chapter.*

10. **Foreshadowing, Irony, and/or Symbolism**   *Explain examples of foreshadowing, irony, and/or symbolism in this story.*

Follow-Up Questions

10 Short Questions

*Select the **best** answer for each.*

____ 1. The Bains are
   a. richer than the Whittakers.
   b. poorer than the Whittakers.
   c. the same as the Whittakers.

____ 2. The Whittakers are
   a. richer than the Bains.
   b. poorer than the Bains.
   c. the same as the Bains.

____ 3. The Old Gentleman is father to
   a. Mrs. Bain.
   b. Mrs Whittaker.
   c. both Mrs. Bain and Mrs. Whittaker.

____ 4. The Old Gentleman lives
   a. with the Bains.
   b. with the Whittakers.
   c. by himself.

____ 5. The Old Gentleman
   a. enjoys his grandson, Paul.
   b. welcomes his grandson, Paul.
   c. drives away his grandson, Paul.

____ 6. Mrs. Bain is
   a. upset that Paul is gone.
   b. happy that Paul is gone.
   c. unconcerned about Paul being gone.

____ 7. The Old Gentleman has
   a. regular meetings with his son, Matt.
   b. been good to his son, Matt.
   c. undermined his son, Matt.

____ 8. The person who sincerely cares about the Old Gentleman is
   a. Mrs. Bain.
   b. Mrs. Whittaker.
   c. Matt.

____ 9. The Old Gentleman will leave his wealth to
   a. Mrs. Bain.
   b. Mrs. Whittaker.
   c. Matt.

____ 10. The Old Gentleman
   a. treats all his children equally.
   b. plays favorites among his children.
   c. is fair to all his children.

5 Significant Quotations

Explain the importance of each of these quotations.

1. "She sniffed loudly and conscientiously, and frequently removed her pince-nez to wipe her eyes with a crumpled handkerchief, gray with damp."

2. "Five years before, Mrs. Whittaker had decided that the Old Gentleman was getting too old to live alone [. . .]. So he had come to live with the Bains."

3. " 'The only thing I could have wished,' Mrs. Bain said, after a pause— 'I could have wished he'd been a little different about Paul.' "

4. " 'Hattie,' she said, 'I suppose—I suppose we'd ought to let Matt know?' "

5. " 'He showed you the will, didn't he, Hat?' asked Mrs. Bain [. . .]."

2 COMPREHENSION ESSAY QUESTIONS

Use specific details and information from the story to answer these questions as completely as possible.

1. What is the irony in this story? Use specific details and information from the story to support your explanation.

2. Who should have inherited the Old Gentleman's wealth and why? Use specific details and information from the story to support your discussion.

DISCUSSION QUESTIONS

Be prepared to discuss these questions in class.

1. How do you feel about the Bains? Mrs. Whittaker? The Old Gentleman? Use specific details from the story to explain your feelings.

2. How does the illustration demonstrate this story? Use specific details from the story to support your ideas.

WRITING

Use each of these ideas for writing an essay.

1. We all have, or know of someone who has, worked hard only to have the reward for that hard work given to another. Write an essay contrasting the worker with the receiver.

2. Many families treat one member differently from another. Write a narrative essay telling about one instance of different treatment in your own family or in a family you know.

Further Writing

1. Compare this story with Alice Walker's "Everyday Use" (page 108).

2. Read and compare Dorothy Parker's "A Telephone Call" with Parker's "New York to Detroit" (both of which are available in a library).

The Ransom of Red Chief

O. Henry

PRE-READING VOCABULARY
CONTEXT

Use context clues to define these words before reading. Use a dictionary as needed.

1. *Kidnapping*, or the taking of someone against her or his will, is a federal offense. *Kidnapping* means _____.

2. When Kelli climbed to the very top of the hill, she had reached the *summit*. *Summit* means _____.

3. Scott is a very honest person and refuses to be part of anything that is *fraudulent*. *Fraudulent* means _____.

4. Vernie had a *scheme* to make a fortune; she would buy old houses, fix them up, and sell them for a profit. *Scheme* means

   _____.

5. Dennis is a *prominent* citizen who has served as mayor, senator, and governor. *Prominent* means _____.

6. In order to get back his rare bird that was stolen, José had to pay a *ransom* of five hundred dollars. *Ransom* means

   _____.

7. Janet decided to drive across the flat fields of Oklahoma and Nebraska, which are part of the American *plains*. *Plains* means

   _____.

8. When Ajay had his head shaved, he looked as if the top of his head was gone and he had been *scalped*. *Scalped* means

   _____.

9. When Rudy bought a new boat, he *christened* it "Weekends" and had this name painted on the back. *Christen* means _____.

10. When Purvi lost her wallet with all her money in it, she was *desperate* to get it back. *Desperate* means _____.

11. After getting lost, Artie had to get out the map and *reconnoiter* to figure out where he was. *Reconnoiter* means _____.

12. Courtney loved the many trees that were around her home and that gave her a rich, *sylvan* view. *Sylvan* means _____.

13. JoAnne *complies* with the law and always obeys the speed limit. *Comply* means _____.

14. Patrick looked at Michael *suspiciously* when he saw Michael's face was covered with chocolate and the new cake was missing. *Suspicious* means _____.

15. Old cowboys in the West sometimes referred to a horse as a *"hoss."* *Hoss* means _____.

16. Carrie thought Reid was trying to cheat her, but then she decided he was being fair and *square*. *Square* means _____.

17. Hal offered a thousand dollars for the car, but the seller offered a *counter-proposition* of two thousand dollars. *Counter-proposition* means _____.

18. The people who live around you are called your *neighbors*. *Neighbor* means _____.

19. Mary was so *liberal* in spreading the jelly that the bread fell apart because of the sheer weight of the jelly. *Liberal* means

_____.

20. After walking on the old wooden boardwalk, Missy had to *abstract* a splinter from her foot. *Abstract* means _____.

Pre-reading Vocabulary
Structural Attack

Define these words by solving the parts. Use the Glossary or a dictionary as needed.

1. self-satisfied
2. semi-rural
3. bloodhound
4. fancier
5. forecloser
6. welter-weight
7. tail-feathers
8. magic-lantern
9. warpath
10. during-dinner
11. war-whoop
12. outlaw
13. indecent
14. terrifying
15. sun-up
16. sleepiness
17. lambkin
18. disappearance
19. earthquake
20. skyrocket
21. parental
22. wildcat
23. hereinafter
24. fence-post
25. postmaster
26. mail-carrier
27. self-defense
28. mad-house
29. counterplot
30. spend-thrift

Pre-reading Questions

Try answering these questions as you read.

What is the plan?

How does the boy react?

What goes wrong?

What is the irony in the story?

The Ransom of Red Chief

O. HENRY

William Sydney Porter was born in 1862 to an educated and comfortable family living in Greensboro, North Carolina, and he grew up in the Reconstruction South. As a result of his mother's early death and his father's alcoholism, he was raised by his aunt, who gave him a love for narration. Like his father, he became a pharmacist's apprentice, and although he did not like the work, his uncle's drugstore provided him with a good vantage point from which to observe the townspeople. In 1882 he married Athol Estes Roach, settled into work at the National Bank of Texas, and bought a printing press to publish his stories in the short-lived The Rolling Stone. He was charged and cleared of embezzlement—a charge he consistently denied. Later, faced with retrial, he fled to New Orleans and then to Honduras, all the while observing others. Returning to Texas because of his wife's failing health and subsequent death, he was retried and sent to the Ohio state penitentiary where he served three years of a five-year sentence. Although it was a dark period in his life, he was again observing and, perhaps, gained his compassion for the underdog, as well as the pen name "O. Henry." In 1902 he moved to New York City to produce weekly stories for the New York Sunday World, and at the turn of the century and amid the streets of New York that were largely filled with immigrants, he found endless stock for his stories. O. Henry died in 1910.

His stories are marked by concise characterizations, concern for working women and the poor, adroit wit, and succinct irony. His many stories and selected sketches are largely based on kernels from his real-life observations and are available in many collections.

I t looked like a good thing: but wait till I tell you. We were down
South, in Alabama—Bill Driscoll and myself—when this kidnapping
idea struck us. It was, as Bill afterward expressed it, "during a moment
of temporary mental apparition;" but we didn't find that out till later.

2   There was a town down there, as flat as a flannel-cake, and called
Summit, of course. It contained inhabitants of as undeleterious and
self-satisfied a class of peasantry as ever clustered around a Maypole.

3   Bill and me had a joint capital of about six hundred dollars, and we
needed just two thousand dollars more to pull off a fraudulent town-lot
scheme in Western Illinois with. We talked it over on the front steps of
the hotel. Philoprogenitoveness, says we, is strong in semi-rural communities; therefore, and for other reasons, a kidnapping project ought
to do better there than in the radius of newspapers that send reporters
out in plain clothes to stir up talk about such things. We knew that
Summit couldn't get after us with anything stronger than constables
and, maybe, some lackadaisical bloodhounds and a diatribe or two in
the *Weekly Farmers' Budget*. So, it looked good.

4   We selected for our victim the only child of a prominent citizen
named Ebenezer Dorset. The father was respectable and tight, a mort-
gage fancier and a stern, upright collection-plate passer and forecloser.
The kid was a boy of ten, with bas-relief freckles, and hair the color of
the cover of the magazine you buy at the news-stand when you want to
catch a train. Bill and me figured that Ebenezer would melt down for a
ransom of two thousand dollars to a cent. But wait till I tell you.

5   About two miles from Summit was a little mountain, covered with
a dense cedar brake. On the rear elevation of this mountain was a cave.
There we stored provisions.

6   One evening after sundown, we drove in a buggy past old Dorset's
house. The kid was in the street, throwing rocks at a kitten on the
opposite fence.

7   "Hey, little boy!" says Bill, "would you like to have a bag of candy
and a nice ride?"

8   The boy catches Bill neatly in the eye with a piece of brick.

9   "That will cost the old man an extra five hundred dollars," says
Bill, climbing over the wheel.

10   That boy put up a fight like a welter-weight cinnamon bear; but, at
last, we got him down in the bottom of the buggy and drove away. We
took him up to the cave, and I hitched the horse in the cedar brake.
After dark I drove the buggy to the little village, three miles away,
where we had hired it, and walked back to the mountain.

11   Bill was pasting court-plaster over the scratches and bruises on his
features. There was a fire burning behind the big rock at the entrance
of the cave, and the boy was watching a pot of boiling coffee, with two

buzzard tail-feathers stuck in his red hair. He points a stick at me when I come up, and says:

12   "Ha! cursed paleface, do you dare to enter the camp of Red Chief, the terror of the plains?"

13   "He's all right now," says Bill, rolling up his trousers and examining some bruises on his shins. "We're playing Indian. We're making Buffalo Bill's show look like magic-lantern views of Palestine in the town hall. I'm Old Hank, the Trapper, Red Chief's captive, and I'm to be scalped at daybreak. By Geronimo! that kid can kick hard."

14   Yes, sir, that boy seemed to be having the time of his life. The fun of camping out in a cave had made him forget that he was a captive himself. He immediately christened me Snake-eye, the Spy, and announced that, when his braves returned from the warpath, I was to be broiled at the stake at the rising of the sun.

15   Then we had supper; and he filled his mouth full of bacon and bread and gravy, and began to talk. He made a during-dinner speech something like this:

16   "I like this fine. I never camped out before; but I had a pet 'possum once, and I was nine last birthday. I hate to go to school. Rats ate up sixteen of Jimmy Talbot's aunt's speckled hen's eggs. Are there any real Indians in these woods? I want some more gravy. Does the trees moving make the wind blow? We had five puppies. What makes your nose so red, Hank? My father has lots of money. Are the stars hot? I whipped Ed Walker twice, Saturday. I don't like girls. You dassent catch toads unless with a string. Do oxen make any noise? Why are oranges round? Have you got beds to sleep on in this cave? Amos Murray has got six toes. A parrot can talk, but a monkey or a fish can't. How many does it take to make twelve?"

17   Every few minutes he would remember that he was a pesky redskin, and pick up his stick rifle and tiptoe to the mouth of the cave to rubber for the scouts of the hated paleface. Now and then he would let out a war-whoop that made Old Hank the Trapper shiver. That boy had Bill terrorized from the start.

18   "Red Chief," says I to the kid, "would you like to go home?"

19   "Aw, what for?" says he. "I don't have any fun at home. I hate to go to school. I like to camp out. You won't take me back home again, Snake-eye, will you?"

20   "Not right away," says I. "We'll stay here in the cave awhile."

21   "All right!" says he. "That'll be fine. I never had such fun in all my life."

22   We went to bed about eleven o'clock. We spread down some wide blankets and quilts and put Red Chief between us. We weren't afraid he'd run away. He kept us awake for three hours, jumping up and

reaching for his rifle and screeching: "Hist! pard," in mine and Bill's ears, as the fancied crackle of a twig or the rustle of a leaf revealed to his young imagination the stealthy approach of the outlaw band. At last, I fell into a troubled sleep, and dreamed that I had been kidnapped and chained to a tree by a ferocious pirate with red hair.

23   Just at daybreak, I was awakened by a series of awful screams from Bill. They weren't yells, or howls, or shouts, or whoops, or yawps, such as you'd expect from a manly set of vocal organs—they were simply indecent, terrifying, humiliating screams, such as women emit when they see ghosts or caterpillars. It's an awful thing to hear a strong, desperate, fat man scream incontinently in a cave at daybreak.

24   I jumped up to see what the matter was. Red Chief was sitting on Bill's chest, with one hand twined in Bill's hair. In the other he had the sharp case-knife we used for slicing bacon; and he was industriously and realistically trying to take Bill's scalp, according to the sentence that had been pronounced upon him the evening before.

25   I got the knife away from the kid and made him lie down again. But, from that moment, Bill's spirit was broken. He laid down on his side of the bed, but he never closed an eye again in sleep as long as that boy was with us. I dozed off for a while, but along toward sun-up I remembered that Red Chief had said I was to be burned at the stake at the rising of the sun. I wasn't nervous or afraid; but I sat up and lit my pipe and leaned against a rock.

26   "What you getting up so soon for, Sam?" asked Bill.

27   "Me?" says I. "Oh, I got a kind of pain in my shoulder. I thought sitting up would rest it."

28   "You're a liar!" says Bill. "You're afraid. You was to be burned at sunrise, and you was afraid he'd do it. And he would, too, if he could find a match. Ain't it awful, Sam? Do you think anybody will pay out money to get a little imp like that back home?"

29   "Sure," said I. "A rowdy kid like that is just the kind that parents dote on. Now, you and the Chief get up and cook breakfast, while I go up on the top of this mountain and reconnoiter."

30   I went up on the peak of the little mountain and ran my eye over the contiguous vicinity. Over towards Summit I expected to see the sturdy yeomanry of the village armed with scythes and pitchforks beating the countryside for the dastardly kidnappers. But what I saw was a peaceful landscape dotted with one man ploughing with a dun mule. Nobody was dragging the creek; no couriers dashed hither and yon, bringing tidings of no news to the distracted parents. There was a sylvan attitude of somnolent sleepiness pervading that section of the external outward surface of Alabama that lay exposed to my view. "Perhaps," says I to myself, "it has not yet been discovered that the

wolves have borne away the tender lambkin from the fold. Heaven help the wolves!" says I, and I went down the mountain to breakfast.

31   When I got to the cave I found Bill backed up against the side of it, breathing hard, and the boy threatening to smash him with a rock half as big as a cocoanut.

32   "He put a red-hot boiled potato down my back," explained Bill, "and then mashed it with his foot; and I boxed his ears. Have you got a gun about you, Sam?"

33   I took the rock away from the boy and kind of patched up the argument. "I'll fix you," says the kid to Bill. "No man ever yet struck the Red Chief but he got paid for it. You better beware!"

34   After breakfast the kid takes a piece of leather with strings wrapped around it out of his pocket and goes outside the cave unwinding it.

35   "What's he up to now?" says Bill, anxiously. "You don't think he'll run away, do you, Sam?"

36   "No fear of it," says I. "He don't seem to be much of a home body. But we've got to fix up some plan about the ransom. There don't seem to be much excitement around Summit on account of his disappearance; but maybe they haven't realized yet that he's gone. His folks may think he's spending the night with Aunt Jane or one of the neighbors. Anyhow, he'll be missed to-day. To-night we must get a message to his father demanding the two thousand dollars for his return."

37   Just then we heard a kind of war-whoop, such as David might have emitted when he knocked out the champion Goliath. It was a sling that Red Chief had pulled out of his pocket, and he was whirling it around his head.

38   I dodged, and heard a heavy thud and a kind of a sigh from Bill, like a horse gives out when you take his saddle off. A rock the size of an egg had caught Bill just behind his left ear. He loosened himself all over and fell in the fire across the frying pan of hot water for washing the dishes. I dragged him out and poured cold water on his head for half an hour.

39   By and by, Bill sits up and feels behind his ear and says: "Sam, do you know who my favorite Biblical character is?"

40   "Take it easy," says I. "You'll come to your senses presently."

41   "King Herod," says he. "You won't go away and leave me here alone, will you, Sam?"

42   I went out and caught that boy and shook him until his freckles rattled.

43   "If you don't behave," says I, "I'll take you straight home. Now, are you going to be good, or not?"

44   "I was only funning," says he, sullenly. "I didn't mean to hurt Old Hank. But what did he hit me for? I'll behave, Snake-eye, if you won't send me home, and if you'll let me play the Black Scout to-day."

45   "I don't know the game," says I. "That's for you and Mr. Bill to decide. He's your playmate for the day. I'm going away for a while, on business. Now, you come in and make friends with him and say you are sorry for hurting him, or home you go, at once."

46   I made him and Bill shake hands, and then I took Bill aside and told him I was going to Poplar Grove, a little village three miles from the cave, and find out what I could about how the kidnapping had been regarded in Summit. Also, I thought it best to send a peremptory letter to old man Dorset that day, demanding the ransom and dictating how it should be paid.

47   "You know, Sam," says Bill, "I've stood by you without batting an eye in earthquakes, fire and flood—in poker games, dynamite outrages, police raids, train robberies, and cyclones. I never lost my nerve yet till we kidnapped that two-legged skyrocket of a kid. He's got me going. You won't leave me long with him, will you, Sam?"

48   "I'll be back some time this afternoon," says I. "You must keep the boy amused and quiet till I return. And now we'll write the letter to old Dorset."

49   Bill and I got paper and pencil and worked on the letter while Red Chief, with a blanket wrapped around him, strutted up and down, guarding the mouth of the cave. Bill begged me tearfully to make the ransom fifteen hundred dollars instead of two thousand. "I ain't attempting," says he, "to decry the celebrated moral aspect of parental affection, but we're dealing with humans, and it ain't human for anybody to give up two thousand dollars for that forty-pound chunk of freckled wildcat. I'm willing to take a chance at fifteen hundred dollars. You can charge the difference up to me."

50   So, to relieve Bill, I acceded, and we collaborated a letter that ran this way:

51   Ebenezer Dorset, Esq.:

52   We have your boy concealed in a place far from Summit. It is useless for you or the most skilful detectives to attempt to find him. Absolutely, the only terms on which you can have him restored to you are these: We demand fifteen hundred dollars in large bills for his return; the money to be left at midnight to-night at the same spot and in the same box as your reply—as hereinafter described. If you agree to these terms, send your answer in writing by a solitary messenger to-night at half-past eight o'clock. After crossing Owl Creek on the road to Poplar Grove, there are three large trees about a hundred yards apart, close to the fence of the wheat field on the right-hand side. At the bottom of the fence-post, opposite the third tree, will be found a small pasteboard box.

53   The messenger will place the answer in this box and return immediately to Summit.

54   If you attempt any treachery or fail to comply with our demand as stated, you will never see your boy again.

55   If you pay the money as demanded, he will be returned to you safe and well within three hours. These terms are final, and if you do not accede to them no further communication will be attempted.

56   Two Desperate Men

57   I addressed this letter to Dorset, and put it in my pocket. As I was about to start, the kid comes up to me and says:

58   "Aw, Snake-eye, you said I could play the Black Scout while you was gone."

59   "Play it, of course," says I. "Mr. Bill will play with you. What kind of a game is it?"

60   "I'm the Black Scout," says Red Chief, "and I have to ride to the stockade to warn the settlers that the Indians are coming. I'm tired of playing Indian myself. I want to be the Black Scout."

61   "All right," says I. "It sounds harmless to me. I guess Mr. Bill will help you foil the pesky savages."

62   "What am I to do?" asks Bill, looking at the kid suspiciously.

63   "You are the hoss," says Black Scout. "Get down on your hands and knees. How can I ride to the stockade without a hoss?"

64   "You'd better keep him interested," said I, "till we get the scheme going. Loosen up."

65   Bill gets down on his all fours, and a look comes in his eye like a rabbit's when you catch it in a trap.

66   "How far is it to the stockade, kid?" he asks, in a husky manner of voice.

67   "Ninety miles," says the Black Scout. "And you have to hump yourself to get there on time. Whoa, now!"

68   The Black Scout jumps on Bill's back and digs his heels in his side.

69   "For Heaven's sake," says Bill, "hurry back, Sam, as soon as you can. I wish we hadn't made the ransom more than a thousand. Say, you quit kicking me or I'll get up and warm you good."

70   I walked over to Poplar Grove and sat around the post-office and store, talking with the chaw-bacons that came in to trade. One whiskerando says that he hears Summit is all upset on account of Elder Ebenezer Dorset's boy having been lost or stolen. That was all I wanted to know. I bought some smoking tobacco, referred casually to the price of blackeyed peas, posted my letter surreptitiously, and came away. The postmaster said the mail-carrier would come by in an hour to take the mail to Summit.

71   When I got back to the cave Bill and the boy were not to be found. I explored the vicinity of the cave, and risked a yodel or two, but there was no response.

72   So I lighted my pipe and sat down on a mossy bank to await developments.

73   In about half an hour I heard the bushes rustle, and Bill wabbled out into the little glade in front of the cave. Behind him was the kid, stepping softly like a scout, with a broad grin on his face. Bill stopped, took off his hat, and wiped his face with a red handkerchief. The kid stopped about eight feet behind him.

74   "Sam," says Bill, "I suppose you'll think I'm a renegade, but I couldn't help it. I'm a grown person with masculine proclivities and habits of self-defense, but there is a time when all systems of egotism and predominance fall. The boy is gone. I sent him home. All is off. There was martyrs in old times," goes on Bill, "that suffered death rather than give up the particular graft they enjoyed. None of 'em ever was subjugated to such supernatural tortures as I have been. I tried to be faithful to our articles of depredation; but there came a limit."

75   "What's the trouble, Bill?" I asks him.

76   "I was rode," says Bill, "the ninety miles to the stockade, not barring an inch. Then, when the settlers was rescued, I was given oats. Sand ain't a palatable substitute. And then, for an hour I had to try to explain to him why there was nothin' in holes, how a road can run both ways, and what makes the grass green. I tell you, Sam, a human can only stand so much. I takes him by the neck of his clothes and drags him down the mountain. On the way he kicks my legs black and blue from the knees down; and I've got to have two or three bites on my thumb and hand cauterized.

77   "But he's gone"—continues Bill—"gone home. I showed him the road to Summit and kicked him about eight feet nearer there at one kick. I'm sorry we lose the ransom; but it was either that or Bill Driscoll to the madhouse."

78   Bill is puffing and blowing, but there is a look of ineffable peace and growing content on his rose-pink features.

79   "Bill," says I, "there isn't any heart disease in your family, is there?"

80   "No," says Bill, "nothing chronic except malaria and accidents. Why?"

81   "Then you might turn around," says I, "and have a look behind you."

82   Bill turns and sees the boy, and loses his complexion and sits down plump on the ground and begins to pluck aimlessly at grass and little sticks. For an hour I was afraid of his mind. And then I told him that my scheme was to put the whole job through immediately and that we would get the ransom and be off with it by midnight if old Dorset fell in with our proposition. So Bill braced up enough to give the kid a weak sort of a smile and a promise to play the Russian in a Japanese war with him as soon as he felt a little better.

83   I had a scheme for collecting that ransom without danger of being caught by counterplots that ought to commend itself to professional

kidnappers. The tree under which the answer was to be left—and the money later on—was close to the road fence with big, bare fields on all sides. If a gang of constables should be watching for any one to come for the note, they could see him a long way off crossing the fields or in the road. But no, sirree! At half-past eight I was up in that tree as well hidden as a tree toad, waiting for the messenger to arrive.

84   Exactly on time, a half-grown boy rides up the road on a bicycle, locates the pasteboard box at the foot of the fence-post, slips a folded piece of paper into it, and pedals away again back toward Summit.

85   I waited an hour and then concluded the thing was square. I slid down the tree, got the note, slipped along the fence till I struck the woods, and was back at the cave in another half an hour. I opened the note, got near the lantern, and read it to Bill. It was written with a pen in a crabbed hand, and the sum and substance of it was this:

86   Two Desperate Men.

87   Gentlemen: I received your letter to-day by post, in regard to the ransom you ask for the return of my son. I think you are a little high in your demands, and I hereby make you a counter-proposition, which I am inclined to believe you will accept. You bring Johnny home and pay me two hundred and fifty dollars in cash, and I agree to take him off your hands. You had better come at night, for the neighbors believe he is lost, and I couldn't be responsible for what they would do to anybody they saw bringing him back. Very respectfully,

88   Ebenezer Dorset

89   "Great pirates of Penzance," says I; "of all the impudent—"

90   But I glanced at Bill, and hesitated. He had the most appealing look in his eyes I ever saw on the face of a dumb or a talking brute.

91   "Sam," says he, "what's two hundred and fifty dollars, after all? We've got the money. One more night of this kid will send me to a bed in Bedlam. Besides being a thorough gentleman, I think Mr. Dorset is a spendthrift for making us such a liberal offer. You ain't going to let the chance go, are you?"

92   "Tell you the truth, Bill," says I, "this little he ewe lamb has somewhat got on my nerves too. We'll take him home, pay the ransom, and make our getaway."

93   We took him home that night. We got him to go by telling him that his father had bought a silver-mounted rifle and a pair of moccasins for him, and we were to hunt bears the next day.

94   It was just twelve o'clock when we knocked at Ebenezer's front door. Just at the moment when I should have been abstracting the fifteen hundred dollars from the box under the tree, according to the original proposition, Bill was counting out two hundred and fifty dollars into Dorset's hand.

95   When the kid found out we were going to leave him at home he started up a howl like a calliope and fastened himself as tight as a leech to Bill's leg. His father peeled him away gradually, like a porous plaster.

96   "How long can you hold him?" asks Bill.

97   "I'm not as strong as I used to be," says old Dorset, "but I think I can promise you ten minutes."

98   "Enough," says Bill. "In ten minutes I shall cross the Central, Southern, and Middle Western States, and be legging it trippingly for the Canadian border."

99   And, as dark as it was, and as fat as Bill was, and as good a runner as I am, he was a good mile and a half out of Summit before I could catch up with him.

The Ransom of Red Chief

JOURNAL

1. **MLA Works Cited**   *Using this model, record this story here.*

   Author's Last Name, First Name. "Title of the Story." Title of the Book.
   3rd ed. Ed. First Name Last Name. City: Publisher, year. Pages of
   the story.

2. **Main Character(s)**   *Describe each main character, and explain why you*
   think each is a main character.

3. **Supporting Characters**   *Describe each supporting character, and explain why*
   you think each is a supporting character.

4. **Setting**   *Describe the setting(s) and any relevant prop(s).*

5. **Sequence** *Outline the events of the story in order.*

6. **Plot** *Tell the story in no more than two sentences.*

7. **Conflicts** *Identify and explain all the conflicts involved here.*

8. **Significant Quotations** *Explain the importance of each of these quotations. Record the page number in the parentheses.*

   a. "Bill and me had a joint capital of about six hundred dollars, and we needed just two thousand dollars more to pull off a fraudulent town-lot scheme in Western Illinois with" (   ).

   b. " 'For Heaven's sake,' says Bill, 'hurry back, Sam, as soon as you can. I wish we hadn't made the ransom more than a thousand' " (   ).

c. " 'Then you might turn around,' says I, 'and have a look behind you' " (   ).

d. " 'You bring Johnny home and pay me two hundred and fifty dollars in cash, and I agree to take him off your hands' " (   ).

e. "[. . .] Bill was counting out two hundred and fifty dollars into Dorset's hand" (   ).

9. **Literary Elements**   *Look at this chapter's title and explain why you think this story is placed in this chapter. Explain in which other chapter(s) you might place this story, as relevant to the literary element(s) of that chapter.*

10. **Foreshadowing, Irony, and/or Symbolism**   *Explain examples of foreshadowing, irony, and/or symbolism in this story.*

FOLLOW-UP QUESTIONS

10 SHORT QUESTIONS

*Select the **best** answer for each.*

_____ 1. Bill and Sam probably
   a. are rich.
   b. are comfortable.
   c. need money.

_____ 2. Johnny Dorset
   a. stays at camp.
   b. has to be forced to stay.
   c. decides to stay home.

_____ 3. When Johnny is with Bill and Sam, he feels
   a. that he is suffering.
   b. as if he is out camping.
   c. homesick.

_____ 4. Bill
   a. pays no attention to Johnny.
   b. enjoys playing with Johnny.
   c. does not enjoy playing with Johnny.

_____ 5. The one who seems to plan the scheme is
   a. Sam.
   b. Bill.
   c. Johnny.

_____ 6. When Sam goes to Poplar Grove, he thinks Summit
   a. is happy or, at least, relieved.
   b. is deeply concerned and upset.
   c. has not heard the news yet.

_____ 7. In fact, Summit probably
   a. is happy or, at least, relieved.
   b. is deeply concerned and upset.
   c. has not heard the news yet.

_____ 8. Bill and Sam ask for a ransom of
   a. $2,000.
   b. $1,500.
   c. $250.

_____ 9. Ebenezer Dorset
   a. rapidly pays the ransom.
   b. sends out the sheriff.
   c. sends a counter-proposition.

_____ 10. In the end, Bill and Sam
   a. gain $2,000.
   b. gain $1,500.
   c. pay out $250.

5 SIGNIFICANT QUOTATIONS

Explain the importance of each of these quotations.

1. "We selected for our victim the only child of a prominent citizen named Ebenezer Dorset."

2. " 'You're a liar!' says Bill. '[. . .]. You was to be burned at sunrise, and you was afraid he'd do it.' "

3. " 'We demand fifteen hundred dollars in large bills for his return [. . .].' "

4. "One whiskerando says that he hears Summit is all upset on account of Elder Ebenezer Dorset's boy having been lost or stolen."

5. " 'I think you are a little high in your demands, and I hereby make you a counter-proposition, which I am inclined to believe you will accept.' "

2 COMPREHENSION ESSAY QUESTIONS

Use specific details and information from the story to answer these questions as completely as possible.

1. What is the irony in this story? Use specific details and information from the story to support your explanation.

2. What are Sam and Bill's mistakes? Use specific details and information from the story to support your explanation.

DISCUSSION QUESTIONS

Be prepared to discuss these questions in class.

1. How does the illustration demonstrate this story? Use specific details from the story to support your ideas.

2. How many ironies can you find in this story? Be prepared to discuss each.

WRITING

Use each of these ideas for writing an essay.

1. The irony here is based on a series of misunderstandings and wrong assumptions. Write about a time that you or someone you know had problems because of misunderstandings or wrong assumptions.

2. The irony in this story is a series of humorous twists. Write about a humorous twist in your life or in the life of someone you know.

Further Writing

1. Compare and contrast Johnny Dorset in this story with Tom Sawyer in the selection by Mark Twain (page 140).

2. Compare and contrast the society in the stories of Mark Twain and O. Henry, which are set in simpler times, with American society today.

Sweat

ZORA NEALE HURSTON

PRE-READING VOCABULARY
CONTEXT

Use context clues to define these words before reading. Use a dictionary as needed.

1. Bill *soiled* his hands when he was digging in the garden and moving dirt around. *Soiled* means _____.

2. Rudy hitched up the horse, put his vegetables in the *buckboard*, and drove it to town. *Buckboard* means _____.

3. Sender used a chair and a long leather *whip* to train the tigers. *Whip* means _____.

4. Sam *truculently* denied the charges, loudly claiming he was innocent. *Truculently* means _____.

5. The wind blew the leaves *helter-skelter*, and it took hours to rake them up. *Helter-skelter* means _____.

6. Liz found, much to her *dismay*, that the jacket she planned to save money on was no longer on sale. *Dismay* means _____.

7. Jacob grew into a strong, *strapping* young man who lettered in football and track. *Strapping* means _____.

8. Akim loved eating and sat down at the dinner table prepared to eat his *vittles*. *Vittles* means _____.

9. The bunny backed up into the protective woods, *cowed* by the large dog's barking. *Cowed* means _____.

10. After the wind storm, Tricia cleared all the broken twigs, leaves, and *debris* that the storm had brought down. *Debris* means _____.

11. Farmers *sow* seeds and *reap* what grows. *Sow* means _____, and *reap* means _____.

12. Andrew was completely *indifferent* and did not care one way or the other if he went to the party. *Indifferent* means

    _____.

13. Allison *abominates* washing dishes and always refuses to wash them. *Abominate* means _____.

14. Josette was in a *fury* when the tax assessor overrated her home by a hundred percent. *Fury* means _____.

15. Much to Edmund's *amazement*, his son surprised him with a totally unexpected party. *Amazement* means _____.

16. The escaped tarantula struck *horror* and *terror* into Chris's heart when he found the spider under the chair. *Horror* and *terror* mean

    _____.

17. Zach *crouched* under the stairs so his friends would not find him and he could surprise them. *Crouch* means _____.

18. Matt is such a good *ventriloquist* that he can make it seem like his dog is talking even though Matt's lips don't move. *Ventriloquist* means

    _____.

19. Edgar was so nervous when he won the award that he spoke *gibberish*, and no one could understand him. *Gibberish* means

    _____.

20. When the fire flared up, the firemen came with water and *extinguished* the fire. *Extinguish* means _____.

PRE-READING VOCABULARY
STRUCTURAL ATTACK

Define these words by solving the parts. Use the Glossary or a dictionary as needed.

1. washwoman
2. mournful
3. washbench
4. scornfully
5. habitual
6. knuckly
7. numerous
8. penniless
9. knotty
10. earthworks
11. biggety
12. swellest
13. work-worn
14. friendliness
15. bloodier
16. underfoot
17. maddened

PRE-READING QUESTIONS

Try answering these questions as you read.

What is Delia like?

What is Sykes like?

What does Sykes do?

What is ironic in the story?

Sweat

Zora Neale Hurston

Zora Neale Hurston was born in 1901 in Eatonville, Florida, the first African American-incorporated town in America. Although her mother died when Hurston was young and she was shifted from relative to relative, Hurston enjoyed a childhood relatively free of the discrimination found elsewhere. Marked by creativity and determination throughout her life, she managed to secure scholarships at the Morgan Academy, Howard University, and Barnard College, where she studied under Franz Boaz, the renown anthropologist. Securing support from the same patron who supported Langston Hughes, Hurston returned to Eatonville to study its stories, melodies, and folkways. She thoroughly believed that the African American experience was both unique and positive, and these small town ways and speech fairly sing through her writing. Her female characters, especially, emerge as intelligent, thoughtful, resourceful, and surviving. However, in presenting too much of the positive and too little of the anger in the African American experience, she was heavily criticized, although today many consider her a forerunner in African American self-recognition. A part of the Harlem Renaissance in the 1920s and a thoughtful writer in the 1930s, she was devoted to recreating the Eatonville experience—a devotion that continued throughout her writing. <u>Their Eyes Were Watching God</u> is her master work. Hurston died in 1960 in Saint Lucie, Florida, of continuing gastrointestinal problems.

I t was eleven o'clock of a Spring night in Florida. It was Sunday. Any other night, Delia Jones would have been in bed for two hours by this time. But she was a washwoman, and Monday morning meant a great deal to her. So she collected the soiled clothes on Saturday when she returned the clean things. Sunday night after church, she sorted them and put the white things to soak. It saved her almost a half day's start. A great hamper in the bedroom held the clothes that she brought home. It was so much neater than a number of bundles lying around.

2   She squatted on the kitchen floor beside the great pile of clothes, sorting them into small heaps according to color, and humming a song in a mournful key, but wondering through it all where Sykes, her husband, had gone with her horse and buckboard.

3   Just then something long, round, limp, and black fell upon her shoulders and slithered to the floor beside her. A great terror took hold of her. It softened her knees and dried her mouth so that it was a full minute before she could cry out or move. Then she saw that it was the big bull whip her husband liked to carry when he drove.

4   She lifted her eyes to the door and saw him standing there bent over with laughter at her fright. She screamed at him.

5   "Sykes, what you throw dat whip on me like dat? You know it would skeer me—looks just like a snake, an' you knows how skeered Ah is of snakes."

6   "Course Ah knowed it! That's how come Ah done it." He slapped his leg with his hand and almost rolled on the ground in his mirth. "If you such a big fool dat you got to have a fit over a earth worm or a string, Ah don't keer how bad Ah skeer you."

7   "You aint got no business doing it. Gawd knows it's a sin. Some day Ah'm gointuh drop dead from some of yo' foolishness. 'Nother thing, where you been wid mah rig? Ah feeds dat pony. He aint fuh you to be drivin' wid no bull whip."

8   "Yo sho is one aggravatin' n——woman!" he declared and stepped into the room. She resumed her work and did not answer him at once. "Ah done tole you time and again to keep them white folks' clothes outa dis house."

9   He picked up the whip and glared down at her. Delia went on with her work. She went out into the yard and returned with a galvanized tub and set it on the washbench. She saw that Sykes had kicked all of the clothes together again, and now stood in her way truculently, his whole manner hoping, praying, for an argument. But she walked calmly around him and commenced to re-sort the things.

10   "Next time, Ah'm gointer to kick 'em outdoors," he threatened as he struck a match along the leg of his corduroy breeches.

11   Delia never looked up from her work, and her thin, stooped shoulders sagged further.

12   "Ah aint for no fuss t'night Sykes. Ah just come from taking sacrament at the church house."

13   He snorted scornfully. "Yeah, you just come from de church house on a Sunday night, but heah you is gone to work on them clothes. You aint nothing but a hypocrite. One of them amen-corner Christians— sing, whoop, shout, then come home and wash white folks clothes on the Sabbath."

14   He stepped roughly upon the whitest pile of things, kicking them helter-skelter as he crossed the room. His wife gave a little scream of dismay, and quickly gathered them together again.

15   "Sykes, you quit grindin' dirt into these clothes! How can Ah git through by Sat'day if Ah don't start on Sunday?"

16   "Ah don't keer if you never git through. Anyhow, Ah done promised Gawd and a couple of other men, Ah aint gointer have it in mah house. Don't gimme no lip neither, else Ah'll throw 'em out and put mah fist up side yo' head to boot."

17   Delia's habitual meekness seemed to slip from her shoulders like a blown scarf. She was on her feet; her poor little body, her bare knuckly hands bravely defying the strapping hulk before her.

18   "Looka heah, Sykes, you done gone too fur. Ah been married to you fur fifteen years, and Ah been takin' in washin' for fifteen years. Sweat, sweat, sweat! Work and sweat, cry and sweat, pray and sweat!"

19   "What's that go to do with me?" he asked brutally.

20   "What's it got to do with you, Sykes? Mah tub of suds is filled yo' belly with vittles more times than yo' hands is filled it. Mah sweat is done paid for this house and Ah reckon Ah kin keep on sweatin' in it."

21   She seized the iron skillet from the stove and struck a defensive pose, which act surprised him greatly, coming from her. It cowed him and he did not strike her as he usually did.

22   "Naw you won't," she panted, "that ole snaggle-toothed black woman you runnin' with aint comin' heah to pile up on *mah* sweat and blood. You aint paid for nothin' on this place, and Ah'm gointer stay right heah till Ah'm toted out foot foremost."

23   "Well, you better quit gittin' me riled up, else they'll be totin' you out sooner than you expect. Ah'm so tired of you Ah don't know whut to do. Gawd! how Ah hates skinny wimmen!"

24   A little awed by this new Delia, he sidled out of the door and slammed the back gate after him. He did not say where he had gone, but she knew too well. She knew very well that he would not return until nearly daybreak also. Her work over, she went on to bed but not to sleep at once. Things had come to a pretty pass!

25   She lay awake, gazing upon the debris that cluttered their matrimonial trail. Not an image left standing along the way. Anything like flowers had long ago been drowned in the salty stream that had been pressed from her heart. Her tears, her sweat, her blood. She had brought love to the union and he had brought a longing for the flesh. Two months after the wedding, he had given her the first brutal beating. She had the memory of numerous trips to Orlando with all of his wages when he had returned to her penniless, even before the first year had passed. She was young and soft then, but now she thought of her knotty, muscled limbs, her harsh knuckly hands, and drew herself up into an unhappy little ball in the middle of the big feather bed. Too late now to hope for love, even if it were not Bertha it would be someone else. This case differed from the others only in that she was bolder than the others. Too late for everything except her little home. She had built it for her old days, and planted one by one the trees and flowers there. It was lovely to her, lovely.

26   Somehow before sleep came, she found herself saying aloud: "Oh well, whatever goes over the Devil's back, is got to come under his belly. Sometime or ruther, Sykes, like everybody else, is gointer reap his sowing." After that she was able to build a spiritual earthworks against her husband. His shells could no longer reach her. *Amen.* She went to sleep and slept until he announced his presence in bed by kicking her feet and rudely snatching the cover away.

27   "Gimme some kivah heah, an' git yo' damn foots over on yo' own side! Ah oughter mash you in yo' mouf fuh drawing dat skillet on me."

28   Delia went clear to the rail without answering him. A triumphant indifference to all that he was or did.

29   The week was as full of work for Delia as all other weeks, and Saturday found her behind her little pony, collecting and delivering clothes.

30   It was a hot, hot day near the end of July. The village men on Joe Clarke's porch even chewed cane listlessly. They did not hurl the cane-knots as usual. They let them dribble over the edge of the porch. Even conversation had collapsed under the heat.

31   "Heah comes Delia Jones," Jim Merchant said, as the shaggy pony came 'round the bend of the road toward them. The rusty buckboard was heaped with baskets of crisp, clean laundry.

32   "Yep," Joe Lindsay agreed. "Hot or col', rain or shine, jes ez reg'lar ez de weeks roll roun' Delia carries 'em an' fetches 'em on Sat'day."

33   "She better if she wanter eat," said Moss. "Syke Jones aint wuth de shot an' powder hit would tek tuh kill 'em. Not to *bub* he aint."

34   "He sho' aint," Walter Thomas chimed in. "It's too bad, too, cause she wuz a right pritty lil trick when he got huh. Ah'd uh mah'ied huh mahseff if he hadnter beat me to it."

35   Delia nodded briefly at the men as she drove past.

36   "Too much knockin' will ruin *any* 'oman. He done beat huh 'nough tuh kill three women, let 'lone change they looks," said Elijah Mosely. "How Syke kin stommuck dat big black greasy Mogul he's layin' roun' wid, gits me. Ah swear dat eight-rock couldn't kiss a sardine can Ah done thowed out de back do' 'way las' yeah."

37   "Aw, she's fat, thass how come. He's allus been crazy 'bout fat women," put in Merchant. "He'd a' been tied up wid one long time ago if he could a' found one tuh have him. Did Ah tell yuh 'bout him come sidlin' roun' *mah* wife—bringin' her a basket uh pee-cans outa his yard fuh a present? Yes-sir, mah wife! She tol' him tuh take 'em right straight back home, cause Delia works so hard ovah dat washtub she reckon everything en de place taste lak sweat an' soapsuds. Ah jus' wisht Ah'd a' caught 'im 'roun' dere! Ah'd a' made his hips ketch on fiah down dat shell road."

38   "Ah know he done it, too. Ah sees 'im grinnin' at every 'oman dat passes," Walter Thomas said. "But even so, he useter eat some mighty big hunks uh humble pie tuh git dat lil' 'oman he got. She wuz *ez pritty ez* a speckled pup! Dat wuz fifteen yeahs ago. He useter be so skeered uh losin' huh, she could make him do some parts of a husband's duty. Dey never wuz de same in de mind."

39   "There oughter be a law about him," said Lindsay. "He aint fit tuh carry guts tuh a bear."

40   Clarke spoke for the first time. "Taint no law on earth dat kin make a man be decent if it aint in 'im. There's plenty men dat takes a wife lak dey do a joint uh sugar-cane. It's round, juicy an' sweet when dey gits it. But dey squeeze an' grind, squeeze an' grind an' wring tell dey wring every drop uh pleasure dat's in 'em out. When dey's satisfied dat dey is wrung dry, dey treats 'em jes lak dey do a cane-chew. Dey thows 'em away. Dey knows whut dey is doin' while dey is at it, an' hates theirselves fuh it but they keeps on hangin' after huh tell she's empty. Den dey hates huh fuh bein' a cane-chew an' in de way."

41   "We oughter take Syke an' dat stray 'oman uh his'n down in Lake Howell swamp an' lay on de rawhide till they cain't say 'Lawd a' mussy.' He allus wuz uh ovahbearin' n——, but since dat white 'oman from up north done teached 'im how to run a automobile, he done got too biggety to live—an' we oughter kill 'im," Old Man Anderson advised.

42   A grunt of approval went around the porch. But the heat was melting their civic virtue and Elijah Moseley began to bait Joe Clarke.

43   "Come on, Joe, git a melon outa dere an' slice it up for yo' customers. We'se all sufferin' wid de heat. De bear's done got *me!*"

44   "Thass right, Joe, a watermelon is jes' whut Ah needs tuh cure de eppizudicks," Walter Thomas joined forces with Moseley. "Come on

dere, Joe. We all is steady customers an' you aint set us up in a long time. Ah chooses dat long, bowlegged Floridy favorite."

45   "A god, an' be dough. You all gimme twenty cents and slice away," Clarke retorted. "Ah needs a col' slice m'self. Heah, everybody chip in. Ah'll lend y'll mah meat knife."

46   The money was quickly subscribed and the huge melon brought forth. At that moment, Sykes and Bertha arrived. A determined silence fell on the porch and the melon was put away again.

47   Merchant snapped down the blade of his jackknife and moved toward the store door.

48   "Come on in, Joe, an' gimme a slab uh sow belly an' uh pound uh coffee—almost fuhgot 'twas Sat'day. Got to git on home." Most of the men left also.

49   Just then Delia drove past on her way home, as Sykes was ordering magnificently for Bertha. It pleased him for Delia to see.

50   "Git whutsoever yo' heart desires, Honey. Wait a minute, Joe. Give huh two bottles uh strawberry soda-water, uh quart uh parched groundpeas, an' a block uh chewin' gum."

51   With all this they left the store, with Sykes reminding Bertha that this was his town and she could have it if she wanted it.

52   The men returned soon after they left, and held their watermelon feast. "Where did Syke Jones git dat 'oman from nohow?" Lindsay asked.

53   "Ovah Apopka. Guess dey musta been cleanin' out de town when she lef'. She don't look lak a thing but a hunk uh liver wid hair on it."

54   "Well, she sho' kin squall," Dave Carter contributed. "When she gits ready tuh laff, she jes' opens huh mouf an' latches it back tuh de las' notch. No ole grandpa alligator down in Lake Bell aint got nothin' on huh."

55   Bertha had been in town three months now. Sykes was still paying her room rent at Della Lewis'—the only house in town that would have taken her in. Sykes took her frequently to Winter Park to "stomps." He still assured her that he was the swellest man in the state.

56   "Sho! you kin have dat lil' ole house soon's Ah kin git dat 'oman outa dere. Everything b'longs tuh me an' you sho' kin have it. Ah sho' 'bominates uh skinny 'oman. Lawdy, you sho' is got one portly shape on you! You kin git *anything* you wants. Dis is *mah* town an' you sho' kin have it.

57   Delia's work-worn knees crawled over the earth in Gethsemane and on the rocks of Calvary many, many times during these months. She avoided the villagers and meeting places in her efforts to be blind and deaf. But Bertha nullified this to a degree, by coming to Delia's house to call Sykes out to her at the gate.

58   Delia and Sykes fought all the time now with no peaceful inter-
ludes. They slept and ate in silence. Two or three times Delia had
attempted a timid friendliness, but she was repulsed each time. It was
plain that the breaches must remain agape.

59   The sun had burned July to August. The heat streamed down like a
million hot arrows, smiting all things living upon the earth. Grass
withered, leaves browned, snakes went blind in shedding and men and
dogs went mad. Dog days!

60   Delia came home one day and found Sykes there before her. She
wondered, but started to go on into the house without speaking, even
though he was standing in the kitchen door and she must either stoop
under his arm or ask him to move. He made no room for her. She
noticed a soap box beside the steps, but paid no particular attention to
it, knowing that he must have brought it there. As she was stooping to
pass under his outstretched arm, he suddenly pushed her backward,
laughingly.

61   "Look in de box dere Delia, Ah done brung yuh somethin'!"

62   She nearly fell upon the box in her stumbling, and when she saw
what it held, she all but fainted outright.

63   "Syke! Syke, mah Gawd! You take dat rattlesnake 'way from heah!
You *gottuh*. Oh, Jesus, have mussy!"

64   "Ah aint gut tuh do nuthin' uh de kin'—fact is Ah aint got tuh do
nothin' but die. Taint no use uh you puttin' on airs makin' out lak you
skeered uh dat snake—he's gointer stay right heah tell he die. He
wouldn't bite me cause Ah knows how tuh handle 'im. Nohow he
wouldn't risk breakin' out his fangs 'gin *yo'* skinny laigs."

65   "Naw, now Syke, don't keep dat thing 'roun' heah tuh skeer me
tuh death. You knows Ah'm even feared uh earth worms. Thass de
biggest snake Ah evah did see. Kill 'im Syke, please."

66   "Doan ast me tuh do nothin' fuh yuh. Goin' 'roun' tryin' to be so
damn asterperious. Naw, Ah aint gonna kill it. Ah think uh damn sight
mo' uh him dan you! Dat's a nice snake an' anybody doan lak 'im kin
jes' hit de grit."

67   The village soon heard that Sykes had the snake, and came to see
and ask questions.

68   "How de hen-fire did you ketch dat six-foot rattler, Syke?" Thomas
asked.

69   "He's full uh frogs so he caint hardly move, thass how Ah eased up
on 'm. But Ah'm a snake charmer an' knows how tuh handle 'em.
Shux, dat aint nothin'. Ah could ketch one eve'y day if Ah so wanted
tuh."

70   "Whut he needs is a heavy hick'ry club leaned real heavy on his
head. Dat's de bes' way tuh charm a rattlesnake."

71   "Naw, Walt, y'll jes' don't understand dese diamon' backs lak Ah do," said Sykes in a superior tone of voice.

72   The village agreed with Walter, but the snake stayed on. His box remained by the kitchen door with its screen wire covering. Two or three days later it had digested its meal of frogs and literally came to life. It rattled at every movement in the kitchen or the yard. One day as Delia came down the kitchen steps she saw his chalky-white fangs curved like scimitars hung in the wire meshes. This time she did not run away with averted eyes as usual. She stood for a long time in the doorway in a red fury that grew bloodier for every second that she regarded the creature that was her torment.

73   That night she broached the subject as soon as Sykes sat down to the table.

74   "Syke, Ah wants you tuh take dat snake 'way fum heah. You done starved me an' Ah put up widcher, you done beat me an Ah took dat, but you done kilt all mah insides bringin' dat varmint heah."

75   Sykes poured out a saucer full of coffee and drank it deliberately before he answered her.

76   "A whole lot Ah keer 'bout how you feels inside uh out. Dat snake aint goin' no damn wheah till Ah gits ready fuh 'im tuh go. So fur as beatin' is concerned, yuh aint took near all dat you gointer take ef yuh stay 'roun' *me*."

77   Delia pushed back her plate and got up from the table, "Ah hates you, Sykes," she said calmly. "Ah hates you tuh de same degree dat Ah useter love yuh. Ah done took an' took till mah belly is full up tuh mah neck. Dat's de reason Ah got mah letter fum de church an' moved mah membership tuh Woodbridge—so Ah don't haftuh take no sacrament wid yuh. Ah don't wantuh see yuh, 'roun' me atall. Lay 'roun' wid dat 'oman all yuh wants tuh, but gwan 'way fum me an' mah house. Ah hates yuh lak uh suck-egg dog."

78   Sykes almost let the huge wad of corn bread and collard greens he was chewing fall out of his mouth in amazement. He had a hard time whipping himself to the proper fury to try to answer Delia.

79   "Well, Ah'm glad you does hate me. Ah'm sho' tiahed uh you hangin' ontuh me. Ah don't want yuh. Look at yuh stringey ole neck! Yo' raw-bony laigs an' arms is enough tuh cut uh man tuh death. You looks jes' lak de devvul's doll-baby tuh *me*. You cain't hate me no worse dan Ah hates you. Ah been hatin' *you* fuh years."

80   "Yo' ole black hide don't look lak nothin' tuh me, but uh passle uh wrinkled up rubber, wid yo' big ole yeahs flappin' on each side lak up paih uh buzzard wings. Don't think Ah'm gointuh be run 'way fum mah house neither. Ah'm goin' tuh de white folks about *you*, mah young man, de very nex' time you lay yo' han's on me. Mah cup is done

run ovah." Delia said this with no signs of fear and Sykes departed from the house, threatening her, but made not the slightest move to carry out any of them.

81   That night he did not return at all, and the next day being Sunday, Delia was glad that she did not have to quarrel before she hitched up her pony and drove the four miles to Woodbridge.

82   She stayed to the night service—"love feast"—which was very warm and full of spirit. In the emotional winds her domestic trials were borne far and wide so that she sang as she drove homeward,

83   "Jurden water, black an' col'
84   Chills de body, not de soul
85   An' Ah wantah cross Jurden in uh calm time."

86   She came from the barn to the kitchen door and stopped.

87   "Whut's de mattah, ol' satan, you aint kickin' up yo' racket?" She addressed the snake's box. Complete silence. She went on into the house with a new hope in its birth struggles. Perhaps her threat to go to the white folks had frightened Sykes! Perhaps he was sorry! Fifteen years of misery and suppression had brought Delia to the place where she would hope *anything* that looked towards a way over or through her wall of inhibitions.

88   She felt in the match safe behind the stove at once for a match. There was only one there.

89   "Dat n—— wouldn't fetch nothin heah tuh save his rotten neck, but he kin run thew whut Ah brings quick enough. Now he done toted off nigh on tuh haff uh box uh matches. He done had dat 'oman heah in mah house, too."

90   Nobody but a woman could tell how she knew this even before she struck the match. But she did and it put her into a new fury.

91   Presently she brought in the tubs to put the white things to soak. This time she decided she need not bring the hamper out of the bedroom; she would go in there and do the sorting. She picked up the pot-bellied lamp and went in. The room was small and the hamper stood hard by the foot of the white iron bed. She could sit and reach through the bedposts—resting as she worked.

92   "Ah wantah cross Jurden in uh calm time." She was singing again. The mood of the "love feast" had returned. She threw back the lid of the basket almost gaily. Then, moved by both horror and terror, she sprang back toward the door. *There lay the snake in the basket!* He moved sluggishly at first, but even as she turned round and round, jumped up and down in an insanity of fear, he began to stir vigorously. She saw him pouring his awful beauty from the basket upon the bed, then she seized the lamp and ran as fast as she could to the kitchen.

The wind from the open door blew out the light and the darkness added to her terror. She sped to the darkness of the yard, slamming the door after her before she thought to set down the lamp. She did not feel safe even on the ground, so she climbed up in the hay barn.

93   There for an hour or more she lay sprawled upon the hay a gibbering wreck.

94   Finally she grew quiet, and after that, coherent thought. With this, stalked through her a cold, bloody rage. Hours of this. A period of introspection, a space of retrospection, then a mixture of both. Out of this an awful calm.

95   "Well, Ah done de bes' Ah could. If things aint right, Gawd knows taint mah fault."

96   She went to sleep—a twitchy sleep—and woke up to a faint gray sky. There was a loud hollow sound below. She peered out. Sykes was at the wood-pile, demolishing a wire-covered box.

97   He hurried to the kitchen door, but hung outside there some minutes before he entered, and stood some minutes more inside before he closed it after him.

98   The gray in the sky was spreading. Delia descended without fear now, and crouched beneath the low bedroom window. The drawn shade shut out the dawn, shut in the night. But the thin walls held back no sound.

99   "Dat ol' scratch is woke up now!" She mused at the tremendous whirr inside, which every woodsman knows, is one of the sound illusions. The rattler is a ventriloquist. His whirr sounds to the right, to the left, straight ahead, behind, close under foot—everywhere but where it is. Woe to him who guesses wrong unless he is prepared to hold up his end of the argument! Sometimes he strikes without rattling at all.

100   Inside, Sykes heard nothing until he knocked a pot lid off the stove while trying to reach the match safe in the dark. He had emptied his pockets at Bertha's.

101   The snake seemed to wake up under the stove and Sykes made a quick leap into the bedroom. In spite of the gin he had had, his head was clearing now.

102   "Mah Gawd!" he chattered, "ef Ah could on'y strack uh light!"

103   The rattling ceased for a moment as he stood paralyzed. He waited. It seemed that the snake waited also.

104   "Oh, fuh de light! Ah thought he'd be too sick"—Sykes was muttering to himself when the whirr began again, closer, right underfoot this time. Long before this, Sykes' ability to think had been flattened down to primitive instinct and he leaped—onto the bed.

105   Outside Delia heard a cry that might have come from a maddened chimpanzee, a stricken gorilla. All the terror, all the horror, all the rage that man possibly could express, without a recognizable human sound.

106   A tremendous stir inside there, another series of animal screams, the intermittent whirr of the reptile. The shade torn violently down from the window, letting in the red dawn, a huge brown hand seizing the window stick, great dull blows upon the wooden floor punctuating the gibberish of sound long after the rattle of the snake had abruptly subsided. All this Delia could see and hear from her place beneath the window, and it made her ill. She crept over to the four-o'clocks and stretched herself on the cool earth to recover.

107   She lay there. "Delia, Delia!" She could hear Sykes calling in a most despairing tone as one who expected no answer. The sun crept on up, and he called. Delia could not move—her legs were gone flabby. She never moved, he called, and the sun kept rising.

108   "Mah Gawd!" She heard him moan, "Mah Gawd fum Heben!" She heard him stumbling about and got up from her flower-bed. The sun was growing warm. As she approached the door she heard him call out hopefully, "Delia, is dat you Ah heah?"

109   She saw him on his hands and knees as soon as she reached the door. He crept an inch or two toward her—all that he was able, and she saw his horribly swollen neck and his one open eye shining with hope. A surge of pity too strong to support bore her away from that eye that must, could not, fail to see the tubs. He would see the lamp. Orlando with its doctors was too far. She could scarcely reach the Chinaberry tree, where she waited in the growing heat while inside she knew the cold river was creeping up and up to extinguish that eye which must know by now that she knew.

Sweat

JOURNAL

1. **MLA Works Cited**   *Using this model, record this story here.*

   Author's Last Name, First Name. "Title of the Story." <u>*Title of the Book*</u>*.
   3rd ed. Ed. First Name Last Name. City: Publisher, year. Pages of
   the story.*

2. **Main Character(s)**   *Describe each main character, and explain why you
   think each is a main character.*

3. **Supporting Characters**   *Describe each supporting character, and explain why
   you think each is a supporting character.*

4. **Setting**   *Describe the setting(s) and any relevant prop(s).*

5. **Sequence**   *Outline the events of the story in order.*

6. **Plot**   *Tell the story in no more than two sentences.*

7. **Conflicts**   *Identify and explain all the conflicts involved here.*

8. **Significant Quotations**   *Explain the importance of each of these quotations. Record the page number in the parentheses.*

   a. " 'Mah sweat is done paid for this house and Ah reckon Ah kin keep on sweatin' in it' " (   ).

   b. "She had brought love to the union and he had brought a longing after the flesh" (   ).

c. " 'Taint no use uh you puttin' on airs makin' out lak you skeered uh dat snake—he's gointer stay right heah tell he die. He wouldn't bite me cause Ah knows how tuh handle 'im' " (   ).

d. " 'Whut's de mattah, ol' satan, you aint kickin' up yo' racket?' She addressed the snake's box. Complete silence" (   ).

e. "She lay there. 'Delia, Delia!' She could hear Sykes calling [. . .]" (   ).

9. **Literary Elements**   *Look at this chapter's title and explain why you think this story is placed in this chapter. Explain in which other chapter(s) you might place this story, as relevant to the literary element(s) of that chapter.*

10. **Foreshadowing, Irony, and/or Symbolism**   *Explain examples of foreshadowing, irony, and/or symbolism in this story.*

FOLLOW-UP QUESTIONS

10 SHORT QUESTIONS

Select the <u>best</u> answer for each.

____ 1. Delia
   a. works hard.
   b. seems to have no job.
   c. seems to be up to no good.

____ 2. Sykes
   a. works hard.
   b. is faithful.
   c. has another woman.

____ 3. Sykes
   a. is kind to Delia.
   b. has beaten Delia.
   c. has not beaten Delia.

____ 4. The town
   a. thinks highly of Sykes.
   b. does not think highly
      of Sykes.
   c. does not know Sykes.

____ 5. Delia
   a. wants a pet snake.
   b. is afraid of snakes.
   c. is not afraid of snakes.

____ 6. Sykes feels he
   a. can handle a rattlesnake.
   b. cannot handle a rattlesnake.
   c. does not want a rattlesnake.

____ 7. Sykes uses the snake because
   a. he likes animals.
   b. he wants Delia to stay.
   c. he wants Delia to leave.

____ 8. Delia plans
   a. to stay.
   b. to leave.
   c. to kill Sykes.

____ 9. When Sykes calls for help,
   Delia
   a. goes to help him.
   b. does not hear him.
   c. does not help him.

____ 10. In the end, Sykes
   a. lives and leaves Delia.
   b. dies.
   c. lives and pushes Delia out.

5 SIGNIFICANT QUOTATIONS

Explain the importance of each of these quotations.

1. " 'Ah been married to you fur fifteen years, and Ah been takin' in washin' fur fifteen years. Sweat, sweat, sweat! Work and sweat, cry and sweat, pray and sweat!' "

2. " 'Oh well, whatever goes over the Devil's back, is got to come under his belly. Sometime or ruther, Sykes, like everybody else, is gointer reap his sowing.' "

3. " 'Syke! Syke, mah Gawd! You take dat rattlesnake 'way from heah! You *gottuh*. Oh, Jesus, have mussy!'"

4. " 'But Ah'm a snake charmer an' knows how tuh handle 'em.' "

5. "Delia could not move—her legs were gone flabby. She never moved, he called, and the sun kept rising."

2 Comprehension Essay Questions

Use specific details and information from the story to answer these questions as completely as possible.

1. What is the irony in this story? Use specific details and information from the story to support your explanation.

2. What might be another title for this story? Use specific details and information from the story to explain your choice.

Discussion Questions

Be prepared to discuss these questions in class.

1. Do you think Delia should have helped Sykes? Use specific details from the story to support your thinking.

2. What qualities does Hurston see in the survivor? Use specific details from the story to support your ideas.

Writing

Use each of these ideas for writing an essay.

1. Whether younger or older, one often has to face something feared. Write an essay telling the story of something you or someone you know has feared and has had to face.

2. Many of us have found ourselves locked in bad relationships. Describe a poor relationship you or someone you know has been in, and describe how you or your friend got out of it.

Further Writing

1. Compare Hurston's irony with that in Dorothy Parker's "The Wonderful Old Gentleman" (page 285).

2. Research spousal abuse, and use Delia's story to offer insight into the question, "Why don't they leave?"

Notes

Chapter 5

Extended Short Story Study

The stories in this chapter, each longer and more complex than the others you have read, combine the elements that you have studied so far. Each offers the opportunity for you to study the thoughts and actions of stirring characters, significant settings and props, well-developed plots and story lines, and ironic twists. Further, each story offers you the opportunity to study complex conflicts.

William Faulkner's "A Rose for Emily" presents several of Faulkner's wonderfully strange characters in a tale steeped in a decaying South. Much as Faulkner denied it, literary symbols seem to appear almost everywhere. **Symbols** are objects or characters that represent something beyond their face value. For instance, an American flag is really nothing more than pieces of cloth sewn together, but an American flag represents the pride, glory, and industry of America. By looking beyond the surface, you will find many symbols in literature.

Nathaniel Hawthorne introduces us to American Gothic in a tale told with a light touch of humor. In a dark and foreboding setting, we watch as Dr. Heidegger offers his guests magic from the Fountain of Youth. Read it to see how well the guests use the magic they are offered.

With Edgar Allan Poe and Herman Melville, we enter the world of the supernatural. In "The Masque of the Red Death," Poe offers many hints that foreshadow events as we come face-to-face with evil, complete with a cryptic figure. In reading the "The Bell-Tower," you should know that a person arrogantly placing herself or himself above the gods or God demonstrates **hubris**, a condition named by the ancient Greeks that means excessive pride. You will see that Melville also offers biblical references to explain the demonic actions and horrible irony of this story.

Look for the conflicts and study the rich details as you read each of these stories.

A Rose for Emily

WILLIAM FAULKNER

PRE-READING VOCABULARY
CONTEXT

Use context clues to define these words before reading. Use a dictionary as needed.

1. *Necro-* means "death" and *-philia* means "love of" or "to love." *Necrophilia* means _____.

2. Juanita caught the first flight after her grandmother died, so that she could attend her *funeral. Funeral* means _____.

3. Penny's *curiosity* got the best of her, and she secretly listened to overhear what her friends said. *Curiosity* means

    _____.

4. Olympic athletes are a very *select* group of the best athletes. *Select* means _____.

5. Ben bought machinery called a *cotton gin* to separate the cotton balls from the seeds inside. *Cotton gin* means _____.

6. When Caesar ruled over most of the known world as emperor of Rome, he held a most *august* position. *August* means

    _____.

7. The dead, rotting snake began to smell as it *decayed* by the side of the road. *Decay* means _____.

8. The old tires and rusty cars that Karl left in the yard around his house were an *eyesore* to the neighborhood. *Eyesore* means

    _____.

9. Since Libby had offered to buy lunch, she fulfilled her *obligation* and paid the bill. *Obligation* means _____.

10. When the Smiths did not have money, their landlord gave them a *dispensation*, and they did not have to pay rent for the month. *Dispensation* means _____.

11. Maura always saves money so that when she receives her *tax notice*, she can pay her taxes right away. *Tax notice* means

_____.

12. For years, the United *Negro* College Fund has made money available for African American students to attend college. *Negro* means

_____.

13. The elderly woman used a slender *cane* made out of oak to help support her as she walked. *Cane* means _____.

14. *Ebony* is a fine hardwood that grows in Africa and turns black when stained. *Ebony* means _____.

15. Jason brought his car to a rapid *halt* when traffic stopped in front of him. *Halt* means _____.

16. Vernie married her high school *sweetheart* whom she had dated all through high school. *Sweetheart* means _____.

17. When the alarm went off, the criminals fled quickly and *deserted* the scene of the crime. *Desert* means _____.

18. Nancy bought a bag full of *lime* powder to sprinkle on the soil when her garden started to smell. *Lime* means _____.

19. *Insanity* occurs when someone can no longer tell reality from fantasy. *Insanity* means _____.

20. The children felt terrible *grief* and sadness when both of their parents died in a crash. *Grief* means _____.

21. Gary had to drive all over town to get to the recycle station so he could *dispose* of his empty paint cans. *Dispose* means

_____.

22. When Susan decided to go horseback riding, she chose to ride the *bay*-colored horse. *Bay* means _____.

23. Construction workers who are paid by the day are considered to be *day laborers*. *Day laborer* means _____.

24. When a person becomes very rich, some believe he or she has a duty to do good things for the community; this duty is called *noblesse oblige*. *Noblesse oblige* means _____.

25. Since Deidre wanted to poison rats, she bought *arsenic* to put on bait for them to kill them. *Arsenic* means _____.

26. Eliot knew the cleaning fluid was poisonous because it had the sign of the *skull and bones* on it. *Skull and bones* means

_____.

27. When Laura was getting married, her friends organized a *bridal* party for her. *Bridal* means _____.

28. When Judy and Mike had been separated for a month and were reunited, they hugged each other at the airport gate in a warm *embrace*. *Embrace* means _____.

29. When Joe's car was struck from behind, the other car left a large *indentation* in the trunk. *Indentation* means _____.

30. The rotting trees in the swamp gave off a sharp, *acrid* smell. *Acrid* means _____.

PRE-READING VOCABULARY
STRUCTURAL ATTACK

Define these words by solving the parts. Use the Glossary or a dictionary as needed.

1. respectful
2. man-servant
3. gardener
4. squarish
5. scrolled
6. repaying
7. dissatisfaction
8. china-painting
9. disuse
10. leather-covered
11. plumpness
12. spokesman
13. invisible
14. graybeards
15. outbuildings
16. foreground
17. horsewhip
18. humanized
19. machinery
20. foreman
21. day laborer
22. kinfolk
23. earthiness
24. druggist
25. eyesockets
26. marrying
27. disgrace
28. blood-kin
29. iron-gray
30. regularity
31. backbone
32. inescapable
33. bottle-neck
34. fleshless

PRE-READING QUESTIONS

Try answering these questions as you read.

Who is Miss Emily?

What do the townspeople see?

What do the townspeople think?

Who is Homer Barron?

What happens to Homer Barron?

A Rose for Emily

WILLIAM FAULKNER

William Faulkner, the great grandson of a Confederate colonel, was born in New Albany, Mississippi in 1897. In 1902 Faulkner's family moved to Oxford, Mississippi in Lafayette County. In addition to being the home of the University of Mississippi and a place Faulkner would continually return to, Oxford and Lafayette County would inspire the fictional Yoknapatawpha County and its county seat, Jefferson, in Faulkner's writing. Faulkner left school after tenth grade, volunteered for the United States Army, and eventually entered the Royal Canadian Air Force during World War I. He then returned home to attend the University of Mississippi, but he did not finish his first year. He became interested in writing, moved to New York City and then to New Orleans, and then toured Europe. He returned to Oxford in 1929 and married Estelle Oldham. Shortly thereafter, he began a writing career marked by spurts and lapses. From 1929 to 1936 he wrote his major works—works that include The Sound and the Fury and Light in August. From 1936 to 1948 he produced little writing, and then in 1949 his writing increased again. Faulkner died in Oxford in 1962.

His complex writing reflects his interests in family relationships, in history, and in the South itself. Often portraying the decay of the old South, Faulkner's writing is as rich as it is shocking. He is credited with developing the narrative technique called **flashback**, wherein a character's present story "flashes back" to a story or stories from her or his past.

When Miss Emily Grierson died, our whole town went to her funeral: the men through a sort of respectful affection for a fallen monument, the women mostly out of curiosity to see the inside of her house, which no one save an old man-servant—a combined gardener and cook—had seen in at least ten years.

2   It was a big, squarish frame house that had once been white, decorated with cupolas and spires and scrolled balconies in the heavily lightsome style of the seventies, set on what had once been our most select street. But garages and cotton gins had encroached and obliterated even the august names of that neighborhood; only Miss Emily's house was left, lifting its stubborn and coquettish decay above the cotton wagons and the gasoline pumps—an eyesore among eyesores. And now Miss Emily had gone to join the representatives of those august names where they lay in the cedar-bemused cemetery among the ranked and anonymous graves of Union and Confederate soldiers who fell at the battle of Jefferson.

3   Alive, Miss Emily had been a tradition, a duty, and a care; a sort of hereditary obligation upon the town, dating from that day in 1894 when Colonel Sartoris, the mayor—he who fathered the edict that no Negro

woman should appear on the streets without an apron—remitted her taxes, the dispensation dating from the death of her father on into perpetuity. Not that Miss Emily would have accepted charity. Colonel Sartoris invented an involved tale to the effect that Miss Emily's father had loaned money to the town, which the town, as a matter of business, preferred this way of repaying. Only a man of Colonel Sartoris' generation and thought could have invented it, and only a woman could have believed it.

4   When the next generation, with its more modern ideas, became mayors and aldermen, this arrangement created some little dissatisfaction. On the first of the year they mailed her a tax notice. February came, and there was no reply. They wrote her a formal letter, asking her to call at the sheriff's office at her convenience. A week later the mayor wrote her himself, offering to call or to send his car for her, and received in reply a note on paper of an archaic shape, in a thin, flowing calligraphy in faded ink, to the effect that she no longer went out at all. The tax notice was also enclosed, without comment.

5   They called a special meeting of the Board of Aldermen. A deputation waited upon her, knocked at the door through which no visitor had passed since she ceased giving china-painting lessons eight or ten years earlier. They were admitted by the old Negro into a dim hall from which a stairway mounted into still more shadow. It smelled of dust and disuse—a close, dank smell. The Negro led them into the parlor. It was furnished in heavy, leather-covered furniture. When the Negro opened the blinds of one window, they could see that the leather was cracked; and when they sat down, a faint dust rose sluggishly about their thighs, spinning with slow motes in the single sun-ray. On a tarnished gilt easel before the fireplace stood a crayon portrait of Miss Emily's father.

6   They rose when she entered—a small, fat woman in black, with a thin gold chain descending to her waist and vanishing into her belt, leaning on an ebony cane with a tarnished gold head. Her skeleton was small and spare; perhaps that was why what would have been merely plumpness in another was obesity in her. She looked bloated, like a body long submerged in motionless water, and of that pallid hue. Her eyes, lost in the fatty ridges of her face, looked like two small pieces of coal pressed into a lump of dough as they moved from one face to another while the visitors stated their errand.

7   She did not ask them to sit. She just stood in the door and listened quietly until the spokesman came to a stumbling halt. Then they could hear the invisible watch ticking at the end of the gold chain.

8   Her voice was dry and cold. "I have no taxes in Jefferson. Colonel Sartoris explained it to me. Perhaps one of you can gain access to the city records and satisfy yourselves."

9   "But we have. We are the city authorities, Miss Emily. Didn't you get a notice from the sheriff, signed by him?"

10   "I received a paper, yes," Miss Emily said. "Perhaps he considers himself the sheriff . . . I have no taxes in Jefferson."

11   "But there is nothing on the books to show that, you see. We must go by the—"

12   "See Colonel Sartoris. I have no taxes in Jefferson."

13   "But, Miss Emily—"

14   "See Colonel Sartoris." (Colonel Sartoris had been dead almost ten years.) "I have no taxes in Jefferson. Tobe!" The Negro appeared. "Show these gentlemen out."

II

15   So she vanquished them, horse and foot, just as she had vanquished their fathers thirty years before about the smell. That was two years after her father's death and a short time after her sweetheart—the one we believed would marry her—had deserted her. After her father's death she went out very little; after her sweetheart went away, people hardly saw her at all. A few of the ladies had the temerity to call, but were not received, and the only sign of life about the place was the Negro man— a young man then—going in and out with a market basket.

16   "Just as if a man—any man—could keep a kitchen properly," the ladies said; so they were not surprised when the smell developed. It was another link between the gross, teeming world and the high and mighty Griersons.

17   A neighbor, a woman, complained to the mayor, Judge Stevens, eighty years old.

18   "But what will you have me do about it, madam?" he said.

19   "Why, send her word to stop it," the woman said. "Isn't there a law?"

20   "I'm sure that won't be necessary," Judge Stevens said. "It's probably just a snake or a rat that n—— of hers killed in the yard. I'll speak to him about it."

21   The next day he received two more complaints, one from a man who came in diffident deprecation. "We really must do something about it, Judge. I'd be the last one in the world to bother Miss Emily, but we've got to do something." That night the Board of Aldermen met—three graybeards and one younger man, a member of the rising generation.

22   "It's simple enough," he said. "Send her word to have her place cleaned up. Give her a certain time to do it in, and if she don't ..."

23   "Dammit, sir," Judge Stevens said, "will you accuse a lady to her face of smelling bad?"

24   So the next night, after midnight, four men crossed Miss Emily's lawn and slunk about the house like burglars, sniffing along the base of the brickwork and at the cellar openings while one of them performed a regular sowing motion with his hand out of a sack slung from his shoulder. They broke open the cellar door and sprinkled lime there, and in all the outbuildings. As they recrossed the lawn, a window that had been dark was lighted and Miss Emily sat in it, the light behind her, and her upright torso motionless as that of an idol. They crept quietly across the lawn and into the shadow of the locusts that lined the street. After a week or two the smell went away.

25   That was when people had begun to feel really sorry for her. People in our town, remembering how old lady Wyatt, her great-aunt, had gone completely crazy at last, believed that the Griersons held themselves a little too high for what they really were. None of the young men were quite good enough for Miss Emily and such. We had long thought of them as a tableau, Miss Emily a slender figure in white in the background, her father a spraddled silhouette in the foreground, his back to her and clutching a horsewhip, the two of them framed by the back-flung front door. So when she got to be thirty and was still single, we were not pleased exactly, but vindicated; even with insanity in the family she wouldn't have turned down all of her chances if they had really materialized.

26   When her father died, it got about that the house was all that was left to her; and in a way, people were glad. At last they could pity Miss Emily. Being left alone, and a pauper, she had become humanized. Now she too would know the old thrill and the old despair of a penny more or less.

27   The day after his death all the ladies prepared to call at the house and offer condolence and aid, as is our custom. Miss Emily met them at the door, dressed as usual and with no trace of grief on her face. She told them that her father was not dead. She did that for three days, with the ministers calling on her, and the doctors, trying to persuade her to let them dispose of the body. Just as they were about to resort to law and force, she broke down, and they buried her father quickly.

28   We did not say she was crazy then. We believed she had to do that. We remembered all the young men her father had driven away, and we knew that with nothing left, she would have to cling to that which had robbed her, as people will.

III

29   She was sick for a long time. When we saw her again her hair was cut short, making her look like a girl, with a vague resemblance to those angels in colored church windows—sort of tragic and serene.

30   The town had just let the contracts for paving the sidewalks, and in the summer after her father's death they began the work. The construction company came with n——s and mules and machinery, and a foreman named Homer Barron, a Yankee—a big, dark, ready man, with a big voice and eyes lighter than his face. The little boys would follow in groups to hear him cuss the n——s, and the n——s singing in time to the rise and fall of picks. Pretty soon he knew everybody in town. Whenever you heard a lot of laughing anywhere about the square, Homer Barron would be in the center of the group. Presently we began to see him and Miss Emily on Sunday afternoons driving in the yellow-wheeled buggy and the matched team of bays from the livery stable.

31   At first we were glad that Miss Emily would have an interest, because the ladies all said, "Of course a Grierson would not think seriously of a Northerner, a day laborer." But there were still others, older people, who said that even grief could not cause a real lady to forget *noblesse oblige*—without calling it *noblesse oblige*. They just said, "Poor Emily. Her kinsfolk should come to her." She had some kin in Alabama; but years ago her father had fallen out with them over the estate of old lady Wyatt, the crazy woman, and there was no communication between the two families. They had not even been represented at the funeral.

32   And as soon as the old people said, "Poor Emily," the whispering began. "Do you suppose it's really so?" they said to one another. "Of course it is. What else could . . ." This behind their hands; rustling of craned silk and satin behind jalousies closed upon the sun of Sunday afternoon as the thin, swift clop-clop-clop of the matched team passed: "Poor Emily."

33   She carried her head high enough—even when we believed that she was fallen. It was as if she demanded more than ever the recognition of her dignity as the last Grierson; as if it had wanted that touch of earthiness to reaffirm her imperviousness. Like when she bought the rat poison, the arsenic. That was over a year after they had begun to say "Poor Emily," and while the two female cousins were visiting her.

34   "I want some poison," she said to the druggist. She was over thirty then, still a slight woman, though thinner than usual, with cold, haughty black eyes in a face the flesh of which was strained across the temples and about the eyesockets as you imagine a lighthouse-keeper's face ought to look. "I want some poison," she said.

35   "Yes, Miss Emily. What kind? For rats and such? I'd recom—"

36   "I want the best you have. I don't care what kind."

37   The druggist named several. "They'll kill anything up to an elephant. But what you want is—"

38   "Arsenic," Miss Emily said. "Is that a good one?"

39   "Is . . . arsenic? Yes, ma'am. But what you want—"

40   "I want arsenic."

41   The druggist looked down at her. She looked back at him, erect, her face like a strained flag. "Why, of course," the druggist said. "If that's what you want. But the law requires you to tell what you are going to use it for."

42   Miss Emily just stared at him, her head tilted back in order to look him eye for eye, until he looked away and went and got the arsenic and wrapped it up. The Negro delivery boy brought her the package; the druggist didn't come back. When she opened the package at home there was written on the box, under the skull and bones: "For rats."

IV

43   So the next day we all said, "She will kill herself"; and we said it would be the best thing. When she had first begun to be seen with Homer Barron, we had said, "She will marry him." Then we said, "She will persuade him yet," because Homer himself had remarked—he liked men, and it was known that he drank with the younger men in the Elks' Club—that he was not a marrying man. Later we said, "Poor Emily" behind the jalousies as they passed on Sunday afternoon in the glittering buggy, Miss Emily with her head high and Homer Barron with his hat cocked and a cigar in his teeth, reins and whip in a yellow glove.

44   Then some of the ladies began to say that it was a disgrace to the town and a bad example to the young people. The men did not want to interfere, but at last the ladies forced the Baptist minister—Miss Emily's people were Episcopal—to call upon her. He would never divulge what happened during that interview, but he refused to go back again. The next Sunday they again drove about the streets, and the following day the minister's wife wrote to Miss Emily's relations in Alabama.

45   So she had blood-kin under her roof again and we sat back to watch developments. At first nothing happened. Then we were sure that they were to be married. We learned that Miss Emily had been to the jeweler's and ordered a man's toilet set in silver, with the letters H. B. on each piece. Two days later we learned that she had bought a complete outfit of men's clothing, including a nightshirt, and we said, "They are married." We were really glad. We were glad because the two female cousins were even more Grierson than Miss Emily had ever been.

46   So we were not surprised when Homer Barron—the streets had been finished some time since—was gone. We were a little disappointed that there was not a public blowing-off, but we believed that he

had gone on to prepare for Miss Emily's coming, or to give her a chance to get rid of the cousins. (By that time it was a cabal, and we were all Miss Emily's allies to help circumvent the cousins.) Sure enough, after another week they departed. And, as we had expected all along, within three days Homer Barron was back in town. A neighbor saw the Negro man admit him at the kitchen door at dusk one evening.

47   And that was the last we saw of Homer Barron. And of Miss Emily for some time. The Negro man went in and out with the market basket, but the front door remained closed. Now and then we would see her at a window for a moment, as the men did that night when they sprinkled the lime, but for almost six months she did not appear on the streets. Then we knew that this was to be expected too; as if that quality of her father which had thwarted her woman's life so many times had been too virulent and too furious to die.

48   When we next saw Miss Emily, she had grown fat and her hair was turning gray. During the next few years it grew grayer and grayer until it attained an even pepper-and-salt iron-gray, when it ceased turning. Up to the day of her death at seventy-four it was still that vigorous iron-gray, like the hair of an active man.

49   From that time on her front door remained closed, save for a period of six or seven years, when she was about forty, during which she gave lessons in china-painting. She fitted up a studio in one of the downstairs rooms, where the daughters and granddaughters of Colonel Sartoris' contemporaries were sent to her with the same regularity and in the same spirit that they were sent to church on Sundays with a twenty-five-cent piece for the collection plate. Meanwhile her taxes had been remitted.

50   Then the newer generation became the backbone and the spirit of the town, and the painting pupils grew up and fell away and did not send their children to her with boxes of color and tedious brushes and pictures cut from the ladies' magazines. The front door closed upon the last one and remained closed for good. When the town got free postal delivery, Miss Emily alone refused to let them fasten the metal numbers above her door and attach a mailbox to it. She would not listen to them.

51   Daily, monthly, yearly we watched the Negro grow grayer and more stooped, going in and out with the market basket. Each December we sent her a tax notice, which would be returned by the post office a week later, unclaimed. Now and then we would see her in one of the downstairs windows—she had evidently shut up the top floor of the house—like the carven torso of an idol in a niche, looking or not looking at us, we could never tell which. Thus she passed from generation to generation—dear, inescapable, impervious, tranquil, and perverse.

52   And so she died. Fell ill in the house filled with dust and shadows, with only a doddering Negro man to wait on her. We did not even know she was sick; we had long since given up trying to get any information from the Negro. He talked to no one, probably not even to her, for his voice had grown harsh and rusty, as if from disuse.

53   She died in one of the downstairs rooms, in a heavy walnut bed with a curtain, her gray head propped on a pillow yellow and moldy with age and lack of sunlight.

V

54   The Negro met the first of the ladies at the front door and let them in, with their hushed, sibilant voices and their quick, curious glances, and then he disappeared. He walked right through the house and out the back and was not seen again.

55   The two female cousins came at once. They held the funeral on the second day, with the town coming to look at Miss Emily beneath a mass of bought flowers, with the crayon face of her father musing profoundly above the bier and the ladies sibilant and macabre; and the very old men—some in their brushed Confederate uniforms—on the porch and the lawn, talking of Miss Emily as if she had been a contemporary of theirs, believing that they had danced with her and courted her perhaps, confusing time with its mathematical progression, as the old do, to whom all the past is not a diminishing road but, instead, a huge meadow which no winter ever quite touches, divided from them now by the narrow bottle-neck of the most recent decade of years.

56   Already we knew that there was one room in that region above stairs which no one had seen in forty years, and which would have to be forced. They waited until Miss Emily was decently in the ground before they opened it.

57   The violence of breaking down the door seemed to fill this room with pervading dust. A thin, acrid pall as of the tomb seemed to lie everywhere upon this room decked and furnished as for a bridal: upon the valance curtains of faded rose color, upon the rose-shaded lights, upon the dressing table, upon the delicate array of crystal and the man's toilet things backed with tarnished silver, silver so tarnished that the monogram was obscured. Among them lay a collar and tie, as if they had just been removed, which, lifted, left upon the surface a pale crescent in the dust. Upon a chair hung the suit, carefully folded; beneath it the two mute shoes and the discarded socks.

58   The man himself lay in the bed.

59   For a long while we just stood there, looking down at the profound and fleshless grin. The body had apparently once lain in the attitude of

an embrace, but now the long sleep that outlasts love, that conquers even the grimace of love, had cuckolded him. What was left of him, rotted beneath what was left of the night-shirt, had become inextricable from the bed in which he lay; and upon him and upon the pillow beside him lay that even coating of the patient and biding dust.

60   Then we noticed that in the second pillow was the indentation of a head. One of us lifted something from it, and leaning forward, that faint and invisible dust dry and acrid in the nostrils, we saw a long strand of iron-gray hair.

A Rose for Emily

JOURNAL

1. **MLA Works Cited** *Using this model, record this story here.*

   *Author's Last Name, First Name. "Title of the Story." <u>Title of the Book</u>.
   3rd ed. Ed. First Name Last Name. City: Publisher, year. Pages of
   the story.*

2. **Main Character(s)** *Describe each main character, and explain why you
   think each is a main character.*

3. **Supporting Characters** *Describe each supporting character, and explain why
   you think each is a supporting character.*

4. **Setting** *Describe the setting(s) and any relevant prop(s).*

5. **Sequence**   *Outline the events of the story in order.*

6. **Plot**   *Tell the story in no more than three sentences.*

7. **Conflicts**   *Identify and explain all the conflicts involved here.*

8. **Significant Quotations**   *Explain the importance of each of these quotations. Record the page number in the parentheses.*
   a. "Only a man of Colonel Sartoris' generation and thought could have invented it, and only a woman could have believed it" (   ).

   b. "The tax notice was also enclosed, without comment" (   ).

c. " 'Dammit, sir,' Judge Stevens said, 'will you accuse a lady to her face of
   smelling bad?' " (   ).

d. " 'I want arsenic' " (   ).

e. "The man himself lay in the bed" (   ).

9. **Literary Elements**   *Look at this chapter's title and explain why you think
   this story is placed in this chapter. Explain in which other chapter(s) you
   might place this story, as relevant to the literary element(s) of that chapter.*

10. **Foreshadowing, Irony, and/or Symbolism**   *Explain examples of foreshadowing,
    irony, and/or symbolism in this story.*

Follow-up Questions

10 Short Questions

*Select the **best** answer for each.*

____ 1. Miss Emily is
   a. very friendly.
   b. very lively.
   c. very reserved.

____ 2. Miss Emily is
   a. a modern woman.
   b. a young woman.
   c. of a past generation.

____ 3. Miss Emily thinks
   a. that she is poor.
   b. that she is rich.
   c. that she is in between.

____ 4. Miss Emily thinks she is
   a. beneath the townspeople.
   b. better than the townspeople.
   c. the same as the townspeople.

____ 5. The servant is
   a. dishonest.
   b. disloyal.
   c. loyal.

____ 6. The servant is
   a. silent.
   b. noisy.
   c. nosy.

____ 7. After her father dies, Miss Emily
   a. easily accepts her father's death.
   b. denies his death.
   c. does not know where her father is.

____ 8. Miss Emily's family
   a. has a history of insanity.
   b. is sane and solid.
   c. is very normal.

____ 9. Miss Emily probably
   a. married Homer.
   b. scared Homer away.
   c. poisoned Homer.

____ 10. Miss Emily's actions seem
   a. normal.
   b. grotesque.
   c. humorous.

5 Significant Quotations

Explain the importance of each of these quotations.

1. "But garages and cotton gins had encroached and obliterated even the august names of that neighborhood; only Miss Emily's house was left [. . .]—an eyesore among eyesores."

2. "On the first of the year they mailed her a tax notice. February came, and there was no reply."

3. "[S]o they were not surprised when the smell developed."

4. " 'Arsenic,' Miss Emily said. 'Is that a good one?' "

5. "Then we noticed that in the second pillow was the indentation of a head."

2 Comprehension Essay Questions

Use specific details and information from the story to answer these questions as completely as possible.

1. What are Miss Emily's relationships with the men in her life? Use specific details and information from the story to support your descriptions.

2. What are the townspeople's perceptions of Miss Emily? Use specific details and information from the story to support your explanation.

Discussion Questions

Be prepared to discuss these questions in class.

1. What elements of foreshadowing are in this story? Use specific details from the story to support your ideas.

2. What events and/or dynamics does Faulkner use to demonstrate the decay of the South? Use specific details from the story to support your ideas.

Writing

Use each of these ideas for writing an essay.

1. Miss Emily's neighbors keep a close watch on Miss Emily. All of us have had interesting neighbors—noisy, nosy, lively, strange, and so forth. Describe an interesting incident that you or someone you know has had with a neighbor.

2. Miss Emily does not handle death well. Think of a loss—the loss of a home when moving, the loss of a favorite thing, the loss of a pet or a loved one—that you or someone you know has experienced. Tell the story of this loss and of how you or someone you know handled the loss.

Further Writing

1. Although Faulkner said he did not use symbols in "A Rose for Emily," many would disagree. Read analyses of this story (available in a library), and relate what you find about symbolism in this story.

2. Read a biography of Lizzie Borden (available in a library), and consider assumptions made about the aristocracy in her case. Compare the defense in the Borden trial with the protection Miss Emily enjoys.

3. Research the generous contributions—*noblesse oblige*—of your favorite rock, sports, or movie stars.

Dr. Heidegger's Experiment

Nathaniel Hawthorne

Pre-reading Vocabulary
Context

Use context clues to define these words before reading. Use a dictionary as needed.

1. The learned wisdom and great dignity of the judge made him a *venerable* person. *Venerable* means _____.

2. After becoming a lieutenant, a captain, and then a major, Juan was made a *colonel* in the Army. *Colonel* means _____.

3. The grape *withered* into a wrinkled little raisin as it sat in the sun. *Withered* means _____.

4. After his father died, Don went to visit his mother who was now a *widow*. *Widow* means _____.

5. With her store selling merchandise valued in the millions, Debbie has become the most successful *merchant* in town. *Merchant* means _____.

6. After losing everything, Chuck became a mere *mendicant*, begging in the streets. *Mendicant* means _____.

7. There are many little-known, *obscure* artists trying to sell their work. *Obscure* means _____.

8. When people learned about the man cheating on his kindly wife, people looked on the affair as *scandalous. Scandalous* means

   _____.

9. When Heather moved into a large home in the country, she became part of the wealthy, landed *gentry. Gentry* means

   _____.

10. Mukendi lost his check records, and his checking account became a *woeful* mess. *Woeful* means _____.

11. The children loved to listen when Purvi read them a wonderful *fable* about a turtle and a rabbit. *Fable* means _____.

12. The museum had *busts*, or statues of the heads and shoulders, of Hippocrates, Plato, and Socrates. *Bust* means _____.

13. Marlen glanced into the *looking glass* to see if she needed to fix her hair. *Looking glass* means _____.

14. Laura's *magnificent* gown was made of golden fabric set with sparkling jewels. *Magnificent* means _____.

15. Jamie decided to hang elegant, heavy satin *brocade* and *damask* drapes. *Brocade* and *damask* means _____.

16. Scott had the *visage* of a happy man as his eyes sparkled, his lips were curved into a smile, and his steps were light. *Visage* means _____.

17. Isabelle had a great *curiosity* about her neighbors and decided to spy on them to learn more. *Curiosity* means _____.

18. The heavy book with its many pages was a sizable *volume* to try to place on the shelf. *Volume* means _____.

19. The adults dressed up as *ghastly* creatures and tried to win the Most Scary prize at the party. *Ghastly* means _____.

20. Jack decorated the top of the drapes with a heavy, braided *festoon*. *Festoon* means _____.

21. On New Year's eve, many drink a bottle of expensive *champagne* to celebrate the evening. *Champagne* means _____.

22. Artie waited for the tomatoes to ripen and turn bright *crimson* before he picked them. *Crimson* means _____.

23. Jay is a master of *deception* and seems to be able to lie about everything and to get away with it. *Deception* means

_____.

24. When Nicole had a cold, the doctor told her to rest and to drink a lot of *fluids*. *Fluid* means _____.

25. Scientists are looking for *rejuvenescent* creams that will make the wrinkles of old age disappear. *Rejuvenescent* means

_____.

26. Mary felt very *repentant* after she broke her mother's vase, and she went everywhere to try to buy a new one. *Repentant* means

_____.

27. After he drank far too much coffee, Hal's *palsied* hands shook uncontrollably. *Palsied* means _____.

28. Donnie and Marie *bestowed* the crown *upon* the new Miss America. *Bestow upon* means _____.

29. The elderly man was old and *decrepit* and could hardly walk without assistance. *Decrepit* means _____.

30. Ann has to have a lot of *patience* to work so long and hard at sewing on beads. *Patience* means _____.

31. Karen was under the *delusion* that she had lost the contest, only to find out later that she had won. *Delusion* means

_____.

32. At twenty-two, Ted is in the *prime* of his life and enjoys perfect health and lots of energy. *Prime* means _____.

33. Loyalty to one's country is called *patriotism*. *Patriotism* means

_____.

34. A *simper* is a silly grin, often following a silly joke. *Simpering* means _____.

35. Joanne's cake completely *vanished*, and not even a crumb was left after the hungry children came home from school. *Vanished* means

_____.

36. The nasty woman *mocked* and made fun of the older woman who moved so slowly. *Mocked* means _____.

37. When Tricia wears her judge's robes and elegantly enters the courtroom, she moves with great *dignity*. *Dignity* means

_____.

38. Anna and Caitlin shared a great *rivalship* when each competed with the other to be prom queen. *Rivalship* means

_____.

39. The young man was absolutely *bewitched* by the young girl's charm and beauty. *Bewitched* means _____.

40. Gloria flirted in playful *coquetry* with every young man she met. *Coquetry* means _____.

41. Dave and Teddy *grappled* with facts and figures as they tried to develop a sales proposal. *Grapple* means _____.

42. The unhappy residents *protested* the new taxes they felt they should not have to pay. *Protest* means _____.

43. Paul mistakenly hit the delicate vase and *dashed* it to the floor. *Dash* means _____.

44. The balloon *shriveled* up after Victoria poked it with a pin and let the air out of it. *Shrivel* means _____.

45. Worry caused deep *furrows* in the old woman's forehead. *Furrow* means _____.

46. Childhood is only a *transient* state, because it disappears in a relatively short time. *Transient* means _____.

47. High fever can cause *delirium*, resulting in one seeing and hearing things that are not really there. *Delirium* means _____.

48. The wealthy woman *lavished* all her wealth on a man who later left her with nothing. *Lavished* means _____.

49. The religious people made a *pilgrimage* to visit the places that they considered to be holy. *Pilgrimage* means _____.

50. The football players took deep *quaffs* of water to satisfy their thirst in the hot sun. *Quaff* means _____.

PRE-READING VOCABULARY
STRUCTURAL ATTACK

Define these words by solving the parts. Use the Glossary or a dictionary as needed.

1. white-bearded	16. chambermaid	31. successive
2. gentlewoman	17. workmanship	32. new-created
3. unfortunate	18. ashen	33. maddened
4. misfortune	19. exceedingly	34. frolicsomeness
5. sinful	20. withered	35. gayety
6. ruined	21. blossomed	36. mischievous
7. infamous	22. faded	37. merriment
8. unfrequently	23. reviving	38. pessimistic
9. recollections	24. deathlike	39. disengage
10. desirous	25. animated	40. livelier
11. old-fashioned	26. improvement	41. threatening
12. besprinkled	27. corpse-like	42. overturned
13. oaken	28. brimful	43. chillness
14. obscurest	29. duskier	44. deepening
15. ornamented	30. joyously	

PRE-READING QUESTIONS

Try answering these questions as you read.

What does Dr. Heidegger have?

What characteristics do Dr. Heidegger's guests have?

How do they change?

How do they stay the same?

Dr. Heidegger's Experiment

NATHANIEL HAWTHORNE

Nathaniel Hawthorne was born in 1804. He came from a prominent family in Salem, Massachusetts. Hawthorne was related to wealthy merchants on his father's side and to working transporters on his mother's side. Hawthorne's family saved money to send him to Bowdoin College in Maine. There he roomed with Franklin Pierce, who would become the fourteenth president of the United States, and met Henry Wadsworth Longfellow. Wishing to become a writer but realizing that writers do not make much money, Hawthorne turned to work in the Boston customhouse and later married Sophia Peabody. Eventually, he returned to Salem and to writing. He later served as President Pierce's consul in Liverpool, England. Hawthorne died of a debilitating disease in 1860.

A friend of Longfellow and of Ralph Waldo Emerson and esteemed by Herman Melville, who dedicated Moby Dick to him, Hawthorne raised questions about the human condition. The Scarlet Letter and The House of Seven Gables remain his masterworks. This story is taken from Twice-Told Tales.

The home that inspired The House of Seven Gables is open to the public, and a visit there offers insight into the mysterious, Gothic, and often eerie world that appears in Hawthorne's writings.

That very singular man, old Dr. Heidegger, once invited four venerable friends to meet him in his study. There were three white-bearded gentlemen, Mr. Medbourne, Colonel Killigrew, and Mr. Gascoigne, and a withered gentlewoman, whose name was the Widow Wycherly. They were all melancholy old creatures, who had been unfortunate in life, and whose greatest misfortune it was that they were not long ago in their graves. Mr. Medbourne, in the vigor of his age, had been a prosperous merchant, but had lost his all by a frantic speculation, and was now little better than a mendicant. Colonel Killigrew had wasted his best years, and his health and substance, in the pursuit of sinful pleasures, which had given birth to a brood of pains, such as the gout, and divers other torments of soul and body. Mr. Gascoigne was a ruined politician, a man of evil fame, or at least had been so till time had buried him from the knowledge of the present generation, and made him obscure instead of infamous. As for the Widow Wycherly, tradition tells us that she was a great beauty in her day; but, for a long while past, she had lived in deep seclusion, on account of certain scandalous stories which had prejudiced the gentry of the town against her. It is a circumstance worth mentioning that each of these three old gentlemen, Mr. Medbourne, Colonel Killigrew, and Mr. Gascoigne, were early lovers of the Widow Wycherly, and had once been on the point of cutting each other's throats for her sake. And, before proceeding further, I will merely hint that Dr. Heidegger and all his four guests were sometimes thought to be a little beside themselves—as is not unfrequently the case with old people, when worried either by present troubles or woeful recollections.

2   "My dear old friends," said Dr. Heidegger, motioning them to be seated, "I am desirous of your assistance in one of those little experiments with which I amuse myself here in my study."

3   If all stories were true, Dr. Heidegger's study must have been a very curious place. It was a dim, old-fashioned chamber, festooned with cobwebs, and besprinkled with antique dust. Around the walls stood several oaken bookcases, the lower shelves of which were filled with rows of gigantic folios and black-letter quartos, and the upper with little parchment-covered duodecimos. Over the central bookcase was a bronze bust of Hippocrates, with which, according to some authorities, Dr. Heidegger was accustomed to hold consultations in all difficult cases of his practice. In the obscurest corner of the room stood a tall and narrow oaken closet, with its door ajar, within which doubtfully appeared a skeleton. Between two of the bookcases hung a looking-glass, presenting its high and dusty plate within a tarnished gilt frame. Among many wonderful stories related of this mirror, it was fabled that the spirits of all the doctor's deceased patients dwelt within its verge, and would stare him in the face whenever he looked thitherward. The opposite side of the chamber was ornamented with the full-length portrait of a young lady, arrayed in the faded magnificence of silk, satin, and brocade, and with a visage as faded as her dress. Above half a century ago, Dr. Heidegger had been on the point of marriage with this young lady; but, being affected with some slight disorder, she had swallowed one of her lover's prescriptions, and died on the bridal evening. The greatest curiosity of the study remains to be mentioned; it was a ponderous folio volume, bound in black leather, with massive silver clasps. There were no letters on the back, and nobody could tell the title of the book. But it was well known to be a book of magic; and once, when a chambermaid had lifted it, merely to brush away the dust, the skeleton had rattled in its closet, the picture of the young lady had stepped one foot upon the floor, and several ghastly faces had peeped forth from the mirror; while the brazen head of Hippocrates frowned, and said—"Forbear!"

4   Such was Dr. Heidegger's study. On the summer afternoon of our tale a small round table, as black as ebony, stood in the centre of the room, sustaining a cut-glass vase of beautiful form and elaborate workmanship. The sunshine came through the window, between the heavy festoons of two faded damask curtains, and fell directly across this

vase; so that a mild splendor was reflected from it on the ashen visages of the five old people who sat around. Four champagne glasses were also on the table.

5   "My dear old friends," repeated Dr. Heidegger, "may I reckon on your aid in performing an exceedingly curious experiment?"

6   Now Dr. Heidegger was a very strange old gentleman, whose eccentricity had become the nucleus for a thousand fantastic stories. Some of these fables, to my shame be it spoken, might possibly be traced back to my own veracious self; and if any passages of the present tale should startle the reader's faith, I must be content to bear the stigma of a fiction monger.

7   When the doctor's four guests heard him talk of his proposed experiment, they anticipated nothing more wonderful than the murder of a mouse in an air pump, or the examination of a cobweb by the microscope, or some similar nonsense, with which he was constantly in the habit of pestering his intimates. But without waiting for a reply, Dr. Heidegger hobbled across the chamber, and returned with the same ponderous folio, bound in black leather, which common report affirmed to be a book of magic. Undoing the silver clasps, he opened the volume, and took from among its black-letter pages a rose, or what was once a rose, though now the green leaves and crimson petals had assumed one brownish hue, and the ancient flower seemed ready to crumble to dust in the doctor's hands.

8   "This rose," said Dr. Heidegger, with a sigh, "this same withered and crumbling flower, blossomed five and fifty years ago. It was given me by Sylvia Ward, whose portrait hangs yonder; and I meant to wear it in my bosom at our wedding. Five and fifty years it has been treasured between the leaves of this old volume. Now, would you deem it possible that this rose of half a century could ever bloom again?"

9   "Nonsense!" said the Widow Wycherly, with a peevish toss of her head. "You might as well ask whether an old woman's wrinkled face could ever bloom again."

10   "See!" answered Dr. Heidegger.

11   He uncovered the vase, and threw the faded rose into the water which it contained. At first, it lay lightly on the surface of the fluid, appearing to imbibe none of its moisture. Soon, however, a singular change began to be visible. The crushed and dried petals stirred, and assumed a deepening tinge of crimson as if the flower were reviving from a deathlike slumber; the slender stalk and twigs of foliage became green; and there was the rose of half a century, looking as fresh as when Sylvia Ward had first given it to her lover. It was scarcely full blown; for some of its delicate red leaves curled modestly around its moist bosom, within which two or three dewdrops were sparkling.

12   "That is certainly a very pretty deception," said the doctor's friends; carelessly, however, for they had witnessed greater miracles at a conjurer's show; "pray how was it effected?"

13   "Did you never hear of the 'Fountain of Youth'?" asked Dr. Heidegger, "which Ponce de Leon, the Spanish adventurer, went in search of two or three centuries ago?"

14   "But did Ponce de Leon ever find it?" said the Widow Wycherly.

15   "No," answered Dr. Heidegger, "for he never sought it in the right place. The famous Fountain of Youth, if I am rightly informed, is situated in the southern part of the Floridian peninsula, not far from Lake Macaco. Its source is overshadowed by several gigantic magnolias, which, though numberless centuries old, have been kept as fresh as violets by the virtues of this wonderful water. An acquaintance of mine, knowing my curiosity in such matters, has sent me what you see in the vase."

16   "Ahem!" said Colonel Killigrew, who believed not a word of the doctor's story: "and what may be the effect of this fluid on the human frame?"

17   "You shall judge for yourself, my dear colonel," replied Dr. Heidegger; "and all of you, my respected friends, are welcome to so much of this admirable fluid as may restore to you the bloom of youth. For my own part, having had much trouble in growing old, I am in no hurry to grow young again. With your permission, therefore, I will merely watch the progress of the experiment."

18   While he spoke, Dr. Heidegger had been filling the four champagne glasses with the water of the Fountain of Youth. It was apparently impregnated with an effervescent gas, for little bubbles were continually ascending from the depths of the glasses, and bursting in silvery spray at the surface. As the liquor diffused a pleasant perfume, the old people doubted not that it possessed cordial and comfortable properties; and though utter sceptics as to its rejuvenescent power, they were inclined to swallow it at once. But Dr. Heidegger besought them to stay a moment.

19   "Before you drink, my respectable, old friends," said he, "it would be well that, with the experience of a lifetime to direct you, you should draw up a few general rules for your guidance, in passing a second time through the perils of youth. Think what a sin and shame it would be, if, with your peculiar advantages, you should not become patterns of virtue and wisdom to all the young people of the age!"

20   The doctor's four venerable friends made him no answer, except by a feeble and tremulous laugh; so very ridiculous was the idea that, knowing how closely repentance treads behind the steps of error, they should ever go astray again.

21   "Drink, then," said the doctor, bowing: "I rejoice that I have so well selected the subjects of my experiment."

22   With palsied hands, they raised the glasses to their lips. The liquor, if it really possessed such virtues as Dr. Heidegger imputed to it, could not have been bestowed on four human beings who needed it more woefully. They looked as if they had never known what youth or pleasure was, but had been the offspring of Nature's dotage, and always the gray, decrepit, sapless, miserable creatures, who now sat stooping round the doctor's table, without life enough in their souls or bodies to be animated even by the prospect of growing young again. They drank off the water, and replaced their glasses on the table.

23   Assuredly there was an almost immediate improvement in the aspect of the party, not unlike what might have been produced by a glass of generous wine, together with a sudden glow of cheerful sunshine brightening over all their visages at once. There was a healthful suffusion on their cheeks, instead of the ashen hue that had made them look so corpse-like. They gazed at one another, and fancied that some magic power had really begun to smooth away the deep and sad inscriptions which Father Time had been so long engraving on their brows. The Widow Wycherly adjusted her cap, for she felt almost like a woman again.

24   "Give us more of this wondrous water!" cried they, eagerly. "We are younger—but we are still too old! Quick—give us more!"

25   "Patience, patience!" quoth Dr. Heidegger, who sat watching the experiment with philosophic coolness. "You have been a long time growing old. Surely, you might be content to grow young in half an hour! But the water is at your service."

26   Again he filled their glasses with the liquor of youth, enough of which still remained in the vase to turn half the old people in the city to the age of their own grandchildren. While the bubbles were yet sparkling on the brim, the doctor's four guests snatched their glasses from the table, and swallowed the contents at a single gulp. Was it delusion? Even while the draught was passing down their throats, it seemed to have wrought a change on their whole systems. Their eyes grew clear and bright; a dark shade deepened among their silvery locks; they sat around the table, three gentlemen of middle age, and a woman, hardly beyond her buxom prime.

27   "My dear widow, you are charming!" cried Colonel Killigrew, whose eyes had been fixed upon her face, while the shadows of age were flitting from it like darkness from the crimson daybreak.

28   The fair widow knew, of old, that Colonel Killigrew's compliments were not always measured by sober truth; so she started up and ran to the mirror, still dreading that the ugly visage of an old woman would

meet her gaze. Meanwhile, the three gentlemen behaved in such a manner as proved that the water of the Fountain of Youth possessed some intoxicating qualities; unless, indeed, their exhilaration of spirits were merely a lightsome dizziness caused by the sudden removal of the weight of years. Mr. Gascoigne's mind seemed to run on political topics, but whether relating to the past, present, or future could not easily be determined, since the same ideas and phrases have been in vogue these fifty years. Now he rattled forth full-throated sentences about patriotism, national glory, and the people's right; now he muttered some perilous stuff or other, in a sly and doubtful whisper, so cautiously that even his own conscience could scarcely catch the secret; and now, again, he spoke in measured accents, and a deeply deferential tone, as if a royal ear were listening to his well-turned periods. Colonel Killigrew all this time had been trolling forth a jolly bottle song, and ringing his glass in symphony with the chorus, while his eyes wandered toward the buxom figure of the Widow Wycherly. On the other side of the table, Mr. Medbourne was involved in a calculation of dollars and cents, with which was strangely intermingled a project for supplying the East Indies with ice, by harnessing a team of whales to the polar icebergs.

29   As for the Widow Wycherly, she stood before the mirror courtseying and simpering to her own image, and greeting it as the friend whom she loved better than all the world beside. She thrust her face close to the glass, to see whether some long-remembered wrinkle or crow's foot had indeed vanished. She examined whether the snow had so entirely melted from her hair that the venerable cap could be safely thrown aside. At last, turning briskly away, she came with a sort of dancing step to the table.

30   "My dear old doctor," cried she, "pray favor me with another glass!"

31   "Certainly, my dear madam, certainly!" replied the complaisant doctor; "See! I have already filled the glasses."

32   There, in fact, stood the four glasses, brimful of this wonderful water, the delicate spray of which, as it effervesced from the surface, resembled the tremulous glitter of diamonds. It was now so nearly sunset that the chamber had grown duskier than ever; but a mild and moonlike splendor gleamed from within the vase, and rested alike on the four guests and on the doctor's venerable figure. He sat in a high-backed, elaborately-carved, oaken arm-chair, with a gray dignity of aspect that might have well befitted that very Father Time, whose power had never been disputed, save by this fortunate company. Even while quaffing the third draught of the Fountain of Youth, they were almost awed by the expression of his mysterious visage.

33   But, the next moment, the exhilarating gush of young life shot through their veins. They were now in the happy prime of youth. Age, with its miserable train of cares and sorrows and diseases, was remembered only as the trouble of a dream, from which they had joyously awoke. The fresh gloss of the soul, so early lost, and without which the world's successive scenes had been but a gallery of faded pictures, again threw its enchantment over all their prospects. They felt like new-created beings in a new-created universe.

34   "We are young! We are young!" they cried exultingly.

35   Youth, like the extremity of age, had effaced the strongly-marked characteristics of middle life, and mutually assimilated them all. They were a group of merry youngsters, almost maddened with the exuberant frolicsomeness of their years. The most singular effect of their gayety was an impulse to mock the infirmity and decrepitude of which they had so lately been the victims. They laughed loudly at their old-fashioned attire, the wide-skirted coats and flapped waistcoats of the young men, and the ancient cap and gown of the blooming girl. One limped across the floor like a gouty grandfather; one set a pair of spectacles astride of his nose, and pretended to pore over the black-letter pages of the book of magic; a third seated himself in an arm-chair, and strove to imitate the venerable dignity of Dr. Heidegger. Then all shouted mirthfully, and leaped about the room. The Widow Wycherly—if so fresh a damsel could be called a widow—tripped up to the doctor's chair, with a mischievous merriment in her rosy face.

36   "Doctor, you dear old soul," cried she, "get up and dance with me!" And then the four young people laughed louder than ever, to think what a queer figure the poor old doctor would cut.

37   "Pray excuse me," answered the doctor quietly. "I am old and rheumatic, and my dancing days were over long ago. But either of these gay young gentlemen will be glad of so pretty a partner."

38   "Dance with me, Clara!" cried Colonel Killigrew.

39   "No, no, I will be her partner!" shouted Mr. Gascoigne.

40   "She promised me her hand, fifty years ago!" exclaimed Mr. Medbourne.

41   They all gathered round her. One caught both her hands in his passionate grasp—another threw his arm about her waist—the third buried his hand among the glossy curls that clustered beneath the widow's cap. Blushing, panting, struggling, chiding, laughing, her warm breath fanning each of their faces by turns, she strove to disengage herself, yet still remained in their triple embrace. Never was there a livelier picture of youthful rivalship, with bewitching beauty for the prize. Yet, by a strange deception, owing to the duskiness of the chamber, and the antique dresses which they still wore, the tall mirror is said to have

reflected the figures of the three old, gray, withered grandsires, ridiculously contending for the skinny ugliness of a shrivelled grandam.

42   But they were young: their burning passions proved them so. Inflamed to madness by the coquetry of the girl-widow, who neither granted nor quite withheld her favors, the three rivals began to interchange threatening glances. Still keeping hold of the fair prize, they grappled fiercely at one another's throats. As they struggled to and fro, the table was overturned, and the vase dashed into a thousand fragments. The precious Water of Youth flowed in a bright stream across the floor, moistening the wings of a butterfly, which, grown old in the decline of summer, had alighted there to die. The insect fluttered lightly through the chamber, and settled on the snowy head of Dr. Heidegger.

43   "Come, come, gentlemen! come, Madam Wycherly," exclaimed the doctor, "I really must protest against this riot."

44   They stood still and shivered; for it seemed as if gray Time were calling them back from their sunny youth, far down into the chill and darksome vale of years. They looked at old Dr. Heidegger, who sat in his carved arm-chair, holding the rose of half a century, which he had rescued from among the fragments of the shattered vase. At the motion of his hand, the four rioters resumed their seats; the more readily, because their violent exertions had wearied them, youthful though they were.

45   "My poor Sylvia's rose!" ejaculated Dr. Heidegger, holding it in the light of the sunset clouds; "it appears to be fading again."

46   And so it was. Even while the party were looking at it, the flower continued to shrivel up, till it became as dry and fragile as when the doctor had first thrown it into the vase. He shook off the few drops of moisture which clung to its petals.

47   "I love it as well thus as in its dewy freshness," observed he, pressing the withered rose to his withered lips. While he spoke, the butterfly fluttered down from the doctor's snowy head, and fell upon the floor.

48   His guests shivered again. A strange chillness, whether of the body or spirit they could not tell, was creeping gradually over them all. They gazed at one another, and fancied that each fleeting moment snatched away a charm, and left a deepening furrow where none had been before. Was it an illusion? Had the changes of a lifetime been crowded into so brief a space, and were they now four aged people, sitting with their old friend, Dr. Heidegger?

49   "Are we grown old again, so soon?" cried they, dolefully.

50   In truth they had. The Water of Youth possessed merely a virtue more transient than that of wine. The delirium which it created had effervesced away. Yes! they were old again. With a shuddering impulse,

that showed her a woman still, the widow clasped her skinny hands before her face, and wished that the coffin lid were over it, since it could be no longer beautiful.

51   "Yes, friends, ye are old again," said Dr. Heidegger, "and lo! the Water of Youth is all lavished on the ground. Well—I bemoan it not; for if the fountain gushed at my very doorstep, I would not stoop to bathe my lips in it—no, though its delirium were for years instead of moments. Such is the lesson ye have taught me!"

52   But the doctor's four friends had taught no such lesson to themselves. They resolved forthwith to make a pilgrimage to Florida, and quaff at morning, noon, and night, from the Fountain of Youth.

53   *Note:* In an English review, not long since, I have been accused of plagiarizing the idea of this story from a chapter in one of the novels of Alexandre Dumas. There has undoubtedly been a plagiarism on one side or the other; but as my story was written a good deal more than twenty years ago, and as the novel is of considerably more recent date, I take pleasure in thinking that M. Dumas has done me the honor to appropriate one of the fanciful conceptions of my earlier days. He is heartily welcome to it; nor is it the only instance, by many, in which the great French romancer has exercised the privilege of commanding genius by confiscating the intellectual property of less famous people to his own use and behoof.

September, 1860.

Dr. Heidegger's Experiment

JOURNAL

1. **MLA Works Cited**   *Using this model, record this story here.*

   Author's Last Name, First Name. "Title of the Story." <u>Title of the Book</u>. 3rd ed. Ed. First Name Last Name. City: Publisher, year. Pages of the story.

2. **Main Character(s)**   *Describe each main character, and explain why you think each is a main character.*

3. **Supporting Characters**   *Describe each supporting character, and explain why you think each is a supporting character.*

4. **Setting**   *Describe the setting(s) and any relevant prop(s).*

5. Sequence   *Outline the events of the story in order.*

6. Plot   *Tell the story in no more than three sentences.*

7. Conflicts   *Identify and explain all the conflicts involved here.*

8. Significant Quotations   *Explain the importance of each of these quotations. Record the page number in the parentheses.*

a. "But it was well known to a be a book of magic [. . .]" (   ).

b. " 'My dear old friends,' repeated Dr. Heidegger, 'may I reckon on your aid in performing an exceedingly curious experiment?' " (   ).

   c. "The crushed and dried petals stirred, and assumed a deepening tinge of
   crimson, as if the flower were reviving from a deathlike slumber [. . .]" (   ).

   d. "But they were young: their burning passions proved them so" (   ).

   e. "But the doctor's four friends had taught no such lesson to themselves" (   ).

9. **Literary Elements**   *Look at this chapter's title and explain why you think
   this story is placed in this chapter. Explain in which other chapter(s) you
   might place this story, as relevant to the literary element(s) of that chapter.*

10. **Foreshadowing, Irony, and/or Symbolism**   *Explain examples of foreshadowing,
   irony, and/or symbolism in this story.*

FOLLOW-UP QUESTIONS

10 SHORT QUESTIONS

*Select the **best** answer for each.*

____ 1. Dr. Heidegger is probably
   a. a doctor of philosophy.
   b. a doctor of medicine.
   c. a doctor of education.

____ 2. Mr. Medbourne was probably
   a. a serious businessman.
   b. an honest businessman.
   c. a dishonest businessman.

____ 3. Colonel Killigrew was probably
   a. a virtuous man.
   b. a minister.
   c. a lady's man.

____ 4. Mr. Gascoigne was probably
   a. an honest politician.
   b. a deceitful politician.
   c. a devoted public servant.

____ 5. Widow Wycherly was probably
   a. a virtuous young woman.
   b. a sincere and serious young woman.
   c. a flirtatious young woman.

____ 6. The mirror seems to
   a. be magical.
   b. reflect reality.
   c. be cracked and useless.

____ 7. The water seems to
   a. be magical.
   b. be infected.
   c. be of no use.

____ 8. The rose that is fifty-five years old is
   a. not kept in the book.
   b. not a reminder of Dr. Heidegger's fiancée.
   c. dried and then becomes fresh again.

____ 9. The four drink the water and
   a. become young again.
   b. become young forever.
   c. become wiser in their youth.

____ 10. The four do not
   a. behave like young fools.
   b. learn from their experiences.
   c. set off to find the Fountain of Youth.

5 SIGNIFICANT QUOTATIONS

Explain the importance of each of these quotations.

1. " 'My dear old friends,' said Dr. Heidegger, motioning them to be seated, 'I am desirous of your assistance in one of those little experiments with which I amuse myself here in my study.' "

2. "The greatest curiosity of the study remains to be mentioned; it was a ponderous folio volume [. . .]."

3. "He uncovered the vase, and threw the faded rose into the water which it contained."

4. "Inflamed to madness by the coquetry of the girl-widow, who neither granted nor quite withheld her favors, the three rivals began to interchange threatening glances."

5. "They resolved forthwith to make a pilgrimage to Florida, and quaff at morning, noon, and night, from the Fountain of Youth."

2 Comprehension Essay Questions

Use specific details and information from the story to answer these questions as completely as possible.

1. How does the title relate to the story? Explain the significance of the title using specific details and information from the story.

2. What are the characters' actions? Use specific details and information from the story to support your explanations.

Discussion Questions

Be prepared to discuss these questions in class.

1. Who is your favorite character? Why? Use specific details from the story to support your choice.

2. Who is your least favorite character? Why? Use specific details from the story to support your choice?

Writing

Use each of these ideas for writing an essay.

1. Dr. Heidegger takes his characters back to their youth. Describe an age or a moment to which you would like to return.

2. If you had the chance to go back and change something or sometime in your life, what would it be? Describe the situation and how you would change it.

Further Writing

1. Read Herman Melville's "The Bell-Tower" (page 398), and contrast, both as scientists and as men, Dr. Heidegger with Bannadonna.

2. Read Nathaniel Hawthorne's "Lady Eleanor's Mantle" (available in a library), and compare this story with Edgar Allan Poe's "The Masque of the Red Death" (page 382).

The Masque of the Red Death

Edgar Allan Poe

Pre-reading Vocabulary
Context

Use context clues to define these words before reading. Use a dictionary as needed.

1. The flu, with aches and fever and dizziness, can be a terrible *pestilence. Pestilence* means _____.

2. When the man rubbed against poison ivy, he got a *hideous* rash of white and red sores over his arms. *Hideous* means

   _____.

3. When the dam broke, the released water was so *profuse* that it flooded the valley below. *Profuse* means _____.

4. When the child dropped the candy in a glass of water, it turned into a *dissolution* of water and sugar. *Dissolution* means

   _____.

5. The store manager put a *ban* on large shopping bags in his store when he thought shoppers were using them to hide stolen goods. *Ban* means _____.

6. When the moth flew into the spider's web, it reached its *termination. Termination* means _____.

7. The king ruled over all his lands and *dominions* with kindness and patience. *Dominion* means _____.

8. If you take your vitamins and eat healthy foods, you will probably be quite *hale* and have few illnesses. *Hale* means

   _____.

9. The king gave the brave *knight* a large piece of land because he had protected the people in the village. *Knight* means

_____.

10. Restaurants usually have an *ingress* door to go into the kitchen and an *egress* door to get out of the kitchen. *Ingress* means

_____ and *egress* means _____.

11. The fans were in a *frenzy* when their favorite group sang their favorite song. *Frenzy* means _____.

12. Flora thought it was sheer *folly* to try to get money from the selfish landlord. *Folly* means _____.

13. Children dress up in different costumes to *masquerade* for Halloween. *Masquerade* means _____.

14. Isabel is usually calm and logical, but when she had a fever with the flu, she talked and acted in a *bizarre* way. *Bizarre* means

_____.

15. The presidential *chambers* are the rooms where the president and his family live in the White House. *Chamber* means

_____.

16. *Ebony* is a fine black wood that grows in Africa. *Ebony* means

_____.

17. The slow drip of the leaking faucet went on and on and on and became *monotonous*. *Monotonous* means _____.

18. The teacher expected the students to use their ears and to *hearken* to her directions. *Hearken* means _____.

19. Dressed in beautiful gowns and formal evening suits, the *waltzers* glided with the music around the ballroom floor. *Waltzer* means

_____.

20. Not knowing what day it was or where he was, Jan felt very confused and *disconcerted* with his surroundings. *Disconcerted* means

    _____.

21. Since all the little girls were giggling and having so much fun at the birthday party, it was hard to tell who was the *giddiest*. *Giddiest* means _____.

22. When the team made the winning touchdown, the crowd went wild, and the noise was *tumultuous*. *Tumultuous* means

    _____.

23. When Gabriella does her yoga exercises, she concentrates deeply in quiet *meditation*. *Meditation* means_____ .

24. All the guests had a wonderful time joining in the party's *revelry*. *Revelry* means _____.

25. Acting like a savage beast is considered *barbaric* behavior. *Barbaric* means _____.

26. The murderer ranted and raved, and his craziness made him seem quite *mad*. *Mad* means _____.

27. For his parents' fiftieth anniversary, Miguel hired a caterer, invited many guests, and planned a grand *fête*. *Fête* means

    _____.

28. The gigantic spider costume with its hairy arms and horrible jaws was *grotesque*. *Grotesque* means _____.

29. When Lusumba could not sleep, he tossed and turned and *writhed* in sleeplessness. *Writhe* means _____.

30. The teacher ordered a *cessation* of all talking, and the room became silent. *Cessation* means _____.

31. Dan dressed as a terrible devil for Halloween, and his *phantasm* scared everyone at the party. *Phantasm* means _____.

32. When Delia went on a diet, she became too thin, and her *gaunt* face looked like a skeleton. *Gaunt* means _____.

33. Dodee went to her closet and carefully chose her *habiliments* for her job interview. *Habiliment* means _____.

34. After their grandfather died, the grandchildren visited his *grave* and planted flowers by the headstone. *Grave* means

_____.

35. You could tell by Elyse's happy *visage* that she was delighted to win the award. *Visage* means _____.

36. After the old man died, his *corpse* was sent to the funeral home. *Corpse* means _____.

37. During a seizure, one may *convulse* with uncontrolled actions. *Convulse* means _____.

38. The dog went crazy when the *intruder* tried to break into our house. *Intruder* means _____.

39. The fans were in *awe* of the rock star who was standing in their presence. *Awe* means _____.

40. The man, intending to stab someone, drew a small *dagger* out of his pocket and was arrested. *Dagger* means _____.

Pre-reading Vocabulary
Structural Attack

Define these words by solving the parts. Use the Glossary or a dictionary as needed.

1. depopulated
2. castellated
3. precaution
4. irregularly
5. disregarded
6. *decora*
7. feverishly
8. whirlingly
9. stiffened
10. thoughtful
11. whisperingly
12. besprinkled
13. reddened
14. nameless
15. maddening
16. hurriedly
17. uninterruptedly
18. unutterable
19. untenanted
20. bedewed
21. illimitable

Pre-reading Questions

Try answering these questions as you read.

What is happening in the story?

Who is Prince Prospero?

What does Prince Prospero try to do?

Who is the figure?

The Masque of the Red Death

EDGAR ALLAN POE

Edgar Allan Poe was born in 1809 and orphaned at a young age. He was adopted by John Allan, a rather militaristic businessman from Richmond, Virginia. Adoption by a person of means was not uncommon and would have been fortunate for the young Poe, except that his free spirit and his father's precision clashed. John Allan provided Poe with study at the University of Virginia—but Poe withdrew, due to drinking problems—and then at West Point—but Poe was dismissed, due to a disciplinary problem. Poe later married his very young cousin, Virginia Clemm, but the probable nonconsummation of this marriage and the early death of young Virginia contributed to Poe's idealization of both real and imagined women. His life, in fact, was one of continual disappointments. After Virginia's death, Poe sank into intermittent depressions, suffered bouts of insanity, and experienced hallucinations. Writing for many others, he wanted to publish his own magazine, but this dissolved in financial failure. He eventually died in Baltimore in 1849.

However, it is from these very problems that Poe's genius soars. He envelops the reader with his perceived worlds of the sane and insane, the rational and macabre, with equal ease. Credited with developing the modern mystery form, Poe's every word and every action draw the reader in, mixing reality with irreality, sane with insane. His other works include "The Pit and the Pendulum" and "The Fall of the House of Usher."

The "Red Death" had long devastated the country. No pestilence had ever been so fatal, or so hideous. Blood was its Avatar and its seal—the redness and the horror of blood. There were sharp pains, and sudden dizziness, and then profuse bleeding at the pores, with dissolution. The scarlet stains upon the body and especially upon the face of the victim, were the pest ban which shut him out from the aid and from the sympathy of his fellow-men. And the whole seizure, progress, and termination of the disease, were the incidents of half an hour.

2   But the Prince Prospero was happy and dauntless and sagacious. When his dominions were half depopulated, he summoned to his presence a thousand hale and light-hearted friends from among the knights and dames of his court, and with these retired to the deep seclusion of one of his castellated abbeys. This was an extensive and magnificent structure, the creation of the prince's own eccentric yet august taste. A strong and lofty wall girdled it in. This wall had gates of iron. The courtiers, having entered, brought furnaces and massy hammers and welded the bolts. They resolved to leave means neither of ingress nor egress to the sudden impulses of despair or of frenzy from within. The abbey was amply provisioned. With such precautions the courtiers might bid defiance to contagion. The external world could take care of itself. In the meantime it was folly to grieve, or to think. The prince had provided all the appliances of pleasure. There were buffoons, there were improvisatori, there were ballet-dancers, there were musicians, there was Beauty, there was wine. All these and security were within. Without was the "Red Death."

3   It was toward the close of the fifth or sixth month of his seclusion, and while the pestilence raged most furiously abroad, that the Prince Prospero entertained his thousand friends at a masked ball of the most unusual magnificence.

4   It was a voluptuous scene, that masquerade. But first let me tell of the rooms in which it was held. There were seven—an imperial suite. In many palaces, however, such suites form a long and straight vista, while the folding doors slide back nearly to the walls on either hand, so that the view of the whole extent is scarcely impeded. Here the case was very different; as might have been expected from the duke's love of the *bizarre*. The apartments were so irregularly disposed that the vision embraced but little more than one at a time. There was a sharp turn at every twenty or thirty yards, and at each turn a novel effect. To the right and left, in the middle of each wall, a tall and narrow Gothic window looked out upon a closed corridor which pursued the windings of the suite. These windows were of stained glass whose color varied in accordance with the prevailing hue of the decorations of the chamber into which it opened. That at the eastern extremity was hung, for

example, in blue—and vividly blue were its windows. The second chamber was purple in its ornaments and tapestries, and here the panes were purple. The third was green throughout, and so were the casements. The fourth was furnished and lighted with orange—the fifth with white—the sixth with violet. The seventh apartment was closely shrouded in black velvet tapestries that hung all over the ceiling and down the walls, falling in heavy folds upon a carpet of the same material and hue. But in this chamber only, the color of the windows failed to correspond with the decorations. The panes here were scarlet—a deep blood color. Now in no one of the seven apartments was there any lamp or candelabrum, amid the profusion of golden ornaments that lay scattered to and fro or depended from the roof. There was no light of any kind emanating from lamp or candle within the suite of chambers. But in the corridors that followed the suite, there stood, opposite to each window, a heavy tripod, bearing a brazier of fire, that projected its rays through the tinted glass and so glaringly illumined the room. And thus were produced a multitude of gaudy and fantastic appearances. But in the western or black chamber the effect of the fire-light that streamed upon the dark hangings through the blood-tinted panes was ghastly in the extreme, and produced so wild a look upon the countenances of those who entered, that there were few of the company bold enough to set foot within its precincts at all.

5   It was in this apartment, also, that there stood against the western wall, a gigantic clock of ebony. Its pendulum swung to and fro with a dull, heavy, monotonous clang; and when the minute-hand made the circuit of the face, and the hour was to be stricken, there came from the brazen lungs of the clock a sound which was clear and loud and deep and exceedingly musical, but of so peculiar a note and emphasis that, at each lapse of an hour, the musicians of the orchestra were constrained to pause, momentarily, in their performance, to hearken to the sound; and thus the waltzers perforce ceased their evolutions; and there was a brief disconcert of the whole gay company; and, while the chimes of the clock yet rang, it was observed that the giddiest grew pale, and the more aged and sedate passed their hands over their brows as if in confused revery or meditation. But when the echoes had fully ceased, a light laughter at once pervaded the assembly; the musicians looked at each other and smiled as if at their own nervousness and folly, and made whispering vows, each to the other, that the next chiming of the clock should produce in them no similar emotion; and then, after the lapse of sixty minutes (which embrace three thousand and six hundred seconds of the Time that flies), there came yet another chiming of the clock, and then were the same disconcert and tremulousness and meditation as before.

6   But, in spite of these things, it was a gay and magnificent revel. The tastes of the duke were peculiar. He had a fine eye for colors and effects. He disregarded the *decora* of mere fashion. His plans were bold and fiery, and his conceptions glowed with barbaric lustre. There are some who would have thought him mad. His followers felt that he was not. It was necessary to hear and see and touch him to be *sure* that he was not.

7   He had directed, in great part, the movable embellishments of the seven chambers, upon occasion of this great *fête*; and it was his own guiding taste which had given character to the masqueraders. Be sure they were grotesque. There were much glare and glitter and piquancy and phantasm—much of what has been since seen in "Hernani." There were arabesque figures with unsuited limbs and appointments. There were delirious fancies such as the madman fashions. There were much of the beautiful, much of the wanton, much of the *bizarre*, something of the terrible, and not a little of that which might have excited disgust. To and fro in the seven chambers there stalked, in fact, a multitude of dreams. And these—the dreams—writhed in and about, taking hue from the rooms, and causing the wild music of the orchestra to seem as the echo of their steps. And, anon, there strikes the ebony clock which stands in the hall of the velvet. And then, for a moment, all is still, and all is silent save the voice of the clock. The dreams are stiff-frozen as they stand. But the echoes of the chime die away—they have endured but an instant—and a light, half-subdued laughter floats after them as they depart. And now again the music swells, and the dreams live, and writhe to and fro more merrily than ever, taking hue from the many-tinted windows through which stream the rays from the tripods. But to the chamber which lies most westwardly of the seven there are now none of the maskers who venture; for the night is waning away; and there flows a ruddier light through the blood-colored panes; and the blackness of the sable drapery appals; and to him whose foot falls upon the sable carpet, there comes from the near clock of ebony a muffled peal more solemnly emphatic than any which reaches *their* ears who indulge in the more remote gaieties of the other apartments.

8   But these other apartments were densely crowded, and in them beat feverishly the heart of life. And the revel went whirlingly on, until at length there commenced the sounding of midnight upon the clock. And then the music ceased, as I have told; and the evolutions of the waltzers were quieted, and there was an uneasy cessation of all things as before. But now there were twelve strokes to be sounded by the bell of the clock; and thus it happened, perhaps, that more of thought crept, with more of time, into the meditations of the thoughtful among those who revelled. And thus too, it happened, perhaps, that before the last

echoes of the last chime had utterly sunk into silence, there were many individuals in the crowd who had found leisure to become aware of the presence of a masked figure which had arrested the attention of no single individual before. And the rumor of this new presence having spread itself whisperingly around, there arose at length from the whole company a buzz, or murmur, expressive of disapprobation and surprise—then, finally, of terror, of horror, and of disgust.

9   In an assembly of phantasms such as I have painted, it may well be supposed that no ordinary appearance could have excited such sensation. In truth the masquerade license of the night was nearly unlimited; but the figure in question had out-Heroded Herod, and gone beyond the bounds of even the prince's indefinite decorum. There are chords in the hearts of the most reckless which cannot be touched without emotion. Even with the utterly lost, to whom life and death are equally jests, there are matters of which no jest can be made. The whole company, indeed, seemed now deeply to feel that in the costume and bearing of the stranger neither wit nor propriety existed. The figure was tall and gaunt, and shrouded from head to foot in the habiliments of the grave. The mask which concealed the visage was made so nearly to resemble the countenance of a stiffened corpse that the closest scrutiny must have had difficulty in detecting the cheat. And yet all this might have been endured, if not approved, by the mad revellers around. But the mummer had gone so far as to assume the type of the Red Death. His vesture was dabbled in *blood*—and his broad brow, with all the features of the face, was besprinkled with the scarlet horror.

10   When the eyes of Prince Prospero fell upon this spectral image (which, with a slow and solemn movement, as if more fully to sustain its *rôle*, stalked to and fro among the waltzers) he was seen to be convulsed, in the first moment with a strong shudder either of terror or distaste; but, in the next, his brow reddened with rage.

11   "Who dares"—he demanded hoarsely of the courtiers who stood near him—"who dares insult us with this blasphemous mockery? Seize him and unmask him—that we may know whom we have to hang, at sunrise, from the battlements!"

12   It was in the eastern or blue chamber in which stood the Prince Prospero as he uttered these words. They rang throughout the seven rooms loudly and clearly, for the prince was a bold and robust man, and the music had become hushed at the waving of his hand.

13   It was in the blue room where stood the prince, with a group of pale courtiers by his side. At first, as he spoke, there was a slight rushing movement of this group in the direction of the intruder, who, at the moment was also near at hand, and now, with deliberate and stately step, made closer approach to the speaker. But from a certain nameless

awe with which the mad assumptions of the mummer had inspired the whole party, there were found none who put forth hand to seize him; so that, unimpeded, he passed within a yard of the prince's person; and, while the vast assembly, as if with one impulse, shrank from the centres of the rooms to the walls, he made his way uninterruptedly, but with the same solemn and measured step which had distinguished him from the first, through the blue chamber to the purple—through the purple to the green—through the green to the orange—through this again to the white—and even thence to the violet, ere a decided movement had been made to arrest him. It was then, however, that the Prince Prospero, maddening with rage and the shame of his own momentary cowardice, rushed hurriedly through the six chambers, while none followed him on account of a deadly terror that had seized upon all. He bore aloft a drawn dagger, and had approached, in rapid impetuosity, to within three or four feet of the retreating figure, when the latter, having attained the extremity of the velvet apartment, turned suddenly and confronted his pursuer. There was a sharp cry— and the dagger dropped gleaming upon the sable carpet, upon which, instantly afterward, fell prostrate in death the Prince Prospero. Then, summoning the wild courage of despair, a throng of the revellers at once threw themselves into the black apartment, and, seizing the mummer, whose tall figure stood erect and motionless within the shadow of the ebony clock, gasped in unutterable horror at finding the grave cerements and corpse-like mask, which they handled with so violent a rudeness, untenanted by any tangible form.

14   And now was acknowledged the presence of the Red Death. He had come like a thief in the night. And one by one dropped the revellers in the blood-bedewed halls of their revel, and died each in the despairing posture of his fall. And the life of the ebony clock went out with that of the last of the gay. And the flames of the tripods expired. And Darkness and Decay and the Red Death held illimitable dominion over all.

The Masque of the Red Death

JOURNAL

1. **MLA Works Cited**   *Using this model, record this story here.*

   Author's Last Name, First Name. "Title of the Story." <u>Title of the Book</u>. 3rd ed. Ed. First Name Last Name. City: Publisher, year. Pages of the story.

2. **Main Character(s)**   *Describe each main character, and explain why you think each is a main character.*

3. **Supporting Characters**   *Describe each supporting character, and explain why you think each is a supporting character.*

4. **Setting**   *Describe the setting(s) and any relevant prop(s).*

5. Sequence   *Outline the events of the story in order.*

6. Plot   *Tell the story in no more than three sentences.*

7. Conflicts   *Identify and explain all the conflicts involved here.*

8. Significant Quotations   *Explain the importance of each of these quotations. Record the page number in the parentheses.*

a. "The 'Red Death' had long devastated the country" (   ).

b. "The prince had provided all the appliances of pleasure" (   ).

c. "It was a voluptuous scene, that masquerade" (   ).

   d. "And, anon, there strikes the ebony clock which stands in the hall of the velvet" (   ).

   e. "And now was acknowledged the presence of the Red Death" (   ).

9. **Literary Elements**   *Look at this chapter's title and explain why you think this story is placed in this chapter. Explain in which other chapter(s) you might place this story, as relevant to the literary element(s) of that chapter.*

10. **Foreshadowing, Irony, and/or Symbolism**   *Explain examples of foreshadowing, irony, and/or symbolism in this story.*

Follow-up Questions

10 Short Questions

*Select the **best** answer for each.*

_____ 1. As a victim of the Red Death bleeds, one
   a. has the help and support of friends.
   b. does not have the help and support of friends.
   c. gets better rapidly.

_____ 2. Prince Prospero
   a. cares about the general population.
   b. is kind to the general population.
   c. shows little concern for the general population.

_____ 3. Prince Prospero
   a. thinks he can escape the Red Death.
   b. thinks he cannot escape the Red Death.
   c. does not know about the Red Death.

_____ 4. He and his court
   a. think they will be infected with the disease.
   b. think they will not be infected with the disease.
   c. do not know about the disease.

_____ 5. The castle rooms are
   a. all the same.
   b. one big room.
   c. separated and different.

_____ 6. The black room's only other color is
   a. white.
   b. blue.
   c. blood red.

_____ 7. The clock has
   a. an unsettling chime.
   b. a pleasant chime.
   c. a sweet, musical chime.

_____ 8. The mummer enters
   a. an afternoon party.
   b. a formal ball.
   c. a masked ball.

_____ 9. The mummer
   a. is wearing a mask.
   b. is not wearing a mask.
   c. is wearing heavy makeup.

_____ 10. The prince and his guests
   a. escape the Red Death.
   b. never see the Red Death.
   c. die from the Red Death.

5 Significant Quotations

Explain the importance of each of these quotations.

1. "No pestilence had ever been so fatal, or so hideous."

2. "When his dominions were half depopulated, he summoned to his presence a thousand hale and light-hearted friends [. . .] and with these retired to the deep seclusion of one of his castellated abbeys."

3. "It was toward the close of [. . .] his seclusion, and while the pestilence raged most furiously abroad, that the Prince Prospero entertained his thousand friends at a masked ball of the most unusual magnificence."

4. "It was in this apartment, also, that there stood against the western wall, a gigantic clock of ebony."

5. "Then, summoning the wild courage of despair, a throng of revellers at once threw themselves into the black apartment, and, seizing the mummer [. . .] gasped in unutterable horror at finding the grave cerements and corpse-like mask [. . .] untenanted by any tangible form."

2 COMPREHENSION ESSAY QUESTIONS

Use specific details and information from the story to answer these questions as completely as possible.

1. How does the black chamber prepare you for the figure's appearance? Use specific details and information from the story to support your explanation.

2. What happens to Prince Prospero? Use specific details and information from the story to support your explanation.

DISCUSSION QUESTIONS

Be prepared to discuss these questions in class.

1. To what current concerns might you compare the masked character? Use specific details from the story to support your ideas.

2. How does the illustration demonstrate this story? Use specific details from the story to support your thinking.

WRITING

Use each of these ideas for writing an essay.

1. We have all been to strange places. Describe a place you have been to that seemed to reek of disease or evil.

2. We have all met scary or gloomy people. Describe your encounter with a scary person and how you handled the situation.

Further Writing

1. Read literary analyses of "The Masque of the Red Death" (available in a library). Then discuss whom or what beyond biological disease the figure of Red Death might represent in this story.

2. Research the AIDS/HIV virus, and use this story in your introduction to your research.

The Bell-Tower

HERMAN MELVILLE

PRE-READING VOCABULARY
CONTEXT

Use context clues to define these words before reading. Use a dictionary as needed. Read Chapters 4 and 5 of Judges in the Bible (available in Appendix A, pages 417–420) to help understand the biblical references in "The Bell-Tower."

1. When Raoul was in ancient Greece, he visited the leftover *ruins* of many ancient buildings. *Ruin* means _____.

2. When Dottie took the clapper out of the bell, the bell would no longer *chime*. *Chime* means _____.

3. Ironically, a *foundling* is a child without parents, while a *foundry* is a place where metals are produced. *Foundling* means _____, and *foundry* means _____.

4. In ancient times, the people of *Babel* tried to build a tower to reach heaven; but the tower was struck down, and the people then talked nonsense. *Babel* means _____.

5. Many campuses have a *bell-tower*, a tall building with a clock that rings out each hour. *Bell-tower* means _____.

6. The *architect* studied art, geology, and physics so that she could design large buildings. *Architect* means _____.

7. When Jorge wanted to build a brick wall, he called the *masons* to build it. *Mason* means _____.

8. The mountain climbers intended to reach the top and refused to stop until they reached the *summit*. *Summit* means

_____.

9. The wrestler *smote* the other wrestler with a folding chair;
   then he turned to *smite* another one. *Smote* and *smite* mean

   _____.

10. When Mom saw the ripped paper all over the floor, she knew the
    puppy was the guilty *culprit*. *Culprit* means _____.

11. The metalworker formed a mold for a vase so that he could pour
    metal into the mold and *cast* many vases. *Cast* means

    _____.

12. The cake that came out of the oven was perfect, except for a bubble
    blemish on the top. *Blemish* means _____.

13. *Homo-* means "man" and *-cide* means "to kill." *Homicide* means

    _____.

14. Arson, armed robbery, and murder are all considered to be *felonies*.
    Felony means _____.

15. Laura kept her valuable jewelry in *seclusion* in a safe hidden inside
    of a closet so that no one could find her jewelry. *Seclusion* means

    _____.

16. The opening at the top of a steeple or tower where a bell hangs
    so that it can ring and be heard is called a *belfry*. *Belfry* means

    _____.

17. The new gloves Ed bought were so soft and *pliant* that they felt like
    a second skin on his hands. *Pliant* means _____.

18. The mayor and the town council members are usually considered
    to be the *magistrates* of the town. *Magistrate* means

    _____.

19. Fatima decided to masquerade as a *domino*, wearing a mask and a long
    cloak; she scared one person after another in a *domino* effect. *Domino*
    means _____ and _____.

20. Marigoula was *apprehensive* about taking another algebra test because she had failed her first two tests. *Apprehensive* means

_____.

21. The lords and ladies, who were born very rich and who lived in large mansions, invited other *nobles* to their parties. *Noble* means _____.

22. *Vulcan*, the ugly Roman god of fire and metalworking, was married to the beautiful Venus. *Vulcan* means _____.

23. In the Bible, *Deborah* is able to see into the future and advises Barak to destroy the evil Sisera. *Deborah* means _____.

24. The man was buried in the churchyard after the *fatal* plane crash. *Fatal* means _____.

25. Although Teddy had been asleep, he awakened when his dog walked around upstairs, and he heard her every *footfall*. *Footfall* means _____.

26. Christians believe that after someone dies, her or his *soul* rises to heaven. *Soul* means _____.

27. In the biblical story of Deborah, *Jael* comes to the rescue and kills the evil Sisera. *Jael* means _____.

28. The criminals were *manacled* by restraining their hands behind their backs when they were arrested. *Manacled* means

_____.

29. Edmund kept the fifteenth-century *arquebuss* in his collection of rare guns. *Arquebuss* means _____.

30. The witnesses were sworn in to *aver* the facts of what they had seen. *Aver* means _____.

31. The drummers who play with the Beach Boys often created a very complex *percussion* beat. *Percussion* means _____.

32. When Francis had a paper to write, he read several books and then took time to *opine* and reflect upon his readings. *Opine* means

_____.

33. The *agent* represented several other people and did their paperwork for them. *Agent* means _____.

34. The car without wheels stood still and had no *locomotion* until Ellen added the wheels and moved it. *Locomotion* means

_____.

35. The giants among the ancient gods were called Titans, and their size was called *titanic*. *Titanic* means _____.

36. *Helots* and *serfs* served as slaves for wealthy nobles. *Helot* and *serf* mean _____.

37. The parents looked on their newborn baby as a gift from God and a *divine creation*. *Divine creation* means _____.

38. Henry Ford's *original* design, the Model A, was the first car built on an assembly line. *Original* means _____.

39. Although they felt they could not wait for the concert to begin, the fans *bided* their time by playing cards. *Bide* means

_____.

40. While her roommates waited to shower for work, Sue was *oblivious* to their needs and spent an hour in the shower. *Oblivious* means

_____.

PRE-READING VOCABULARY
STRUCTURAL ATTACK

Define these words by solving the parts. Use the Glossary or a dictionary as needed.

1. immeasurable	21. spring-like	41. unbeknown
2. lengthening	22. unease	42. becloaked
3. lessening	23. earthen	43. uplifted
4. falsity	24. artistic	44. uncertainty
5. metallic	25. unemployed	45. steely
6. mechanician	26. restlessness	46. sword-blade
7. snail-like	27. milder	47. upward
8. overtopped	28. innumerable	48. rehooded
9. self-esteem	29. footfall	49. unavoidably
10. climax-stone	30. fore-looking	50. unscientific
11. unrailed	31. unusual	51. indirectly
12. prosperously	32. encamp	52. comparatively
13. bell-tower	33. blindwork	53. elephantine
14. clock-tower	34. suspiciously	54. erroneous
15. state-bell	35. feverish	55. craziest
16. undeterred	36. foretell	56. irrationality
17. mythological	37. hair's breadth	57. vice-bench
18. sickly	38. scarcely	58. railway
19. assistance	39. blankly	59. clangorous
20. withdrew	40. unforeseen	60. superstructure

Try defining this word by using the other words in Melville's sentence.

"*Talus*, iron slave to Bannadonna, and through him, to man."

Talus means _____.

PRE-READING QUESTIONS

Try answering these questions as you read.

Who is Bannadonna?

What does Bannadonna propose to do?

Who is Haman?

What happens to Bannadonna?

The Bell-Tower

HERMAN MELVILLE

Herman Melville was born in New York City in 1819 to a prosperous family with roots in the American Revolution and the Boston Tea Party. Melville enjoyed his early schooling. However, failing family finances, the family's move to Albany, and his father's mental instability and early death left Melville in personal and career confusion. After working briefly as an accountant and then as a teacher, Melville took to the sea, sailing around the Pacific from 1841 to 1846. During this period, he gained his richest material. In 1847 he married Elizabeth Knopp Shaw, the daughter of a close family friend, and left the sea for a more sedate life that enabled him to write. Between 1846 and 1851 he produced his major novels, including Moby Dick. From 1850 to 1851 he lived close to and visited with Nathaniel Hawthorne, whom he highly respected; in fact, he dedicated Moby Dick to Hawthorne. He returned to New York City, living out his life as a customs inspector. Preceded by two of his sons, Melville died in 1891.

His complex works can be read as narratives and as **allegories**, or symbolic tales, that concern good and evil and often center on relationships with God and the devil. "The Bell-Tower" takes on the very taboo of creation and is filled with rich biblical references (see Judges 4 and 5 in Appendix A, pages 417–420) and references to the Renaissance and to ancient Greece.

I n the south of Europe, nigh a once frescoed capital, now with dank mould cankering its bloom, central in a plain, stands what, at distance, seems the black mossed stump of some immeasurable pine, fallen, in forgotten days, with Anak and the Titan.

2   As all along where the pine tree falls, its dissolution leaves a mossy mound—last-flung shadow of the perished trunk; never lengthening, never lessening; unsubject to the fleet falsities of the sun; shade immutable, and true gauge which cometh by prostration—so westward from what seems the stump, one steadfast spear of lichened ruin veins the plain.

3   From that tree-top, what birded chimes of silver throats had rung. A stone pine; a metallic aviary in its crown: the Bell-Tower, built by the great mechanician, the unblest foundling, Bannadonna.

4   Like Babel's, its base was laid in a high hour of renovated earth, following the second deluge, when the waters of the Dark Ages had dried up, and once more the green appeared. No wonder that, after so long and deep submersion, the jubilant expectation of the race should, as with Noah's sons, soar into Shinar aspiration.

5   In firm resolve, no man in Europe at that period went beyond Bannadonna. Enriched through commerce with the Levant, the state in which he lived voted to have the noblest Bell-Tower in Italy. His repute assigned him to be architect.

6   Stone by stone, month by month, the tower rose. Higher, higher; snail-like in pace, but torch or rocket in its pride.

7   After the masons would depart, the builder, standing alone upon its ever-ascending summit, at close of every day, saw that he overtopped still higher walls and trees. He would tarry till a late hour there, wrapped in schemes of other and still loftier piles. Those who of saints' days thronged the spot—hanging to the rude poles of scaffolding, like sailors on yards, or bees on boughs, unmindful of lime and dust, and falling chips of stone—their homage not the less inspirited him to self-esteem.

8   At length the holiday of the Tower came. To the sound of viols, the climax-stone slowly rose in air, and, amid the firing of ordnance, was laid by Bannadonna's hands upon the final course. Then mounting it, he stood erect, alone, with folded arms, gazing upon the white summits of blue inland Alps, and whiter crests of bluer Alps off-shore— sights invisible from the plain. Invisible, too, from thence was that eye he turned below, when, like the cannon booms, came up to him the people's combustions of applause.

9   That which stirred them so was, seeing with what serenity the builder stood three hundred feet in air, upon an unrailed perch. This none but he durst do. But his periodic standing upon the pile, in each stage of its growth—such discipline had its last result.

10   Little remained now but the bells. These, in all respects, must correspond with their receptacle.

11   The minor ones were prosperously cast. A highly enriched one followed, of a singular make, intended for suspension in a manner before
unknown. The purpose of this bell, its rotary motion, and connection
with the clock-work, also executed at the time, will, in the sequel,
receive mention.

12   In the one erection, bell-tower and clock-tower were united, though,
before that period, such structures had commonly been built distinct; as
the Campanile and Torre del 'Orologio of St. Mark to this day attest.

13   But it was upon the great state-bell that the founder lavished his
more daring skill. In vain did some of the less elated magistrates here
caution him; saying that though truly the tower was Titanic, yet limit
should be set to the dependent weight of its swaying masses. But unde-
terred, he prepared his mammoth mould, dented with mythological
devices; kindled his fires of balsamic firs; melted his tin and copper,
and, throwing in much plate, contributed by the public spirit of the
nobles, let loose the tide.

14   The unleashed metals bayed like hounds. The workmen shrunk.
Through their fright, fatal harm to the bell was dreaded. Fearless as
Shadrach, Bannadonna, rushing through the glow, smote the chief culprit with his ponderous ladle. From the smitten part, a splinter was
dashed into the seething mass, and at once was melted in.

15   Next day a portion of the work was heedfully uncovered. All
seemed right. Upon the third morning, with equal satisfaction, it was
bared still lower. At length, like some old Theban king, the whole
cooled casting was disinterred. All was fair except in one strange spot.
But as he suffered no one to attend him in these inspections, he concealed the blemish by some preparation which none knew better to
devise.

16   The casting of such a mass was deemed no small triumph for the
caster; one, too, in which the state might not scorn to share. The homicide was overlooked. By the charitable that deed was but imputed to
sudden transports of esthetic passion, not to any flagitious quality. A
kick from an Arabian charger; not sign of vice, but blood.

17   His felony remitted by the judge, absolution given him by the
priest, what more could even a sickly conscience have desired.

18   Honoring the tower and its builder with another holiday, the
republic witnessed the hoisting of the bells and clock-work amid
shows and pomps superior to the former.

19   Some months of more than usual solitude on Bannadonna's part
ensued. It was not unknown that he was engaged upon something for
the belfry, intended to complete it, and surpass all that had gone before.

Most people imagined that the design would involve a casting like the bells. But those who thought they had some further insight, would shake their heads, with hints, that not for nothing did the mechanician keep so secret. Meantime, his seclusion failed not to invest his work with more or less of that sort of mystery pertaining to the forbidden.

20   Ere long he had a heavy object hoisted to the belfry, wrapped in a dark sack or cloak—a procedure sometimes had in the case of an elaborate piece of sculpture, or statue, which, being intended to grace the front of a new edifice, the architect does not desire exposed to critical eyes, till set up, finished, in its appointed place. Such was the impression now. But, as the object rose, a statuary present observed, or thought he did, that it was not entirely rigid, but was, in a manner, pliant. At last, when the hidden thing had attained its final height, and, obscurely seen from below, seemed almost of itself to step into the belfry, as if with little assistance from the crane, a shrewd old blacksmith present ventured the suspicion that it was but a living man. This surmise was thought a foolish one, while the general interest failed not to augment.

21   Not without demur from Bannadonna, the chief-magistrate of the town, with an associate—both elderly men—followed what seemed the image up the tower. But, arrived at the belfry, they had little recompense. Plausibly entrenching himself behind the conceded mysteries of his art, the mechanician withheld present explanation. The magistrates glanced toward the cloaked object, which, to their surprise, seemed now to have changed its attitude, or else had before been more perplexingly concealed by the violent muffling action of the wind without. It seemed now seated upon some sort of frame, or chair, contained within the domino. They observed that nigh the top, in a sort of square, the web of the cloth, either from accident or design, had its warp partly withdrawn, and the cross threads plucked out here and there, so as to form a sort of woven grating. Whether it were the low wind or no, stealing through the stone lattice-work, or only their own perturbed imaginations, is uncertain, but they thought they discerned a slight sort of fitful, spring-like motion, in the domino. Nothing, however incidental or insignificant, escaped their uneasy eyes. Among other things, they pried out, in a corner, an earthen cup, partly corroded and partly encrusted, and one whispered to the other, that this cup was just such a one as might, in mockery, be offered to the lips of some brazen statue, or, perhaps, still worse.

22   But, being questioned, the mechanician said, that the cup was simply used in his founder's business, and described the purpose; in short, a cup to test the condition of metals in fusion. He added, that it had got into the belfry by the merest chance.

23   Again, and again, they gazed at the domino, as at some suspicious incognito at a Venetian mask. All sorts of vague apprehensions stirred them. They even dreaded lest, when they should descend, the mechanician, though without a flesh and blood companion, for all that, would not be left alone.

24   Affecting some merriment at their disquietude, he begged to relieve them, by extending a coarse sheet of workman's canvas between them and the object.

25   Meantime he sought to interest them in his other work; nor, now that the domino was out of sight, did they long remain insensible to the artistic wonders lying round them; wonders hitherto beheld but in their unfinished state; because, since hoisting the bells, none but the caster had entered within the belfry. It was one trait of his, that, even in details, he would not let another do what he could, without too great loss of time, accomplish for himself. So, for several preceding weeks, whatever hours were unemployed in his secret design, had been devoted to elaborating the figures on the bells.

26   The clock-bell, in particular, now drew attention. Under a patient chisel, the latent beauty of its enrichments, before obscured by the cloudings incident to casting, that beauty in its shyest grace, was now revealed. Round and round the bell, twelve figures of gay girls, garlanded, hand-in-hand, danced in a choral ring—the embodied hours.

27   "Bannadonna," said the chief, "this bell excels all else. No added touch could here improve. Hark!" hearing a sound, "was that the wind?"

28   "The wind, Excellenza," was the light response. "But the figures, they are not yet without their faults. They need some touches yet. When those are given, and the —— block yonder," pointing towards the canvas screen, "when Haman there, as I merrily call him,—him? *it*, I mean —— when Haman is fixed on this, his lofty tree, then, gentlemen, will I be most happy to receive you here again."

29   The equivocal reference to the object caused some return of restlessness. However, on their part, the visitors forbore further allusion to it, unwilling, perhaps, to let the foundling see how easily it lay within his plebeian art to stir the placid dignity of nobles.

30   "Well, Bannadonna," said the chief, "how long ere you are ready to set the clock going, so that the hour shall be sounded? Our interest in you, not less than in the work itself, makes us anxious to be assured of your success. The people, too,—why, they are shouting now. Say the exact hour when you will be ready."

31   "To-morrow, Excellenza, if you listen for it,—or should you not, all the same—strange music will be heard. The stroke of one shall be the first from yonder bell," pointing to the bell adorned with girls and garlands, "that stroke shall fall there, where the hand of Una clasps Dua's.

The stroke of one shall sever that loved clasp. To-morrow, then, at one o'clock, as struck here, precisely here," advancing and placing his finger upon the clasp, "the poor mechanic will be most happy once more to give you liege audience, in this his littered shop. Farewell till then, illustrious magnificoes, and hark ye for your vassal's stroke."

32   His still, Vulcanic face hiding its burning brightness like a forge, he moved with ostentatious deference towards the scuttle, as if so far to escort their exit. But the junior magistrate, a kind-hearted man, troubled at what seemed to him a certain sardonical disdain, lurking beneath the foundling's humble mien, and in Christian sympathy more distressed at it on his account than on his own, dimly surmising what might be the final fate of such a cynic solitaire, not perhaps uninfluenced by the general strangeness of surrounding things, this good magistrate had glanced sadly, sideways from the speaker, and thereupon his foreboding eye had started at the expression of the unchanging face of the Hour Una.

33   "How is this, Bannadonna?" he lowly asked, "Una looks unlike her sisters."

34   "In Christ's name, Bannadonna," impulsively broke in the chief, his attention, for the first attracted to the figure, by his associate's remark, "Una's face looks just like that of Deborah, the prophetess, as painted by the Florentine, Del Fonca."

35   "Surely, Bannadonna," lowly resumed the milder magistrate, "you meant the twelve should wear the same jocundly abandoned air. But see, the smile of Una seems but a fatal one. 'Tis different."

36   While his mild associate was speaking, the chief glanced, inquiringly, from him to the caster, as if anxious to mark how the discrepancy would be accounted for. As the chief stood, his advanced foot was on the scuttle's curb.

37   Bannadonna spoke:

38   "Excellenza, now that, following your keener eye, I glance upon the face of Una, I do, indeed perceive some little variance. But look all round the bell, and you will find no two faces entirely correspond. Because there is a law in art—but the cold wind is rising more; these lattices are but a poor defense. Suffer me, magnificoes, to conduct you, at least, partly on your way. Those in whose well-being there is a public stake, should be heedfully attended."

39   "Touching the look of Una, you were saying, Bannadonna, that there was a certain law in art," observed the chief, as the three now descended the stone shaft, "pray, tell me then—."

40   "Pardon; another time, Excellenza;—the tower is damp."

41   "Nay, I must rest, and hear it now. Here,—here is a wide landing, and through this leeward slit, no wind, but ample light. Tell us of your law; and at large."

42   "Since, Excellenza, you insist, know that there is a law in art, which bars the possibility of duplicates. Some years ago, you may remember, I graved a small seal for your republic, bearing, for its chief device, the head of your own ancestor, its illustrious founder. It becoming necessary, for the customs' use, to have innumerable impressions for bales and boxes, I graved an entire plate, containing one hundred of the seals. Now, though, indeed, my object was to have those hundred heads identical, and though, I dare say, people think them so, yet, upon closely scanning an uncut impression from the plate, no two of those five-score faces, side by side, will be found alike. Gravity is the air of all; but, diversified in all. In some, benevolent; in some, ambiguous; in two or three, to a close scrutiny, all but incipiently malign, the variation of less than a hair's breadth in the linear shadings round the mouth sufficing to all this. Now, Excellenza, transmute that general gravity into joyousness, and subject it to twelve of those variations I have described, and tell me, will you not have my hours here, and Una one of them? But I like—."

43   "Hark! is that—a footfall above?"

44   "Mortar, Excellenza; sometimes it drops to the belfry-floor from the arch where the stone-work was left undressed. I must have it seen to. As I was about to say: for one, I like this law forbidding duplicates. It evokes fine personalities. Yes, Excellenza, that strange, and—to you—uncertain smile, and those fore-looking eyes of Una, suit Bannadonna very well."

45   "Hark!—sure we left no soul above?"

46   "No soul, Excellenza; rest assured, no *soul*.—Again the mortar."

47   "It fell not while we were there."

48   "Ah, in your presence, it better knew its place, Excellenza," blandly bowed Bannadonna.

49   "But, Una," said the milder magistrate, "she seemed intently gazing on you; one would have almost sworn that she picked you out from among us three."

50   "If she did, possibly, it might have been her finer apprehension, Excellenza."

51   "How, Bannadonna? I do not understand you."

52   "No consequence, no consequence, Excellenza—but the shifted wind is blowing through the slit. Suffer me to escort you on; and then, pardon, but the toiler must to his tools."

53   "It may be foolish, Signor," said the milder magistrate, as, from the third landing, the two now went down unescorted, "but, somehow, our great mechanician moves me strangely. Why, just now, when he so superciliously replied, his walk seemed Sisera's, God's vain foe, in Del Fonca's painting. And that young, sculptured Deborah, too. Ay, and that—."

54   "Tush, tush, Signor!" returned the chief. "A passing whim. Deborah?—Where's Jael, pray?"

55   "Ah," said the other, as they now stepped upon the sod, "Ah, Signor, I see you leave your fears behind you with the chill and gloom; but mine, even in this sunny air, remain. Hark!"

56   It was a sound from just within the tower door, whence they had emerged. Turning, they saw it closed.

57   "He has slipped down and barred us out," smiled the chief; "but it is his custom."

58   Proclamation was now made, that the next day, at one hour after meridian, the clock would strike, and—thanks to the mechanician's powerful art—with unusual accompaniments. But what those should be, none as yet could say. The announcement was received with cheers.

59   By the looser sort, who encamped about the tower all night, lights were seen gleaming through the topmost blind-work, only disappearing with the morning sun. Strange sounds, too, were heard, or were thought to be, by those whom anxious watching might not have left mentally undisturbed—sounds, not only of some ringing implement, but also—so they said—half-suppressed screams and plainings, such as might have issued from some ghostly engine, overplied.

60   Slowly the day drew on; part of the concourse chasing the weary time with songs and games, till, at last, the great blurred sun rolled, like a football, against the plain.

61   At noon, the nobility and principal citizens came from the town in cavalcade, a guard of soldiers, also, with music, the more to honor the occasion.

62   Only one hour more. Impatience grew. Watches were held in hands of feverish men, who stood, now scrutinizing their small dial-plates, and then, with neck thrown back, gazing toward the belfry, as if the eye might foretell that which could only be made sensible to the ear; for, as yet, there was no dial to the tower-clock.

63   The hour hands of a thousand watches now verged within a hair's breadth of the figure 1. A silence, as of the expectation of some Shiloh, pervaded the swarming plain. Suddenly a dull, mangled sound—naught ringing in it; scarcely audible, indeed, to the outer circles of the people—that dull sound dropped heavily from the belfry. At the same moment, each man stared at his neighbor blankly. All watches were upheld. All hour-hands were at—had passed—the figure 1. No bell-stroke from the tower. The multitude became tumultuous.

64   Waiting a few moments, the chief magistrate, commanding silence, hailed the belfry, to know what thing unforeseen had happened there.

65   No response.

66   He hailed again and yet again.

67   All continued hushed.

68   By his order, the soldiers burst in the tower-door; when, stationing guards to defend it from the now surging mob, the chief, accompanied by his former associate, climbed the winding stairs. Half-way up, they stopped to listen. No sound. Mounting faster, they reached the belfry; but, at the threshold, started at the spectacle disclosed. A spaniel, which, unbeknown to them, had followed them thus far, stood shivering as before some unknown monster in a brake: or, rather, as if it snuffed footsteps leading to some other world. Bannadonna lay, prostrate and bleeding, at the base of the bell which was adorned with girls and garlands. He lay at the feet of the hour Una; his head coinciding, in a vertical line, with her left hand, clasped by the hour Dua. With downcast face impending over him, like Jael over nailed Sisera in the tent, was the domino; now no more becloaked.

69   It had limbs, and seemed clad in a scaly mail, lustrous as a dragon-beetle's. It was manacled, and its clubbed arms were uplifted, as if, with its manacles, once more to smite its already smitten victim. One advanced foot of it was inserted beneath the dead body, as if in the act of spurning it.

70   Uncertainty falls on what now followed.

71   It were but natural to suppose that the magistrates would, at first, shrink from immediate personal contact with what they saw. At the least, for a time, they would stand in involuntary doubt; it may be, in more or less of horrified alarm. Certain it is, that an arquebuss was called for from below. And some add, that its report, followed by a fierce whiz, as of the sudden snapping of a main-spring, with a steely din, as if a stack of sword-blades should be dashed upon a pavement, these blended sounds came ringing to the plain, attracting every eye far upward to the belfry, whence, through the lattice-work, thin wreaths of smoke were curling.

72   Some averred that it was the spaniel, gone mad by fear, which was shot. This, others denied. True it was, the spaniel never more was seen; and, probably, for some unknown reason, it shared the burial now to be related of the domino. For, whatever the preceding circumstances may have been, the first instinctive panic over, or else all ground of reasonable fear removed, the two magistrates, by themselves, quickly rehooded the figure in the dropped cloak wherein it had been hoisted. The same night, it was secretly lowered to the ground, smuggled to the beach, pulled far out to sea, and sunk. Nor to any after urgency, even in free convivial hours, would the twain ever disclose the full secrets of the belfry.

73   From the mystery unavoidably investing it, the popular solution of the foundling's fate involved more or less of supernatural agency. But some few less unscientific minds pretended to find little difficulty in otherwise accounting for it. In the chain of circumstantial inferences drawn, there may, or may not, have been some absent or defective links. But, as the explanation in question is the only one which tradition has explicitly preserved, in dearth of better, it will here be given. But, in the first place, it is requisite to present the supposition entertained as to the entire motive and mode, with their origin, of the secret design of Bannadonna; the minds above-mentioned assuming to penetrate as well into his soul as into the event. The disclosure will indirectly involve reference to peculiar matters, none of the clearest, beyond the immediate subject.

74   At that period, no large bell was made to sound otherwise than as at present, by agitation of a tongue within, by means of ropes, or percussion from without, either from cumbrous machinery, or stalwart watchmen, armed with heavy hammers, stationed in the belfry, or in sentry-boxes on the open roof, according as the bell was sheltered or exposed.

75   It was from observing these exposed bells, with their watchmen, that the foundling, as was opined, derived the first suggestion of his scheme. Perched on a great mast or spire, the human figure, viewed from below, undergoes such a reduction in its apparent size, as to obliterate its intelligent features. It evinces no personality. Instead of bespeaking volition, its gestures rather resemble the automatic ones of the arms of a telegraph.

76   Musing, therefore, upon the purely Punchinello aspect of the human figure thus beheld, it had indirectly occurred to Bannadonna to devise some metallic agent, which should strike the hour with its mechanic hand, with even greater precision than the vital one. And, moreover, as the vital watchman on the roof, sallying from his retreat at the given periods, walked to the bell with uplifted mace, to smite it, Bannadonna had resolved that his invention should likewise possess the power of locomotion, and, along with that, the appearance, at least, of intelligence and will.

77   If the conjectures of those who claimed acquaintance with the intent of Bannadonna be thus far correct, no unenterprising spirit could have been his. But they stopped not here; intimating that though, indeed, his design had, in the first place, been prompted by the sight of the watchman, and confined to the devising of a subtle substitute for him: yet, as is not seldom the case with projectors, by insensible gradations, proceeding from comparatively pigmy aims to Titanic ones, the original scheme had, in its anticipated eventualities, at last, attained to

an unheard of degree of daring. He still bent his efforts upon the loco-motive figure for the belfry, but only as a partial type of an ulterior creature, a sort of elephantine Helot, adapted to further, in a degree scarcely to be imagined, the universal conveniences and glories of humanity; supplying nothing less than a supplement to the Six Days' Work; stocking the earth with a new serf, more useful than the ox, swifter than the dolphin, stronger than the lion, more cunning than the ape, for industry an ant, more fiery than serpents, and yet, in patience, another ass. All excellences of all God-made creatures, which served man, were here to receive advancement, and then to be combined in one. Talus was to have been the all-accomplished Helot's name. Talus, iron slave to Bannadonna, and, through him, to man.

78   Here, it might well be thought that, were these last conjectures as to the foundling's secrets not erroneous, then must he have been hope-lessly infected with the craziest chimeras of his age; far outgoing Albert Magus and Cornelius Agrippa. But the contrary was averred. However marvelous his design, however apparently transcending not alone the bounds of human invention, but those of divine creation, yet the proposed means to be employed were alleged to have been confined within the sober forms of sober reason. It was affirmed that, to a degree of more than skeptic scorn, Bannadonna had been without sympathy for any of the vain-glorious irrationalities of his time. For example, he had not concluded, with the visionaries among the metaphysicians, that between the finer mechanic forces and the ruder animal vitality some germ of correspondence might prove discoverable. As little did his scheme partake of the enthusiasm of some natural philosophers, who hoped, by physiological and chemical inductions, to arrive at a knowledge of the source of life, and so qualify themselves to manufac-ture and improve upon it. Much less had he aught in common with the tribe of alchemists, who sought, by a species of incantations, to evoke some surprising vitality from the laboratory. Neither had he imagined, with certain sanguine theosophists, that, by faithful adoration of the Highest, unheard-of powers would be vouchsafed to man. A practical materialist, what Bannadonna had aimed at was to have been reached, not by logic, not by crucible, not by conjuration, not by altars; but by plain vice-bench and hammer. In short, to solve nature, to steal into her, to intrigue beyond her, to procure someone else to bind her to his hand;—these, one and all, had not been his objects; but, asking no favors from any element or any being, of himself, to rival her, outstrip her, and rule her. He stooped to conquer. With him, common sense was theurgy; machinery, miracle; Prometheus, the heroic name for machinist; man, the true God.

79   Nevertheless, in his initial step, so far as the experimental automaton for the belfry was concerned, he allowed fancy some little play; or, perhaps, what seemed his fancifulness was but his utilitarian ambition collaterally extended. In figure, the creature for the belfry should not be likened after the human pattern, nor any animal one, nor after the ideals, however wild, of ancient fable, but equally in aspect as in organism be an original production; the more terrible to behold, the better.

80   Such, then, were the suppositions as to the present scheme, and the reserved intent. How, at the very threshold, so unlooked for a catastrophe overturned all, or rather, what was the conjecture here, is now to be set forth.

81   It was thought that on the day preceding the fatality, his visitors having left him, Bannadonna had unpacked the belfry image, adjusted it, and placed it in the retreat provided—a sort of sentry-box in one corner of the belfry; in short, throughout the night, and for some part of the ensuing morning, he had been engaged in arranging everything connected with the domino; the issuing from the sentry-box each sixty minutes; sliding along a grooved way, like a railway; advancing to the clock-bell, with uplifted manacles; striking it at one of the twelve junctions of the four-and-twenty hands; then wheeling, circling the bell, and retiring to its post, there to bide for another sixty minutes, when the same process was to be repeated; the bell, by a cunning mechanism, meantime turning on its vertical axis, so as to present, to the descending mace, the clasped hands of the next two figures, when it would strike two, three, and so on, to the end. The musical metal in this time-bell being so managed in the fusion, by some art, perishing with its originator, that each of the clasps of the four-and-twenty hands should give forth its own peculiar resonance when parted.

82   But on the magic metal, the magic and metallic stranger never struck but that one stroke, drove but that one nail, severed but that one clasp, by which Bannadonna clung to his ambitious life. For, after winding up the creature in the sentry-box, so that, for the present, skipping the intervening hours, it should not emerge till the hour of one, but should then infallibly emerge, and, after deftly oiling the grooves whereon it was to slide, it was surmised that the mechanician must then have hurried to the bell, to give his final touches to its sculpture. True artist, he here became absorbed; and absorption still further intensified, it may be, by his striving to abate that strange look of Una; which, though, before others, he had treated with such unconcern, might not, in secret, have been without its thorn.

83   And so, for the interval, he was oblivious of his creature; which, not oblivious of him, and true to its creation, and true to its heedful

winding up, left its post precisely at the given moment; along its well-oiled route, slid noiselessly towards its mark; and, aiming at the hand of Una, to ring one clangorous note, dully smote the intervening brain of Bannadonna, turned backwards to it; the manacled arms then instantly up-springing to their hovering poise. The falling body clogged the thing's return; so there it stood, still impending over Bannadonna, as if whispering some post-mortem terror. The chisel lay dropped from the hand, but beside the hand; the oil-flask spilled across the iron track.

84   In his unhappy end, not unmindful of the rare genius of the mechanician, the republic decreed him a stately funeral. It was resolved that the great bell—the one whose casting had been jeopardized through the timidity of the ill-starred workman—should be rung upon the entrance of the bier into the cathedral. The most robust man of the country round was assigned the office of bell-ringer.

85   But as the pall-bearers entered the cathedral porch, naught but a broken and disastrous sound, like that of some lone Alpine land-slide, fell from the tower upon their ears. And then, all was hushed.

86   Glancing backwards, they saw the groined belfry crashed sideways in. It afterwards appeared that the powerful peasant, who had the bell-rope in charge, wishing to test at once the full glory of the bell, had swayed down upon the rope with one concentrate jerk. The mass of quaking metal, too ponderous for its frame, and strangely feeble somewhere at its top, loosed from its fastening, tore sideways down, and tumbling in one sheer fall, three hundred feet to the soft sward below, buried itself inverted and half out of sight.

87   Upon its disinterment, the main fracture was found to have started from a small spot in the ear; which, being scraped, revealed a defect, deceptively minute, in the casting; which defect must subsequently have been pasted over with some unknown compound.

88   The remolten metal soon reassumed its place in the tower's repaired superstructure. For one year the metallic choir of birds sang musically in its belfry-bough-work of sculptured blinds and traceries. But on the first anniversary of the tower's completion—at early dawn, before the concourse had surrounded it—an earthquake came; one loud crash was heard. The stone-pine, with all its bower of songsters, lay overthrown upon the plain.

89   So the blind slave obeyed its blinder lord; but, in obedience, slew him. So the creator was killed by the creature. So the bell was too heavy for the tower. So the bell's main weakness was where man's blood had flawed it. And so pride went before the fall.

The Bell-Tower

JOURNAL

1. **MLA Works Cited**   *Using this model, record this story here.*

   *Author's Last Name, First Name. "Title of the Story." <u>Title of the Book</u>.
   3rd ed. Ed. First Name Last Name. City: Publisher, year. Pages of
   the story.*

2. **Main Character(s)**   *Describe each main character, and explain why you
   think each is a main character.*

3. **Supporting Characters**   *Describe each supporting character, and explain why
   you think each is a supporting character.*

4. **Setting**   *Describe the setting(s) and any relevant prop(s).*

5. **Sequence**   *Outline the events of the story in order.*

6. **Plot**   *Tell the story in no more than three sentences.*

7. **Conflicts**   *Identify and explain all the conflicts involved here.*

8. **Significant Quotations**   *Explain the importance of each of these quotations. Record the page number in the parentheses.*

   a. "In firm resolve, no man in Europe at that period went beyond Bannadonna" (   ).

   b. "In the one erection, bell-tower and clock-tower were united, though, before that period, such structures had commonly been built distinct [. . .]" (   ).

c. "Fearless as Shadrach, Bannadonna, rushing through the glow, smote the chief culprit with his ponderous ladle" (   ).

d. "At last, when the hidden thing had attained its final height, and, obscurely seen from below, seemed almost of itself to step into the belfry, as if with little assistance from the crane, a shrewd old blacksmith present ventured the suspicion that it was but a living man" (   ).

e. "He lay at the feet of the hour Una; his head coinciding, in a vertical line, with her left hand, clasped by the hour Dua. With downcast face impending over him, like Jael over nailed Sisera in the tent, was the domino [. . .]" (   ). [Note: You will find that reading Judges 4 and 5 (Appendix A, pages 417–420) may help you explain the importance of this quotation.]

9. **Literary Elements**   *Look at this chapter's title and explain why you think this story is placed in this chapter. Explain in which other chapter(s) you might place this story, as relevant to the literary element(s) of that chapter.*

10. **Foreshadowing, Irony, and/or Symbolism**   *Explain examples of foreshadowing, irony, and/or symbolism in this story.*

FOLLOW-UP QUESTIONS

10 SHORT QUESTIONS

Select the __best__ answer for each.

____ 1. Bannadonna is
   a. just starting his career.
   b. a recognized artisan.
   c. not a recognized artisan.

____ 2. Bannadonna
   a. is comfortable in his tower.
   b. is not comfortable in his tower.
   c. does not go up in his tower.

____ 3. The bell has a flaw because
   a. it is too large.
   b. it has different figures.
   c. a man has been killed and melted in the process.

____ 4. The figures are designed to unclasp hands so that
   a. each may stand alone.
   b. the bell will sound differently at each hour.
   c. they may move more easily.

____ 5. Haman seems
   a. to move alone.
   b. not to move alone.
   c. never to move at all.

____ 6. Una's face seems to
   a. look happy.
   b. look like her sisters.
   c. predict a fatal future.

____ 7. The younger magistrate
   a. has suspicions about what Bannadonna is doing.
   b. does not have suspicions about what Bannadonna is doing.
   c. gets killed.

____ 8. Haman relates to
   a. Jael.
   b. Bannadonna.
   c. Sisera.

____ 9. In mechanical terms, Bannadonna
   a. should have oiled Haman's path more.
   b. does not oil Haman's path enough.
   c. oils Haman's path too well.

____ 10. In mystical terms, the creation
   a. is ruled by the creator.
   b. slays the creator.
   c. is good to the people.

5 SIGNIFICANT QUOTATIONS

Explain the importance of each of these quotations.

1. "But it was upon the great state-bell that the founder lavished his more daring skill."

2. "The homicide was overlooked."

3. " 'When those are given, and the—block yonder,' pointing towards the canvas screen, 'when Haman there, as I merrily call him,—him? *it*, I mean—when Haman is fixed on this, his lofty tree, then, gentlemen, will I be most happy to receive you here again.' "

4. "He lay at the feet of the hour Una; his head coinciding, in a vertical line, with her left hand, clasped by the hour Dua. With downcast face impending over him, like Jael over nailed Sisera in the tent, was the domino; now no more becloaked."

5. "In short, to solve nature, to steal into her, to intrigue beyond her, to procure someone else to bind her to his hand;—these, one and all, had not been his objects; but, asking no favors from any element or any being, of himself, to rival her, outstrip her, and rule her."

2 COMPREHENSION ESSAY QUESTIONS

Use specific details and information from the story to answer these questions as completely as possible.

1. How does the title relate to the story? Explain the significance of the title using specific details and information from the story.

2. Hubris means self-pride wherein a person arrogantly thinks he or she is better than God. How does hubris relate to this story? Use specific details and information from the story.

DISCUSSION QUESTIONS

Be prepared to discuss these questions in class.

1. The ancients said that hubris, or wrongful pride, could destroy a person. How does this relate to this story?

2. In a Hegelian dialetic, a given (the thesis) produces that which will destroy it (the antithesis) and this results in a whole new construct (the synthesis). How does this story demonstrate this dialectic form?

WRITING

Use each of these ideas for writing an essay.

1. Think of one machine you depend on, and write an essay explaining both the good side and the bad side of your dependence.

2. Think of a machine that you wish you had or perhaps one you might invent. Describe the machine, and explain specifically how this machine would help you.

Further Writing

1. Research current genetic studies, and explain how new research relates to Bannadonna.

2. Read Judges 4 and 5 from the Bible (Appendix A, pages 417–420), and relate these chapters to Bannadonna.

3. Read Sophocles' <u>Oedipus Rex</u> (available in a library), and compare the consequences of the hubris of Oedipus and that of Bannadonna.

APPENDIX A

Judges

CHAPTER 4

¹Deborah and Barak deliver them from Jabin and Sisera. ¹⁸Jael killeth Sisera.

♦♦¹And the children of Israel again did evil in the sight of the LORD when Ehud was dead. ²And the LORD sold them into the hand of Jabin king of Canaan, who reigned in Hazor, the captain of whose host was Sisera, who dwelt in Harosheth of the Gentiles. ³And the children of Israel cried unto the LORD; for he had nine hundred chariots of iron, and twenty years he mightily oppressed the children of Israel.

⁴And Deborah, a prophetess, the wife of Lapidoth, judged Israel at that time. ⁵And she dwelt under the palm tree of Deborah between Ramah and Bethel in Mount Ephraim, and the children of Israel came up to her for judgment. ⁶And she sent and called Barak the son of Abinoam out of Kedesh-naphtali, and said unto him, "Hath not the LORD God of Israel commanded, saying, 'Go and draw near Mount Tabor, and take with thee ten thousand men of the children of Naphtali and of the children of Zebulun; ⁷and I will draw unto thee Sisera, the captain of Jabin's army, with his chariots and his multitude to the River Kishon;* and I will deliver him into thine hand'?"
♦ ⁸And, Barak said unto her, "If thou wilt go with me, then I will go; but if thou wilt not go with me, then I will not go." ⁹And she said, "I will surely go with thee. Notwithstanding, the journey that thou takest shall not be for thine honor, for the LORD shall sell Sisera into the hand of a woman." And Deborah arose, and went with Barak to Kedesh. ¹⁰And Barak called Zebulun and Naphtali to Kedesh, and he went up with, ten thousand men at his heels; and Deborah went up with him. ¹¹(Now Heber the Kenite, who was of the children of Hobab the father-in-law of Moses,* had severed himself from the Kenites and pitched his tent unto the plain of Zaanaim, which is by Kedesh.)

¹²And they showed Sisera that Barak the son of Abinoam had gone up to Mount Tabor. ¹³And Sisera gathered together all his chariots, even nine hundred chariots of iron, and all the people who were with him, from Harosheth of the Gentiles unto the river of Kishon. ¹⁴And Deborah said unto Barak, "Up! For this is the day, in which the LORD hath delivered Sisera into thine hand. Has not the LORD gone out before thee?" So Barak went down from Mount Tabor, and ten thousand men after him. ¹⁵And the LORD discomfited Sisera and all his chariots and all his host with the edge of the sword before Barak, so that Sisera alighted down off his chariot and fled away on his feet.* ¹⁶But Barak pursued after the chariots and after the host unto Harosheth of the Gentiles; and all the host of Sisera fell upon the edge of the sword, and there was not a man left.

*7 Ps 83:9–10. *11 Num 10:29. *15 Ps 83:10.

¹⁷However, Sisera fled away on his feet to the tent of Jael the wife of Heber the Kenite, for there was peace between Jabin the king of Hazor and the house of Heber the Kenite. ¹⁸And Jael went out to meet Sisera, and said unto him, "Turn in, my lord, turn in to me. Fear not." And when he had turned in unto her into the tent, she covered him with a mantle. ¹⁹And he said unto her, "Give me, I pray thee, a little water to drink; for I am thirsty." And she opened a bottle of milk, and gave him drink, and covered him.* ²⁰Again he said unto her, "Stand in the door of the tent, and it shall be, when any man doth come and inquire of thee and say, 'Is there any man here?' that tho, shalt say, 'No.'" ²¹Then Jael, Heber's wife, took a nail of the tent and took a hammer in her hand, and went softly unto him and smote the nail into his temples, and fastened it into the ground; for he was fast asleep and weary. So he died. ²²And behold, as Barak pursued Sisera, Jael came out to meet him and said unto him, "Come, and I will show thee the man whom thou seekest." And when he came into her tent, behold, Sisera lay dead, and the nail was in his temples.

²³So God subdued on that day Jabin the king of Canaan before the children of Israel. ²⁴And the hand of the children of Israel prospered, and prevailed against Jabin the king of Canaan, until they had destroyed Jabin king of Canaan.

CHAPTER 5

¹The song of Deborah and Barak.

¹Then sang Deborah and Barak, the son of Abinoam, on that day, saying:
² "Praise ye the LORD for the avenging of Israel,
    when the people willingly offered themselves.

³ Hear, O ye kings;
    give ear, O ye princes.
  I, even I, will sing unto the LORD;
    I will sing praise to the LORD God of Israel.

⁴ "LORD, when Thou wentest out of Seir,*
    when Thou marched out of the field of Edom,
  the earth trembled and the heavens dropped,
    the clouds also dropped water.
⁵ The mountains melted from before the LORD,*
    even that Sinai, from before the LORD God of Israel.*

⁶ "In the days of Shamgar the son of Anath,*
  in the days of Jael,*
    the highways were unoccupied,
    and the travelers walked through byways.
⁷ The inhabitants of the villages ceased,
  they ceased in Israel,
    until I, Deborah, arose,
    I arose a mother in Israel.
⁸ They chose new gods;
  then was war in the gates.
    Was there a shield or spear seen
    among forty thousand in Israel?

*19 Jdg 5:25. *4 Dt 4:11. *5a Ps 97:5. *5b Ex 19:18. *6a Jdg 3:31. *6b Jdg 4:18.

⁹My heart is toward the governors of Israel
that offered themselves willingly among the people.
    Bless ye the LORD.

¹⁰"Speak, ye that ride on white asses,
    ye that sit in judgment and walk by the way.
¹¹They that are delivered from the noise of archers
  in the places of drawing water,
        there shall they rehearse the righteous acts of the LORD,
    even the righteous acts toward the inhabitants
  of His villages in Israel.
        Then shall the people of the LORD go down to the gates.

¹²"Awake, awake, Deborah!
    Awake, awake, utter a song!
  Arise, Barak, and lead thy captivity captive,
    thou son of Abinoam.

¹³"Then He made him that remaineth have dominion
  over the nobles among the people;
        the LORD made me have dominion over the mighty.
¹⁴Out of Ephraim was there a root of them against Amalek;
    after thee, Benjamin, among thy people;
  out of Machir came down governors,
        and out of Zebulun they that handle the pen
    of the writer.
¹⁵And the princes of Issachar were with Deborah,
    even Issachar, and also Barak;
  he was sent on foot into the valley.
        In the divisions of Reuben there were great thoughts of
        heart.
¹⁶Why abodest thou among the sheepfolds,
  to hear the bleatings of the flocks?
        In the divisions of Reuben there were great
        searchings of heart.
¹⁷Gilead abode beyond the Jordan;
    and why did Dan remain in ships?
  Asher continued on the seashore
    and abode in his sheltered coves.
¹⁸Zebulun and Naphtali were a people
    that jeopardized their lives unto the death
    in the high places of the field.

¹⁹"The kings came and fought;
    then fought the kings of Canaan
    in Taanach by the waters of Megiddo;
    they took no gain of money.
²⁰They fought from heaven;
    the stars in their courses fought against Sisera.
²¹The river of Kishon swept them away,
  that ancient river, the river Kishon.
        O my soul, thou hast trodden down strength!

22 Then were the horsehoofs broken
   by the means of the prancings,
      the prancings of their mighty ones.
23 " 'Curse ye Meroz,' said the angel of the LORD;
      'curse ye bitterly the inhabitants thereof,
   because they came not to the help of the LORD,
      to the help of the LORD against the mighty.'

24 "Blessed above women
   shall Jael the wife of Heber the Kenite be;
      blessed shall she be above women in the tent.
25 He asked water, and she gave him milk;
      she brought forth butter in a lordly dish.
26 She put her hand to the nail,
      and her right hand to the workmen's hammer.
   And with the hammer she smote Sisera;
      she smote off his head, when she had pierced and
      stricken through his temples.
27 At her feet he bowed, he fell, he lay down;
   at her feet he bowed, he fell;
      where he bowed, there he fell down dead.

28 "The mother of Sisera looked out at a window,
   and cried through the lattice:
      'Why is his chariot so long in coming?
      Why tarry the wheels of his chariots?'
29 Her wise ladies answered her,
      yea, she returned answer to herself:
30 'Have they not sped?
      Have they not divided the prey:
   to every man a damsel or two,
      to Sisera a prey of divers colors,
      a prey of divers colors of needlework,
   of divers colors of needlework on both sides,
      meet for the necks of them that take the spoil?'

31 "So let all Thine enemies perish, O LORD!
      But let them that love Him be as the sun
      when he goeth forth in his might."

And the land had rest forty years.

APPENDIX B

How *I* Use This Book

This section is *not* intended to tell anyone how to use this book, but rather it is intended to offer insight into some of the many options and possibilities in this book. I am often asked to demonstrate the comprehensive pedagogical apparatus surrounding each story and, since I cannot come out and meet with all of you, this section is an attempt to present at least one instructor's—my!—approach to this book. I truly hope, hope, hope that you use this book as you see fit. The following are simply strategies I use and are offered in response to the many enthusiastic questions I receive.

As has been continually noted, I designed this book most carefully to maximize student learning and teacher efficiency simultaneously. Every entry, every exercise, every word has been most carefully weighed. Following this list, I will explain each entry. However, to streamline this whole section, here are my steps for each story, in a nutshell:

1. First, I do the Sample Lesson with the class, step-by-step, assigning the students to complete the incomplete exercises on their own. I then review, discuss, and/or have students tear out the completed exercises so that I can assess their first journey into this book.

2. Second, with students now ready to start the actual stories, I assign the chapter introduction and the first story in each chapter, then second, and so forth. I introduce any given story via the biographical blurb. Because the blurbs are purposefully written at a more sophisticated level to initiate students into collegiate reading, encourage students to look up words, and so forth, these blurbs are a good place to start discussion. I then assign all vocabulary exercises, pre-reading exercises, and journal exercises, either individually or in groups, depending on the story and the class. Students are to predefine, pre-think, read, and then reflect upon each story.

3. Third, after each story the students complete, I have students tear out selected pages (one page from vocabulary and one from the Journal selected at random, so that text is protected and students have to do all the work, because they never know what I will want them to pull out) and I collect the above exercises. By collecting these exercises, I gain insight into each student's progress and proficiency, I gain necessary and consistent diagnostic and assessment instruments, and I gain

students who are well prepared, because they know they will be responsible for their work.

4. Fourth, with exercises collected, I quiz and collect the 10 Short Questions. Although seemingly simplistic, these short questions offer a very efficient measure of each student's comprehension. With students' baseline exercises and comprehension testing collected, I then discuss the story and the correct and/or acceptable answers, as well as relevant test-taking strategies, with the students. These exercises are designed for efficient assessment, so I am then easily able to numerically grade and return all assignments by the next class.

5. Fifth, depending on the story and the class, I then assign the 5 Significant Quotations, the Comprehension Essay Questions, and/or the Discussion Questions to be completed individually, in groups, or through class-wide discussion. These are intended to be highly flexible and to be used at your discretion.

6. Sixth, for writing classes I then continue on to discuss and assign the relevant writing prompts (Writing is intended for developmental students, while Further Writing is intended for more advanced composition courses).

7. Seventh, as the semester progresses and some students truly start to excel, I follow the same procedures above but now may do so on an individualized basis, assigning the more demanding stories at the back of the book individually to the more capable students.

There it is briefly. By the time the students have completed each story, they have applied, hands-on, an entire complex of cognitive skills and I have multiple diagnostic and assessment tools. You, of course, should use this book any way you see fit and I hope the above list is merely a concise summary of how I use it. Should you care to read further, here are some more insights I most humbly offer.

In general, I believe that we often learn by doing and that many of our students are capable learners who simply have learned and/or adopted many counter-productive habits. Initiate and then reinforce productive habits by hands-on application and reapplication and students prosper. To this end, the apparatus surrounding each story is consistent. Students rather rapidly learn appropriate ways to approach stories and, because the apparatus is not only consistent but also most carefully designed to maximize learning, students are learning, prospering, and forming new and more productive habits that will improve all their reading skills and endeavors. Further, among the now several thousand students who have field-tested this book, using this book has dramatically increased performance for both reading and writing students.

Concerning **vocabulary** specifically, the very simple axiom applies that if one cannot understand the words, one cannot read. Reading is a split-second, reception-retrieval-synthesis process. Not knowing words interrupts and thereby breaks down the process. To demonstrate this, try reading this:

Guardare the chaînon with pithecanthropus, the discovery of zinjanthropus
semble démarquer a significato gradino in poursuite.

Now, we are all well-versed, well-read, and hopefully learned, yet unless
one is familiar with French, Italian, and some basic cultural anthropology
concepts, this is relatively unfathomable, albeit unreadable. Yet this is
exactly what collegiate reading material looks like to many of our entering
students—every few words have no meaning and the sum total becomes
unreadable.

For this reason, each story starts with words in **Context** that are not
necessarily the hardest words in the story, but rather that are the most necessary to understanding the story. Thus, in addition to applying context
solution skills, each context section also presents the students with the
words they will need to know to approach the story, and does so before the
students read. While I do not know if each student does the vocabulary
before or after each reading, I do know that those who do a poor job or who
do not do these exercises at all invariably have problems understanding the
given story. These exercises, therefore, simultaneously reinforce context
solving skills for each student while providing you with insight into each
student's proficiencies.

Similarly, the **Structural Attack** words apply attack skills for the students and also provide you with insight into each student's proficiencies.
These words are chosen because they best apply structural attack skills
but, unlike the words in context, these words are not necessarily essential
for understanding the story. These exercises also encourage students to use
the Glossary and/or a dictionary, therein applying referencing skills.

Concerning **Pre-reading Questions**, these questions are intended to be
simplistic and to set the students up for reading efficiently. After using this
consistent and tactile model, in time students learn to frame their own
pre-reading questions.

Concerning each **biographical blurb**, I often use the blurb to introduce
the story. As noted, each blurb is purposefully written at a sophisticated
level to link students to collegiate vocabulary and concepts. Because of
this, the blurbs often need explanation. Further, each blurb is intended to
provide the students with background before reading and referrals for
further readings.

Concerning the **Journal**, what can I say? This, to me, is the engine of
this book. Here students record, outline, summarize, reflect upon, make
sense out of, and even apply MLA documentation format to every story.
This is a strenuous and tactile cognitive workout for students as they apply
multiple skills, processes, and dynamics to complete it. I always collect the
Journal and it is very easy for me to note those students who are having
trouble; the Journal clearly demonstrates student acuity, effort, and insight.

Concerning the **Follow-up Exercises**, I quiz and collect the **10 Short
Questions** while I collect the vocabulary and journal exercises and before I
discuss the story. I give a few minutes in class for those who have already
done the questions at home to review their answers and for those who have

not done the questions to complete them. While we might assume that students would all do the work beforehand, I am regularly surprised not so much by those who do the questions ahead, as I am by those who do not. I collect this section before discussion for a very simple reason: diagnostically, I need to know what each student has gotten out of the story on her or his own and without my information and/or prompting. These seemingly simplistic questions often demonstrate real confusion and offer invaluable insight into increasing and/or static student proficiencies.

With Pre-reading and Journal exercises and 10 Short Questions collected (which are, again, designed most carefully to be efficient measurement tools and which I will, therefore, easily be able to return by the next class), I now thoroughly discuss the story—and relevant test-taking strategies—with students. I also now turn to the other sections. Depending on the story and/or the class, I may assign the **5 Significant Quotations** and/or the **Comprehension Essay Questions**, or I may use them for discussion. I may assign the **Discussion Questions**, or I may use them for discussion. As noted above, this is a totally fluid area that I designed for your individual discretion. I may choose to use these for discussion in a reading class, and I may choose to assign them for writing in a writing class, or vice versa. These are truly intended to offer you many options.

Finally, the **Writing** prompts speak for themselves. Many of you have commented on how much you like them and there are, again, many options here. I have been privileged to initiate and to chair our learning community program from its very inception. In this program, I teach the same students both reading and writing curricula, and the writing prompts are a natural extension of every story. As noted above, with the now several thousand students who have field-tested this book, we have seen dramatic improvements in both reading and writing students' performances. In fact, many writing instructors are now using this book as the base text in writing courses.

So there it is. This book is designed to meet many, many student needs and to offer a great variety of teaching options. I hope, no matter what ways you choose to use this book, that your students prosper and that you enjoy the book.

Yvonne Collioud Sisko
Old Bridge, New Jersey

Glossary of Prefixes and Suffixes

Some words in the **Pre-Reading Vocabulary—Structural Attack** are simple words that have been combined or have extra syllables, which make these words look strange or difficult. When you take these words apart, they are usually quite simple to define.

When two or more words are combined to form a new word, the new word is called a **compound word**. By combining the meaning of each of the words, you can define the new word. Look at the word *everyday*. Here, two simple words—*every* and *day*—combine to mean "all the time." Look at the word *worn-whiskered*. *Worn* means "tired" or "old," and *whiskered* implies "old man" or "mature man." Thus, *worn-whiskered* is a word used to describe an old man.

Another way to build a new word is to add a prefix or suffix to a **root** word, or a core word. A **prefix** is a syllable added to the front of the root word that often changes the meaning of the word. A **suffix** is a syllable added to the end of the root word that may alter the use or the meaning of the word. Prefixes and suffixes are called **affixes**. As you define the words in the Pre-reading Vocabulary—Structural Attack exercises, look for and define the root word, and then define the affixes added onto the root word.

For instance, look at the word *provider*. *Provide* is the root word and is a verb that means "to supply." The suffix *-er* at the end means "one who." Thus, the verb *provide* becomes a person, and the noun *provider* means "a person who supplies something." Now, look at the word *nonprovider*. The prefix *non-* at the beginning means "not" and greatly changes the meaning of the word. *Nonprovider* means "a person who does *not* supply something."

To define the words in Pre-Reading Vocabulary—Structural Attack, you need to know the prefixes and suffixes that are listed in Tables G-1 and G-2. Prefixes are defined and are listed in alphabetical order. Suffixes are arranged alphabetically in definition groups. Use the lists to help you in defining these words.

Prefixes

A **prefix** is added to the beginning of a root word. A prefix usually changes the meaning of the root word. *Be especially aware of prefixes because they can greatly change the meaning of a word.* Note that some prefixes have more than one meaning and these meanings may be different.

TABLE G-1
Prefixes

Prefix	Meaning	Application
a-	full of	*Acrawl* means "creeping or spreading everywhere." The town was *acrawl* with gossip when people learned the mayor was arrested.
a-	total absence	*Amoral* means "totally unable to tell right from wrong." When a shark kills, it is *amoral* because a shark does not know right from wrong.
ante-	before	*Antecedent* means "that which comes before." An unkind act may be the *antecedent* to a quarrel.
anti-	against	*Antifreeze* means "a substance that works against or prevents freezing." Vernie uses *antifreeze* in her car during the winter.
be-	full of	*Beloved* means "very much loved." The soldier dearly missed his *beloved* wife.
counter-	against	*Counterplot* means "a plan to work against another plan." The police developed a *counterplot* to ruin the criminals' robbery plan.
de-	against, wrong	*Deform* means "to form badly or wrongly." The fire *deformed* the house and left it twisted and falling down.
de-	out of	*Deplane* means "to get off the airplane." The team claimed their luggage after they *deplaned*.
dis-	not, against	*Distrust* means "not to trust." Allison felt *distrust* toward the salesman who lied to her.
en-	within, into	*Encircle* means "to place in the middle" or "to surround." The floodwaters *encircled* the house.
il-	not	*Illegal* means "not legal." Many laws state that stealing is *illegal* and will put you in jail.
il-	more so	*Illuminate* means "to light up brightly." The fireworks *illuminated* the night sky so brightly that it looked like daylight.
im-	not	*Immeasurable* means "not able to be measured." The joy Teddy felt when he won the championship was *immeasurable*.
im-	more so	*Impoverished* means "very poor." The *impoverished* family did not even have enough money for food.
in-	not	*Incurable* means "not able to be healed." Doug caught an *incurable* disease, which he will have for the rest of his life.

TABLE G-1 (Cont'd)

Prefix	Meaning	Application
in-	in, into	*Inside* means "in the side" or "through the side." Michelle walked through the door to get *inside* the room.
inter-	between, among	*Intercollegiate* means "between two or more colleges." Michigan defeated Alabama in *intercollegiate* football.
intra-	within	*Intracollegiate* means "within one college." The red shirts played the blue shirts in the *intracollegiate* gym class competition.
kin-	relative	*Kinfolk* means "the people you are related to or your family." All my *kinfolk* will gather together at Thanksgiving for a family reunion.
non-	not	*Nonaccompanied* means "no company or alone." Bill preferred to attend the party alone, *nonaccompanied* by others.
pre-	before	*Predictable* means "able to be told beforehand." Tom's speeding ticket was *predictable* because he always drives too fast.
re-	again	*Refamiliarize* means "become familiar with again." To pass the test, Sue will *refamiliarize* herself with her notes.
self-	alone, one's own	*Self-satisfied* means "satisfied with oneself." After passing the test, Robert felt good about himself and was quite *self-satisfied*.
semi-	half	*Semiconscious* means "only half or partly aware." With all the noise at the concert, Jake was only *semiconscious* of the sirens outside.
sub-	under	*Subway* means "a road that goes underground." When there is too much traffic on the city roads, it is easier to take the *subway*.
super-	larger, above	*Superman* means "a man larger or better than other men." Bravely running into a burning building to help others is the act of a *superman*.
un-	not	*Unperceived* means "not noticed." Geri usually notices everything, but this time the dirty room went *unperceived*.
under-	below	*Underbrush* means "low shrubs and bushes that grow under the trees." Tony decided to cut the *underbrush* that was growing under his shade trees.
trans-	across	*Transoceanic* means "across the ocean." Aley will catch a *transoceanic* flight from New York to Paris.

Suffixes

A **suffix** is added to the end of a root word. A suffix may have very little effect on the meaning of a word, but a suffix will often change the part of speech of a root word.

What is the part of speech of a word? The **part of speech** of a word is, very simply, the function or use of the word. For instance, look at the word *ski*. In the sentence "Laura's *ski* was damaged," *ski* is a noun—the thing Laura had that was damaged. In "Laura and Ted *ski* downhill," *ski* is a verb—the action Laura and Ted do. In "Laura took *ski* lessons," *ski* is an adjective that describes the kind of lessons that Laura took. The word *ski* remains the same three letters, but the function it serves and the information it communicates change slightly depending on the part of speech it demonstrates. Note that although the use changes—from thing to action to description—the basic idea of a downhill sport remains the same.

In the same way, a suffix may often change the part of speech of a root word while leaving the root word's basic meaning largely unchanged. For instance, if we add *-ed* to the noun and say, "Ted *skied* down the hill," the noun becomes a verb, and the action is in the past. Thus, Ted is still involved with skiing, but now he has done it in the past.

In Table G-2, suffixes you will need to know are listed alphabetically within definition groups and with the relevant parts of speech noted. You will see several words from Pre-Reading Vocabulary—Structural Attack.

TABLE G-2
Suffixes

Suffix   Application

The following suffixes mean "one who" or "that which." Each turns a root word into a noun because the root word becomes the person or the thing that does something.

-ant   A *servant* is "one who serves." The *servants* cleaned the mansion before the guests arrived.

-ary   A *visionary* is "one who sees clearly or into the future." Einstein was a *visionary* and saw the future uses of nuclear energy.

-ee   A *payee* is "one to whom things are paid." When Dodee owed her brother money, she wrote a check to him and made him the *payee*.

-ent   A *student* is "one who studies." College *students* are usually serious about their studies and work for good grades.

-er   A *fancier* is "one who fancies or likes something." Reid is a proven cat *fancier* and currently has four cats that he loves living in his home.

-ess   A *princess* is "a female who acts like a prince." The *princess* sat on the throne next to her husband, the prince.

TABLE G-2 (Cont'd)

Suffix	Application
-folk	*Townsfolk* are "people of the town." The *townsfolk* held a general meeting so that they could all welcome the new mayor.
-ian	A *musician* is "one who plays music." Renée hired several *musicians* so that people would be able to dance at her party.
-ist	A *futurist* is "one who predicts the future on the basis of current trends." *Futurists* advise those in the government in Washington about issues on which it may someday need to enact laws.
-man	A *horseman* is "a person who is skilled at riding and driving horses." Dave is a fine *horseman* who often rides his horse around the park.
-or	A *survivor* is "one who survives or lasts." Rich lasted the longest on the deserted island and was named the *survivor*.

The following suffixes make a root word an adjective, and each changes the meaning of the root word.

-able	*Distinguishable* means "able to be told apart or distinguished." The greasy spots made the dirty clothes *distinguishable* from the clean clothes.
-er	*Lovelier* means, by comparison, "more lovely than another." Missy's garden, filled with blooms, is *lovelier* than Margaret's weed patch.
-est	*Kindliest* means, by comparison, "the most kind of all." The mother's gentle pat was the *kindliest* touch of all.
-ful	*Frightful* means "full of fright or awful." With all its costumes and noisy bell-ringing, Halloween is a *frightful* night.
-less	*Hapless* means "without happiness or luck" or "unfortunate." The *hapless* student had two flat tires and got a headache on his way to school.
-most	*Uppermost* means "most high" or "important." With a record of no accidents for two years, safety is the company's *uppermost* concern.
-ous	*Nervous* means "full of nerves" or "tense." Kirk was so *nervous* before his test that his hands were shaking.

The following suffixes mean "related to," "like," or "having the quality of" and generally change the meaning of a root word very little. Mostly, they change the parts of speech of the root word.

-al	The noun *cone* means "a form that comes to a circular point" and becomes the adjective *conical*. The tip of the space shuttle is rounded and *conical*.
-ance	The verb *repent* means "to feel sorry about" and becomes the noun *repentance*. After he broke his Mom's favorite vase, John felt awful and was filled with *repentance*.
-ant	The verb *observe* means "to see" and becomes the adjective *observant*. Carrie watches everything closely and is very *observant*.
-ed	The noun *candy* means "something sweet" and becomes the adjective *candied*. Mom used lots of sugar to sweetly coat the *candied* apples.

TABLE G-2 (Cont'd)

Suffix	Application
-ed	The noun *ink* means "writing fluid" and becomes the past-tense verb *inked*. Jefferson took pen and *inked* his signature on the Declaration of Independence that he wrote.
-en	The verb *choose* means "select" and becomes the adjective *chosen*. He had joined the Marines and became one of the *chosen* few.
-ence	The verb *depend* means "to rely on" and becomes the noun *dependence*. When Lisa paid her own bills, she knew her *dependence* on her parents would end.
-ic	The noun *metal* means "shiny element" and becomes the adjective *metallic*. Laura's silvery dress had a *metallic* shine.
-ing	The verb *terrify* means "to scare" and becomes the adjective *terrifying*. The *terrifying* thunder scared all of us as it seemed to shake the whole house.
-ish	The noun *fever* means "internal heat" and becomes the adjective *feverish*. Joel felt *feverish* from the heat of his sunburn.
-ism	The adjective *ideal* means "perfect" and becomes the noun *idealism*, which means "belief in perfection." George's *idealism* often leaves him disappointed because things are not always perfect.
-ity	The adjective *stupid* means "unthinking" and becomes the noun *stupidity*. Alice could not believe her *stupidity* when she locked her keys in the car.
-ive	The noun *feast* means "cheerful meal" and becomes the adjective *festive*. The wedding, with all its foods and colorful flowers, was a most *festive* affair.
-ly, -ily	The adjective *stealthy* means "moving quietly" and becomes the adverb *stealthily*. Bob crept so *stealthily* in the back door that no one knew he had entered the house.
-ment	The verb *confine* means "to restrain" and becomes the noun *confinement*. When the children misbehaved, Dad sent them to their rooms for silent *confinement*.
-ness	The adjective *nervous* means "tense" and becomes the noun *nervousness*. It was very hard for the groom to overcome his *nervousness* on his wedding day.
-tation	The adjective *ornamental* means "decorated" and becomes the noun *ornamentation*. Her diamond rings and pearl necklaces created *ornamentation* fit for a queen.
-ty	The adjective *frail* means "delicate" and becomes the noun *frailty*. At Aunt Alice's ninetieth birthday, we were all concerned about her *frailty*.
-y	The noun *stone* means "hard item" and becomes the adjective *stony*. The policeman had a *stony* look when the boy who was driving did not have a license.

Credits

Chapter 1: *Page 28:* "A Worn Path" from *A Curtain of Green and Other Stories*. Copyright 1941 and renewed 1969 by Eudora Welty. Reprinted by permission of Harcourt, Inc. *Page 44:* "Yoruba" by Migene Gonzalez-Wippler. *Page 62:* "Two Kinds", from The Joy Luck Club by Amy Tan, copyright © 1989 by Amy Tan. Used by permission of G. P. Putnam's Sons, a division of Penguin Group (USA) inc. *Page 80:* "The Tell-Tale Heart" by Edgar Allan Poe. *Page 93:* "There Will Come Soft Rains" by Ray Bradbury is reprinted by permission of Don Congdon Associates, Inc. Copyright © 1950 by Crowell-Collier Publishing, renewed 1977 by Ray Bradbury.

Chapter 2: *Page 108:* "Everyday Use" from In Love & Troubles: Stories of Black Women, copyright © 1973 by Alice Walker, reprinted by permission of Harcourt, Inc. *Page 125:* "Bone Girl" by Joseph Bruchac. From Earth Son, Sky Spirit (1993, Anchor Books). *Page 140:* "Strong Temptations—Strategic Movements—The Innocents Beguiled" by Mark Twain. *Page 154:* "The Cask of Amontillado" by Edgar Allan Poe. *Page 169:* "To Build a Fire" by Jack London.

Chapter 3: *Page 193:* "The Kiss" by Kate Chopin. *Page 204:* "Salvation" from *Short Stories* by Langston Hughes. Copyright © 1996 by Ramona Bass and Arnold Rampersad. Reprinted by permission of Hill and Wang, a division of Farrar, Straus & Giroux, LLC. *Page 215:* "Wine on the Desert" by Max Brand. Copyright © 1940 by United Newspapers Magazine Corporation. Copyright © renewed 1968 by the Estate of Frederick Faust. Reprinted by arrangement with Golden West Literary Agency. All rights reserved. *Page 231:* "The Last Leaf" by O. Henry. *Page 245:* "The Lady or the Tiger?" by Frank Stockton.

Chapter 4: *Page 261:* "The Story of an Hour" by Kate Chopin. *Page 272:* "Gifts of the Magi" by O. Henry. *Page 285:* The Wonderful Old Gentleman," copyright 1926, renewed © 1954 by Dorothy Parker, from *The Portable Dorothy Parker* by Dorothy Parker. Used by permission of Viking Penguin, a division of Penguin Putnam, Inc. *Page 304:* "The Ransom of Red Chief" by O. Henry. *Page 322:* "Sweat" as taken from *The Complete Stories* by Zora Neale Hurston.

Chapter 5: *Page 344:* "A Rose for Emily" from *Collected Short Stories of William Faulkner* by William Faulkner. Copyright © 1930 and renewed 1958 by William Faulkner. Reprinted by permission of Random House, Inc. *Page 363:* "Dr. Heidegger's Experiment" by Nathaniel Hawthorne. *Page 382:* "The Masque of the Red Death" by Edgar Allan Poe. *Page 398:* "The Bell-Tower" by Herman Melville.

Notes

Index of
Authors, Titles, and Terms